MEDIAMERICA

Form, Content, and Consequence
of Mass Communication

WADSWORTH SERIES IN MASS COMMUNICATION
Rebecca Hayden, Senior Editor

General

The New Communications by Frederick Williams

Mediamerica: Form, Content, and Consequence of Mass Communication, 3d, by Edward Jay Whetmore

The Interplay of Influence: Mass Media & Their Publics in News, Advertising, Politics by Kathleen Hall Jamieson and Karlyn Kohrs Campbell

Mass Communication and Everyday Life: A Perspective on Theory and Effects by Dennis K. Davis and Stanley J. Baran

Mass Media Research: An Introduction by Roger D. Wimmer and Joseph R. Dominick

The Internship Experience by Lynne Schafer Gross

Telecommunications

Stay Tuned: A Concise History of American Broadcasting by Christopher H. Sterling and John M. Kittross

Writing for Television and Radio, 4th, by Robert L. Hilliard

Communicating Effectively on Television by Evan Blythin and Larry A. Samovar

World Broadcasting: A Comparative Analysis, by Sydney W. Head

Broadcast/Cable Programming: Strategies and Practices, 2d, by Susan Tyler Eastman, Sydney W. Head, and Lewis Klein

Advertising in the Broadcast and Cable Media, 2d, by Elizabeth J. Heighton and Don R. Cunningham

Strategies in Broadcast and Cable Promotion by Susan Tyler Eastman and Robert A. Klein

Modern Radio Station Practices, 2d, by Joseph S. Johnson and Kenneth K. Jones

The Magic Medium: An Introduction to Radio in America by Edward Jay Whetmore

Audio in Media by Stanley R. Alten

Television Production Handbook, 4th, by Herbert Zettl

Sight-Sound-Motion: Applied Media Aesthetics by Herbert Zettl

Electronic Cinematography: Achieving Photographic Control over the Video Image by Harry Mathias and Richard Patterson

Journalism

Media Writing: News for the Mass Media by Doug Newsom and James A. Wollert

Excellence in College Journalism by Wayne Overbeck and Thomas M. Pasqua, Jr.

When Words Collide: A Journalist's Guide to Grammar & Style by Lauren Kessler and Duncan McDonald

News Editing in the '80s: Text and Exercises by William L. Rivers

Reporting Public Affairs: Problems and Solutions by Ronald P. Lovell

Newswriting for the Electronic Media: Principles, Examples, Applications by Daniel E. Garvey and William L. Rivers

Free-Lancer and Staff Writer: Newspaper Features and Magazine Articles, 3rd, by William L. Rivers and Shelley Smolkin

Magazine Editing in the '80s: Text and Exercises by William L. Rivers

This is PR: The Realities of Public Relations, 3rd, by Doug Newsom and Alan Scott

Writing in Public Relations Practice: Form and Style by Doug Newsom and Tom Siegfried

Creative Strategy in Advertising, 2d, by A. Jerome Jewler

MEDIAMERICA
Form, Content, and Consequence of Mass Communication

Third Edition

Edward Jay Whetmore
University of San Francisco

Wadsworth Publishing Company
A Division of Wadsworth, Inc. • Belmont, California

Senior Editor: Rebecca Hayden
Production Editor: Leland Moss
Managing Designers: Detta Penna and Andrew H. Ogus
Designer: Wendy Calmenson
Copy Editor: Anne Montague
Time Line Illustrator: Masami Sam Daijogo
Cover: Andrew H. Ogus
Cover Photograph: Marshall Berman

Printed in the United States of America
3 4 5 6 7 8 9 10—89 88 87 86

ISBN 0-534-03390-3

Library of Congress Cataloging in Publication Data

Whetmore, Edward Jay.
  Mediamerica: form, content, and consequence of mass communication.

  Includes bibliographies and index.
  1. Mass media—United States. 1. Title.
P92.U5W48 1985   001.51′0973   84–7350
ISBN 0–534–03390–3

This book is dedicated to my mother, Phyllis JoAnn Armstrong (1923–1970), who was an amazing lady and continues to be a guiding spirit in my life. It was she who first helped me understand the beauty and excitement of life in Mediamerica.

ABOUT THE AUTHOR

EDWARD JAY WHETMORE (Ph.D., University of Oregon) teaches at the University of San Francisco. Prior to his academic career, he was actively involved in the media as a radio news director, announcer, DJ, and media consultant. He is the author of *The Magic Medium: An Introduction to Radio in America* (Wadsworth) as well as numerous articles and papers on media topics.

Contents in Brief

Part One
Print: The Gutenberg Gallery   1

1   Welcome to Mediamerica   3
2   Books: The Permanent Press   17
3   Newspapers, Part One:
    The Evolution of American
    Journalism   29
4   Newspapers, Part Two:
    Soft News and Contemporary
    American Journalism   55
5   Magazines: A Mass Menagerie   69

Part Two
Electronic Media:
Edison Came to Stay   91

6   Radio: The Magic Medium   93
7   The Sound of Music   125
8   Television, Part One:
    Structures and Strategies   147
9   Television, Part Two:
    Patterns and Programs   169
10 Sunsets and Scenarios:
    Film as Popular Art   203

Part Three
Beyond the Media:
The Phenomena of Mass
Communication   235

11 And Now the News . . .   237
12 Advertising and Public Relations:
    The Pretty Package   259
13 The Global Village:
    Popular Culture and
    International Mass Communication   289
14 Mass-Communication Research:
    A Beginner's Guide   307
15 New Technologies and the
    Future of Mass Communication   341

Index   361

Acknowledgments

Columbia Pictures Industries, Inc.; © 1966 Cotillion Music/Springalo Toones/Ten-East Music. All rights reserved. (p. 3)
Historical Pictures Service, Inc. (pp. 4, 25, 41, 78, 95, 99, 126, 208, 210, 211, 249)
Shirley Polykoff Advertising, Inc. (p. 19)
USA TODAY (pp. 31, 32)
Excerpt from "The Shooting Script" by Herman J. Mankiewicz and Orson Welles, as published in *The Citizen Kane Book;* copyright 1971 by Bantam Books, Inc. (pp. 42–43)
RKO General Pictures (pp. 42, 216)
CBS News (pp. 45, 238, 282)
Harte-Hanks Newspapers, Inc. (p. 48)
The *National Enquirer* (p. 58)
Ann Landers/Field Newspaper Syndicate (p. 60)
Audit Bureau of Circulations (p. 70)
TV/Cable Week (p. 75)
Triangle Publications, Inc.; Copyright © 1983 by Triangle Publications, Inc., Radnor, Pennsylvania. Reprinted with permission from *TV Guide*® Magazine. (p. 75)
Journal of Popular Culture, © 1975 (pp. 76–77)
Time (p. 81)
IEEE *Spectrum* Magazine (p. 82)
Changing Times (p. 83)
Mad Magazine, © 1980 by E. C. Publications, Inc. (p. 84)
Bronze Thrills (p. 86)
Compressed Air (p. 86)
American Blade (p. 86)
Broadcast Pioneers (pp. 100, 131)
Huber Ellingsworth (pp. 102–103)
National Broadcasting Company, Inc., NBC Radio Division, and Don Imus (p. 104)
KSFO (p. 106)
KFWB, Los Angeles, California (p. 107)
Watermark Productions, Inc. (p. 109)
KOIT (p. 111)
KANG Radio (p. 116)
Scientific American, December 22, 1877 (p. 126)
Singular Publishing Co.; lyrics by David White (p. 130)
"Eve of Destruction" by P. F. Sloan, © 1965 by American Broadcasting Music, Inc. All rights reserved. (p. 132)
Elektra Records (p. 133)

Warner Brothers/Sire Records (p. 135)
Deborah Gordon (pp. 136–138)
Lyrics from pp. 351–352 of *Ball Four* by Jim Bouton; © 1970 by Jim Bouton. Used by permission of Thomas Y. Crowell Company, Inc. (p. 141)
Don Weller (pp. 141–142)
Children's Television Workshop (pp. 160, 161)
Cover of paperback edition of *How to Talk Back to Your Television Set,* reproduced by permission of Bantam Books, Inc. (p. 164)
Nicholas Johnson (p. 164)
Sullivan Productions (p. 175)
WNET/13, New York (pp. 178, 196, 253)
Viacom Enterprises (p. 182)
Gene Roddenberry (p. 183)
NBC Television (pp. 190, 195)
Merv Griffin Productions (p. 191)
The Museum of Modern Art/Film Stills Archive (pp. 206, 214)
Patrick Smith (pp. 224–225)
Lucasfilm, Ltd.; © Lucasfilm Ltd. (LFL) 1983. All rights reserved. Used courtesy of Lucasfilm Ltd. (p. 226)
Jack Anderson (p. 240)
Edwin Ginn Library, Tufts University (p. 246)
Turner Broadcasting System, Inc. (p. 252)
Creamer Advertising (pp. 262–263)
Radio Advertising Bureau (p. 265)
Advertising Council (p. 268)
Ralston Purina Company (p. 270)
Luigi & Allessandra MacLean Manca (pp. 272–274)
Jaguar Rover Triumph, Inc. (p. 273)
Jaeger International (p. 274)
Seagram Distillers Company (p. 275)
Oneida Ltd., © 1976 (p. 276)
Philip Morris, Inc. (p. 277)
Chevrolet Motor Division, General Motors Corporation (p. 278)
Marshall Fishwick (pp. 296–297)
Western Electric (p. 346)
U. S. Satellite Broadcasting (p. 350)
Warner/Amex Cable (p. 352)
Sony Corporation of America (p. 354)
RCA Corporation (p. 355)
The Magnavox Company (pp. 356–357)

Detailed Contents

Preface   xvii

Part One
Print: The Gutenberg Gallery   1

1 Welcome to Mediamerica   3

The Birth of Mass Communication   3
Defining Communication   4
Form: Mass Media   6
Content: Mass Message   7
Consequence: Mass Culture   8
The Technological Embrace   9
Competing Technologies in Mass
  Communication   9
The Cone Effect: Understanding
  Mediated Reality   10
Media Education and Research   12
Queries and Concepts   14
Readings and References   15

2 Books: The Permanent Press   17

The Permanent Press   17
The Gutenberg Legacy   18
The Permanent Press in America   20
The Business of Books   23
Issues and Answers:
  Purity in Print   24
Queries and Concepts   27
Readings and References   27

3 Newspapers, Part One:
  The Evolution of American
  Journalism   29

Hard and Soft News   30
Mass and Special-Interest Audiences   33
What You See Is What You Get   33
Business Trends in Newspaper
  Publishing   34
Time Line: Five Eras of American
  Newspaper Journalism   36
Five Eras of American Newspaper
  Journalism   38
Press, Public, and Government   46
Issues and Answers:
  A Question of Balance   50
Queries and Concepts   52
Readings and References   52

4 Newspapers, Part Two:
  Soft News and Contemporary
  American Journalism   55

What Really Happened?   55
Editors and Readers:
  A New Social Contract   56
Supermarket Sensationalism   57
Sorting Out the Soft News   59
Comics: You're Significant,
  Charlie Brown!   61

Issues and Answers:
Love, Law, and Libel—The
Private Lives of Public People 64
Queries and Concepts 66
Readings and References 66

5 Magazines: A Mass Menagerie 69

The Mass Menagerie 69
History: The Good Old Days 70
**Time Line: The History of
American Magazines** 72
These Days: Magazines Since 1950 74
A Portrait: The Death of *Life* 74
Guest Essay by John Brady:
The Nude Journalism 76
Specialization and Marketing Trends 79
What, No Advertising? 80
Writing for Magazines 83
Issues and Answers:
Professional Print—The Curious
Collective 87
Queries and Concepts 88
Readings and References 88

**Part Two
Electronic Media:
Edison Came to Stay** 91

6 Radio: The Magic Medium 93

Pioneers and Programmers 94
The Golden Age of Radio (1926–1948) 95
**Time Line: The History of
American Radio** 96
The Big Change: Radio after
Television 100
Meet the Deejay 101
Guest Essay by Huber Ellingsworth:
Entertainment Radio in the
1950s: More Than an Afterglow
of the Golden Age 102

The People You Never Hear 105
Music Formats 106
News and News-Talk: The
Information Exchange 113
The Numbers Game: Ratings and
Radio 114
Educational and Public Radio 115
"That Other Band": FM Radio 117
Whither Radio? 118
Issues and Answers:
Regulation of Radio:
The Zigzag Trail 118
Queries and Concepts 121
Readings and References 121

7 The Sound of Music 125

The Fabulous Phonograph 126
Popular Music in the 1940s 128
The Birth of Rock 128
The British Are Coming! 130
The Rock Renaissance 131
The Diffusion of Rock 132
New Music and the 1980s 133
Rock and Rote: The Themes
of Rock Music 135
Guest Essay by Deborah Gordon:
The Image of Women in
Contemporary Music 136
Country and Western Music 139
Soul Music 140
Issues and Answers
Guest Essay by Don Weller:
"And the Hits Just Keep on
Comin' " 141
Queries and Concepts 144
Readings and References 144

**8 Television, Part One:
Structures and Strategies** 147

Pioneers 148
The Growth of Television 148
The Ratings War 149

**Time Line: The History of
American Television**   150
Rating the Ratings: Problems and
Paradoxes   152
The Economics of Network
Programming   154
TV as Movie   155
Movie as TV   155
Network Decision Makers   157
Public TV   158
UHF and LPTV   159
Issues and Answers:
Who's in Charge Here?   163
Queries and Concepts   165
Readings and References   166

**9 Television, Part Two:
Patterns and Programs**   169

Now Back to *Maverick*   169
TV's Mediated Reality   170
From Sitcom to *Star Trek:*
The Genres of Prime Time   171
Daytime TV and the Common Cold   184
Talk Shows   190
Children's Shows   191
Sports   193
Real Life as Mediated Reality   194
Issues and Answers:
Roots, Mass Audience, and Social
Awareness   197
Queries and Concepts   198
Readings and References   198

**10 Sunsets and Scenarios:
Film as Popular Art**   203

The Audiovisual Record   203
Life Is Like a Movie   204
**Time Line: The History of Film in
America**   205
The Magic Lantern   207
The Quiet Years   209
The Star Is Born   211

The Movies Learn to Talk   212
1930s: The Sound and the Cinema   213
Gone with the Wind   213
1940s: *Citizen Kane* and the
American Dream   214
Humphrey Bogart and the Detective
Movie   217
1950s: A New Film Audience   219
1960s: The Young and the Restless   220
1970s: Snatching Victory from the
Jaws of Disaster   222
Nashville and *Network*   222
The 1980s: Simple Stories and
Galactic Allegories?   223
Guest Essay by Patrick Smith:
Understanding the Movies:
Another View   224
The Critics, Promotion, and Success   227
Issues and Answers:
The Regulation of Self   229
Queries and Concepts   231
Readings and References   231

**Part Three
Beyond the Media:
The Phenomena of
Mass Communication**   **235**

11 And Now the News . . .   **237**

What's News?   237
Good News Is No News   239
Newspapers   241
The Newspaper You Never See   241
Newspaper Layout: The Eyes
Have It   242
Straight from the Wires   243
Radio: The New Kid in Town   244
Rip and Read   245
The Commentators   246
Television News: The Tossed Salad   248
Friendly Teamness . . . Teeming
Friendliness   250

TV News in the 1980s 252
Broadcast Editorials 254
Issues and Answers:
Who Owns the Media? 255
Queries and Concepts 256
Readings and References 257

**12 Advertising and Public
Relations: The Pretty Package** 259

The Information Environment 259
The Advertising Business Develops 260
Early Excesses 261
Truth in Advertising 261
Radio Advertising 264
Television: The Ultimate
Advertising Medium 264
Save Me a Spot 265
Advertising: Making a Living 265
Case in Point:
The Great Pet-Food War 267
Form and Content:
How Advertising Works 270
**Guest Essay by Luigi Manca and
Allessandra MacLean Manca:**
The Siren's Song: A Theory
of Subliminal Seduction 272
Public Relations:
Mastering the Subtle Semantics 278
Press-Agentry Pioneers:
P. T. Barnum & Co. 279
Public Relations in the Global
Village 280
Ethics, Journalists, and PR 280
Issues and Answers:
The Selling of the President 281
Queries and Concepts 284
Readings and References 284

**13 The Global Village:
Popular Culture and
International Mass
Communication** 289

Defining Popular Culture 290

Popular Culture and Mass
Communication 291
Icons and Artifacts 294
The Events of Popular Culture 295
The Cult in Popular Culture 295
Guest Essay by Marshall Fishwick:
God and the Super Bowl 296
Issues and Answers:
The Dilemma of Popular Culture 298
International Media Systems 298
The United Kingdom: Media in the
Motherland 298
The Canadian Compromise 299
The Mexican Challenge:
Serving All the People 300
The Netherlands:
Print Leads the Way 301
Back in the USSR: The Soviet Model 301
Made in Japan: Technology and More 302
The Global Village 303
Queries and Concepts 303
Readings and References 303

**14 Mass-Communication
Research: A Beginner's
Guide** 307

Patterns in Mass-Communication
Research 307
Procedures and Problems of
Communication Research 308
A Sampler of Research Studies 310
Television Network News Reporting
by Female Correspondents:
An Update
by Loy A. Singleton and
Stephanie L. Cook 311
The Treatment and Resolution of Moral
Violations on Soap Operas
by John C. Sutherland and
Shelley J. Siniawsky 317
Popular Music: Resistance to
New Wave
by James Lull 326

Issues and Answers:
Mass-Communication Research
and You   338
Queries and Concepts   338
Readings and References   339

**15 New Technologies and the Future
of Mass Communication**   341
Linkups: The Foundation of the
Communications Revolution   342
Cable TV   342

Satellite Communication   344
The Computer Age   351
Home Video: The Consumer Takes
Control   353
Issues and Answers:
The Communications Future   358
Queries and Concepts   359
Readings and References   360

Index   361

Preface

The original idea for *Mediamerica* grew out of some frustrations I had experienced as a teacher. I looked in vain for a text that communicated to students some of the excitement I've experienced in my involvement with the media—a text that went beyond facts and figures and delivered something about the heart and soul of mass communication. Finding none, I decided to attempt a text of my own. With the help of the excellent staff at Wadsworth, the first edition of *Mediamerica* appeared in 1979, a second in 1982. The book has been used in hundreds of colleges and universities in almost every state across the nation. I have received feedback from thousands of students. Most have commented that they enjoyed reading a "different" kind of media book.

As with most texts, you'll find names, places, and statistics here, but I think history is most relevant when it relates to what is happening now. In short, my emphasis in this text is on what *is* happening as well as what *has* happened. We will explore the *whys* as well as the *whats*. Why has MTV become such a phenomenal success? Why has the Super Bowl come to dominate the American sports scene? Why did *M*A*S*H* become such a hit? All *mediated* phenomena offer clues about ourselves and our culture.

As I read through competing texts, I notice that many authors prefer not to acknowledge the existence of the *National Enquirer*, TV commercials, and rock and roll music. If they are mentioned at all, it is in a condescending manner. I have included at least some discussion of each of these because, for better or worse, they are part of our culture. To ignore them is to ignore many of the most important aspects of Mediamerica.

So we'll deal with *Return of the Jedi*, new wave music, and *Mad* magazine along with more traditional topics, because they all play an important part in our mass-communication system. You may not be completely happy with the content of mass media; none of us is. But if you're going to try to change it, first you must examine *what* it is and *why* it is.

That theme remains constant throughout the three parts of *Mediamerica*. The first deals with print: books, newspapers, and magazines. The second offers some insights into the electronic media, which have become an increasingly important part of our lives. In the final section we'll explore some media-related phenomena: news, advertising and public relations, popular culture, and international communication. We'll also take a look at the new media technologies and explore some of the ways they're changing our media habits and our everyday lives as well.

The changes in this third edition are far more than cosmetic. The final chapter was totally revised from the previous editions and virtually all of the other chapters were updated to reflect the rapid changes in the world of mass communication. Those familiar with the second edition will find new studies in Chapter 14 and extra help for students in understanding the complex process of media-related research.

All in all, *Mediamerica* is quite different this time around, but we've worked hard to keep the spirit that many felt helped make the first two editions so widely read.

When I was in college, my teachers seemed to have largely negative opinions about mass media. We read texts and listened to lectures about how bad newspapers, magazines, radio, and especially television were. There are many problems with mass media, but I just cannot accept this antimedia perspective. Perhaps I'm too optimistic. I find the form and content of mass media fascinating, but fascination need not mean bias. I don't think I am handicapped in helping you to develop your critical perspective as a media consumer.

During the last decade or so, I have worked professionally as a disc jockey and also in advertising, public relations, and television. I've included a few of these personal media experiences here. This is a textbook, not an autobiography, but I hope my own experiences as a producer and consumer of mass information will help you understand your own experiences. So overwhelming are the forces of mass communication that we are all involved, whether we like it or not.

I hope to hear from you and your instructors about your reactions to the book. Use the form at the back; I'll be glad to respond to any questions or comments you may have.

Acknowledgments

In a project of this size it is virtually impossible to thank everyone who has helped, but there are several I especially want to acknowledge. *Mediamerica* owes its existence to Rebecca Hayden, Senior Editor at Wadsworth, more than anyone else. She recently celebrated her silver anniversary at Wadsworth, and I wasn't kidding when I told her that I looked forward to the next 25 years. A special bond forms between an author and an editor, and her kind and gentle feedback throughout each edition has helped make the book what it is.

I want to thank all those who worked on the first two editions. Much of their hard work and effort still shines through in this latest effort. This time around I appreciate the guidance extended by the many instructors who answered a questionnaire about their experiences with *Mediamerica*, and in particular special thanks to third-edition reviewers who offered many helpful suggestions: Patricia Bowie Orman and Glenn Miller of the University of Southern Colorado, Michael Porte of the University of Cincinnati, and Willis A. Selden of Olivet College. I am also grateful to James R. Smith of SUNY–New Paltz for his detailed review of Chapter 15 on the new technologies.

I want to thank Stacy Lynn for her help with the new-wave section of Chapter 7. Thanks also to Production Editor Leland Moss. Kudos to the late Marshall McLuhan for inspiration and to "Seth" for explaining, at last, why we are all here.

Finally, a special thanks to all of my students at the University of San Francisco who have read the book and offered suggestions for the new edition. I am continually and pleasantly surprised by their enthusiasm for what I have tried to do with *Mediamerica*.

Edd Whetmore

Note to the Instructor: An instructor's manual is available to instructors adopting *Mediamerica* as a required text, as is a color videotape on "Future Prospects: The Communications Revolution in Mediamerica." For further information, write to Senior Editor, Mass Communications, Wadsworth Publishing Company, Belmont, CA 94002.

MEDIAMERICA
Form, Content, and Consequence
of Mass Communication

PART ONE
Print:
The Gutenberg Gallery

IT'S BEEN ROUGHLY 550 YEARS SINCE GUTENBERG CAME up with the idea of a mass-produced form of communication. What changes we've been through since then! Today satellites circle the globe, sending billions of bits of information down to us daily. Gutenberg could hardly have known he was setting such a revolution in motion, yet his early efforts were indeed the first attempt to disseminate information "to the masses."

Media analysts often speculate about what might have happened had Gutenberg invented television instead of movable type. Would there still have been wars, famines, kings and queens, Linda Ronstadt, and David Bowie? No one really knows, but most agree that the print media have exerted a tremendous influence on our social and cultural development.

In Part One, I have devoted one chapter each to books and magazines and two chapters to newspapers. This is not to say that any one medium is more important than another. But, for many, newspapers seem to be a basis of comparison, the yardstick for all mass media. Even defining what constitutes a newspaper can be troublesome. Is *Rolling Stone* a newspaper or a magazine? Actually *Rolling Stone*, the *National Enquirer*, and other publications like them are *tabloids*, a newspaper-magazine hybrid, which do not necessarily belong to either camp. I have included tabloids with newspapers for reasons of *form* rather than *content*. Their format is borrowed from successful daily newspapers like the *New York Daily News*.

1

The most frustrating thing about writing a general text is the space limitation. I would have liked to devote a dozen chapters to each medium, but of course that is not practical. I hope that the queries and source material at the end of each chapter will lead you to the further exploration so necessary to developing a real understanding of each medium.

Welcome to Mediamerica

IN 1436, JOHANNES GUTENBERG WAS BROKE, BUT THE INVENTOR was not used to asking for handouts. He had moved from his native Mainz to Strasbourg with servants and plenty of capital. His sudden need for funds had sprung from a desire to develop what he called a "secret art."

Before long, he was able to find several partners who were interested in this mysterious new art. Among them was Andreas Dritzehen, who mortgaged his property and borrowed on his inheritance to invest in Gutenberg's idea. He had boasted to a friend that the project "will not fail us; before a year is passed we shall have our capital again." Such candor was rare among the investors in Gutenberg's project. When asked about their investment, they avoided mentioning printing specifically, instead speaking vaguely of "the work" or "the adventure and art."

Historians now know that the art involved a set of molds that could be arranged and rearranged to print virtually any message. Gutenberg's secret was a new kind of printing press using movable type, which would greatly expand the dissemination of the printed word (see 1.1). No longer would printers have to carve a new set of molds for each page.

THE BIRTH OF MASS COMMUNICATION

The invention of the Gutenberg press with its movable type made possible mass literacy and the birth of what we call "mass communication." The term *mass* is of critical importance. In earlier days, the masses could communicate only by using the oral, or story, form, since most books were handwritten and very expensive. Gutenberg's press changed all that.

**There's something happening here
What it is ain't exactly clear . . .
I think it's time to stop/
Hey what's that sound
Everybody look what's going down . . .**

STEPHEN STILLS

1.1

Gutenberg demonstrates his new movable type to investors.

Culture, history, and religion, preserved on the pages of books, could now conceivably be made available to everyone. It was the beginning of mass culture. (See Chapter 13.)

During its first 200 years, the publishing business was usually the tool of the church and state. Early books and pamphlets encouraged readers to accept the doctrine of the ruling elite. But mass literacy brought with it a more sophisticated and questioning media consumer. Eventually, many people, encouraged by their new literacy, began to question the divine right of rule and authority. It is no accident that the rise of printed literature coincided with the Renaissance and the Reformation.

DEFINING COMMUNICATION

What we know about the form and content of mass media is part of a larger field of study we call *communication*. Communication researcher Frank E. X. Dance offers fifteen separate definitions of communication. One says:

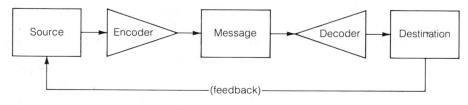

1.2

Shannon/Weaver model of the communication process (from Wilbur Schramm and Donald F. Roberts, eds., The Process and Effects of Mass Communication. *Copyright 1972, University of Illinois Press. Used by permission.).*

The connecting thread appears to be the idea of something being transferred from one person to another. We use the word communication sometimes to refer to what is so transferred, sometimes to the means by which it is transferred, and sometimes to the whole process.

We refer to what is being transferred as the *content.* For example, so far the content of this chapter can be summarized as:

1 A brief historical sketch of how the Gutenberg press came into being.

2 A brief discussion of the significance of Gutenberg's invention.

3 A definition of *communication.*

So the message of this book is the content of its communication. *Form* involves how a message is being transferred. There are many ways to send a message. We can whisper, shout, write, dance, or paint. We might choose to use any number of technological devices.

The model in 1.2 by Shannon and Weaver is a simple representation of how communication works. Such a model can be used to represent all three of the major types or *modes* of communication: intrapersonal, interpersonal, and mass.

Intrapersonal communication involves the messages we send to ourselves. You are reading this book in the library when suddenly you realize you are hungry. You put the book down and go off to a vending machine. Through a complex series of cybernetics, your internal system has motivated you to seek food. A countless number of such messages happen within you every day. One part of your system acts as the source: It encodes the message "I am hungry" and sends it to your brain, where it is decoded on arrival. When the message reaches its final destination, you put down the book and act on the message.

Interpersonal communication happens when two or more beings are involved. Assuming that you are no longer hungry, you return to the library and begin to read again. Suddenly a friend comes in, sees you, and says "Hello!" At this point, he or she becomes the source, encoding the message "Hello!" and then saying the word. Through a complex process involving language as well as nonverbal cues, you decode the message and it arrives at its destination, namely you.

In *mass* communication, the source may be one person, but more often it is a group of people. In print, there are writers, editors, typesetters, distributors, and many more. In electronic media, there are script writers, actors, directors, and others. Each group becomes a source. The encoding process involves a media form like a book, radio, or television set. The message is decoded by the media consumer, who may or may not offer feedback to the source.

Encoding and decoding are very important links in the communication processes. The advertising campaign that uses the wrong medium is a failure. The government agency that sends health-care books to a remote South American village where the people can't read has not communicated successfully.

Accuracy is another factor essential to the success of a particular act of communication. In *Speech Communication, Concepts and Behavior*, authors Frank E. X. Dance and Carl E. Larson define accuracy in each of the three communication modes:

In very general terms we may say that intrapersonal communication is accurate to the extent that what an individual tells himself approximates "reality." On the interpersonal level, we may say that communication is accurate to the extent that one person understands another's sentiments, preferences, values and so on. On the person to persons (or mass) level . . . accuracy is often viewed (as) the extent to which information transmitted by a source has been acquired and retained by members of an "audience."

Communication researcher Harold Lasswell feels that the basic components of the communication process are identified in one question: *Who* says *what* through what *channel* to *whom?*

Consequences, or effects, involve every step of the process. Form involves *how* the message is communicated; content involves *what* is communicated. A consequence can be the result of either or of both. But to understand effects fully, we need to examine all components of the communication process.

Another way of looking at the conse-

quences or effects of communication in each of the three communication modes can be found in the Whetmore Grid for Understanding Communication Relationships (see 1.3). In this model, the intrapersonal mode is described as internal reality, the interpersonal as external reality, and the mass as mediated reality. Each dimension has unique characteristics described in several different ways. From a psychosocial point of view, we use intrapersonal communication to perceive the world. Our communication with others helps us relate to what we perceive in a meaningful way. Mass communication brings about a linking process that enables us to feel connected to the population as a whole.

From a philosophical point of view, we begin with our internal instincts and habits. These often come under scrutiny when we take them into the "real world," where the interpersonal mode frequently provides an antithesis. How often have you found your ideas or beliefs challenged in a classroom discussion or even a casual conversation with a friend? Mediated reality often acts to bring about a synthesis. A close examination of the values espoused in TV's prime-time programs, for example, yields the fact that we all hold pretty much the same set of values: Crime doesn't pay, love conquers all, good deeds are rewarded, bad ones are punished, and so on. Whether these things are true or not, most of us like to believe that they're true; mediated reality often provides us with a reinforcement of that belief.

FORM: MASS MEDIA

We call a medium a "mass medium" if it meets two requirements:

1 *It must reach many people.* Gutenberg's press made books a mass medium. Later

1.3
The Whetmore Grid for Understanding Communication Relationships

Reality Level	Reality Dimension	Communication Mode	Psychosocial Mode	Philosophical Mode
Internal reality	Inside dimension	Intrapersonal communication	Perceiving	Thesis
External reality	Outside dimension	Interpersonal communication	Relating	Antithesis
Mediated reality	Collective dimension	Mass communication	Linking	Synthesis

came other media: newspapers, magazines, radio, and television, to name a few. All are mass media because they can reach many people simultaneously.

2 *It requires the use of some technological device, located between source and destination.* Mass media can be illustrated in much the same way as interpersonal communication. Let me use this book as an example of how mass media fit the Shannon/Weaver model. The thoughts you're reading now come from me, the source. I encode them using the English language and my typewriter. From here, they go by mail to my publisher, arriving (I hope) on time. They are edited, changes are made, and finally they go to the printer. The technological device used by these modern-day Gutenbergs represents the medium. It comes after encoding and before decoding. That technological device is *the book.*

Now you go to the bookstore, wait in line, buy the book, and open it to the first page. There you begin *decoding* my message by reading it. Finally my thoughts have reached you, their destination.

So this book qualifies as a mass medium because it is designed to reach many people and uses a technological device between source and receiver.

CONTENT: MASS MESSAGE

Controversial communication researcher Marshall McLuhan's favorite slogan was "The medium is the message." (For more on McLuhan, see Chapter 13.) He believed that since all mass messages pass through a technological device, they are no longer the same message at all but have been radically changed. His slogan is an exaggerated plea for examining the form of mass messages as well as their content.

From the very beginning of the process, mass messages are different from interpersonal ones. A source who designs a mass message realizes that it will be altered by the

Drawing by Koren; © 1980, The New Yorker Magazine, Inc.

"My friend, you are weighty in form but light in content."

medium. Try to imagine Billy Joel suddenly blurting out "I love you just the way you are" to his wife-to-be on their first date. It would seem a little awkward. Yet the thought "I love you just the way you are," which was transmitted from the source to the receiver via record and radio, was one of the more successful messages in the history of mass communication!

CONSEQUENCE: MASS CULTURE

A good deal of mass-communication research involves mass culture. We use the term *mass culture* to identify the *effects* of mass media. In the Billy Joel example, the media were radio and records. But you would not be familiar with "Just the Way You Are," or even with Billy Joel, unless you were a participant in mass culture. Mass culture involves a body of knowledge that you *share* with others in your environment.

Communication researcher Alex Gode points out that all communication "makes common to two or several what was the monopoly of one or some." In other words, a central purpose of communication is to establish some common ground between people. Mass culture, made possible by mass communication, is shared by virtually everyone. This sharing process opens up many possibilities, and not all of them are pleasant. Critics worry about the possible effects of TV violence on the nation's children. Will children's beliefs and attitudes about violence be affected by their endless diet of cops and robbers? Are we becoming so mesmerized by the *mediated* world of commercial products that we forget that material goods are not everything in life? Have we forgotten "quality art" and its importance in a world filled with the popular art found in mass media?

Other critics worry that the mass audience is too easily swayed, that the era of the individual is over. On the one hand, we may be trading our individualism for a more collective, tribal identity we don't yet completely understand. On the other hand, we may simply be on the verge of a new kind of individualism. Futurist Alvin Toffler contends that products like home video and audio recorders will bring about more diverse media content that will "un-mass" the mass media. In either case, there can be no doubt that this is a time of transition. No person or nation can afford to be self-oriented as in the past. In the world of instantaneous communication, everything we do affects everyone else all the time. And that is what mass culture is all about.

THE TECHNOLOGICAL EMBRACE

Can you imagine a world without mass communication? There would be no newspapers, radios, television sets, or McDonald's golden arches. Before Gutenberg, the myths, proverbs, and fairy tales that were used to pass wisdom from one generation to the next were limited by their channel capacity. *Channel capacity* is the term communication researcher Wilbur Schramm and others use to describe the ability of a particular medium to transfer a message successfully.

Remember the parlor game in which each person whispers a story to the next? The end version is usually entirely different from the original. Obviously, verbal exchange is not necessarily the best way to transfer a story. We cannot remember long messages exactly, and we tend to embellish or exaggerate some details and omit others. Naturally, the ability to remember exact words differs for every individual. Gutenberg's printing offered everyone a *precise* method of exchanging information. You can still go back and read the original Gutenberg Bibles if you can read Latin. They haven't changed. Nor have the handwritten books from before Gutenberg's time, but those books could reach only one reader at a time.

Chaucer's *Canterbury Tales* offers an example of a series of folk tales that became part of the mass culture thanks to the printing press. Though they were written some 80 years before Gutenberg's invention, once they were set in type, they became standard literature for the information-hungry mass audience. The tales remain intact and are still literary standards in our society. There are more recent examples of the same basic phenomenon: Superman, E.T., Archie Bunker, Elvis Presley, Devo, Richard Nixon, Shangri-La, Volkswagen, and Luke Skywalker were all brought to us in whole or in part via mass communication. How have we changed as a result of these mass-communication experiences?

McLuhan contended that we now live in a "global village" where we share our hopes, dreams, and fears in a "worldpool" of information. He said that in the global village, the old social, racial, and ethnic barriers of the past will break down, and media will eventually help us achieve world peace and harmony. Others disagree, citing the social unrest of the 1960s, the Vietnam War, and Watergate as examples of problems created and nurtured, at least in part, by mass media. Just about everyone agrees that mass media have altered our evolution and destiny, but no one is quite sure how.

COMPETING TECHNOLOGIES IN MASS COMMUNICATION

One of the most intriguing theories about how mass media affect our lives involves competing communication technologies. In certain time periods, one particular medium seems to dominate. Thus, we speak of the pre-Gutenberg oral or folk period, the rise of print, the golden age of radio, and so on.

Most of us spend more time watching television than reading. This shift of our attention away from books has disturbed many people. What effect might it have on our attitudes and beliefs? To cite one example, our decisions in the voting booth are probably influenced heavily by the 30-second campaign commercials we see on TV. Do these give candidates enough time to discuss the complex issues of our society, or do they reduce the political arena to a world of meaningless slogans and redundant clichés? In the 1960s, David Brinkley gave this reaction to surveys showing that most Americans relied almost solely on television news: "Then they're getting damn little news."

One thing is certain: In many ways, print and electronic media compete with each other. Their form and content represent different approaches to delivering entertainment, reporting the news, and distributing vital information.

A book is something we experience alone, often in a quiet, isolated environment. Remember the last time you sat next to someone who was whispering in the library? It probably distracted you. Yet loud audience reaction is common in most movie theaters. Even when the audience is silent, the film is a shared experience. We can experience radio and television equally well alone or with others. Rivalry between different media, then, is a rivalry of different *forms*. The form of a mass medium directly affects what the message will be, how we perceive and understand the message, and how that message affects us.

THE CONE EFFECT: UNDERSTANDING MEDIATED REALITY

The *cone effect*, named after the two cones that make up its design (see 1.4), is another way of examining the effects of mass media on our lives. It involves the relationship between *mediated reality* and real life. In 1.4 we see that everything begins in the circle labeled "real life." Real life represents all life experiences that do not *directly* involve a mass medium. For example, we may take a walk in the park on a sunny day and eat a sandwich. We all had these kinds of real-life experiences long before there were any mass media.

Certain aspects of real-life experience are then used by a communicator to form *constructed mediated reality* (CMR). CMR may consist of a TV show, magazine ad, or any other media message. It's important to remember that, even though CMR is taken from real life, there are many differences between the two. Basically, CMR tends to be funnier, sexier, more intense, more colorful, and more violent than real life. After all, nobody ever wrote a song about an ordinary relationship. Songs are written about special relationships, ones that have a great degree of intensity. Television situation comedies may picture dozens of funny and entertaining things happening every half hour, but in real life we are lucky if one funny thing happens to us in an average day. Novels are written about larger-than-life people, those who have special qualities.

Because CMR is real life "blown up," the mere fact that something appears as part of CMR triggers audience expectations about its larger-than-life qualities. We *expect* CMR to offer us things that are out of the ordinary. If it didn't, there would be no reason to suspend real life long enough to experience mediated reality.

In many ways, this book is really a study of various mass media and their competing CMRs. You'll learn how and why these are constructed as they are. In our society, many mass media vie for the attention of the consumer. More often than not, CMR is designed in such a way so as to attract and hold the

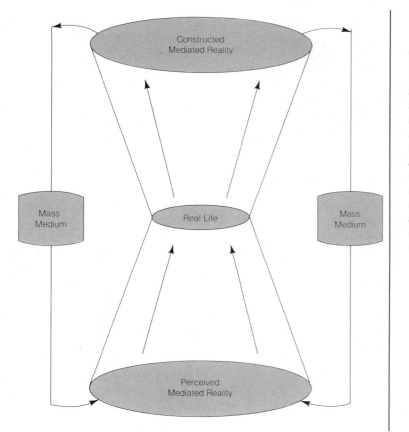

1.4

The cone effect is one way to represent the processes involved in bringing you mass messages. Note that the information must pass from Real Life to the Constructed Mediated Reality and then through a Mass Medium to the audience. The consumers make it part of their Perceived Mediated Reality and eventually incorporate it into their own lives.

largest possible portion of the mass audience.

Once CMR is completed, it is transmitted to the audience. We call the audience perception *perceived mediated reality* (PMR). We perceive mediated information in many ways. We can listen intently to a song on the radio (foreground), or we can use the mediated reality of a radio station as background while we concentrate on other tasks. A magazine advertisement can be studied closely or simply glanced at as we turn the page.

Whatever the case, our perception of mediated reality takes up a great part of each day. With the average TV set on more than six hours every day and our radios and stereos going constantly, it's obvious that we're exchanging an increasing amount of our real life for various PMRs.

It should be noted that PMR is a highly *selective* process. We choose what we wish to perceive by choosing our medium. Once connected with that source, we also choose what to retain. We may regard something as memorable and pay close attention to it, even taking notes or recording it for later review. Or we can disregard it. How many times has someone asked you about a particular TV show or movie you saw recently, but, try as you might, you simply could not remember the details?

The final step in the process involves the relationship between PMR and real life. We often take information gleaned from mediated reality and apply it to our real lives. Often this process can be disappointing. After all, how many people do we meet who are as attractive as those on *Magnum, P.I.*, or *Dynasty*? How often do we have a love affair that is as dramatic as those depicted in the songs routinely played on the radio? The fact is that real life often cannot measure up to the more glamorous and intense world of mediated reality.

Perhaps the single most important thing to remember about the cone effect—and mass media in general—is that mediated reality and real life are indeed worlds apart, and that's the way it has to be. Indeed, if real life and mediated reality were the same, there would be no reason for us to seek out mass-mediated information. Mediated reality must remain a place where significant and exciting things are constantly happening. As long as we understand why this is, media can provide us with a world of fascinating, informative, and entertaining stimuli. However, the confusion between mediated reality and real life can lead to serious consequences. You can't expect every doctor to treat you with the tender loving care of a Trapper John, M.D., or every wealthy person to be as flamboyant and mysterious as the Great Gatsby.

The cone effect applies equally to all mass media. In books, magazines, radio, and TV, there is always a mediated reality exerting some degree of influence over the mass audience.

MEDIA EDUCATION AND RESEARCH

Relationships between the mass audience and mediated reality with its form, content, and consequence are often difficult to understand. So much is happening so fast that tra-

ditional approaches are often obsolete. Many college and university departments have begun to erase established boundaries and experiment with multidisciplinary approaches to understanding communications. A new word, *communicology*, is appearing more often. Communicology is the study of intrapersonal, interpersonal, and mass-communication processes under what is called the "communication umbrella." The umbrella has many supportive ribs, including journalism, theater arts, speech and rhetoric, technical writing, advertising, broadcasting, public relations, and popular culture.

Most educators now agree that technology is reshaping our environment so fast that teaching specific vocational skills to communication students is only part of the job. The study of communication also involves teaching students how to land on their feet in unforeseen communication situations. We can train students to operate today's television cameras, but tomorrow's cameras will be different. Cable TV may revolutionize the commercial broadcast system we now study. Satellites could provide daily programs from foreign countries.

Mediamerica and You

Many of you will never become involved in the production of mass-media messages, but all of you will continue to be message consumers. Directly or indirectly, you will have a hand in deciding the future of mass media and the way they shape your life. This book is part historical and part exploratory. It offers historical information as a backdrop to how we got here. We'll explore what is happening now and speculate on what is to come. This is not an encyclopedia of mass communication, nor could it be. But I hope it will be a catalyst to start you thinking about mass media. You don't have to think very hard to come up with ways media *directly* affect our lives. Examples are everywhere.

Part One includes chapters on the print media. These media have a rich history, and you will meet some of the more important contributors in their 500 years. Of course, print media started with books, the "permanent press," and books are still the most revered of all mass media.

Separate chapters deal with the two worlds of the newspaper: "hard" and "soft" news. In recent years, the function of the newspaper has changed. Readers' needs have been affected by the appearance of other mass media. Serious questions about the newspaper's relationships with government and the public have arisen. America's concept of freedom of the press has changed.

Magazines are the most rapidly changing of all print media. Their trends often provide early clues to changes in the characteristics of the mass audience. Dozens of new magazines appear each year, and dozens of others disappear.

Part Two, "Electronic Media: Edison Came to Stay," is about all the media that rely on electric power to get their message to you. No one invented electricity, of course, and several people had a hand in harnessing it, but Edison's contribution in coupling it with message delivery was unsurpassed.

First came record players and films, but in the beginning these were regarded as mere amusement. Radio became the first mass medium to link the source and the destination simultaneously; it played an important part in the social and political development of its day. A separate chapter deals with the recording industry and music itself. Contemporary music enjoys a unique relationship with the youth culture and dominates radio's entertainment programming.

Two chapters deal with television. The structure of the medium is analyzed to help you understand how our commercial television system has developed. You'll also learn about those troublesome Nielsen ratings and how they influence network decision makers.

Often when we think of television, we think of the programs that led former Federal Communications Commission (FCC) Chairman Newton Minow to call the medium "the vast wasteland." Writer Horace Newcomb, among others, has a different perspective. He feels that television is an art form, the nation's most popular and meaningful experience.

Film, like television, is an audiovisual medium, but it delivers larger-than-life people and has been described as the "American dream machine." Since it has been around longer than any other electronic medium, we have developed a more serious attitude about its status.

In Part Three, "The Phenomena of Mass Communication," we cover some issues related to the growing power of the mass media. Many feel that the most important function of mass media is to deliver the news. Do media really keep us up to date with what's happening in our rapidly shrinking world? We explore how that job gets done and learn about some issues facing those who do it and the rest of us as well.

Advertising and public relations are completely dependent on mass media for their existence. People working in these industries are media specialists who design the pretty packages for information consumers.

Popular culture is not an industry but a social by-product of mass media. Virtually everything we see, touch, smell, hear, and taste has something to do with mass media. These mass-mediated experiences make up our life-styles and culture.

In Chapter 14, "Mass-Communication Research: A Beginner's Guide," we examine several research studies that address crucial issues in mass communication. You'll discover how research is conducted and what it can tell us.

Finally, we look into the mediated future. How will new technologies change society? In the world of mass communication, some of yesterday's dreams included:

1 A wire service that would give the small-town newspaper a reporter in every news capital on the globe.

2 A radio news network that would let all Americans hear a speech by their President at the same time it was being given.

3 A communication device that could bring sound and pictures simultaneously into every American home.

These dreams are now realities. New predictions for mass communication—its form, content, and consequence—challenge the imagination.

QUERIES AND CONCEPTS

1 If you had to give up all mass media, which one would you miss the *most*? Which one would you miss the *least*? Why?

2 Pick a topical news story aired on tomorrow's TV newscast. Then listen for the same story on radio and also clip it out of the newspaper. Which facts are common to all stories? Which are missing from at least one story?

3 List five questions about a mass medium you would like to have answered. Which involve form? Content? Consequence?

4 Using the Shannon/Weaver model in 1.2, define how each component could be applied to a newspaper, magazine article, radio program, television program, and/or movie. Does the model work more effectively for some media than for others?

5 Using the Whetmore grid in 1.3, can you think of specific examples where mass-communication content has performed the linking and synthesis functions? Are some media more adept at these tasks than others?

READINGS AND REFERENCES

The Birth of Mass Communication

Elizabeth Geck
Johannes Gutenberg: From Lead Letter to the Computer. Bad Godesberg, Germany: Inter Natione Books, 1968.

An interesting account of Gutenberg's life and his influence on the rise of mass communication. Easy to read and comprehensive enough for everyone.

Defining Communication

Frank E. X. Dance
"The 'Concept' of Communication." *Journal of Communication*, June 1970, pp. 201–10.

Every definition of communication you ever wanted, along with a bibliography of original sources. The article is tough to read, but the definitions will make you stop and think.

Frank E. X. Dance
Carl E. Larson
The Functions of Human Communication: A Theoretical Approach. New York: Holt, Rinehart & Winston, 1976.

An advanced look at the formulation of communication theory. In the relatively new field of communication theory, this book is considered a classic. Includes sections on theoretical strategy, the functions of communication, and theoretical formulations.

Frank E. X. Dance
Carl E. Larson
Speech Communication: Concepts and Behavior. New York: Holt, Rinehart & Winston, 1972.

Though speech communication is the central topic here, the theoretical structures presented are useful in looking at the mass-communication process. Particularly strong on the three modes of communication.

Mass Message;
Mass Culture;
The Technological Embrace;
The Cone Effect

See Chapter 13, "Popular Culture and International Mass Communication," and the readings and references at the end of that chapter.

Media Education and Research

See Chapter 14, "Mass-Communication Research: A Beginner's Guide," and the readings and references at the end of that chapter.

Books:
The Permanent Press

HUNDREDS OF COLLEGES AND UNIVERSITIES USED THE FIRST two editions of this book. Thousands of students read it. Since 1979 I have received countless letters, phone calls, and "feedback sheets" from students like you all over the country and all over the world, from Brooklyn, New York, to Bombay, India. At the end of the book you will find your own postage-free feedback sheet.

Needless to say, I am gratified by all this reaction, but it pales when compared with the response to other successful texts in many fields. It is estimated that one popular psychology text has reached over a million students in the last two decades. Indeed, the power of print is very evident in textbooks, which sell by the thousands each day. And a successful novel or exercise book might sell millions of copies in a year. All of this adds up to an unrelenting onslaught of print in our culture.

McLuhan said that writing "has the power to translate man from the tribal to the civilized sphere." There can be no civilized society without reading and writing.

THE PERMANENT PRESS

Print is the keeper of records, great literature, and all accomplishments. It is the medium that, more than all others, daily dictates the fortunes and failures of men and women. Teachers who publish flourish; those who don't, perish. Students who read the right books go to the head of the class, meet the right people, and go on to the right colleges.

Print is the Supreme Court, the ultimate arbiter, of our culture. If we want to know who is the best at a particular activity, we consult a copy of the *Guinness Book of World Records*. From the pages of books flows truth, the answer to any

> He had grown up to
> a thousand books,
> a thousand lies;
> he had listened
> eagerly to people who
> pretended to know,
> who knew nothing. . . .
> F. SCOTT FITZGERALD

17

conceivable question. When we say we are doing it "by the book," we mean we are doing it in a civilized, correct, coherent, logical manner.

Bookbinding is also powerful. It adds an additional touch of respectability to print. The hardback book is considered the ultimate reliable source, followed in order by the paperback book, the magazine, and finally the newspaper. The better the binding, the greater the credibility! All of these print forms are somehow perceived as preferable to the electronic media, which seem fleeting and unstable. Print is for keeps! (See 2.1.)

For most of the history of mass communication, the book was the only readily accessible means of storing information and retrieving it at will. Of course, the proliferation of microfilm, microfiche, video cassettes, audio cassettes, and so on is changing that. Nevertheless, the dominance of the book in our culture as a means of storing and retrieving information is undeniable.

We do not only *what* books tell us, but *how* they tell us. We perform most activities the same way we read, in a *linear* fashion. Linear (from *line*) means one thing at a time, one job at a time, one spouse at a time. This seems quite normal; in fact, we are so conditioned to doing things one at a time that any other way seems absurd. Yet in preliterate cultures, people tend to do many things simultaneously. Hawaiians never had a written language until the missionaries came in the 19th century. Perhaps that is why things on the Islands are still done according to what they call "Hawaiian time," involving hours of delay. If you are to meet some people at one o'clock, it may be two or later before they show up.

McLuhan predicted that as literate societies spend less time with books and more time with electronic media, they will return to this preliterate state. He said, "Ours is a brand new world of all-at-once-ness, time has ceased, space has vanished." Our concepts of time and space are influenced by the *form* of our dominant media. The real message of the book medium may not be *what* it says, but *how* it says it. While books deliver their messages one thought at a time, one word at a time, television and electronic media have a kind of simultaneous approach, delivering many kinds of information in a rapid-fire manner. These differences have had important consequences in our mass culture. Yet despite McLuhan's observations we are still a print-oriented culture in many ways.

THE GUTENBERG LEGACY

When Gutenberg's movable type ushered in the new era of mass communication, he was totally unaware of it. He was more interested in deriving some creative pleasure from the experience and turning a profit for his investors. What happened was of considerably greater consequence. Often inventors and other technological pioneers receive little recognition in their lifetime. We are numb to our changing environment, much too preoccupied with day-to-day problems to get "the big picture."

Look around the room where you are right now. Take a good look. You are at home, in a classroom, in a library. No doubt you've been here many times before. Yet have you ever noticed the pattern on the ceiling? The small holes in the wall? The plaster chips on the floor? The linoleum pattern? The trademark on the desk in front of you? By stopping and looking at these things, you are really seeing them for the first time, getting a glimpse of the "invisible environment" that always surrounds you. Our information environment, created by books and other mass media, is very much like that. It surrounds us constantly, leaving no part of us unaltered or

If your product needs a reflective audience, a selective audience PRINT IT!

If the purchase requires deliberation— or liberation from the accepted way of doing things, nothing performs like print.

Print it. Print is for keeps.

Shirley Polykoff
Copywriter
and President
Shirley Polykoff
Advertising, Inc.

Magazine Publishers Association, Inc. 575 Lexington Avenue, New York, N.Y. 10022

2.1

Print is for keeps. Magazine publishers naturally choose print for their message, an implied disparagement of the electronic media.

untouched. Yet we are completely oblivious to it. We think that, if we're not reading at the moment, books have no influence on us.

We human beings have always had the urge to keep records of ourselves, our friends, our dreams. Inside each of us is a secret archivist; we like to collect things that prove our accomplishments are of lasting value. Books perform a different function than the newspapers and magazines we chew up and recycle daily: They provide a permanent record.

No one really knows how long books have been around, but the earliest records show that there were clay tablets in Babylonia about 4,500 years ago. Chinese scholars may have invented the first books, a series of bamboo strips tied together. But bamboo, clay, and stone were impractical and not easily transported. According to most accounts, the Chinese were the first to invent paper, but the earliest inexpensive writing materials were made by Egyptians from the papyrus plants growing along the Nile River.

The Romans invented codex, a kind of binding that allowed them to organize laws and other important materials into easily transportable form. Some early forms of paper appeared in Italy and Spain in the 12th century. At that time, books were handwritten primarily on vellum or parchment (both made from lambskin or calfskin), and that practice continued into the 15th century. In fact, in some parts of Europe, vellum and parchment are still used today. At the end of the 15th century, Gutenberg used paper along with movable type and an old wine press to print his first book, a Bible.

It is estimated that more than 30,000 titles were printed in the first 50 years of mass-produced books (1450–1500). Early works were law books, Bibles, and other religious publications. Later came folklore, stories, and verse, such as Chaucer's *Canterbury Tales*. The costly hand-copied manuscripts that had been the exclusive property of the ruling elite gave way to mass-produced works that encouraged literacy among the general populace. In fact, it can be argued that books were the first mass-produced "product" and forerunners of the industrial age.

The mechanical procedures of printing changed very little during the first 350 years. All type had to be set by hand and each sheet pressed separately. About 1800, the French invented a machine that made paper in one continuous roll. In England, the first successful iron press replaced the old wooden ones. In 1810, a steam-powered press replaced earlier hand-operated models. In 1884, Ottmar Mergenthaler, a German-born American, invented the Linotype. Now type could be set by machine, greatly speeding production.

In recent years, a number of technological developments have sped up the printing process. Computer typesetting, for example, may eventually have a much greater impact than the Linotype did on the distribution of the printed word.

THE PERMANENT PRESS IN AMERICA

Books landed at Plymouth Rock with the Pilgrims in 1620. Twenty years later, Stephen Day was commissioned to print one of the first books published in the New World, *The Whole Booke of Psalms*. Just as in Europe, most early books in America were about law or religion. The Bible was the most popular of all.

Benjamin Franklin's *Poor Richard's Almanack*, a collection of tide tables, harvest suggestions, and proverbs like "Early to bed and early to rise makes a man healthy, wealthy, and wise," was the rage from 1733 to 1758. Franklin also started the first subscription library in the colonies. In many ways, his was the first American mass-communication success story.

Until 1800, the price of books kept them out of the hands of many U.S. citizens. Books cost a dollar or more, which amounted to a week's pay for the average wage earner. During the next 50 years, many cities started compulsory public schools, and a new generation grew up hungry for the printed word. Heavy demand for books plus technological innovation helped lower the price. It is important to remember that in America, reading was considered the right of everyone. Though many successful publishers were upper-class Americans, printing was not controlled by the ruling elite because the new nation had established freedom of the press in its Bill of Rights. Education of the masses posed no threat to a nation that had already rejected a king.

By the mid-1800s, the price of some books was down to ten cents. Horatio Alger and

2.2
Horatio Alger and the American Dream

Perhaps the most successful of all the 19th-century novelists was Horatio Alger (1834–1899). Though the literary merit of his work was subject to criticism, his writings were both abundant and widely read. His 120 titles sold around 30 million copies. The name Horatio Alger became synonymous with the American struggle for upward social mobility. Here's the philosophy of the Alger novel in a nutshell, taken from his first book, *Ragged Dick:* "'I hope, my lad,' Mr. Whitney said, 'you will prosper and rise in this world. You know in this free country poverty is no bar to a man's advancement.'"

Alger's belief in piety, purity, frugality, and hard work was a legacy from his conservative father, a Unitarian minister in Revere, Massachusetts. For a time Horatio thought that he too would have a career as a minister, and he graduated from Harvard Divinity School before his success with *Ragged Dick.*

Alger eventually moved to New York and became somewhat of a celebrity, lending his name to a number of reform and antivice crusades, including the New York Society for the Suppression of Vice.

All the Alger novels idolized the self-made man. The hero was "a bright-looking boy with brown hair, a ruddy complexion, and dark blue eyes, who looked, and was, frank and manly. . . ." The villain was often another boy, son of a rich but corrupt family. He often had a "slender form and sallow complexion, and dressed with more pretension than taste. . . ." Inevitably, the hero triumphed.

Alger's own life story mirrored the success of his heroes, but though his books brought him fame and fortune, he did know sorrow. Alger's father talked him out of marrying his "one true love" at 17 because he was too young. And Alger longed to write "one great book," to be applauded by the critics who scoffed at his "boys' stories." That book was never written, though he once chose a title: *Tomorrow.*

The important cultural contribution of the Alger novel had

OUR HERO

nothing to do with literary quality. Popular media reflect the emotions and ideologies of their times. Alger's ideas were already in the thoughts and feelings of Americans. Though his medium and message may no longer dominate the social landscape, the implications of Alger's work have helped form our cultural legacy. His millions of readers have grown up and passed that legacy along to succeeding generations.

other authors of this era stressed action, romance, adventure, and the puritan ethic of honesty and hard work (see 2.2). The message of these inexpensive novels became part of the American culture. People across the country shared the same romantic notions, agonies, and ecstasies through the pages of the books they read.

By 1900, nine out of every ten Americans could read, and read they did. Naturally, not all of the social and political events of that day were triggered by books, but the medium's influence was great. Just as *Uncle Tom's Cabin* had aided the cause of freedom for slaves before the Civil War, Upton Sinclair's *The Jungle* exposed the wretched conditions of Chicago's meat-packing plants at the turn of the century. During the 1930s, John Steinbeck's *The Grapes of Wrath* sensitized many to the plight of those who fled the Dust Bowl during the Depression. All of these books had a lasting impact on the consciousness of the nation.

In the 1940s, paperbacks changed the role of books in America. First popular more than 100 years ago, paperbacks have had escalated sales since World War II. With gross annual sales at $500 million, paperbacks now account for a major portion of all book sales, and they no longer deal only with "lighter" material. Almost all of the world's literature, from Shakespeare to Saul Bellow, now appears in paperback. Even that once stalwart hardback, the textbook, has yielded. The evidence is in your hands.

For many years paperbacks were largely reprints of material already available in hardback, but costs for the rights to reprint hardback materials have now escalated astoundingly. When the paperback rights to Judith Krantz's hardback best-seller *Princess Daisy* were auctioned off, the bidding was brisk. Eventually they brought $3.2 million, the highest ever for such a sale.

These huge bidding wars have forced most major companies to rely on paperback originals as a strong source of income. John Jakes's series of novels about the Kent family and the Harlequin romance series are recent examples of such works, which have provided excellent profit margins to help offset hefty production and promotion costs in other areas.

Many bookstores now derive half or more of their gross income from paperback books, while used-book stores have given over shelf after shelf to paperbacks. The average paperback now costs over three dollars, up from 50 cents during the 1950s. Still, most magazines cost a dollar or more, and paperbacks have a much longer life.

Speedy production of paperbacks has made possible the "instant book." Often based on a political event, the instant book appears within a few weeks of the event's hitting the headlines. Such was the case in 1978, when several paperbacks were produced within a week of the tragedy in Jonestown, Guyana. These included eyewitness accounts and photographs. While some of these books were credited to one author, most were actually put together by special staffs prepared to be geared up almost immediately by major paperback companies.

Gross annual sales for all books exceeded $3 billion for the first time in the early 1970s. Of these books, nearly half were educational in nature, including textbooks and legal, medical, and other professional works. Millions of copies of popular paperbacks, such as *Roots*, were also sold as required reading in courses.

Book clubs accounted for another 10 percent of the total, offering highly touted selections to members at discount prices. Authors know that selection as a "Book of the Month" can mean instant success.

The goal of commercial publishers is to get their titles on the influential best-seller lists, particularly the one published in the *New York Times*. Yet sources inside the industry reveal that such lists are inaccurate at best. One bookseller said, "If George Gallup conducted his political polls the same way, we'd have Harold Stassen, Mary Tyler Moore, Al Capone, and Rin Tin Tin as America's favorite candidates for the presidency." Best-seller lists never include books like *The Living Bible*, for example, despite the fact that it sold more copies than any other book one year. Also missing are dictionaries, cookbooks, and titles that sell well in rural locations, which are seldom polled. Most of the confusion could be cleared up if commercial publishing houses were willing to disclose sales figures, but most don't want the competition to know exactly how they're doing.

Some writers are now receiving more royalties from the sale of film rights than from the books themselves. Sometimes the film is made first and a book is then based on the film. *Love Story*, written by Erich Segal, a Yale professor, was originally a screenplay and was later marketed as a novel. Both versions enjoyed tremendous success. *Time* magazine has labeled this film-to-book process the "bovie." Examples of successful bovies include *Saturday Night Fever*, *E.T.*, and *Return of the Jedi*.

Despite the paperback boom and increasing total book sales, America's love affair with books may have gone sour. According to *Library Trends*, although 78 percent of Americans 18 years and older read a newspaper every day, fewer than one in five could answer yes to the question, "Do you happen to be reading any books or novels at the present?" A Gallup survey reveals that about one in four adults is a hard-core book reader. A little less than half of the adults in the survey reported that they "read occasionally—perhaps at the rate of one book a year." Only one in four possesses a library card.

Critics are disturbed by this, particularly those in the academic community whose business it is to assess the impact of mass media. Many decry the time Americans spend with electronic media. If we spent more time reading, they say, we would be much improved. Usually the argument stops there, for it is always assumed that information derived from books is far more valuable than that derived from other mass media. Perhaps it's because we hold books in such high regard.

The more we learn about all mass media, the more we know that each medium has a different impact and delivers certain kinds of information more effectively than others.

Media forms may compete with one another, but there's also a potential symbiosis. Eventually we may discover which medium performs which information tasks most effectively. Considerably more empirical research needs to be done before we can assume that any single medium will enable us to be "much improved."

THE BUSINESS OF BOOKS

Media analyst Charles Madison lists four major eras in American book publishing. *The colonial era* lasted from the 17th century until about 1865. Early colonial publishers in Philadelphia, New York, and Boston tended to come from the upper classes. Men like Matthew Carey, Charles Wiley, and James Monroe were well-educated aristocrats who thought the books they published should offer something of lasting value. Periodicals, they felt, catered to the desire for instant gratification that might be harmful to the masses. In those days, publishing was something of a private club; there were so few publishers that most knew each other by their first names.

The Gilded Age (1865–1900) brought an abrupt change. The number of publishers mushroomed, and with the arrival of the dime novel, publishing became big business. George P. Munro was a six-dollar-a-week clerk when he convinced his employer's brother to publish cheap reprints of pirated editions of popular fiction. Thirty years later he left an estate valued at more than $10 million. The Munro story was typical of this era, when publishing experienced its most rapid growth.

The commercialization of literature (1900–1945) was a period of great technological advance. The antiquated printing practices of the 18th and 19th centuries were set aside for streamlined commercial procedures more in keeping with the Industrial Revolution. Bookselling, as well as publishing, had become big business.

Famous authors found publishers less willing to meet their financial demands as competition increased and publishing costs skyrocketed. The unknown author was having an increasingly difficult time breaking into print. A new, untested book required substantial financial commitment. Most publishing companies were cutting back and trying to ensure success with the books they did publish.

The era of *publishing goes public* (1945–present) encompasses the biggest changes in business practice in publishing's history. The postwar era brought another boom in the demand for books as veterans flocked into American classrooms. The textbook business flourished. Older family-type publishing houses sold stock and became corporations.

Ultimately, book publishing is both a business and a cultural enterprise. It is important to remember that *cultural* means all culture and not only what some would call "high" or "elite" culture. Dr. Spock's *Baby and Child Care* and Shakespeare are both part of the cultural stew. The book medium is used to convey messages of every imaginable description. Each makes some contribution to the American experience. Examination of each can yield interesting and worthwhile data about the complex nature of American society.

ISSUES AND ANSWERS: PURITY IN PRINT

As long as there have been books, there has been censorship. King Henry VIII of England issued a list of prohibited books in 1529, and for the next 170 years, each English monarch issued a similar list. Those caught reading or circulating prohibited works were subject to fines and imprisonment. Thousands of titles were in print in Europe by 1600. As literacy and information spread, the threat of revolution swept Europe. Books sparked increasing demands for social, religious, and political freedom. The ruling elite were losing the battle for control of the printing presses.

Many people feel that the days of book banning have passed. Science fiction author Ray Bradbury's *Fahrenheit 451* (the title refers to the temperature at which paper catches fire), about a society where all books were burned, shocked and dismayed many readers. Was it science fiction or wasn't it?

The banning and burning of books have been commonplace in America. Historian Paul Boyer has speculated on the reasons behind this. His theory is that, while America developed a unified identity after the Civil War, it also developed a unified conscience. This new collective conscience encouraged certain religious and social groups to feel that they should have the power to decide what was and was not appropriate reading material for everyone.

In 1873, Anthony Comstock (see 2.3) founded a nonprofit social organization known as the New York Society for the Suppression of Vice. He headed that controversial group for 40 years. According to Boyer, the vice-society movement

. . . was in response to the deep-seated fears about the drift of urban life in the post–Civil War years. The origin of Comstock's society, the first of its kind in America, is illustrative. Throughout the nineteenth century, as today, New York City possessed a magnetic attraction for ambitious and restless young men from other parts of the country. The metropolis which held so much promise

2.3

Anthony Comstock and the Suppression of Vice

Anthony Comstock arrived in New York, "the wickedest city in the world," shortly after the Civil War, in 1867. He had been born in 1844 to devout Connecticut parents.

According to his biographers, he worked in a dry-goods store until 1872, when he noticed that "shocking" literature was being passed around by other employees. Until then there was little or no enforcement of the antismut laws in New York City, but Comstock brought suit and had a fellow employee arrested for distributing such material. As it turned out, that was only the beginning. His Society for the Suppression of Vice was backed by most of the New York aristocracy, and Comstock became legendary in his self-appointed task of "cleaning the filth out of this town."

Sporting thick muttonchop sideburns, a pot belly, thick neck, and jutting jaw, he railed against what he called the "base villains" of pornography and their "pathetic and awful" cases. In 1893 he greeted a roomful of reporters with an

impromptu belly dance to illustrate graphically the evils of the Chicago World's Fair. It must have been quite a sight!

for these youths, however, was also somehow threatening. The familiar sources of guidance and support—family, church, close-knit community—had been left behind, and often it seemed that the city offered nothing in their place.

Book censorship was a paternalistic approach. The reader was to be protected from falling to the depths of depravity. The problem, then as now, was figuring out exactly what constitutes the "depths," or even "depravity." The Supreme Court has never successfully defined obscenity.

During the 1920s, the term *banned in Boston* described literature of "questionable taste." Authors whose works were banned in Boston included H. G. Wells, John Dos Passos, Theodore Dreiser, Sinclair Lewis, Upton Sinclair, Ernest Hemingway, and Robert W. Service. Upton Sinclair didn't seem to mind; he mused, "We authors are using America as our sales territory and Boston as our advertising department." The mass audience has always expressed a pronounced curiosity about forbidden literature, and this curiosity can lead to increased sales.

The Nazi book burnings of the 1930s and the Soviet suppression of books today may seem far removed from American society. Yet in 1953, more than 100 titles were banished from the worldwide libraries of the United States Information Service after "exposure" by Senator Joseph McCarthy's congressional subcommittee. Among them were the works of American patriot Thomas Paine. McCarthy contended the books were "procommunist," and several public book burnings were held. *Saturday Review* editor Norman Cousins moaned, "What do we do about the charge that a nation that became great because of a free flow of ideas has itself become frightened of ideas?"

There are still stories of school boards prohibiting certain books in school libraries, or teachers being fired for requiring reading of controversial texts. In a poetry class I took as a community college student, the instructor assigned Allen Ginsberg's *Howl and Other Poems*. The bookstore refused to carry it, so the instructor supplied the copies himself. When we read it aloud in class, he closed all the doors and urged us not to report it to the local chapter of the John Birch Society, which had been placing students with tape recorders in some controversial classes.

In March of 1976, several members of the Island Trees School District Board of Education in New York entered a high school library and confiscated 60 books they later said were "anti-American, anti-Semitic, anti-Christian, and just plain filthy." Removed were Pulitzer Prize winners *The Fixer* and *Laughing Boy*. Also banned were Kurt Vonnegut Jr.'s *Slaughterhouse-Five*, Desmond Morris's *The Naked Ape*, and *Go Ask Alice*, which makes a strong statement against the use of drugs by teenagers.

The board's action stirred quite an uproar in the small Long Island town. Eventually New York City's WCBS radio aired an editorial condemning such actions as "prejudgments of the worst kind." In its opinion: "The idea of students getting off on this forbidden literature suits us just fine!"

The president of the school board went on the air to reply, contending that "what is taught in schools should reflect local values" and that "one of the purposes of a board of education is to see that local control is maintained and that the will of the majority prevails." He also emphasized: "Education is supposed to be an uplifting experience, but if you have to get down into the gutter to do it, then it is just not worth it. For as the twig is bent, so grows the tree." The New York Civil Liberties Union filed a class-action suit demanding that the books be returned to the library and contending that no board of education had the right to go over the heads of administrators to blacklist certain works.

After a long series of delays, the case wound up before the U.S. Supreme Court, and in 1982, in a 5–4 decision, the court held that "local boards may not remove books from library shelves simply because they dislike the ideas contained in those books and seek by their removal to prescribe what shall be orthodox in politics, nationalism, religion or matters of opinion."

Pornography is often a big part of the censorship question. Community and national standards change from day to day. *Ulysses* (1922), the famous novel by James Joyce, was once banned in this country. There was some banning of *Lolita*, *Tropic of Cancer*, *Fanny Hill*, *Candy*, and other novels that seem tame by today's standards.

During the 1950s, the liberal Earl Warren Supreme Court struck down most state obscenity laws as being too vague and subjective. The more conservative Warren Burger court of the 1970s reversed the Warren rulings and in *Miller* v. *California* it struck down all national standards, reestablishing the right of local juries to apply local community standards in judging obscenity. Now local governments are again arresting editors and publishers, and there have been some convictions by local juries. Some of these cases are on appeal, and it will be many years before all the results are in. In fact, the results will probably never be "all in." The war between government and "obscene" publishers seems to be a never-ending one.

QUERIES AND CONCEPTS

1 What would our culture be like if we weren't doing it by the book? What if we were doing it by the TV or by the radio? What would happen to our relationships with government? With one another?

2 A survey project: Poll your ten favorite people by posing the age-old cliché: "Read any good books lately?" How many have they read in the last six months? How many are of the "pop" variety?

3 What is the single book that has had the greatest influence on *your* life? Why?

4 The qualities that make America unique are embodied in American myths and stories like those of Horatio Alger. Make a list of other stories and myths that seem to be a vital part of the American character. How many are closely related to a mass medium?

5 Can you think of any sentences, words, or phrases that should not be allowed in print? Should there be an age limit on the freedom to read any kind of information? If so, draw up some guidelines. If not, what about books on how to make bombs and set them off by remote control? Do you want your local terrorist to have that information?

6 What is the last book you read "for the fun of it"? Describe that experience. How was it different from books you are assigned to read in school? How did it compare with other media experiences you may have recently had? The last movie you saw? The last record album you listened to?

READINGS AND REFERENCES

The Gutenberg Legacy

S. H. Steinberg
Five Hundred Years of Printing. New York: Criterion Books, 1959.
    Though old, this brief book is really not out of date, since it concentrates on the visual aspects of print and how they developed. Technical advances in the printing press are also treated.

The Permanent Press in America

John C. Oswald
Benjamin Franklin, Printer. Detroit: Gale Research, 1974.
    Of all the Franklin biographies, this is perhaps the most reverent. Originally published in 1917, it is still easy to read. The author often uses language from the colonial era to describe his subject.

Lawrence C. Wroth
The Colonial Printer. Charlottesville:
University Press of Virginia, 1964.
    This book describes printing in the pre–
    Revolutionary War period, including
    discussions of Franklin, Day, and
    others. A very thorough and in-depth
    look at the colonial printer.

The Business of Books

Benjamin M. Compaine
*The Book Industry in Transition: An
Economic Study of Book Distribution and
Marketing.* White Plains, N.Y.: Knowl-
edge Industry Publishing, 1978.
    Concentrates on the economic facets of
    book publishing and distribution. Chap-
    ters on libraries, mass-market paper-
    backs, outlets, formats, and much
    more.

Lewis A. Coser
Charles Kadushin
Walter W. Powell
*Books: The Culture and Commerce of
Publishing.* New York: Basic Books, 1982.
    The most current and up-to-date book
    available at this time. Covers the entire
    book and publishing landscape, includ-
    ing sections on history, economics, how
    publishing companies are organized,
    channels of distribution, and virtually
    every other important aspect of the
    industry.

Charles A. Madison
Book Publishing in American Culture.
New York: McGraw-Hill, 1966.

There is ample material on book publishing in America in just about any
library, and I reviewed a dozen books
or so until I found Madison's. It has a
good index of all publishers, with a couple of paragraphs on each if you are
curious about any specific company. The
best material is on the earlier eras of
publishing, and I recommend that you
go to a more recent source for current
data, sales figures, and other information. *Writer's Market* (see Chapter 5)
lists the kinds of books each major
house publishes and the number of
titles each produces yearly.

David Shaw
"Book Business Best Sellers: Are They
Really?" *Los Angeles Times* News Ser-
vice, October 24, 1976.

**Issues and Answers:
Purity in Print**

Paul S. Boyer
*Purity in Print: The Vice Society Move-
ment and Book Censorship in America.*
New York: Scribner's, 1968.
    This is probably the liveliest and most
    thorough book in the area. Boyer is a
    scholar with a sense of humor who
    delivers the problems of book censor-
    ship with gusto. The author brings out
    details about historical characters that
    make them come alive.

Newspapers, Part One: The Evolution of American Journalism

3

IN THE FALL OF 1982, *USA TODAY* BEGAN TO APPEAR ON America's newsstands. Subscriptions weren't available, but anyone who wished to have a copy needed only to deposit some money in one of the high-tech boxes emblazoned with the *USA Today* logo and the words *by satellite.*

Those who ventured a quarter were treated to a newspaper that bore only a slight resemblance to their hometown paper. *USA Today* divides the day's events into four distinct sections: the headline news "of the USA" in Section One, followed by sections devoted to "Money," "Sports," and "Life." The stories, brief and direct, are surrounded by splashy graphics, full color in every section, and a dizzying array of charts and graphs to simplify the day's events for the reader.

The decision to attempt a national newspaper had been made late in 1981 by the board of directors of Gannett Company, Inc., one of the country's most successful publishing conglomerates. (Circulation for all Gannett papers exceeds 3.5 million nationwide.) It was thoroughly researched, of course, and by April 1983, *USA Today*'s press run exceeded 1.5 million copies, with audited circulation well above 1 million. Those who had predicted failure for the new paper were astonished. In 1977 the *National Observer*, a weekly national newspaper, had folded after 15 consecutive years in the red. In 1981 alone, 45 daily newspapers, many in America's largest markets, had gone under. Facing such overwhelming odds, how could *USA Today* succeed in an uncertain economy?

Gannett research had shown that 15 percent of all U.S. households bought a paper that was not produced in their county. This indicated that many people in rural areas were buying a major metropolitan paper to get something the local paper wasn't giving them. In addition, Gannett board chairman Allen Neuharth stressed that *USA Today* would be a "second buy" for

> **Fairly soon the press began to sense that news was not only to be reported but also gathered, and, indeed, to be made. What went into the press was news. The rest was not news.**
>
> MARSHALL McLUHAN

many newspaper readers, to supplement the information they were getting in their local paper.

The technology that makes *USA Today* is almost as flashy as the color features and in-depth sports coverage of the paper itself. The paper is put together in Washington, D.C.; the final copy, ads and all, is transmitted by satellite to 15 locations across the country, where it is automatically turned into printing plates. Then the presses roll.

This was relatively easy for Gannett to accomplish, since it owns more newspapers (many with printing facilities) than any other newspaper chain—108 in all. Many of the Gannett papers are published in the after-noon, leaving the presses free for an early-morning run.

Such a huge undertaking is not entirely without problems. When Gannett announced plans to attempt a national newspaper, its stock tumbled to a twelve-month low. In areas where Gannett didn't own a paper it was forced to rent press facilities, often at inflated costs. Publishers in each of the target markets have resisted the new competition. In Los Ange-les, Tom Johnson, publisher of the *Los Ange-les Times*, vowed to "go rack for rack" with *USA Today*'s ambitious marketing strate-gies. Everywhere the paper has appeared, the competition has been forced to take note.

Whatever the ultimate fate of *USA Today*, it has certainly shaken up the journalism establishment. Criticism has been heavy, especially concerning the perceived "frivo-lous" nature of the paper's content. Readers get lots of information about the activities of Kenny Rogers and Reggie Jackson, and a decidedly less detailed account of world events. News of the day is capsulized in the "Newsline" section, the left column of the front page. Also on the front page is "USA Snap-shots," a graphics display of "the statistics that shape our lives." According to *Business*

Week magazine, *USA Today*'s "emphasis on color photos, sports and business appeals to a generation hooked on TV" (see 3.1).

At least one publisher has admitted to stealing the idea of *USA Today*'s color weather map (see 3.2). In addition, many newspapers have moved toward more color graphics and color photos and are imitating *USA Today*'s use of blue throughout.

Yet *USA Today* has only capitalized on a growing newspaper trend, that of emphasiz-ing "soft news," entertainment and feature stories, to gain new readers and hold on to existing subscribers. This trend is not new— in fact, the battle between hard news and soft news is at the very heart of the history of American journalism.

HARD AND SOFT NEWS

Hard news is factual accounting; soft news is the background information. It's hard news when the mayor has a heart attack, but soft news when her husband is interviewed in the next room. Hard news is facts and statistics: temperature, box scores, the number of votes cast for a candidate. Soft news is opinion and color: columns, comics, editorials, "Dear Abby."

Hard news, in theory, *is* the story. Soft news is nice if there is space, but isn't essen-tial. Many stories contain both hard and soft news. The shotgun murderer who kills six people is hard news. His neighbors describ-ing him as one who worshiped Hitler is soft news. Hard-news events are often serious matters of importance to everyone. Soft-news events are the stuff of human-interest and feature stories.

The *New York Times* carries a lot of hard news, the *New York Daily News* very little. Each has cultivated an audience that expects the balance between fact and feature found

Please see COVER STORY next page ►

3.1

Highly colorful, highly visual, and highly profitable, USA Today is an American success story. The publishers, however, might find that description unusual: The word America never appears in USA Today. It's always life "in the U.S.A."

3.2

In USA Today even the weather is subject to splashy graphics and alliteration. Note how the "violent storms snap summer's sultry grip"!

there. Readers depend on their chosen newspaper to deliver a particular blend of hard and soft news about the world around us. In doing so, newspapers help us develop a sense of participation in the global village. They are an important part of our social and cultural identity.

MASS AND SPECIAL-INTEREST AUDIENCES

Newspapers are our "cultural bath." We immerse ourselves in the massive amounts of information they offer. Few people read the newspaper from cover to cover; it would take most of the day. Most of us read the newspaper selectively.

All media deal with two audiences: the mass audience and the special-interest audience. Media consumers are members of both. Newspapers run stories of general interest to everyone; they also run sports, stocks, and features for various special-interest audiences. The wide variety of their articles gives newspapers what communication authors John Merrill and Ralph Lowenstein call "internal specialization," allowing the newspapers to appeal to a large, diverse audience. In this way, newspapers are like some magazines—*Reader's Digest*, for example—which draw a large readership of people with different age, educational, and social backgrounds.

The newspaper format sets an information *agenda* by grading events according to how important or interesting they may be to the reader. Perhaps this function was best described by media researcher Bernard Cohen in his book *The Press and Foreign Policy:* "The press may not be successful much of the time in telling people what to think, but it is stunningly successful in telling its readers what to think about."

In most newspapers, important stories are displayed prominently on or near the front. The lead story is supposed to be the day's most significant event. Inside the paper, the special interest reader finds information in neatly divided sections: sports, editorial, family, and business. This helps readers set their own agendas. Some may read their horoscope first, then work the crossword puzzle, and never get around to the front page. A stockbroker may go straight to the business section.

Of course, sometimes special-interest news makes it to the front page. So many people have become fans that sports news often appears there. If Wall Street has its worst day in 20 years, most of us will read about it. But on a normal day, only the special-interest audience will pore over the day's stock quotations.

The more successfully a newspaper meets the mass and special-interest needs, the higher its circulation. The higher the circulation, the greater the revenues. Advertising revenues make it possible for you to buy the paper at a fraction of its production cost. Advertising also makes daily delivery possible. A newspaper is a *mass* medium that depends on mass circulation—a large audience—to make a profit.

WHAT YOU SEE IS WHAT YOU GET

Americans have an insatiable appetite for printed news. There is a need to know what's happening and a feeling that it hasn't happened unless it has appeared in the paper. Why read the full newspaper account of the baseball or football game you saw last night? You want to match your perceptions with those of a professional observer who was on the scene.

The event described in a newspaper story is not the original event at all, but a constructed mediated reality. Newspaper stories are condensed versions of the real thing. A quote standing alone, for example, with no explanation of events preceding or following it, may appear absurd or sensational. Politicians are often irritated when they see their words in the morning paper. Their immediate response is that the words were "taken out of context."

In a sense, all speeches are taken out of context, since they have been taken from one medium (interpersonal speech) and put into another (print). Tape-record a conversation at random. Then transcribe the first several sentences. What you write on paper will seem very different from what you overheard. If it were printed, the difference would be greater still. We don't *talk* the way we *read*. Talk, as they say, is cheap. But print has a finality, a permanence about it that can change the meaning of events and messages, making them appear different from the original.

In addition, reporters bring their own perspective to a story. No matter how hard they try to remain objective, they inevitably develop opinions about a newsmaker. Whether reporters are aware of it or not, personal bias can play a major role in how they "see" a news event.

Nor is the reporter the only person who influences the news. A story must pass through many hands before it appears in print. There are copy editors who correct errors and edit for easier comprehension. Perhaps a photographer assigned to a story turns in a picture that tells a "different story" from the reporter's. Very few reporters write their own headlines, and headlines can reflect still another point of view.

Media consumers need to be aware of these variables before making decisions based on information received from the newspaper.

BUSINESS TRENDS IN NEWSPAPER PUBLISHING

According to *Editor & Publisher*, there are more than 1,750 daily newspapers and more than 8,000 nondailies published in the United States today. Of these, about 150 are metropolitan dailies. In many major cities, the number of "metros" has been decreasing. For example, in New York in 1900 there were 14 English-language dailies. In 1981 there were only five left. Why the decrease?

For one reason, the metros have been particularly hard hit by rising labor costs. Printing-plant workers have joined truck drivers and construction workers as among the most highly paid blue-collar workers in America. Another problem is the skyrocketing cost of newsprint. In 1940, newsprint cost about $50 per short ton; by 1984, it had climbed to $425.

One way the metros have dealt with rising production costs has been to raise the selling price of the paper. In the last ten years, the street price of most papers has risen from 10 cents to 20 or even 25 cents. The cost of advertising has also gone up.

Most newspapers get about 75 percent of their income from advertising, which means that the paper you buy for 25 cents probably costs about a dollar to make. This reliance on ad income also means that more than half of the space in most newspapers is devoted to ads. It may surprise you to learn that production of the day's newspaper begins in the advertising department. The ads are placed, and then the news must fit *around* the ads in the space that's left. More ads sell on Sunday; that's why there's more to read that day. In addition, advertisers may specify stories that they do or don't want to run with their ads. An airline might prohibit plane crash stories on the same page with its ad. A real estate advertiser may be promised a related news story on the real estate market.

Another problem facing metros is circulation. Although the total circulation of most metros continues to rise, it is not keeping up with the rise in population. Metro owners have paid for exhaustive marketing studies to find out why there is less interest in their product. They found that some age groups (20–29 years, for example) and special-interest groups (blacks and Hispanics, for example) feel there is nothing for them in the paper.

Metros are also threatened by the suburban dailies, whose numbers have increased in recent years. As city dwellers move to the suburbs, they often prefer the dailies that are particularly relevant to their communities. The smaller local newspaper is one of the few forums where citizens can exchange information with one another on a community-wide basis. Suburban dailies can deal directly with community issues that metros cannot or will not cover. Classified and local advertisers reach their target market.

However, some metros have moved to minimize this competition by publishing regional editions that concentrate more on local news. Morning papers have countered afternoon papers by publishing later editions with up-to-date sports results. Afternoon papers are publishing morning editions specifically aimed at suburban markets.

Any discussion of the decline of the metros is incomplete without mentioning the impact of electronic media. In the early 1970s, a Roper poll reported that 49 percent of the population felt that television was the most believable news source, whereas 20 percent cited newspapers. A 1980 Roper poll asked "Where do you usually get most of the news about what's going on in the world today?" People were allowed to respond in multiple categories; 64 percent cited TV, 44 percent newspapers, 18 percent radio, 5 percent magazines, and 4 percent "talking to people."

Other studies have found that Americans get more news from newspapers than they actually think they do. A Simmons Market Research/Roper study conducted in 1982 indicates that many Americans get more news from newspapers than from TV, despite what they might perceive they're getting.

Electronic media deliver the up-to-the-minute kind of news once covered by the extra newspaper edition. Are we giving up newspapers in favor of electronic media? Many blame television for the plight of the metros and for what they feel is a poorly informed citizenry.

It is often assumed that any decrease in the number of newspapers or in their circulation translates into a less-informed public. But there may be a *symbiosis*, or mutually beneficial process, at work here, too: Newspapers provide a wide range of news, opinion and interpretation, radio a quick summary of the headlines, and television a brief eyewitness account of the day's events. All perform different news-related functions while covering the same events. The consumer receiving information from all media is probably better informed than the one who insists that a single medium is the "best" way to get the news. For that matter, researcher Leo Bogart determined that most people who watched TV news found that it increased their desire to read the newspaper. Newspapers can provide details missing from 30-minute TV newscasts.

The newspaper format is not fixed and frozen. The appearance and success of *USA Today* indicates that newspapers can and will adjust to changing consumer information habits.

Despite all of the changes of the last 300 years, the newspaper continues to exert a tremendous influence on our daily lives. Most of us take a daily plunge in the information bath of newspapers. This ritual is likely to continue.

3.3

Time Line: Five Eras of American Newspaper Journalism

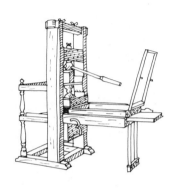

The Early Years

1690 *Publick Occurrences both Forreign and Domestick* is the first U.S. newspaper; it folds after one issue.

1721 James and Benjamin Franklin are early colonial printers. James starts the *New England Courant.*

1735 John Peter Zenger is acquitted of charges of seditious libel, thus setting precedence for truth as defense in libel cases.

1767 John Dickinson writes his series of "Letters from a Farmer in Pennsylvania" in the *Pennsylvania Chronicle,* characterizing the political nature of early papers.

1783 *The Pennsylvania Evening Post and Daily Advertiser* is the first American daily newspaper.

1798 The Sedition Act marks the effort to suppress the young nation's free press.

1808 First on-the-spot correspondents in Washington report political news for the papers back home.

1820s A colorful era for an information-starved public. Seacoast city papers hire boats to meet incoming ships carrying news. Pony express riders race each other from Washington to Boston and New York to carry congressional news.

The Penny Press

1833 Benjamin Day begins the *New York Sun.* Now everyone can afford a daily paper. His success is soon imitated by dozens of others.

1835 James Gordon Bennett launches the *New York Herald.*

1841 Horace Greeley starts the *New York Tribune.* Nine years later it is the first major newspaper to come out for the abolition of slavery. It is the first to develop the editorial page as we know it today.

1844 Samuel Morse invents the telegraph, wires are strung between major cities, and news now travels instantaneously.

1848 The Associated Press is founded. It serves papers of many political persuasions, so encourages reporters to write stories more objectively.

1865 After the Civil War, industrialization invades the press room and newspapers become increasingly mechanized.

Yellow Journalism

1878 Joseph Pulitzer founds the *St. Louis Post-Dispatch.*

1883 Pulitzer's *New York World* brings what was eventually called yellow journalism to America's largest city.

1886 The *World* tops 250,000 in circulation and surpasses the *Daily News* as New York's most widely read newspaper.

1887 William Randolph Hearst is put in charge of the *San Francisco Examiner.* Long an admirer of Pulitzer, he imitates *World* style and the *Examiner* prospers.

1895 Hearst comes to New York, buys the *New York Journal,* and hires away many *World* staffers.

1896 Circulation war between the *Journal* and *World.* Within 12 months, the *Journal* has the top circulation.

1896–98 Stories in the yellow press whip up public sentiment for a war with Spain.

1900 One-third of all metropolitan dailies practice yellow journalism.

1900 President McKinley is assassinated. The Hearst papers are blamed for inspiring the murderer.

1901–10 Circulation of most yellow papers falls and yellow journalism rapidly disappears.

Objective Journalism

1896 Adolph Ochs takes over the *New York Times.*

1900 The Associated Press moves to New York and expands.

1914 The *New York Times* begins a policy of publishing important documents in their entirety.

1923 The Canons of Journalism adopted by the American Society of Newspaper Editors stress the social responsibility of newspapers and reporters to report the news "fairly."

1933 The American Newspaper Guild is founded as the first union for news people.

1941 *The Wall Street Journal* is taken over by Bernard Kilgore. Circulation soars as the *Journal* practices detached reporting with emphasis on financial news and detailed analyses of economic events.

1942 Voluntary "Code of Wartime Practices for the American Press" is issued by government; the press is willing to cooperate.

1947 Hutchins Commission report is critical of press practices. It argues for tighter regulation of print journalism.

1958 United Press and International News Service combine to form United Press International.

The New Journalism

1958 Both major wire services begin running more "interpretative" articles and columns.

1960 The *New York Herald Tribune* begins using a magazine-style layout—more pictures and a lighter writing style.

1960s American metros lose circulation in many cities. Many combine to save press and circulation expenses. Many dailies in business for 60 years or more fold.

1962 Tom Wolfe, the father of the new journalism, joins the staff of the *New York Herald Tribune.*

1963 Sportswriter Jimmy Breslin begins column for the *Herald Tribune,* using writing techniques borrowed from fiction.

1968 Some Democratic convention reporters find they need more than objectivity to tell the story.

Domestic violence and increasing hostility over the Vietnam War make "objective" reporting difficult.

1968–69 Underground newspapers like the *Los Angeles Free Press* and the *Village Voice* experience rapid circulation increases.

1971 President Nixon temporarily blocks *New York Times, Washington Post,* and *Boston Globe* publication of the Pentagon Papers.

1972 Hunter Thompson's *Fear and Loathing: On the Campaign Trail 1972* appears as a series of articles in *Rolling Stone.*

1972 Bob Woodward and Carl Bernstein's *Washington Post* articles help expose Watergate scandals.

1974 President Nixon resigns.

1978 Over 60 percent of U.S. dailies are owned by large chains. Daily circulation of the 1,764 English-language dailies nears 62 million.

1980 The *Berkeley Barb,* one of the last surviving underground newspapers that began in the 1960s, prints its final issue.

1980s Journalists fear the worst as U.S. Supreme Court decisions appear to narrow the constitutional definitions of freedom of the press.

1983 Just one year after its inception, *USA Today* circulation tops 1 million.

FIVE ERAS OF AMERICAN NEWSPAPER JOURNALISM

Historians differ over the best way to divide the history of newspaper journalism. The five-way division in 3.3 appeared for the first time (as far as I know) in this book and merits some explanation. The eras alternate between an emphasis on objective or factual reporting and on subjective or advocacy reporting. The early, "yellow," and new-journalism eras are dominated by the subjective opinions of reporters, editors, and owners. The penny press and objective eras are characterized by more dispassionate attempts to report the news. Any division suffers to some degree from oversimplification, but this one does point out a continuing historical cycle that I believe is significant.

The Early Years

During the first years of American newspapers, opinions of the owner-editors were paramount in deciding how a story was to be "played." There were several small papers in each metropolitan area, and each reflected a particular point of view. Owner-editors usually printed stories to appeal to the faithful and bring new subscribers into the fold. Newspapers crusaded for political causes and decried political injustice. Editorial opinion did not appear on a special page, but came within a story, often in the lead paragraph, sometimes in italics. Since editors and reporters were advocates for a point of view, we refer to this period as the beginning of *advocacy journalism.*

The most heated debates appeared in the letters-to-the-editor column. Historian Frank Luther Mott notes that letters were often contributed by editors as well as readers. After the Revolution, debate centered on the adoption of a federal constitution, taxes, the treaty with England, and problems with the French.

Did newspapers in the new nation really have freedom of the press? Massachusetts adopted a tax on newspapers, and later on newspaper advertising, that smacked of state control. New printers were often poor and susceptible to promises of lucrative government printing contracts or post office appointments. In 1798 Congress passed the Sedition Act. It provided that "any person . . . writing, printing or uttering any false, scandalous or malicious statement against the Government of the United States . . . should be imprisoned not over two years and pay a fine not exceeding $2,000." This was interpreted by most editors as direct censorship, since those likely to be punished were those who disagreed with the powerful Federalist Party.

There were several trials under the act, and a few prominent printers were fined and sent to prison. But when Thomas Jefferson was elected President in 1800, he pardoned the prisoners, and the House Judiciary Committee denounced the Sedition Act as unconstitutional. All fines collected were returned with interest.

The last 30 years of the early period have been called the dark ages of partisan journalism. The profession was rife with corruption, and attacks on political leaders grew increasingly vicious. The personal lives of prominent figures were considered fair game, and Jefferson probably suffered the most. Andrew Jackson was never a favorite of journalists either, but he knew how to use the press to his own advantage. In 1830 he endowed the *Washington Globe* with a federal printing contract, and it became the official organ of the Jackson administration.

The Penny Press

Until this time, newspapers had been sold by yearly subscription, although several pub-

3.4

Independence Day at the New York Sun

"Police Office" was one of the most popular columns in the *Sun*. This sample is from the July 4, 1834, issue as reproduced in Frank Luther Mott's *American Journalism*. Note the occasional editorial quip.

Police Office

Margaret Thomas was drunk in the street—said she never would get drunk again "upon her honor." Committed, "upon honor."

William Luvoy got drunk because yesterday was so devilish warm. Drank 9 glasses of brandy and water and said he would be cursed if he wouldn't drink 9 more as quick as he could raise the money to buy it with. He would like to know what right the magistrate had to interfere with his private affairs. Fined $1—forgot his pocketbook, and was sent over to bridewell.

Bridget McMunn got drunk and threw a pitcher at Mr. Ellis, of 53 Ludlow st. Bridget said she was the mother of 3 little orphans—God bless their dear souls—and if she went to prison they would choke to death for the want of something to eat. Committed.

Catharine McBride was brought in for stealing a frock. Catharine said she had just served out 6 months on Blackwell's Island, and she wouldn't be sent back again, for the best glass of punch that ever was made. Her husband, when she last left the penitentiary, took her to a boarding house in Essex st., but the rascal got mad at her, pulled her hair, pinched her arm, and kicked her out of bed. She was determined not to bear such treatment as this, and so got drunk and stole the frock out of pure spite. Committed.

Bill Doty got drunk because he had the horrors so bad he couldn't keep sober. Committed.

Patrick Ludwick was sent up by his wife, who testified that she had supported him for several years in idleness and drunkenness. Abandoning all hopes of a reformation in her husband, she bought him a suit of clothes a fortnight since and told him to go about his business, for she would not live with him any longer. Last night he came home in a state of intoxication, broke into his wife's bedroom, pulled her out of bed, pulled her hair, and stamped on her. She called a watchman and sent him up. Pat exerted all his powers of eloquence in endeavoring to excite his wife's sympathy, but to no purpose. As every sensible woman ought to do who is cursed with a drunken husband, she refused to have anything to do with him hereafter—and he was sent to the penitentiary.

From Frank Luther Mott, *American Journalism, a History.* Copyright 1962 Macmillan Publishing Company, Inc. Used by permission.

---

lishers (including Horace Greeley) tried unsuccessfully to publish a cheap daily paper that could be sold on the streets for as little as two cents a copy. But the going price for most dailies was still six cents. At last, in 1833, thanks to technical improvements that sped production and distribution, Benjamin Day was able to bring the price of the *New York Sun* down to a penny a copy.

Advocacy journalism did not magically disappear in 1833, but the "penny press" did help develop a different kind of newspaper. The *New York Sun* offered to "lay before the public, at a price well within the means of everyone, all the news of the day. . . ." In contrast to the advocacy journals, the *Sun* was really apolitical. It offered very little political news, but reported short, breezy items about local people and domestic events. One of the most popular features was the "Police Office" report, which carried a long list of local people who had been arrested for drunkenness and rowdy behavior (see 3.4).

Within a few months, the *Sun*'s circulation surpassed all others in New York. Since the *Sun* did not depend on any one political constituency, it appeared to present the news impartially to all. Its overnight success prompted a number of imitators, including the *New York Herald* and the *New York Tribune*. All sold for a penny, and all were successful. Soon the penny press appeared in

Philadelphia and Baltimore. Penny-press owners seldom had an ax to grind; their purpose was to provide the public with the news at the cheapest possible price and, of course, to show a profit.

This is not to say the penny-press papers did not take positions. Greeley's *New York Tribune* printed his famous articles on the suffering in the New York slums in 1837–38; Greeley called his paper "the great moral organ," claiming it was on a much higher ethical plane than competing penny papers. The *Tribune* did much to convince religious and community leaders that the cheap newspaper could be an instrument for good and that journalism was not the exclusive bailiwick of sensation-seeking commercial publishers. But none of Greeley's opinion articles appeared on the news pages. In fact, the *New York Tribune* was the first paper to develop an editorial page as we know it today.

Mott credits the penny press with changing the concept of news. Newspapers of the early era had emphasized politics and events in Europe. The penny press shifted attention to hometown events, particularly those involving crime and sex. There was also the human-interest story—forerunner of today's soft news.

Another blow to advocacy journalism came with the invention of the telegraph in 1844 and the founding of the Associated Press (AP) four years later. The AP would provide all news stories for a fee, but what about a political slant? It was decided that events would be reported as dispassionately as possible, so as not to offend any subscriber. Organized as a cooperative and owned by its member publications, the AP offered its service to newspapers of every political persuasion.

Yellow Journalism

The slavery issue and the threat of civil war heated up political debate in the late 1850s.

More and more penny-press space was given over to political news. Later, battles between the Yankee and rebel armies were reported in detail. After the war, a young ex-soldier named Joseph Pulitzer (see 3.5) arrived in St. Louis to seek his fortune. Almost immediately he became involved in local politics and to everyone's surprise was elected to the state legislature. There he became an ardent spokesman for the common people, fighting graft and corruption.

In 1878 Pulitzer bought the *St. Louis Dispatch* at a sheriff's auction and combined it with the *Post*. The new *Post-Dispatch* enlivened its columns with crusades against lotteries, tax evasion, and the city administration.

Buoyed by his success, Pulitzer moved east and acquired the *New York World*, which had been losing $40,000 a year. Pulitzer promptly announced that the *World*, under his leadership, would "expose all fraud and sham, fight all public evils and abuses . . . and battle for the people in earnest sincerity."

The phenomenal success of this formula changed journalism forever. The news reporter searched for an "unusual" slant to the story; there were stunts and "people's crusades." One reporter feigned insanity to be admitted to a state asylum and then exposed conditions there. *World* crusades against telephone and railroad monopolies were incessant. Most articles featured diagrams, illustrations, and, later, photographs. The *World* made daring use of the editorial cartoon.

Pulitzer's fiercest rival was William Randolph Hearst, who bought the competing *New York Journal* in 1895. In two years the *Journal* surpassed Pulitzer's *World* circulation. Money was no object, and Hearst hired the best writers and illustrators away from his competition. Like Pulitzer's, his paper embarked on large-scale crusades, but none more extravagant than the publicity he bought

3.5
Personal Profile: Joseph Pulitzer

Every year on his birthday Joseph Pulitzer gave each of his friends a little gift and passed out cigars to his top executives. This reverse of the usual practice made sure that no one forgot his birthday, but it also said something about the paradoxical nature of one of history's most influential journalists.

His was a Horatio Alger story. He started out penniless, worked hard, and saved his money. He turned the *St. Louis Post-Dispatch* into one of the finest newspapers in America in less than five years. Then he moved on to New York, where he boosted the *New York World*'s circulation from 20,000 to more than 250,000.

Though what he did was amazing, the way he did it was even more notable. Both his papers were examples of yellow journalism. The "yellows" had a lively and uncompromising style that included the world of emotion as well as that of fact. No political party or candidate felt safe from the sting of the *World*.

Pulitzer was careful to distinguish his brand of advocacy journalism from Hearst's. The Hearst papers, he explained, were simply "malicious and hateful." In all fairness, Hearst's own political ambitions may have sparked his most vicious attacks, while Pulitzer's worst ulterior motive was to increase circulation. But contemporary critics see very little difference between the practices of the two yellow-journalism giants.

A colorful character in his own right, Pulitzer was often cantankerous and arbitrary, demanding superhuman performance from his workers, who often put in 16-hour days. Ironically, the originally penniless trustbuster became part of the capitalistic establishment he criticized with such vehemence, and his profits from the *World* helped buy a yacht and hire personal servants. But his paper never wavered from the original editorial commitments that had been made when Pulitzer took command in 1883. It continued to crusade for social and economic equality. It is this spirit that is embodied in the most coveted awards in American journalism, the Pulitzer Prizes.

During the final 20 years of his life, Pulitzer was virtually blind and seldom came to the *World* offices, gaining a reputation as an eccentric recluse. The reputation was well deserved. During the summer of 1911 he mused, "From the day on which I first consulted the oculist up to the present time I have only been three times in the *World* building. Most people think I'm dead. . . ." Before the end of the year, he was.

3.6
Citizen Kane and His Declaration of Principles

The office is dark except for the dim light from a gas lamp. Charles Foster Kane has taken over the *New York Inquirer* and moved into the office, bag and baggage, reminding a befuddled editor that "the news goes on 24 hours a day and I want to be here for all of it." In his first 24 hours he has fired that editor, dropped the price of the *Inquirer* from three cents to two, and remade the front page four times. He is joined by his business manager, Mr. Bernstein, and his best friend, Jed Leland:

Bernstein: You just made the paper over four times tonight, Mr. Kane—that's all.

Kane: I've changed the front page a little, Mr. Bernstein. That's not enough—there's something I've got to get into this paper

besides pictures and print—I've got to make the *New York Inquirer* as important to New York as the gas in that light.

Leland: What're you going to do, Charlie?

Kane: My Declaration of Principles—don't smile, Jed. (Getting the idea) Take dictation, Mr. Bernstein.

Bernstein: I can't write short-hand, Mr. Kane.

Kane: I'll write it myself. (Kane grabs a piece of rough paper and a grease crayon. Sitting

for the *Journal* itself: full-page ads in other publications and giant billboards and notices plastered everywhere. Through it all, Hearst maintained that profits were secondary. His was a mission to defend "the average person" (see 3.6).

Like Pulitzer, Hearst was not above using stunts in the pursuit of circulation and even of news itself. According to legend, Hearst sent an illustrator named Remington to Havana to document atrocities and cover the "war" that was soon to break out there. Remington cabled:

HEARST, JOURNAL, NEW YORK
EVERYTHING IS QUIET. THERE IS NO
TROUBLE HERE. THERE WILL BE NO WAR.
WISH TO RETURN. REMINGTON.

To which Hearst replied:

REMINGTON, HAVANA
PLEASE REMAIN. YOU FURNISH THE
PICTURES AND I'LL FURNISH THE WAR.
HEARST.

No one knows whether the story is true. But it is true the Hearst papers helped convince

down on the bed next to Bernstein, he starts to write.)

Bernstein: (Looking over his shoulder) You don't wanta make any promises, Mr. Kane, you don't wanta keep.

Kane: (As he writes) These'll be kept. (Stops and reads what he has written) I'll provide the people of this city with a daily paper that will tell all the news honestly. (Starts to write again, reading as he writes) I will also provide them . . .

Leland: That's the second sentence you've started with "I."

Kane: (Looking up) People are going to know who's responsible. And they're going to get the news—the true news—quickly and simply and entertainingly. (With real conviction) And no special interests will be allowed to interfere with the truth of that news. (Writes again, reading as he writes) I will also provide them with a fighting and tireless champion of their rights as citizens and human beings—Signed—Charles Foster Kane.

Leland: Charlie . . . (Kane looks up)

Leland (continuing): Can I have that?

Kane: I'm going to print it. (Calls) Mike!

Mike: Yes, Mr. Kane.

Kane: Here's an editorial. I want to run it in a box on the front page.

Mike: (Very wearily) Today's front page, Mr. Kane?

Kane: That's right. We'll have to remake again—better go down and let them know.

Mike: All right, Mr. Kane. (He starts away)

Leland: Just a minute, Mike. (Mike turns)

Leland (continuing):When you're done with that, I'd like to have it back. (Mike registers that this, in his opinion, is another screwball and leaves. Kane looks at Leland.)

Leland (continuing): I'd just like to keep that particular piece of paper myself. I've got a hunch it might turn out to be one of the important papers—of our time. (A little ashamed of his ardor) A document—like the Declaration

of Independence—and the Constitution—and my first report card at school. (Kane smiles back at him, but they are both serious. The voices of the newsboys fill the air.)

That scene, from perhaps the greatest American film ever made, *Citizen Kane,* is fantasy, of course. But it captures precisely the image of the crusading editor that we all carry around in our heads. The editor who fights for the public's rights "as citizens and human beings" is part of the folklore of American journalism and is based on the real-life stories of men like Hearst (who served as the obvious model for *Citizen Kane*) and Pulitzer.

Though journalism has changed in many ways since the beginning of the century, most of us still think of newspaper work as romantic, glamorous, and socially vital. Films like *Citizen Kane* (the crusading publisher) and *All the President's Men* (the crusading reporters) reinforce that image.

Americans that their pride and freedom were threatened; before long, America was at war with Spain.

In 1895 the Hearst-Pulitzer battle centered on the Sunday editions. The *World* was the undisputed leader in that area. Sunday supplements were costly to produce but very profitable. They featured large, sensationalized articles and drawings about science or pseudo-science, along with crime, sports, society news, and color comics.

Most renowned of all *World* cartoonists was Richard Outcault, whose *Yellow Kid* comic strip depicted local scenes and situations and soon became the city's favorite. This prompted Hearst to hire Outcault away from Pulitzer and feature the strip in his competing Sunday *Journal.* Pulitzer claimed he had sole rights and hired another artist to draw his own version of the strip. For a while New York had two *Yellow Kids.* So famous was the character, the strip, and the story of the competing journalists that critics began to call both "yellow papers." Eventually the term *yellow journalism* was used to describe this era of American journalism.

Objective Journalism

Not everyone was happy with yellow journalism. Some readers boycotted the *Journal* and *World*, and some libraries and clergymen canceled their subscriptions. They believed that the exploitation of sex and crime news was a public menace. Critics cited Hearst's involvement in the Spanish-American War as one of the dangers of yellow journalism.

But other things were also happening in New York. In 1896, Adolph Ochs rescued the *New York Times* from bankruptcy. Within a few years, he made it one of the country's most successful newspapers without the help of yellow journalism, ushering in a new era of objective journalism. By 1914, the *Times* had a policy of printing speeches, treaties, and government documents *in full*, the ultimate expression of objectivity.

Reporters were professional observers whose role was limited to reporting "just the facts." The period after 1900 saw journalism move from a vocation to a profession. Journalism schools began springing up across the country. The approach that most schools taught as "proper reporting" is perhaps summarized best in George Fox Mott's *New Survey of Journalism*. According to Mott, the beginning reporter should realize at the outset that

. . . there is little or no opportunity in the reporting of news for the writer to give rein to his innermost thoughts, however high, or his deepest feelings, however subtle. . . . reporting the news, even the hot news, is a coldly impersonal job. The Editor wants to find the facts in the story and not the writer's personal impressions or emotions. He has learned from long experience that effective newswriting must be objective.

In 1923, the American Society of Newspaper Editors stated rather concretely what was already the credo of most major American newspapers: "A journalist who uses his power for any selfish or otherwise unworthy purpose is faithless to a high trust." This "selfishness" included slanting stories to a particular political perspective.

Not all journalists would agree that slanted reporting had disappeared entirely. *Time* magazine often came under criticism from those who felt it presented certain political biases, particularly during the post–World War II period. Until its demise in 1971, *I. F. Stone's Weekly* followed earlier traditions of advocacy journalism. Still, most editors insisted on objectivity and got it. Objectivity became synonymous with good journalism, and few challenged it. Papers still conducted crusades, of course, but journalists were careful to print both sides of an issue wherever possible, and they generally bent over backward to double-check facts and figures before printing them.

Modern journalistic business methods reinforce the practice of objective reporting. Local ownership of the metropolitan daily has rapidly become a thing of the past. Large chains like the Newhouse and Gannett groups have bought up dozens of major newspapers. Often this means that one chain owns both major newspapers in a city. (Newhouse, for example, owns both the *Oregonian* and the *Oregon Journal* of Portland; the Gannett group owns both the *Advertiser* and the *Star Bulletin* of Honolulu.) These large corporations are seldom overtly concerned with national political matters and are primarily interested in making a profit. As for local political issues, top management is often thousands of miles away and does not wish to get involved. Of course, most papers do take sides on local and national issues on the editorial pages, and local editors and reporters do have a stake in the community. But there is not the kind of all-out pressure that comes from an owner-editor on the scene.

3.7

Army Counsel Joseph Welch (left) and Wisconsin's Senator Joseph McCarthy during the 1954 hearings that were McCarthy's final turn in the spotlight.

The New Journalism

Not all would agree that objective journalism is a blessing. Some feel, for example, that an insistence on two sides to every story may have prevented journalists from doing what print does best, describing the complexities of an issue or event. According to Marshall McLuhan:

The old (objective) journalism tried to give an objective picture of the situation by giving the pro and the con. It was strangely assumed that there were two sides to every case. It never occurred to them that there might be 40 sides, 1,000 sides . . . no, only two sides.

During the McCarthy hearings of the early 1950s, the press was careful to maintain its objectivity. Senator Joseph McCarthy from Wisconsin was making serious allegations about communists in the United States. Most journalists disagreed with McCarthy and his methods but feared taking him on directly in their stories; however, a few did not. The *New York Times* editorialized against McCarthy.

Columnist Drew Pearson and broadcast journalist Edward R. Murrow were among those who vehemently denounced McCarthy's tactics. Murrow's famous *See It Now* broadcast, using clips from the senator's own speeches, seemed to help turn the public tide against McCarthy.

At this point, the press began to seriously reexamine the role of the reporter (see 3.7). Perhaps facts alone weren't enough. The public had a right to get *more* than the facts. Veteran reporters were in a position to make value judgments about the facts as well as report them.

In 1958, both the Associated Press and the new United Press International (UPI) began running more interpretative articles and columns on their wires. The use of large pictures and more visually attractive magazine-style layouts became common practice in most metros. A band of renegade journalists began experimenting with the *new journalism*, the new nonfiction. Theirs was a subjective, no-holds-barred writing style. Objectivity, they said, had been a sacred cow long enough—

truth was best reported by those who let their emotions become *part* of the story.

In the 1960s, dozens of underground newspapers like the *East Village Other*, *Los Angeles Free Press*, and *Berkeley Barb* appeared. These had a definite left-of-center political viewpoint, and their bias showed in almost every article. The underground press was irreverent, funny, frank, and often outrageous. It was also very popular. Apparently, there was an audience for subjective journalism.

The new journalism is still more at home in underground newspapers and magazines than on the front pages of metros. But the underground press left its mark on those "above ground." Newspapers now devote more space to soft news and new-journalism stories than ever before, and reporters are not as timid about expressing their points of view. Today, every issue of the *Los Angeles Times* carries a soft news-analysis story on the front page. The reporter's point of view is often part of the story.

The Evolution of American Journalism

Each of the five eras of American journalism had its own distinct flavor. All contributed to and reflected the social order of their day.

Early newspapers were formed in a new society, still seeking a political and social direction. They were chaotic and sometimes bitter, and so were their readers. The penny press resulted from advances in technology and mechanization. Penny papers may have served the first real popular desire for equality and honest government. Their zeal in this pursuit reflects the zeal of the times. The objective years may have been a necessary consequence of yellow journalism. The more sophisticated reader expected something less

sensational. It is probably too early to pass judgment on the new journalism, but it was born of the social and political chaos of the 1960s and is changing modern news practices. Critics worry that readers spotting a bias in a story may grow to distrust newspapers and reporters as much as they now distrust the politicians the stories are often about.

Newspaper messages are vital clues to the social norms and behaviors of their times. The newspaper, like all mass media, contributes to and amplifies those behaviors. In every case, an important part of this contribution involves *how* a subject is presented as well as *what* is presented, *form* as well as *content*, *medium* as well as *message*.

PRESS, PUBLIC, AND GOVERNMENT

Like all freedoms, the freedom to print information must be tempered by a certain responsibility. Most of us think of freedom as absolute, yet freedom of speech does not include the right to yell "fire" in a crowded theater.

The entire problem of freedom of the press involves relationships between three entities: press, public, and government. Each of these three entities has certain rights guaranteed under the Constitution. The public has a "right to know," and thus the press has a constitutional right to gather information and print it for public consumption. But the "public" can also include one or more parties accused of a crime. The accused also have a number of rights under the Constitution, such as the right to a trial by an unbiased jury of their peers. Since the news media play such a large role in determining what potential jurors might hear about a case, there is often a conflict between the press's right to obtain and print information and the rights of the accused to an unbiased jury. Obviously if everyone in town reads all about the "guilt" of an accused criminal before he or she is brought to trial, it will be difficult to find 12 "unbiased" peers to serve on a jury.

In a larger context, the duties of various branches of the government can conflict with the duty of the press to report information to the public. When there is conflict between the press and the government, it is generally resolved through the courts.

Thus when a reporter declines to name a source to an investigating government agency, such as a grand jury, the matter is eventually resolved in the courts. When the police want access to a reporter's information regarding, say, an investigation of a crime, the reporter might refuse and once again the matter must be decided by the courts.

In recent decades a number of key Supreme Court decisions have spoken to these issues. These decisions are particularly crucial, since the court interprets the Constitution and makes the final decision in selected cases. These rulings are then *interpreted* by lower courts. Hence, one Supreme Court decision might eventually affect hundreds of cases in the lower courts.

In general, Supreme Court decisions made in the 1960s tended to favor the press, and they offered journalists a much broader protection from government interference than had been possible earlier. All of that changed, however, during the 1970s and early 1980s, when the court handed down a number of decisions that were seen as more severely limiting the freedom of the press when it conflicts with the duties of various branches of federal, state, and local governments.

A number of decisions involved reporters' access to court proceedings and the trials of accused criminals. The court is interested in protecting the rights of the accused and

ensuring a fair trial. Reporters are interested in preserving the public's right to know by reporting all of the aspects of the case to the public.

Two of the more controversial cases were *Gannett Co., Inc.* v. *DePasquale* (1979) and *Richmond Newspapers, Inc.* v. *Virginia* (1980). In *DePasquale* the court ruled 5–4 that a pretrial suppression-of-evidence hearing in a murder case could be closed to the public and the press. What worried journalists most was the language of the majority decision. Writing in the *Columbia Journalism Review* (September-October 1980), Bruce Sanford said that the language of the decision "suggests that even trials may be closed to the public and the press whenever the defendant and the judge agree to do so."

A year later, however, a 7–1 majority ruled in the *Richmond Newspapers* case that "absent an overriding interest articulated in findings, the trial of a criminal case must be open to the public" and the press. Chief Justice Warren Burger said that "people in an open society do not demand infallibility from their institutions, but it is difficult for them to accept what they are prohibited from observing." This opinion seemed in marked contrast to *DePasquale*, but the court was careful to distinguish between pretrial hearings and actual trials. While journalists could take some comfort from *Richmond Newspapers*, many contended that it did not completely undo the damage done to the newsgathering process by *DePasquale*. What matters most, of course, is whether lower courts will use this decision to bar the press from judicial proceedings, and how seriously that will affect the public's right to know (see 3.8).

When it comes to protecting a journalist's sources, however, the press has had little to be joyous about. Beginning in the early 1970s, a number of decisions seemed to deeply

3.8

This ad, sponsored by the Harte-Hanks newspaper group, points up the continuing friction between reporters trying to cover criminal cases in court and judges who banish the press from the courtroom in an attempt to protect the defendant's right to trial by an unbiased jury. The "Fresno Four" case was a celebrated example of reporters' being jailed for refusing to disclose their confidential sources while being questioned under oath.

undercut the traditional right of reporters to maintain the confidentiality of their sources. In *Zurcher* v. *Stanford Daily* (1978), the court upheld the right of the Santa Clara County Sheriff's Department, armed with a search warrant, to "rummage through" the files of the Stanford University paper in a search for "criminal evidence." At issue were photographs taken during a campus demonstration. The Sheriff's Department contended that, since the paper had covered the demonstration and since a number of photographs had been taken but not published, deputies should be allowed to inspect any and all files in the *Stanford Daily*'s newsroom to look for the pictures. The idea was that the photos *might* reveal some wrongdoing on the part of the demonstrators. The department convinced a judge to issue a search warrant and spent several days searching the newsroom. Ironically, it found nothing that could help it. However, the newspaper contended that this search was a violation of the First Amendment, which prohibits government infringement of freedom of the press, because:

1 The presence of the police in the newsroom disrupted editorial processes of the paper.

2 Reporters' confidential notes and other materials covering unrelated matters would be examined by the police. Hence reporters could no longer guarantee confidentiality to their sources.

The court disagreed, however, ruling that, where the rights of the government to conduct a "good-faith" investigation of criminal activity and the rights of the press to keep a newsroom off limits to police and other investigating agents came into conflict, it is the right of the press that must give way. In a dissenting opinion, Justice Potter Stewart suggested that such materials should be obtained by issuing a court subpoena, rather than a search warrant. A subpoena directs that specific materials be submitted for inspection. A newspaper would also have the right to petition the court and argue its side of the story before giving up the disputed documents. Thus there would be a hearing with both sides represented, and a judge would make a final determination based on the facts in that specific case.

Press reaction to the *Stanford Daily* decision was swift and decidedly negative. Paul Davis, then president-elect of the Radio-Television News Directors Association, said, "I am convinced that we will see more newsroom search warrants in the near future and that sometimes unintentionally, sometimes intentionally, abuse will come as quickly." Jack C. Landau, of the Reporters Committee for Freedom of the Press, noted that "the fabric of journalism on a daily basis is so intertwined with obtaining information of a confidential nature that permitting police to search through a newsroom jeopardizes the relationships of every reporter in the newsroom. . . ."

Journalists' reactions to the decision were also heard in Washington, where Senator Birch Bayh, an Indiana Democrat, introduced a bill during the 1980 session that restricted surprise police searches of newsrooms. A modified version of that bill became law in 1981.

Other recent court decisions seem to have further eroded reporters' relationships with confidential sources. The *Reporters Committee for Freedom of the Press* v. *American Telephone & Telegraph Co. et al.* decision (1979) found that the telephone company's routine practice of supplying various government investigative agencies with the telephone records of certain journalists was indeed constitutional and did not significantly abridge the freedom of the press to gather information. The court again held that government interests in the process of conducting "good faith felony investigations" "always override a journalist's interests in protecting his source." The court said further that "in our view, plaintiff's position is based on erroneous propositions. First, the so-called right of journalists to gather information from secret sources does not include a right to maintain the secrecy of sources in the face of good faith felony investigations."

Perhaps the most controversial of all the decisions in this area came in the matter of *New York Times Co.* v. *New Jersey* (1978).

Myron Farber, a reporter for the *Times*, wrote a series of articles investigating "mysterious deaths" at a hospital in New Jersey. The stories were widely read and reprinted and eventually led to the 1976 indictment of Dr. Mario E. Jascalevich on charges of poisoning five patients. In the pretrial hearing, Jascalevich's lawyers asked the court to subpoena the reporter's notes and other related materials to examine them for potential use in defending their client. When Farber refused to give them up, the judge found him and the *Times* guilty of contempt of court and sentenced the reporter to six months in jail with the sentence to begin *after* he gave up the notes. Meanwhile, Farber was ordered to jail and held there without bail. In addition, the *Times* was ordered to pay a fine of $100,000 per day plus $5,000 for each day that passed until the notes were surrendered.

The case went through the courts, and finally the Supreme Court upheld the lower court actions, again ordering Farber to jail. While the case was still pending, the *Times* commented in an editorial: "The loss of this case on the merits would be a serious blow to all newsgathering. The present trial by nights in jail is itself a dangerous infringement on the right to publish." What was particularly disturbing to journalists about this case was that it was tried in New Jersey, a state that has one of the toughest "shield laws"

in the nation. Many states have passed such laws in recent years. They are intended specifically to protect reporters' confidential notes and sources. By letting the lower court decision stand, the Supreme Court said that when a shield law and a defendant's rights under the U.S. Constitution collide, a shield law must yield. The lower court further questioned certain aspects of the shield law and concluded that they might violate existing citizen guarantees as granted under the United States and New Jersey constitutions.

In matters concerning reporter access to criminal proceedings, government access to reporters' confidential notes and sources, and press responsibility for potentially libelous stories (see Chapter 4), the courts have usually found in recent years against the press. Many journalists feel that there is a decidedly antipress sentiment in the Supreme Court as it is presently constituted and that this is, in part, a reflection of the beliefs of justices appointed by Richard Nixon.

Whatever the reason, it is clear that the court's decisions over the last decade or so may have seriously hindered journalists in their work and may indeed be narrowing our concept of freedom of the press. How seriously these decisions will hamper reporters in the future and the extent to which the public's right to know will be diminished remain to be seen.

ISSUES AND ANSWERS: A QUESTION OF BALANCE

Over the years, the balance of power between press, public, and government has shifted. During the colonial years, the King of England determined what colonists could read. The new nation established freedom

of the press as a cornerstone of its democracy with the First Amendment, which flatly declared that "Congress shall make no law . . . abridging the freedom of speech, or of the press . . . ," but unrestricted press freedom posed some problems. The balance of power has shifted to reflect current social and political trends.

The excesses of the early years and yellow journalism prompted reform movements within newspapers themselves. Competing publishers stepped in and reformed news practices in response to public demand. The government has, for the most part, stayed out of the business of reforming the press. But as mass media have grown in power and status, there have been calls for the government to "do something."

The 1947 Hutchins Commission on Freedom of the Press concluded: "It becomes an imperative question whether the performance of the press can any longer be left to the unregulated initiative of the few who manage it." The commission's skepticism reflects the growing power of mass media to determine our political and social attitudes and beliefs. Press coverage of a political candidate may mean the difference between victory and defeat. Thus there is a delicate balance between the power of the press to determine the outcome of an election and the perceived "rightful outcome" of such an event.

Most observers agree that the balance today is weighted heavily in favor of the press. Prepublication censorship is unknown, and obscenity remains the only area in which there is systematic government intervention. Though cries of censorship are heard whenever anyone suggests government regulation, the growing power of mass media seems to demand some shift in the balance. Many interpret recent Supreme Court decisions limiting freedom of the press as a response to this.

If we are to limit the freedom of the press for the benefit of all, should we also limit who may practice journalism? Since report-

ers and editors determine the content of the information we get for making important decisions, should we require some credentials from them to make sure they operate in our best interests? Doctors and lawyers must pass rigorous government exams to be admitted to practice. Medical and bar associations police their own ranks, weeding out the occasional incompetent or unethical member. (Of course this doesn't guarantee that all incompetents will be dismissed, but it helps.)

The beginning reporter can be a high school dropout or a Ph.D., a highly ethical person or one willing to exploit her position for personal or political purposes. There are journalism associations, fraternal codes, ethics committees, and the like, but none has the power to purge its ranks of incompetent or unethical members.

Since journalists have not acted to regulate themselves, some contend that it is the business of government to do so. They envision a regulatory agency similar to those that police the legal and medical professions.

Most journalists abhor the thought of any government regulation, maintaining it would violate freedom of the press. How can the government have such power over media when media are supposed to act as watchdogs? It might be easy for government to blunt press criticism by punishing it through a regulatory agency. Yet will any private business regulate itself in the public interest without the threat of external control?

Many books have been written about these press-public-government relationships; this has been a very simple overview. I hope that it will start you thinking about these issues and encourage you to do additional reading. A good starting point is the references at the end of this chapter.

QUERIES AND CONCEPTS

1 Delve into your own local newspaper, sifting the hard news from the soft. What is the balance of the front section in numbers of stories? How many total column inches are devoted to each?

2 How many people in your class read at least one story from a newspaper every day? Which section do they prefer and why?

3 Pick your favorite character from the history of American journalism and find a biography. Write a brief portrait along the lines of the story on Pulitzer in this chapter.

4 Citizen Kane's crusade and the Watergate reporters represent two of the images we have about journalism as a career. Can you think of others? Where did they come from?

5 Does the same company control all print news outlets in your nearest big city? Does it have any interests in the broadcast media?

6 Contact a local reporter, a government official, and a consumer advocate. Do they think the government should license or regulate reporters?

7 If *USA Today* is available in your area, compare the coverage of national and international hard-news stories with that of your local daily newspaper. How do they differ? Can you speculate as to why those differences exist? What the long-term impact might be on readers who rely on one or the other for all their news coverage?

READINGS AND REFERENCES

Hard and Soft News

William L. Rivers
The Mass Media: Reporting, Writing, Editing, 2d ed. New York: Harper & Row, 1975.
　　This is a complete *reporter's* handbook that covers all media. See especially "The World of the Journalist" and "Writing." The latter offers a "straight news" formula for carefully separating fact from opinion.

Michael Schudson
Discovering the News: A Social History of American Newspapers. New York: Basic Books, 1978.

The author deals explicitly with the various definitions of objectivity throughout journalism's history. The book is a series of essays covering the entire range of that history, but the most telling analyses of the objectivity question come in the section covering the 20th century.

Paul V. Sheehan
Reportorial Writing. Radnor, Pa.: Chilton Books, 1972.
　　This book will give you an idea of what the hard news reporter's goals are. Sheehan's approach is based on the assumption that most news is hard

news, though he does allow for the "human interest story" and the "interesting angle."

Mass and Special-Interest Audiences

Allen Kirschner and Linda Kirschner, eds. *Journalism: Readings in the Mass Media.* Indianapolis, Ind.: Odyssey Press, 1971.
  This anthology is full of useful articles about the role of the press in society and its audiences. See especially "Audience and Effect."

What You See Is What You Get

Marshall McLuhan
Understanding Media, 2d ed. New York: McGraw-Hill, 1964. (Also available in paperback from New American Library, 1973.)
  Much of McLuhan's work deals with the permanence of print and the unique characteristics of the newspaper form. See especially Chapters 9 ("The Written Word: An Eye for an Ear"), 16 ("The Print: How to Dig It"), 18 ("The Printed Word: Architect of Nationalism"), and 21 ("The Press: Government by News Leak").

Business Trends in Newspaper Publishing

Editor & Publisher. New York: Editor & Publisher, annual.
  As far as facts and figures are concerned, this is the bible of newspaper and magazine publishing. Available in most libraries.

Five Eras of American Newspaper Journalism

Journalists are preoccupied with their history. There have been hundreds, maybe thousands of books published on the subject. Those selected here are included for their comprehensiveness and readability. Use the bibliographies to pursue specific historical eras or personalities if you wish. None of these really covers the fifth era: the new journalism. See also the readings and references in Chapter 4.

Edwin Emery
Michael Emery
The Press and America: An Interpretative History of Journalism, 4th ed. Englewood Cliffs, N.J.: Prentice-Hall, 1978.
  A thorough and comprehensive history of journalism in the United States. Events are given more or less in chronological order. Thirty chapters, over 750 pages, everything you always wanted to know. . . .

Frank Luther Mott
American Journalism. Riverside, N.J.: Macmillan, 1962.
  A complete treatment of American journalism. Very popular among journalists and journalism history teachers. The excellent index enables you to go to your area of interest.

Robert A. Rutland
The Newsmongers: Journalism in the Life of the Nation, 1690–1972. New York: Dial Press, 1973.
  A breezier and more up-to-date version of journalism history than Mott's. More lively and readable, though less comprehensive.

W. A. Swanberg
Citizen Hearst. New York: Scribners,
1961. *Pulitzer*. New York: Scribners,
1972.

> Swanberg is a biographer who makes
> his characters come alive, and both vol-
> umes illuminate the subject matter in a
> way few others do. As interesting as
> any biographies you will find, each of
> these books has a useful bibliography
> and index.

Press, Public and Government

The *Columbia Journalism Review* is the
best single source for interpretative articles dealing with court actions affecting
newspapers and reporting. The material
presented in this section was drawn
largely from the following *Review* articles:

Bruce W. Sanford
"No Quarter from This Court," Septem-
ber-October 1979, pp. 59–63. "The Press
and the Courts: Is News Gathering
Shielded by the First Amendment?",
November-December 1978, pp. 43–50.
"Richmond Newspapers: End of a Zigzag
Trail?", September-October 1980, pp. 46–
47.

> When journalism writers are not busy
> writing about history, they are writing
> about government and the press. Again,
> there are dozens of books available, and
> the criteria for inclusion here are compre-
> hensiveness and readability.

Jerome A. Barron
Freedom of the Press for Whom? The

Right of Access to Mass Media. Blooming-
ton: Indiana University Press, 1973.

> Includes sections on campus press,
> underground press, crime, citizens'
> groups, and television. Media access is
> presented as a prime issue.

Georgetown Law Journal
*Media and the First Amendment in a
Free Society*. Amherst: University of Mas-
sachusetts Press, 1973.

> An anthology with contributions by
> Walter Cronkite and former Senator
> Sam Ervin, among others. Use the
> table of contents to go right to the area
> that interests you. This is a potpourri
> designed to have something for just
> about everybody.

Wayne Overbeck
Rick D. Pullen
Major Principles of Media Law. New
York: Holt, Rinehart & Winston, 1982.

> An excellent text that bridges the gap
> between law-student use and journal-
> ism-student use. Describes the Ameri-
> can legal system and then meticulously
> applies that system and its laws to the
> various issues surrounding freedom of
> the press.

Don R. Pember
Mass Media Law, 2d ed. Dubuque, Iowa:
Wm. C. Brown, 1981.

> Similar in scope and approach to Over-
> beck and Pullen. Separate chapters on
> gathering news and information, inva-
> sion of privacy, free press/fair trial,
> obscenity, and more.

Newspapers, Part Two: Soft News and Contemporary American Journalism

4

ON APRIL 22, 1983, THE WEST GERMAN MAGAZINE *STERN* announced a dramatic journalistic coup. It had come into possession of 62 volumes of Adolf Hitler's "personal diaries" that had been recovered surreptitiously from a 1945 plane crash. The volumes, now stored in a bank vault in Zurich, had been "authenticated" by several experts.

Newspapers and magazines in Great Britain, France, and Italy scrambled to secure the serial rights to the diaries. Headlines around the world heralded the story with zest and zeal. Extra newspapers and magazines were sold by the million as public interest in the newly found diaries swelled. *Newsweek* featured the diaries on its cover.

But a chemical analysis done on the diaries shortly after *Stern*'s publication of the first parts of them indicated clearly that they had been produced during the 1960s by a clever forger. A great number of newspapers and magazines had been hoaxed. And, of course, so had the public.

WHAT REALLY HAPPENED?

Time magazine was quick to point out that this was not the first such large-scale journalistic swindle. In 1928 the *Atlantic Monthly* published a series of articles on "Lincoln the Lover," based on some recently discovered letters that also proved to be fakes.

In a more recent example, Clifford Irving tried to convince the world and McGraw-Hill Publishing Company that he and reclusive billionaire Howard Hughes had agreed to coauthor Hughes' autobiography. When he produced a manuscript, the revelations made headlines. Again they were proved false. Ir-

> **The New York Times slogan, "all the news that's fit to print," advertises the fact that news is actually fiction.**
>
> MARSHALL McLUHAN

ving eventually served a prison term as a result of his escapades, and wrote a book, *The Hoax*, detailing his exploits in the case.

At the heart of such cases is the ethical obligation of any publication to authenticate such documents before rushing to press. Yet financial considerations can sway even the most cautious of editors. *Stern* was said to have paid some 4 million dollars for the rights to the diaries; had they been authentic, it might have been a good investment. The sale of syndication rights to other publications could well have exceeded that figure.

In a cover story on the fake diaries, *Time* warned the public to beware of such practices. "At least equally forewarned should be any editor foolish enough to emulate those at *Stern*, who so recklessly placed journalistic expediency above society's overriding need for accurate history. There is never a need, nor a justification for 'publishing first and authenticating later.' "

The nature of journalism, especially of the brand practiced by daily newspapers, makes authenticating every word difficult and time-consuming. But according to Donald D. Jones, a journalist and ombudsman who listens to complaints from the public about the *Kansas City Star*, "Errors of fact do more to undermine the trust and confidence of readers than any other sin we commit."

The public's insistence on "being the first to know" also figures in this issue. The editor or reporter who is blamed for rushing a story into print that later proves false is also praised for being first with a story that proves to be accurate. Perhaps it's human nature to want to be one of the insiders who possesses information ahead of the next person. But everyone should realize that such privilege can also exact a price. This is only one of a number of complex issues surrounding the relationship between newspaper editors and newspaper readers.

EDITORS AND READERS: A NEW SOCIAL CONTRACT

Two differing perceptions of what constitutes news in newspapers were very evident in a recent study commissioned by the American Society of Newspaper Editors. It describes the problem in detail: "There is indeed a serious gap between editors and readers, and it is much more than a simple difference of opinion between what editors think is new and interesting and what people want in their newspapers. It is a failure of communication and therefore of basic understanding."

What is happening, according to the study, is the emergence of a new "social contract," which readers seem to understand fully but which editors have not yet come to grips with. The social contract contains a number of needs that readers feel should be addressed by their local papers. Paramount among these is the need for self-fulfillment, for a "focus on self." One reader put it this way: "Editors live in one world, I live in another. They're worried about the Middle East and I'm worried about meeting my bills." Articles that emphasize self-help in one form or another seem to address these needs.

Readers interested in the study also expressed a deep, if subconscious, desire for a more *personal* type of journalism. "In a television age when personalities dominate and credibility depends on the chemistry between anchorman and viewer, it is not surprising that readers want to know who is speaking to them through their newspapers! How can I believe you if I don't know who you are, they ask." The popularity of local columnists and feature reporters is yet another indication of this need for communication on a one-to-one level.

Readers also expressed a desire for more local coverage and less emphasis on national and international affairs. "Whatever the importance of national news, strong local coverage still produces the strongest ties between readers and editors." It is these ties that bring about a stable circulation base for many newspapers.

The study concluded that readers still demand some hard news, but it must be accompanied by features—and a lot of them. They find features easier to read than news, partly because they are written in a personal and conversational style, but mostly because they are often aimed at the individual interests of the "Me" generation: health, diet, money management, self-improvement. A related complaint was that there is far too much emphasis on negative news, perhaps because standard beats such as the police beat are keyed to trouble. Readers pleaded for more positive news about their communities, more personal coverage through human-interest reporting and local columnists, and more service information to help them in their daily lives.

The message of the study is loud and clear. Editors have reacted with varying degrees of concern. *The New Yorker* magazine deplored the study, saying that if editors heeded it, newspaper content would become simply stories about readers and reporters. The logical conclusion would be a newspaper that becomes a "closed world," characterized by "an uninterrupted one-to-one relationship from which word of events in the larger world—what used to be called 'the news'—is shut out."

Despite this warning, one glance at your local newspaper will probably reveal an increasing amount of soft news and other materials speaking to the needs articulated in the study. Once, it was up to the editor to decide what was news, and the readers could take it or leave it. Now it appears that the readers have taken charge, largely because

of the fiscal realities of running a newspaper. Newspapers are, after all, a business. And businesses, at least in America, must make a profit or die.

SUPERMARKET SENSATIONALISM

The desire people have to read about other people may explain the success of the largest-selling newspaper in America, the *National Enquirer* (4.1), and its imitators, the *Star*, the *National Tattler*, and *Midnight*. These can usually be found at supermarket checkout counters; for this reason they represent "supermarket journalism."

Their marketing method guarantees them enormous exposure. Their subject matter, too, is designed to appeal to the largest possible audience. They feature gossip about Hollywood stars and other national and international celebrities. In addition, there are weekly stories about cancer discoveries, arthritis breakthroughs, and common but overlooked diseases "you can diagnose by taking a simple test right in the privacy of your own home." There are stories involving UFOs and astrological predictions. Faith healers who routinely perform miracles are also given space. In each issue, the *Enquirer* polls readers about their favorite TV shows. Every subject is chosen for its popular appeal. The *National Tattler* calls it "people-to-people journalism."

Publisher Generoso Pope paid $75,000 for the *National Enquirer* in 1952, when its circulation was only 17,000. Right away the *National Enquirer* began to offer up massive helpings of sex and gore (headlines screamed "I Cut Out Her Heart and Stomped on It"; "Mom Boiled Her Baby and Ate Her"), and in time, circulation rose to just over 1 million, where it stayed for a while. Then, in a stroke of marketing genius, Pope "cleaned up" the *Enquirer* in 1968, and circulation has been

4.1

Bold headlines and close-up pictures of the stars characterize the National Enquirer's brand of "supermarket journalism." The Enquirer's approach to reporting "intimate secrets" of celebrities took a severe blow in 1981 when a Los Angeles jury awarded Carol Burnett $1.6 million in damages for a 1976 item which reported her drunk and disorderly in a Washington restaurant. The libel suit has blazed the trail for other stars who have suits pending against the Enquirer. Like Burnett, they claim the tabloid fabricates stories about them which damage their reputation.

NATIONAL   40¢

ENQUIRER
LARGEST CIRCULATION OF ANY PAPER IN AMERICA

MARY TYLER MOORE TRAGEDY

Too Busy to Give Him Love He Craved—Son Killed Himself

Double Heartbreak

Violence by
Women Linked
To Menstruation
page 62
* * *
Lana Turner
Rescued From
Life as a Boozing,
Burned-Out Wreck
page 2
* * *
Look Slimmer
By Wearing the
Right Fashion
Accessories
page 42
* * *
New Predictions
By World's Most
Successful Psychic
page 52
* * *
How to Put Your
Budget on a Diet
— And Save $$
page 20

Angie Dickinson's Mom Dies & Hubby Falls for Another Woman

climbing ever since. Today, "America's liveliest newspaper" sells about 4 million copies a week.

Pope accounts for his success by saying the *Enquirer* gives the people what they want. "What you see on page one of the *New York Times* does not really interest most people, and interest is our only real rule." As for his critics, he says, "I don't care if other media respect us or not; a Pulitzer Prize ain't going to win us two readers."

The *Enquirer* relies heavily on human-interest stories. Supermarket journalism seldom lets the reporter become part of the story. Instead, reporters try to "help" subjects tell it in their own words. One memo from Pope's office told writers to "prod, push and probe the main characters in your stories, help them frame their answers. Ask leading questions like, 'Do you ever go into the corner and cry?'" In fact, like the yellow papers, the *Enquirer* will do anything to get a story. Pope admits a certain affection for the stunts of the old Hearst-Pulitzer days and pays writers up to $50,000 a year to dream them up. When Greek shipping tycoon Aristotle Onassis died, the *Enquirer* sent 21 reporters and photographers to cover the funeral. The tab was an estimated $50,000.

Enquirer stories have a definite point of view. The *Enquirer* world is one of modest heroes, brutal killers, brilliant astrologers, and sophisticated stars. Research shows that these are the stereotypes that most intrigue the consumers of supermarket journalism. Like all successful mass media, the *National Enquirer* anticipates trends in popular tastes and provides gratification for the mass audience. The object, of course, is an enormous circulation, and the formula has paid off. It appears that most of us do have an interest in the occult, the unknown, Hollywood stars, and the like. The *Enquirer* also delivers dozens of moral lessons that reflect popular myths and beliefs. *Enquirer* stories satisfy the hopes of their readers and justify their view of the world: The policewoman in New York teaches blind children to read in her spare time; the handicapped mother of six refuses welfare.

But there's a dark side too—government officials (the *Enquirer* calls them "burrocrats") are crooks living off the sweat of the working people, while the courts set criminals free to roam the streets and prey on their unsuspecting victims, who are often *Enquirer* readers. For better or worse, these beliefs are held by a lot of people, and the *National Enquirer* offers proof for only 65 cents a week.

SORTING OUT THE SOFT NEWS

How different is your local daily newspaper from the *National Enquirer*? Your local editors would maintain that the *Enquirer* is totally "soft" and that its only goal is financial profit, whereas their daily provides important hard news and operates by a strict set of journalistic ethics.

Yet the overwhelming majority of news in the local paper is soft: features, syndicated material, and columns. What's more, readership studies indicate that soft news enjoys a much larger following than hard news. If this were not so, there would not be so much of it, and the *National Enquirer* would not be America's best-selling newspaper.

Even in the dailies, many front-page stories are not all hard news. Often there is a large photograph, a colorful description, or a human-interest piece. After the first few pages, news-section content typically includes a detailed story about drugs, or a plea for the paper's latest crusade to send poor children to summer camp.

The editorial section is filled with interpretative and passionate pronouncements on the issues of the day from both editor and reader. Most papers now run an *op-ed* page (meaning opposite the editorial page). First-person narratives, stories about "interesting" important people, and detailed discussions of cultural trends appear here.

The real estate section contains large ads for new housing projects next to "news" stories about those same projects. There is an entertainment section filled with advertising for TV shows and films plus reviews of those same TV shows and films.

The family section is chock full of helpful household hints. Here you'll find columns by Erma Bombeck, Ann Landers, and syndicated gossip columnists (see 4.2). Most papers now include a midweek food section with recipes, restaurant and wine reviews, and, of course, the inevitable supermarket and restaurant ads. Meanwhile, life-style features teach readers how to balance their checkbooks in a new, creative way. Consumer features advise which type of automobile or food processor may be the best value.

4.2
Ask Ann Landers

She is the most widely read newspaperwoman in the world. Her column runs in some 800 newspapers, and according to a poll taken by United Press International, she is considered one of the world's ten most influential women. In any given week, her mailbox is stuffed with more than 7,000 letters from readers, most pleading for advice.

She is Ann Landers, the queen of the advice columnists (the closest competition is her twin sister, Abigail "Dear Abby" Van Buren). Both were raised in Sioux City, Iowa, and were taught the old-fashioned American virtues of hard work, honesty, and sexual restraint. Though Ann turned 65 in 1983, there is no sign she is about to retire. She brags she can "run rings around" her secretaries, primarily because they smoke and/or drink. Ann does neither.

Unabashedly she exclaims, "How do I feel about being a square? . . . Why, I think that's just fine. . . . I am a square and that squareness has paid off in ways that are very important to me." To teenagers contemplating premarital sex, she has her "three commandments": (1) four feet on the floor, (2) all hands on deck, and (3) no fair sitting in the dark.

For years her own nuptial bliss served as an example to those who felt marriage might be an outmoded institution. But after 36 years with Jules Lederer (founder of the Budget Rent-a-Car chain), divorce came in 1975. Though she gave the news to readers in one of her columns, she now rebuffs those who wonder why the answer lady had no answer for her own marital problems with a curt "M.Y.O.B.B." That's Ann Landers lingo for "mind your own business, buster!"

Dear Ann Landers:
You stated in your column recently that the executive who exposed himself to two neighborhood females was "mentally ill." Will you please explain?

Does this mean that all people who have the desire to display their bodies are ill in the same way? What about the folks who frequent nudist camps? And the ones who like swimming in the nude? And the nude dancers—both male and female?

Are these people sick? If so, where can they get help? Please print this letter, Ann. It is very important that I get answers to these questions, and there is nowhere I can go but to you.—Wondering in U.S.A.

Dear U.S.A.:
The executive who exposed himself to the neighborhood girls is indeed sick. The poor fellow needs psychiatric help. This illness is called exhibitionism. The man is intensely insecure about his sexuality and gets his jollies from the startled reactions of females who come upon the sight of him unexpectedly. It reassures him that he is male.

Nudists and strippers and people who enjoy swimming in the buff run the gamut from free spirits to nature-lovers. They may be a little far-out, but they are not necessarily in need of a head doctor. There's a big difference between showing off a good body and flashing one's genitals.

Dear Ann Landers:
I don't know where "Your Friendly Neighborhood Bank Teller" works, but he should try making it in the bank where I am employed.

I'd be happy if my customers only gave me their money upside down and backwards. How about the people who pull bills out of their shoes, bras and pouches under their armpits?

I wish those boobs who scream at the teller because they have to wait in line so long would scream at the rummies ahead of them who don't have their forms filled out properly, or who get right up to the teller's cage before they realize they haven't made out a deposit slip.

While I'm at it, I'd like to say "Thanks" to all the nice customers who make my job a pleasure. There are more of them than the other kind.—I Could Write a Book

Dear I.C.:
Why don't you? You're pretty funny.

Dear Ann Landers:
Don't back off. There IS a way to get your name off the junk mailer's list. It worked for me.

Take the time to open the packet and find the postage-free response envelope. Stuff it full of their material, plus any other junk mail you want to get rid of. Seal it and throw it in the mailbox.

When the junk dealer pays double or triple postage to receive his own junk back (it helps to write in big, bold letters "TAKE MY NAME AND ADDRESS OFF YOUR LIST"), he will probably comply with your request.—Judy R. in Elmhurst

Dear Judy:
Thanks for what sounds like a logical solution to the problem. I am going to try it myself and will report back in six months to let you know if it worked for me.

CONFIDENTIAL to Corpus Christi on the Fence:
Your fears are unfounded. The major difference between a man of 65 and a man of 35 is 30 years of experience.

© 1980 Field Enterprises Inc.

In other words, excepting obituaries, tide tables, weather, and a few paragraphs on the front pages, most newspapers deal primarily in soft news. It's their bread and butter, since it is often the reason readers subscribe in the first place. So in that respect, the content of your local paper is probably not that different from that of the *National Enquirer*, though there is a difference in style.

Professional journalists who feel that newspapers are primarily filled with hard news live in a fantasy world. Attention to hard news and the real complexities of national affairs is not what sells most newspapers. Most readers seek personalities, not politics; simple explanations, not exhaustive analyses. Faced with losses in circulation, newspaper editors have been forced to give readers more of what they want and less of what editors think they *should* have. After all, news is entertainment, and it has been since the days of the penny press.

COMICS: YOU'RE SIGNIFICANT, CHARLIE BROWN!

Among the most loved of all newspaper features is the comic strip. Arthur Asa Berger, who teaches at San Francisco State University, points out that comic strips and comic books have long "been part of the American imagination." It is strange that so little academic attention has been given them, because there is much to be learned from studying this medium and its audience. Some comics appeal to almost all of us (*Garfield*) and some appeal to only a few (*Gordo*), but in each case a special relationship forms between consumer and strip.

The forerunners of American comic strip artists were the great British caricaturists of the 18th and 19th centuries. James Gillray, Thomas Rowlandson, and George Cruik-shank pioneered in telling stories with a *series* of pictures. Rowlandson was among the first to use speech balloons to give his characters a voice of their own. Most of these early strips dealt exclusively with politics. By the end of the 19th century, American comic pioneer Richard Outcault was drawing a regular humorous strip for the *New York World*. Rudolph Dirks's *Katzenjammer Kids* were pulling tricks on the Captain as early as 1897 in the *New York Journal*. Names like *Oliver's Adventures*, *The Yellow Kid*, *The Gungles*, and *Dixie Dugan* will ring no bells unless you are a real old-time comic buff. On the other hand, many strips that started as early as the 1930s and 1940s or even earlier are still with us today. These include Chic Young's *Blondie* (which first appeared in 1930—she married Dagwood later that same year), *Dick Tracy*, *Gasoline Alley*, and a host of others.

Most of us tend to think of comic strips as either humorous or serious. Certainly *B.C.*, *Broom Hilda*, and *Miss Peach* are humorous, whereas *Brenda Starr*, *Mary Worth*, and *Apartment 3G* are more serial than strip. But what do we do with strips like *Feiffer* and the more recent *Doonesbury* (see 4.3)? Perhaps the "social" comics need a category of their own.

Another category might include the action-adventure strips like *Steve Canyon* and *Dick Tracy*, but these are seen less and less often on the newspaper comic pages. Action-adventure heroes seem to survive with greater dignity in other media. Superheroes Superman, Batman, and Captain Marvel still have a faithful audience who follow their adventures in comic books. Superheroes like the Incredible Hulk have also been found on television in their own series.

Many comic strips faithfully depict real-life characters in more or less realistic situations (*Rex Morgan, M.D.* and *Mary Worth*). Others caricature human facial or body features in a distinctive way (*Cathy*, *Dennis the*

4.3
Doonesbury and His Heritage

DOONESBURY   **by Garry Trudeau**

In 1968, the *Yale Daily News* began running an occasional comic strip by undergraduate Garry Trudeau. Initially, it depicted the antics of B.D., the mythical star quarterback of the Yale football team. The student audience quickly connected B.D. with Brian Dowling, who was, in fact, the captain of the Yale football team. Before long Trudeau was adding new characters: Mike Doonesbury, the make-out king who never quite made out; Bernie, the science major who revealed casually that he had been weird since age four when he ate an entire outboard motor; and Megaphone Mark, the campus radical.

The strip was picked up by Universal Press Syndicate in 1970, and Trudeau began to add non-campus characters like Joanie Caucus, the "liberated" ex-housewife, Phred the Terrorist, a lovable North Vietnamese soldier; and Uncle Duke, a drug-crazed reporter for *Rolling Stone*.

Almost immediately, *Doonesbury* became the most talked-about strip since *Peanuts*. It was earthy, contemporary, political, and funny. Real-life characters began making appearances in the strip: Dan Rather speaking from Zonker's television set and Richard Nixon, Gerald Ford, Jimmy Carter, and Ronald Reagan from inside the White House. A series of strips on Watergate won Trudeau the first Pulitzer Prize for editorial cartooning ever given to a daily comic strip artist.

Trudeau's insistence on delving into political issues has not been totally without consequence for the strip itself. During the Watergate affair, a number of newspapers refused to run strips they deemed too controversial. Others shifted *Doonesbury* to the editorial page and some left it there. Similar responses came when the strip discussed the political fortunes of then–California governor Jerry Brown in 1980. Through it all, Trudeau remained stoic and enigmatic, choosing to let the strip do his talking for him.

In 1982 *Doonesbury* fans were shocked when Trudeau announced he would be taking a "sabbatical" at the end of the year to work on other projects and that the strip would not be appearing again for at least two years. Trudeau claimed that the break was necessary to give

BLOOM COUNTY   by Berke Breathed

© 1983, The Washington Post Company. Reprinted with permission.

him time to help his characters make the transition from "draft beer and mixers to cocaine and herpes."

In *Doonesbury*'s absence, many fans turned to *Bloom County*, a *Doonesbury*-like strip created by 26-year-old Trudeau devotee Berke Breathed. Though the two strips look remarkably alike, Breathed maintains that the artistic similarities between them are "cosmetic." Like Trudeau, Breathed got his start cartooning at college; he says it was the one thing he did there that "immediately got me all this attention."

Perhaps Breathed can identify with Trudeau's need for a sabbatical. He was quoted in a recent interview as saying that "we're living in the dullest times in the past 45 or 50 years. The only change occurring is tech-

nological . . . I'm having a hard time finding good material to satirize and to comment on. . . ."

Whatever happens from here, *Doonesbury* and *Bloom County* have left their mark on the evolution of the American cartoon strip. The cartoonists' willingness to comment on social issues has brought a new dimension to the genre. The "funny papers" will never be quite the same again.

Menace). There are also strips that allow us to enter a world where animals talk and think in very human terms (*Bloom County* and *Garfield*).

For many years most leading cartoonists were men. This began to change in the 1970s, however, when women became more prominent on the comic pages just as they did in all other areas of media. Cathy Guisewite's *Cathy* provides realistic and humorous glimpses into the world of the working woman. In *For Better or Worse*, Lynn Johnston depicts home and family problems as grist for humor, from the point of view of a wife and mother.

Why do most of us devote a part of our day to these cartoon fantasies? Because they are a source of diversion and escape, and for many they supply the heroes and heroines that are all too rare in real life. Action-adventure comics have pure heroes and pure villains. In the end, the bad guys are caught and punished while the good guys win out. Even TV isn't that clear-cut anymore.

Another reason we read comic strips is because they give us a chance to become involved morally. Cartoonists receive hundreds of letters when they "kill off" a popular character. When Mary Worth dispenses folksy common sense to ease the troubled lives of her fellow characters, thousands write to agree or disagree with her advice.

The comic pages are replete with perennial losers. Charlie Brown and Dagwood cannot seem to win no matter how they try. Often they are rejected by their friends for reasons beyond their control. We sit helplessly by and watch it happen, but perhaps we chuckle. We have been in similar situations, and it's good to see somebody else lose for a change. We can identify because we've all been rejected, lonely, afraid.

It is no secret that most of us derive a certain pleasure from vicarious experience. We like to look in on other people's lives, to share in their victories and defeats. Comic strips afford us that opportunity in a safe and comfortable way.

ISSUES AND ANSWERS: LOVE, LAW, AND LIBEL— THE PRIVATE LIVES OF PUBLIC PEOPLE

Late one July night in 1975, reporter Jay Gourley stepped very carefully onto the patio of a Georgetown home. His mission: to steal the garbage of then–Secretary of State Henry Kissinger. His employer: the *National Enquirer*. When Gourley was confronted by several Secret Service men, he explained he was engaging in "garbology," the study of notables according to what they throw away.

His was not the first garbage search. Some time before, an article had been written about Bob Dylan's trash. Dylan ignored it, but Kissinger was not so charitable. Threatening a lawsuit, he demanded his garbage back and got it. Most of it, anyway.

These incidents involve a fundamental question in reporting: Where does the public's right to know or the reporter's right to find out end and the privacy of a well-known personality begin?

Libel laws were designed to give the individual recourse against damaging statements in the press. Since all parties may not agree on what is fair and unfair, the courts have handed down three guidelines for the reporter anxious to avoid libel suits.

1 Is it true?

2 Is it privileged?

3 Is it fair comment and criticism?

Truth was established as a defense of libel in 1735. That landmark decision acquitted New York printer John Peter Zenger of libel charges brought by the Royal Governor, who had often been a target of criticism from Zenger's press. Though existing law forbade such criticism, Zenger's lawyer argued that the statements were true and therefore not libelous.

Privileged information includes charges or statements made as part of the official record during court trials or legislative sessions. If one senator calls another a crook during a speech on the floor of the Senate, a newspaper may print it without fear of libel. If the senator does so outside in the hallway, reporters publishing it *could* be subject to a libel suit, even though they are quoting a source.

The standard for "fair comment and criticism" rests on intent. In *New York Times Co.* v. *Sullivan* (1964), the Supreme Court held that the Constitution "prohibits a public official from recovering damages for a defamatory falsehood relating to his official conduct unless he proves the statement was made with actual malice." The court felt newspaper reporters were bound to make some errors in reporting the facts. Even if charges as printed were eventually proved false, the plaintiff must prove that the reporter knew they were false and wrote the story with "malicious intent."

New York Times Co. v. *Sullivan* started

a trend of giving the press every benefit of the doubt in potentially libelous situations. This decision wiped out almost any chance for public officials to recover damages in libel suits and gave the press wide latitude in covering those officials. In later years the courts have interpreted "public officials" to include not only those in government, but all public figures in all matters of public interest. This drastically reduced the number of libel suits filed against the press each year. The more liberal Supreme Court justices would like to see libel laws, as they relate to the press, completely abolished. Justice Hugo Black once wrote: "The First Amendment [guaranteeing freedom of the press] was intended to leave the press free from the harassment of libel judgments."

When being interviewed by David Frost, former President Richard Nixon cited *New York Times Co.* v. *Sullivan* as the reason he could not sue *Washington Post* reporters Bob Woodward and Carl Bernstein for what he called "factual errors" in their book *The Final Days*. Nixon and the press have never been fond of one another, and it comes as no surprise that the Nixon Supreme Court appointees may be changing the Supreme Court position. With Justice Black and liberal champion William O. Douglas dead, more-recent decisions have allowed writers less latitude in what they may say about public and government officials.

Most notable among these were the decisions in *Hutchinson* v. *Proxmire* (1979) and *Wolston* v. *Reader's Digest Association, Inc.* (1979). In both instances, the court narrowed significantly the broad definition of what constitutes a "public figure." In *Wolston*, the court found that a mere accusation of criminal activity does not make one a "public figure." This severely limits newspapers' attempts to report on criminal proceedings, since they must constantly write their stories with an eye to being sued for libel by the defendant, whether or not he or she is eventually found guilty.

All this probably adds up to trouble for newspapers in the future. These recent decisions have not yet been completely interpreted by the lower courts, but when they are, many newspapers may face huge libel suits. With some papers, both large and small, operating on razor-thin budgets, such costly suits could eventually determine the difference between survival and bankruptcy.

QUERIES AND CONCEPTS

1 Get a copy of the *National Enquirer* and examine story content. Is there a particular point of view in most stories? Is it direct or implied?

2 Now use that same copy of the *Enquirer* and compare story categories (crime, violence, occult, and others) with story categories in your local city newspaper. What are the major differences?

3 What is your favorite comic strip? Would it fall into any of the categories defined in the text? Do you identify in any direct way with any of the characters? What is it about them that you enjoy?

4 Can you find at least one article in your local paper that may contain some libel? Apply the three criteria from the text.

5 You're the editor of a major newspaper. You've been approached by a source who claims he can deliver the "authentic" personal diaries of John Lennon. What do you do?

READINGS AND REFERENCES

What Really Happened?

"Hitler's Forged Diaries." *Time*, May 16, 1983.

**Editors and Readers:
A New Social Contract**

Ruth Clark
Changing Needs of Changing Readers, A Qualitative Study of the New Social Contract Between Newspaper Editors and Readers. Reston, Va.: American Society of Newspaper Editors, 1979.

The complete report as cited, with research work done by Yankelovich, Skelly, and White, is available for five dollars from the American Society of Newspaper Editors, c/o the Charlotte Observer, P.O. Box 32188, Charlotte, N.C. 28232.

**Supermarket
Sensationalism**

"From Worse to Bad." *Newsweek*, September 8, 1969, p. 75.

"Goodbye to Gore." *Time*, February 21, 1972, pp. 64–65.

Elizabeth Peer
William Schmidt
"The Enquirer: Up From Smut." *Newsweek*, April 21, 1975, p. 62.

Sorting Out the Soft News

Harry F. Waters
Martin Weston
"Don't Ask Ann." *Newsweek*, July 14, 1975, pp. 53–55.

Linda Witt
"Ann Landers: 'Let's Hear It For Us Squares.'" *Today's Health*, January 1974, pp. 38–41.

Comics: You're Significant, Charlie Brown!

Arthur Asa Berger
The Comic-Stripped American: What Dick Tracy, Blondie, Daddy Warbucks and Charlie Brown Tell Us About Ourselves. New York: Penguin Books, 1974.
   The sociological end of the comic-strip business. Berger examines some mainstream comics and explores audience identification with each. The context is popular culture. Chapters on *Blondie, Dick Tracy, Buck Rogers*, underground comics, and more. In paperback; no bibliography or index.

Berke Breathed
Bloom County: Loose Tails. New York: Little, Brown, 1983.
   The first collection of *Bloom County* strips.

Reinhold C. Reitberger
Wolfgang J. Fuchs
Comics: Anatomy of a Mass Medium. Boston: Little, Brown, 1972.

First published in Germany, this stands as the most comprehensive *historical* portrait of the comic strip and comic book. Most major strips are covered. Useful index and reading list.

Garry Trudeau
The Doonesbury Chronicles. New York: Holt, Rinehart & Winston, 1975.
   The ultimate collection of *Doonesbury* cartoons from the early days at Yale to 1975, some in color. A short but interesting introduction and discussion of the significance of *Doonesbury* as a new force in the comic world.

Doonesbury's Greatest Hits. New York: Holt, Rinehart & Winston, 1978.
   The second collection.

The People's Doonesbury. New York: Holt, Rinehart & Winston, 1981.
   The final "large format" collection before the sabbatical period, this covers strips which appeared in the 1978–80 period. Includes a widely publicized "annotated conversation with the author." (Trudeau rarely grants interviews.)

Issues and Answers: Love, Law, and Libel— The Private Lives of Public People

Nelson and Teeter's *Law of Mass Communications*, 4th ed. (Mineola, N.Y.: Foundation Press, 1981) and Gillmor and Barron's *Mass Communication Law*, 4th ed. (St. Paul, Minn.: West Publishing, 1984) are both excellent sources for more detailed accounts of libel cases and related issues. For the historical perspective, check under "libel" in the index of Frank L. Mott's *American Journalism* (Riverside, N.J.: Macmillan, 1962).

A good introduction to mass-communication law for the beginner can be found in *Major Principles of Media Law* by Wayne Overbeck and Rick D. Pullen (New York: Holt, Rinehart & Winston, 1982). The organization of the text enables you to go to precisely the aspect of mass-communication law you wish to investigate.

For more-recent cases, see the *Reader's Guide to Periodical Literature*. There are usually a few major libel cases each year, and court rulings constantly reinterpret existing libel laws.

5

Magazines:
A Mass Menagerie

MAGAZINES FORM A WILD AND UNPREDICTABLE COLLECTION of publications—colorful, competitive, and exciting. Magazines are a *mass* menagerie because without a mass audience they wouldn't survive. Their existence says a lot about how we spend our leisure time, and we have more of that than ever before.

THE MASS MENAGERIE

According to the Magazine Publishers Association's newsletter, in 1982 over 250 million magazine copies were published each month (see 5.1). In addition, the average magazine was read by 3.8 persons; thus, a million-circulation magazine probably reached almost 4 million people.

Ninety-four percent of the nation's population 18 years of age and older reads magazines during an average month. Each one reads an average of 11.6 different magazine copies a month. Thus, it can be safely concluded that Americans have a voracious appetite for the printed word in general and for magazines in particular.

Relationships between magazines and readers reveal changing trends and patterns in social behavior. Like all commercial mass media, magazines create and reflect popular beliefs and tastes. The success—and profits—of a magazine depend on how well it can anticipate those tastes and deliver an information package the audience will buy.

All popular magazines in America *specialize* in some way. In fact, they are the most specialized of all mass media. Researchers John C. Merrill and Ralph L. Lowenstein point out that a magazine may have either unit specialization or internal specialization. *Unit specialization* occurs in *Personal Computing, Gourmet,* and others that appeal to a particular group of readers who have common interests. The magazine as a whole

The whole tendency of this age is magazineward.
EDGAR ALLAN POE, 1824

5.1
National Circulation of Leading U.S. Magazines

This table indicates the national circulation of the U.S. magazines with circulation in excess of 2 million. The Magazine Publishers Association estimates that the average magazine is read, in part, by 3.8 persons. (Think of all those old magazines in doctors' and dentists' waiting rooms!) If it is right, then the actual readership of these magazines is about four times the number indicated. Also note that the Audit Bureau of Circulation considers the *National Enquirer* a magazine, but I have chosen to include it as a tabloid newspaper in Chapter 4. The debate about its proper category continues.

Based on Audit Bureau of Circulation's FAS-FAX Report for six months ending December 31, 1982. Used by permission.

Magazine	Total Circulation (in millions)
Reader's Digest	17.9
TV Guide	17.0
National Geographic	10.6
Better Homes and Gardens	8.1
Family Circle	7.4
Woman's Day	6.9
McCall's	6.3
Good Housekeeping	5.5
Ladies' Home Journal	5.1
National Enquirer	5.1
Playboy	4.5
Time	4.5
The Star	4.0
Redbook	3.9
Penthouse	3.8
Newsweek	3.0
Cosmopolitan	2.9
Scholastic Magazine	2.9
People	2.7
Prevention	2.6
Sports Illustrated	2.4
U.S. News and World Report	2.2
Globe	2.2
Southern Living	2.1
Glamour	2.1
Field and Stream	2.0

appeals to a special-interest group. *Internal-specialization* publications, like *Reader's Digest*, appeal to a larger audience, offering a wide variety of articles and letting readers choose those they find interesting. The specialization occurs within the magazine in individual articles.

HISTORY:
THE GOOD OLD DAYS

The earliest American magazines were local journals of political opinion. None circulated far beyond its geographic origin; most were monthlies. In 1741, Andrew Bradford's *American Magazine* was the first magazine to appear in the Colonies, beating Benjamin Franklin's *General Magazine and Historical Chronicle* by three days (see 5.2). Both folded within six months.

For the next 130 years, magazines came and went. All were aimed at the local audience; most sold advertising and were published monthly. In 1879, Congress lowered the postal rates for periodicals to encourage broader distribution of magazines and newspapers.

In 1893, S. S. McClure founded *McClure's* magazine and priced it at 15 cents for those who could not afford the usual 25 or 30 cents. His strategy was simple: deliver an entertaining, easy-to-read magazine to the masses. Thus armed with a large circulation, the magazine could make profits from advertising revenues.

McClure's gained fame through a journalistic practice known as *muckraking*. Muckraking stories generally exposed some political or social injustices. Two early exposés in *McClure's* that helped the magazine gain notoriety were Ida M. Tarbell's "History of the Standard Oil Company" and Lincoln Steffens's "The Shame of the Cities."

The chief competitor of *McClure's* was Frank Munsey's magazine (*Munsey's*), which dropped its price to 10 cents in 1893. Like the newspaper yellow journalists, Munsey stopped at nothing to increase circulation. When he died in 1925, one critic wrote: "Frank Munsey contributed to the journalism of his day the talent of a meat packer, the morals of a money changer, and the manner of an undertaker." While other publishers made speeches about getting quality reading to the masses, Munsey was primarily concerned with making money.

Though muckraking was common among magazines of this period, only a few magazines carry on this tradition today. Among them is *Mother Jones*, which first became recognized nationally for its articles charging that some Ford Pintos posed a fire hazard.

In 1897, Cyrus Curtis bought the floundering *Saturday Evening Post* for $1,000. That year, its circulation was 2,200, and advertising revenues were just under $7,000. *Printer's Ink*, a trade paper, described the investment as "an impossible venture." But Curtis developed just the right combination of fact, fiction, and folk story. Within five years, circulation had risen to more than 300,000, and ad revenues to $360,000. By 1912, circulation neared 2 million, and ad revenues soared accordingly.

McClure's, *Munsey's*, the *Saturday Evening Post*, and many more ushered in the era of the mass-circulation magazine. Readers regularly supplemented news from their daily paper with the in-depth articles and fiction of their favorite magazines.

During the 1930s, many successful magazines ran quality fiction to boost sales. The *Saturday Evening Post*, *Esquire*, and even *Look* and *Life* were showcases for the shorter fiction of writers like Ernest Hemingway and F. Scott Fitzgerald. Technical developments in photography and typography also increased magazines' appeal.

From 1900 to 1950, the number of "magazine families" subscribing to one or more periodicals rose from 200,000 to more than 32 million. This magazine boom came in spite of the introduction of film, radio, television, and the paperback book.

After World War I, new magazines appeared by the hundreds. *Time* presented a capsulized version of the week's news. Within a year after its first issue, it was financially in the black. *Life* appeared in 1936 at 10 cents a copy. Offering bold, imaginative photography and tremendous visual impact, it was soon equally successful.

By the beginning of World War II, most of the earlier mass-circulation magazines had died, including *Munsey's* and *McClure's*. Some, like the *Saturday Evening Post*, *Collier's*, *Cosmopolitan*, and *McCall's*, remained, but many were in financial trouble. Publishers had used profits from successful magazines to finance less successful new ones. Since magazines are among the freest of the free-market enterprises, those that command adequate circulation and attract advertisers survive, and those that don't, perish.

5.2
Time Line: The History of American Magazines

1710   Several American printers collect essays and print them in newspaper format.

1741   Benjamin Franklin's *General Magazine and Historical Chronicle* and Andrew Bradford's *American Magazine* are the first regularly published magazines in America; neither is financially successful.

1821   The *Saturday Evening Post* is founded, appealing to both women and men.

1824   Magazine editor Edgar Allan Poe predicts, "This is the age of magazines; the whole tendency of this age is magazineward."

1857   *Harper's Weekly* begins publication and offers engravings that add visual depth to stories; it immediately becomes the country's largest-selling magazine.

1865   Beginning of the first magazine boom. In the next 20 years the number of periodicals increases from 700 to 3,300.

1865   E. L. Godkin founds *The Nation,* a journal of news and a forerunner of magazines like *Time* and *Newsweek.*

1879   The federal government decreases postal rates for magazines and other publications to encourage wider circulation.

1880s   Women's magazines *Ladies' Home Journal* and *Good Housekeeping* begin to have major market impact.

1893   *McClure's* is the first cheap mass-circulation magazine at 15 cents a copy.

1893   *Munsey's* magazine cuts its price from 25 cents to 10 cents to compete with *McClure's.*

1897   Cyrus Curtis takes charge of the *Saturday Evening Post.*

1903–12   Magazine muckrakers expose unethical practices in business and government.

1907   The *Saturday Evening Post* is one of the first magazines to top $1 million in annual advertising revenues.

1918   William Randolph Hearst hires Ray Long to edit his *Cosmopolitan.* Long becomes the highest-paid editor of the era and gains a reputation for his uncanny ability to predict public reading tastes.

1920   Gross annual revenues in magazine advertising top $129 million.

1922   DeWitt Wallace founds *Reader's Digest.* His idea: Take the best articles from other magazines and reprint them in condensed form. Articles must be "constructive, of lasting value, and applicable to readers."

1923   Henry Luce and Briton Hadden found *Time* magazine, an overnight success.

1925   *The New Yorker* begins publication and becomes the most successful metropolitan magazine.

1925   Many magazines shift emphasis from subscription to newsstand sales to increase profits.

1930 Gross annual revenues in magazine advertising peak near $200 million, then fall to less than $100 million in 1933.

1930s Magazine circulation greatly increases from sales in grocery stores.

1933 *Esquire's* first issue appears, and at 50 cents a copy it is the most expensive of its day.

1936 *Vanity Fair,* perhaps the most elite and "cultural" mass circulation magazine of its era, ceases publication after 22 years.

1936 *Life* magazine founded; first issue sells for 10 cents.

1937 *Look* magazine appears as a frank imitator of *Life.*

1940s The heyday of the big general-interest magazines. *Life, Look, Saturday Evening Post, Reader's Digest,* and *Collier's* show healthy profits while expanding; black and white is replaced with new color format.

1947 *Reader's Digest* becomes the first magazine with a circulation of more than 9 million.

1948 *TV Guide* founded for New York viewers; later expands to national publication.

1951 Gross annual revenues in magazine advertising exceed $500 million.

1952 William Gaines starts *Mad* magazine.

1953 Hugh Hefner founds *Playboy;* Marilyn Monroe is the first centerfold.

1954 Time Inc. founds *Sports Illustrated.*

1955 Rising production costs force *Reader's Digest* to accept advertising for the first time.

1956 *Collier's* is the first modern mass-circulation, general-interest magazine to go bankrupt and cease publication.

1967 *Look* magazine publishes its first "demographic" edition in an attempt to reach various special-interest readers and advertisers.

1970s *Cosmopolitan* leads the way to more explicit magazines for women. Burt Reynolds is the first centerfold.

1971 *Look* magazine ceases publication.

1972 *Life* magazine prints its final regular issue.

1972 *Ms.* magazine is published, devoted to women's rights and the women's movement; an overnight success.

1974 Time Inc. founds *People* magazine, a smaller, livelier and more "show biz" version of *Life.*

1974 *TV Guide* overtakes *Reader's Digest* as the largest-selling magazine in America.

1978 Time Inc. announces *Life* will begin publication again—as a monthly.

1980s Demographics is "the name of the game" as magazines' content and marketing strategies are aimed at the special audience.

1983 *Vanity Fair* is resurrected by Conde Nast publishing company.

1983 Time Inc. launches *TV-Cable Week* in April to compete with *TV Guide,* but it ceases publication in September 1983.

THESE DAYS:
MAGAZINES SINCE 1950

Nostalgia buffs would have us believe that the "good old days" of magazines are gone forever. They wail that there will never be another *Look*, or *Collier's*. Their concern for the old has prompted special "nostalgia" issues of magazines like *Liberty*. The *Saturday Evening Post* now publishes nine special issues each year, which really makes it the *Almost Monthly Post*.

What happened to these magazines? The world of mass communication is one of mass change. Public tastes and information needs shift over the years; some magazines couldn't or wouldn't shift with them. Of course, the influence of television was felt by many; *Life*, for example, which had provided its audience a pictorial window on the world, was clearly upstaged by the newer medium. Other problems were increased postal rates, paper costs, salaries, and other production costs and poor management. Most important was probably the loss of advertising revenue to other media. Why should advertisers pay almost eight dollars to reach 1,000 *Life* readers when a minute of television time cost approximately four dollars per every 1,000 viewers?

Of course, not all the older magazines have died. Among those still doing well are *National Geographic*, *Better Homes and Gardens*, and *Ladies' Home Journal*. And if some former giants have died, hundreds of new magazines have sprung up to take their place (or part of their place) or establish new places of their own (see 5.1). Recent success stories include *Ms.*, *Penthouse*, the new *Cosmopolitan*, *TV Guide* (see 5.3), and *People*. The point is not that magazines are dying, but reader needs are changing.

Figures alone don't tell the survival story in today's mass menagerie. Magazines are people: owners, editors, writers, and readers. These people represent a coalition of diverse interests that make a magazine live. Two of the biggest stories during the menagerie's last 30 years have been the rise of *Playboy* and the death of *Life*. The *Playboy* story is one of manners, morals, and ingenuity (see the guest essay by John Brady on page 76). The *Life* story is one of visual splendor and harsh fiscal reality.

A PORTRAIT:
THE DEATH OF *LIFE*

To see life; to see the world; to eyewitness great events . . . to see strange things—machines, armies, multitudes, shadows in the jungle and on the moon; to see man's work—his paintings, towers, and discoveries; to see things thousands of miles away, things hidden behind walls and within rooms, things dangerous to come to; the women that men love and many children; to see and take pleasure in seeing; to see and be amazed; to see and be instructed. Thus to see, and to be shown, is now the will and new expectancy of half mankind.
—Henry R. Luce, 1936

Henry Luce, cofounder of Time Inc., shared this vision for a new magazine with potential advertisers and financial backers in 1936 (see 5.4). The nation was still in an economic depression, but Luce sensed that technological development had made possible a new kind of journalism. Paper was cheap and photographs were increasingly appealing to readers. Why not a magazine that would provide a weekly "window on the world" for a mass audience starved for visual information?

Life's initial success was so overwhelming that it nearly killed the magazine. Luce had contracted with advertisers anticipating a circulation of 250,000 for the first year. To his delight and dismay, circulation was twice that

5.3
Taking on *TV Guide:* A Brief Bright Star on the Video Horizon

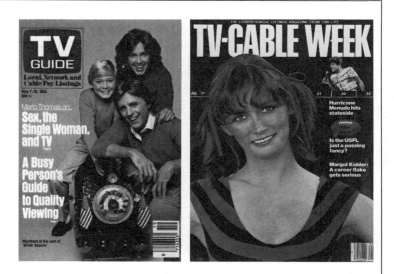

In April 1983, Time Inc. mailed the first issue of *TV-Cable Week* to 150,000 subscribers in five test markets. At stake was $100 million, the largest sum ever spent to launch a magazine. But the rewards might have been equally great, as *TV-Cable Week* aimed for a piece of the $240 million in annual advertising revenues enjoyed by *TV Guide.*

TV Guide began in 1953 with 1.5 million subscribers. Its circulation is now over 17 million, though it has dipped from its all-time high of 19 million in 1980. In 1974 it became, for several years, the largest-selling magazine in America, replacing the *Reader's Digest* in that coveted position.

But the people at Time Inc. felt that *TV Guide* had been too slow to respond to the video revolution. Many cable subscribers found they could not readily identify all of their channel choices using *TV Guide*'s regular listings. By catering specifically to the cable subscriber, *TV-Cable Week* hoped to slowly gather a large, loyal readership.

Of course, *TV Guide* did not take this lying down. In 1982 it spent $40 million to expand its cable listings; now beneath the familiar *TV Guide* logo we also find the words "Local, Network and Cable/Pay Listings." All of this was accomplished before the first issue of *TV-Cable Week* was in the mail. Nevertheless, the new publication still offered a more complete picture of the myriad choices confronting the cable subscriber.

When the first issue of *TV-Cable Week* came out, *TV Guide* editorial director Merrill Panitt didn't seem too worried. He told *Newsweek,* "Competition is fine, it wakes everybody up!" Indeed, it appeared that the impending arrival of new competition had woken up the folks at *TV Guide.* With their new cable-listings section in place, they were able to do a successful end run around Time's marketing strategies.

In September 1983, just five months after its debut, it was announced that *TV-Cable Week* had published its final issue. The staff, numbering some 250, was laid off. The still unfinished offices in New York were closed. Total 1983 losses had been close to $50 million. There were a lot of reasons given for the failure of *TV-Cable Week,* but in the end it was yet another victim of the fierce competition in the mass menagerie of the magazine marketplace.

Guest Essay by John Brady

The Nude Journalism

John Brady is former editor of Writer's Digest *and author of* The Craft of Interviewing. *This is an excerpt from an article that first appeared in* The Journal of Popular Culture *in 1974.*

For the past 25 years a gaunt, pipe-smoking, Pepsi-swigging man in Chicago has edited a magazine that was never intended for female chauvinist sows or for the little old ladies of Dubuque. Along the way he has been called—among lesser delicacies—"the Crusader Rabbit of Sex," "the Norman Vincent Peale of Erotica," and "the man who started the loosening of sexual attitudes in America." If, as Emerson suggested, "an institution is the lengthened shadow of one man," *Playboy* magazine is surely one Hugh Marston Hefner.

Hefner's success is even more remarkable because it came at a time when American magazine journalism was, at best, risky. The period, in fact, is a mausoleum for once-successful publications—*Collier's, Saturday Evening Post, Look,* and *Life*—while hundreds of lesser magazines slipped quietly into unmarked graves. Yet *Playboy* prospered. The Hefner-

ian secret? "I invented sex," the publisher wryly observed on a recent TV talk show. And, to an extent, it's true—at least insofar as publishers are concerned. Hefner led the way. He gave popular culture a sex life. The Nude Journalism. But of course!

No other magazine in America has had an impact to match *Playboy*'s. "*Playboy* is probably the most influential publication of my lifetime," say Gay Talese, now working on a book of his own called *Sex in America.* [This later became *Thy Neighbor's Wife,* published in 1980.] "It has influenced middle America. It has recorded and been in the vanguard of change, sexually, in this country. . . . Hefner will probably go down in modern history as one of the most influential men of the 1960s and 70s."

Whether the magazine fostered the revolution or the revolution nurtured the magazine is debatable. "*Playboy* came at the right time, when the United States was experiencing a sexual revolution," says Hefner. "My naked girls became a symbol of disobedience, a triumph of sexuality, an end of puritanism." It seems safe to conclude, however, that *Playboy* at least helped bring about a cultural change in our society much more rapidly than would have occurred otherwise. Hefner's magazine became the foremost chronicler of sexual change throughout this period. Thus, following closely on the heels of Dr. Kinsey, and paralleling

the development of The Pill, *Playboy* served as midwife while the age of sexual candor was born unto the popular press in America.

In 1952, only two major publications could be called general magazines for men—*Esquire* and the now-defunct *Gentry.* Other magazines that featured female nudity were a pretty seamy lot in general. The remaining men's magazines emphasized the great outdoors. Hefner found them "asexual at best, and maybe homosexual. With the outdoor and hunting and adventure things in which the place for the woman was in the kitchen while you hung out with the guys and played poker or went out on a hunting trip to chase the abominable snowman."

The first issue of *Playboy* was put together with paste pot and scissors on a bridge table in Hefner's kitchen. The publisher's personal investment was $600, which he obtained by mortgaging furniture and borrowing from friends. He also sold $10,000 in stock to random social acquaintances.

"I'm sitting in my studio one day and in comes this skinny, intense, wild-eyed guy," recalls Arthur Paul, then a young Chicago freelance artist. "He showed me this magazine he had put together. He had done all the artwork by himself, and it was awful. But he looked at my work and asked me to redesign his magazine." Of course, Hefner had no money. "I took on the job," adds Paul, "accepting private shares of stock in the company he was founding, instead of salary"—and it was probably the best thing that ever happened to him.

Sales mushroomed. By the end of 1954, monthly circulation was 104,189; one year later that figure had more than tripled, and by December 1956, sales averaged 795,965 monthly.

Each month the book became thicker and slicker as profits were plowed back into the product. Not until 1956, though, did *Playboy* attract advertisers in large numbers—partly because conservative accounts were reluctant to be associated with a "skin" magazine, but mostly because Hefner rejected some 80 percent of the advertising submitted for publication, including ads for firearms, weight reducers, acne and baldness cures, correspondence courses, trusses, athlete's foot powder, sex manuals, "lifelike" inflatable dolls, vibrators, and whatnot.

"Right from the start, he knew it would be fatal in the long run to carry the kind of schlock ads that usually go in pin-up magazines," says a longtime associate of the publisher. "It was the best decision he ever made." *Playboy*'s former advertising director Howard Lederer added: "We create a euphoria and we want nothing to spoil it. We don't want a reader to come suddenly on an ad that says he has bad breath. We don't want him to be

reminded of the fact, though it may be true, that he is going bald."

Now that the field suddenly belonged to *Playboy,* the magazine began to change. "I've always edited on the assumption that my tastes are pretty much like those of our readers," said Hefner in 1955. "As I develop, so will the magazine." One of the first things to develop was the centerfold. Although the feature had begun with Marilyn Monroe as "Sweetheart of the Month" ("Playmate" did not appear until the second issue), subsequent centerfolds were nameless. "In the early days, when it was hard to get a decent girl to pose in the nude," observed J. Anthony Lukas, "a few of the Playmates looked as though they might feel at home on a barstool."

Critic Benjamin DeMott pointed out that the Playmate, generally chosen from a middle-income background, could be *any* girl with an attractive figure. *Playboy,* he said, undertakes "to establish that the nude in Nassau and the stenotypist in Schenectady—the sex-bomb and the 'ordinary girl'—are actually one creature. Essential Woman."

Today, of course, when one passes the men's-magazine section of a newsstand, *Playboy* is pictorially tame compared with publications that seem to have staff gynecologists rather than art directors. "*Playboy* has become part of the Establish-

ment," says Bob Guccione, editor of *Penthouse,* a younger, more virile *Playboy.*

Whether *Playboy* has gone Establishment is debatable, but clearly many of the causes the magazine once fought have either been won or forgotten. The magazine's circulation, which once flirted with 7 million, has fallen back to some 5 million monthly—mostly because *Playboy* has fallen behind in the commodity its publisher invented: sex. Despite the criticism, the competition, and the awareness that the *Playboy* phenomenon has probably peaked, Hugh Marston Hefner's place as a journalist of distinction and of influence is rather secure. "All history," said Emerson, "resolves itself very easily into the biography of a few stout and earnest persons." In the annals of popular culture and The Nude Journalism, Hefner is surely the publisher who led the change. "I'm sure that I will be remembered as one significant part of our time," Hefner told an interviewer a few years ago. "We live in a period of rapid sociological change, and I am on the side of the angels."

5.4

Henry R. Luce, founder of Life, *at a banquet with Elsa Maxwell, the songwriter, radio star, and syndicated columnist.*

almost immediately. This meant double production costs without higher advertising rates. *Life* lost $6 million before appropriate adjustments could be made. Luce should have learned a lesson from *Munsey's* and *McClure's;* both magazines had experienced the same problem 40 years earlier.

In its early years, *Life* was often controversial. A 1938 issue featured a photo essay (the term itself was a *Life* invention) on the birth of a baby. Some readers were shocked, and the magazine was banned in 33 cities. Though Luce maintained that *Life's* photo essays would "begin in delight and end in wisdom," some critics disagreed. One described the *Life* photo formula as "equal parts of the decapitated Chinaman, the flogged Negro, and the rapidly slipping chemise." As years went by, *Life* did provide a certain amount of sex appeal, and pin-up pictures of Rita Hayworth and others often created a stir.

Life was also a news magazine. During the Spanish Civil War, World War II, and the Korean War, readers depended on *Life* to be there, to help them witness these important world events in a way no other medium could. In 1969 *Life* brought the Vietnam War home by running pictures of 217 Americans killed during a single week of combat.

But there was more to *Life* than news and photographs. Some of the world's first-rate authors published original stories there, including Ernest Hemingway, Graham Greene, Norman Mailer, and James Dickey. *Life* carried the memoirs of the famous, including Winston Churchill, Harry S. Truman, Charles de Gaulle, Dwight Eisenhower, and Nikita Khruschev.

A generation that had grown up with the institution called *Life* was dismayed when Time Inc. announced abruptly that *Life's* 1972 year-end issue would be its last. Many *Life* staffers were no less surprised, though rumors had been circulating for some time. *Look* had stopped publishing in 1971, and many had said that *Life* would soon follow.

What really killed *Life*? *Life* writer and longtime staffer Tommy Thompson said: "We lost our focus, we didn't know who we were writing to. We continued to try to put out a mass magazine when America was not a *mass* any more, but divergent groups of specialized interests." Perhaps the needs of a "mass" audience were now better served by television. In 1952, when *Life* published color pictures of the coronation of Elizabeth II in only ten days, readers were amazed; but a few years later, television was bringing viewers similar events instantly. Of course, television is not exactly, nor can it replace, photojournalism. *Life*'s pictures captured the moment and could be enjoyed again and again.

Columnist Shana Alexander rejected the doomsday theories of those who felt *Life*'s demise foretold shifting trends in American taste: "Photojournalism is not dead, and the American people have not stopped reading, nor have they lost interest in the world around them. What died at *Life* was an appropriate and responsible relationship between editors and management."

During its final three years, *Life* swam in a sea of red ink, losing some $30 million. A conservative management rejected numerous plans from editors and other staffers to "save" the magazine. *Life* could have gone to a smaller format (its large size made postal rate increases disastrous) or shifted its balance between photo and story content. It could have trimmed from its circulation list those whom demographers did not consider prime targets for potential advertisers, thereby cutting circulation costs and increasing advertiser appeal. But this would have meant a major shift in editorial policy and the very concept of the magazine. In the end, *Life* did nothing, and died.

In death it was remembered as a social force of unparalleled magnitude. William Shawn, managing editor of *The New Yorker*, said: "*Life* invented a great new form of jour-

nalism. It contributed much to the American community that was valuable, often reaching moments of brilliance and beauty." Poet James Dickey noted, "I can't begin to calculate all of the things I have learned from *Life*. I'm not quite the same person I was because of what I read and saw in its pages." Indeed, hundreds of millions of *Life* readers had their lives transformed in some way. For 36 years *Life* was an information source that expanded its readers' vision of the world around them. It continued that mission through a number of special issues during the mid-1970s. The success of these issues prompted an announcement by Time Inc. in 1978 that *Life* would return as a monthly. Perhaps the reports of the death of *Life* had been greatly exaggerated after all!

The new monthly *Life* has become solidly entrenched in the current magazine scene, and *Life* still sets the standard for excellence in photojournalism. Still, it doesn't seem to have quite the impact of its previous incarnation, perhaps in part because it relies on street sales rather than subscriptions. Whatever the ultimate destiny of *Life*, it is a monument to an era of magazine journalism that may never come again.

SPECIALIZATION AND MARKETING TRENDS

Are you a regular reader of *The Peanut Farmer*? Maybe not, but former President Jimmy Carter probably is, along with more than 28,000 others. *Writer's Market* lists over 100 magazines that deal with farming, soil management, poultry, dairy farming, and rural life. Farming magazines are one example of special-interest publications, which account for more than 90 percent of the total number of magazines published today.

Other vocations have their magazines as well (*The Iron Worker*, *Bank Systems &*

Equipment, American Shipper). Many magazines appeal to readers' ethnic background (*Ebony, Southern Jewish Weekly*), age (*Children's Digest*), sex (*Man to Man*), religion (*Gospel Carrier*), geographic location (*Golden Gate North, Gulfshore Life, Nashville!*), hobbies (*Biker/Hiker*), or point of view (*Ideals*). Not surprisingly, magazines come and go according to changes in demographics and interest patterns around the world. In the mid–1980s, there seems to be a glut of magazines devoted to video games and microcomputers. Magazines like *Byte, Compute!, Creative Computing*, and *Popular Computing* have circulations in the hundreds of thousands and can be found at newsstands everywhere. While mass-circulation magazines give us a sense of global participation, special-interest publications allow us to share our individual concerns with people like ourselves.

Special-interest magazines have flourished, partly because of the success of their general-interest big brothers and sisters. Since mass-circulation magazines print millions of copies, they must charge extremely high advertising rates. Only a handful of advertisers can afford to pay $30,000 to $85,000 for a full page in a mass-circulation magazine. As a result, many smaller companies have turned to less expensive special-interest magazines, where their ads will be seen by fewer but more receptive readers.

Of course, general-interest magazines have not calmly stood by and watched their revenues disappear. Magazines such as *Time* offer local companies reduced rates for regional "breakouts"—ads that will appear only in copies sent to a specific geographic region. This gives smaller companies a chance to appear in a national magazine at a rate they can afford.

But geography is only one of the special-interest trends in magazine marketing. *Time* offers advertisers the opportunity to reach subscribers who are doctors, members of top management, students or educators, or even those who live in special high-income and "ultra-high income" areas (see 5.5). This trend toward demographic breakouts began in 1967 when *Look* published its first *demo-edition*.

Magazines have also developed a "floating rate base" to help combat advertisers' urge to spend money on flashier TV campaigns. A floating rate base guarantees that advertisers will pay to reach only those who actually receive a given magazine. It works like this: When advertisers buy TV time, they are gambling that the ratings for a given show will be as high as they have been in the past. Otherwise, they are paying too much money to reach too few people. Magazine circulations tend to be more stable than TV ratings. Thus magazines can claim that the floating rate base takes the gamble out of magazine advertising.

In the near future, increasing audience specialization seems a certainty (see 5.6). Already *Newsweek* offers advertisers a chance to reach only their "working women" subscribers, and the day may not be far away when magazines can promise an advertiser that its message will reach, for example, only scotch-drinking readers. In any event, demographic breakouts work well because they're easy for agencies to sell clients; it is as if a special service is being performed just for them. Breakouts offer the advertiser a way to reach a desirable audience in a prestigious national magazine at a reduced rate—altogether an irresistible proposition for those interested in making sure that their messages are noticed.

WHAT, NO ADVERTISING?

Once upon a time, there were a number of magazines that survived without any advertising at all. They were able to make enough

5.5

This special rate card is distributed to agencies and potential advertisers to give them some idea of how much it will cost to reach a special portion of Time *readership. For example, 300,000 top-management people can be reached with a full-page, four-color ad for $14,840 on a one-time basis. The same ad in all U.S. editions of* Time *would cost over three times that amount. Ad rates have risen about 25% since this 1980 rate card was in effect.*

Demographic Editions

TIME U.S. Ex-TIME B
Rate Base: 2,700,000
Space available every other week starting with the January 7, 1980 issue. (See pages 4-5, Cycle D.) **Seven week closing date** all colorations, full pages only. (See page 3.)

	1X	13X	17X	26X	39X	52X
Page B & W	$29,565	$28,380	$27,935	$27,195	$26,605	$26,015
Page B & 1C	36,955	35,475	34,920	33,995	33,255	32,520
Page 4C	46,120	44,275	43,580	42,430	41,505	40,585

TIME B (Business Edition)
Rate Base: 1,550,000
Space available every other week starting with the January 7, 1980 issue. (See pages 4-5. Cycle D.) **Five week closing date** B & W and B & 1C, **seven week closing date** 4C. (See page 3.)

	1X	13X	17X	26X	39X	52X
Page B & W	$24,585	$23,600	$23,230	$22,615	$22,125	$21,630
Page B & 1C	30,730	29,500	29,035	28,270	27,655	27,040
Page 4C	38,350	36,815	36,240	35,280	34,515	33,745
2 cols B & W	18,435	17,695	17,420	16,960	16,590	16,220
2 cols B & 1C	23,045	22,120	21,775	21,200	20,740	20,275
1 col B & W	9,830	9,435	9,285	9,040	8,845	8,650
1 col B & 1C	12,290	11,795	11,610	11,305	11,060	10,815
½ col B & W	6,145	5,895	5,805	5,650	5,530	5,405
½ col B & 1C	7,680	7,370	7,255	7,065	6,910	6,755

TIME Z
(High Income Zip Code Areas)
Rate Base: 1,200,000
Space available in 1980 issues dated: January 28, February 25, March 10, 24, April 7, 21, May 5, 19, June 2, 30, July 28, August 25, September 8, 22, October 6, 20, November 3, 17, December 1, 15. (See pages 4-5.) **Seven week closing date** all colorations, full pages only. (See page 3.)

	1X	13X	17X	26X	39X	52X
Page B & W	$21,495	$20,635	$20,310	$19,775	$19,345	$18,915
Page B & 1C	26,865	25,790	25,385	24,715	24,175	23,640
Page 4C	33,530	32,185	31,685	30,845	30,175	29,505

TIME A+ (Ultra High Income Professional/Managerial Households)
Rate Base: 600,000
Space available in 1980 issues dated: January 14, February 11, March 10, 24, April 7, 21, May 5, 19, June 2, 16, July 14, August 11, September 8, 22, October 6, 20, November 3, 17, December 1, 15. (See pages 4-5.) **Seven week closing date** all colorations, full pages only. (See page 3.)

	1X	13X	17X	26X	39X	52X
Page B & W	$11,980	$11,500	$11,320	$11,020	$10,780	$10,540
Page B & 1C	14,975	14,375	14,150	13,775	13,475	13,175
Page 4C	18,685	17,935	17,655	17,190	16,815	16,440

TIME Student/Educator
Rate Base: 550,000
Space available in 1980 issues dated: February 18, March 17, April 14, May 12, September 15. October 13, November 10. (See pages 4-5.) **Five week closing date** B & W and B & 1C. **seven week closing date** 4C (See page 3.)

	1X	13X	17X	26X	39X	52X
Page B & W	$10,295	$ 9,880	$ 9,725	$ 9,470	$ 9,265	$ 9,055
Page B & 1C	12,865	12,350	12,155	11,835	11,575	11,320
Page 4C	16,060	15,415	15,175	14,775	14,450	14,130
2 cols B & W	7,720	7,410	7,295	7,100	6,945	6,790
2 cols B & 1C	9,650	9,260	9,115	8,875	8,685	8,490
1 col B & W	4,115	3,950	3,885	3,785	3,700	3,620
1 col B & 1C	5,145	4,935	4,860	4,730	4,630	4,525
½ col B & W	2,570	2,465	2,425	2,360	2,310	2,260
½ col B & 1C	3,215	3,085	3,035	2,955	2,890	2,825

TIME T (Top Management)
Rate Base: 300,000
Space available every other week starting with January 7, 1980 issue. (See pages 4-5, Cycle D.) **Five week closing date** B & W and B & 1C. **seven week closing date** 4C (See page 3.)

	1X	13X	17X	26X	39X	52X
Page B & W	$ 9,515	$ 9,130	$ 8,990	$ 8,750	$ 8,560	$ 8,370
Page B & 1C	11,890	11,410	11,235	10,935	10,700	10,460
Page 4C	14,840	14,245	14,020	13,650	13,355	13,055
2 cols B & W	7,135	6,845	6,740	6,560	6,420	6,275
2 cols B & 1C	8,920	8,560	8,425	8,205	8,025	7,845
1 col B & W	3,805	3,650	3,595	3,500	3,420	3,345
1 col B & 1C	4,755	4,560	4,490	4,370	4,275	4,180
½ col B & W	2,375	2,280	2,240	2,185	2,135	2,090
½ col B & 1C	2,970	2,850	2,805	2,730	2,670	2,610

TIME Doctors'
Rate Base: 165,000
Space available in 1980 issues dated: January 21, February 4, March 3, 31, April 28, May 26, June 9, 23, July 21, August 18, September 1, 29, October 27, November 24, December 8. (See pages 4-5.) **Seven week closing date** all colorations, full pages only. (See page 3.)

	1X	13X	17X	26X	39X	52X
Page B & W	$4,825	$4,630	$4,555	$4,435	$4,340	$4,245
Page B & 1C	6,030	5,785	5,695	5,545	5,425	5,305
Page 4C	7,525	7,220	7,110	6,920	6,770	6,620

Courtesy Time, Inc. Used by permission.

5.6

Spectrum *magazine advertises a special "upscale-consumer" edition that enables advertisers to reach a carefully selected portion of subscribers.*

from subscription and newsstand revenues to cover production costs and still make a profit. In recent years, however, skyrocketing production costs have made this all but impossible. *Reader's Digest* resisted selling advertising for more than 30 years until rising costs finally forced it to give in; *Changing Times* (see 5.7) recently began accepting advertising for the first time; *Mad* magazine, unique in a number of ways, now stands alone as the only large-circulation magazine that refuses to accept advertising (see 5.8).

Like newspapers, most magazines have suffered heavily from inflation in recent years. And no wonder—magazine production is a very costly business, and it is getting more

5.7
Changing Times *accepted no advertising for 33 years, but the economic realities of magazine publishing finally caught up with it in 1979. In this ad, designed to reach potential advertisers, it compares its situation with that of* Reader's Digest, *which began accepting advertising in 1955.*

expensive all the time. The paper must be of better quality than newsprint, so it is considerably more expensive. In order to remain competitive, virtually all general-interest magazines and many special-interest magazines must feature color photographs. This, too, means extra costs.

Recent technological innovations such as computerized typesetting and the use of video display terminals in the editorial process have reduced production costs to some extent. But a glance at the price of your favorite magazine now, as compared with five years ago, should be enough to convince you that magazines, like everything else, cost more all the time.

WRITING FOR MAGAZINES

Rising production costs are not the only problem for general-interest magazines. A local newspaper will always have some loyal readers simply because it covers events in a given

5.8

Mad Magazine: "What, Me Worry?"

William Gaines's *Mad* magazine is mostly a journal of satire. Though it started as a comic-book-size publication in 1952, it soon grew to its present format. *Mad*'s success reflects its unique ability to satirize the very products others rely on for advertising revenues. *Mad* gleefully attacks drug, automotive, and household products. Any medium is a likely target, including film, television commercials, and other magazines. *Mad* has even been known to satirize itself. These "attacks" are not malicious, but they point out the absurdity of our heavy reliance on advertising and the products it promotes. Ironically, the offices of *Mad* are on Madison Avenue, giving staffers a bird's-eye view of the advertising industry.

During the 1950s the "sick humor" of *Mad* was attacked by many parent and teacher groups. But what was once counterculture has now become a part of the mainstream, and *Mad* seems harmless, if frivolous, to most parents. For them, more radical humor magazines like the *National Lampoon* pose a greater threat. *Mad*'s readers, once almost exclusively teenagers, now include people of all ages.

Alfred E. Neuman, the fictitious publisher of *Mad,* has become so widely recognized that he is a cult hero. His motto, "What, me worry?" may describe the *Mad* approach to the complexities of the technological and materialistic American culture that the magazine satirizes so successfully.

geographic area. For the general-interest magazine, the "local area" is the entire country. To get readers, each magazine develops a "formula" for the type of material it publishes. This formula is passed along to staff writers and to the freelancers (independent writers who are paid by the article) who write the majority of magazine stories.

Most beginning freelancers shoot for the mass-circulation magazines, which, they assume, will pay well for their stories. Some do. *Reader's Digest* and *Playboy* pay about $3,000 per story; *TV Guide*, however, may pay as little as $500. More likely markets for the beginner are the special-interest magazines, which pay anywhere from nothing to $250. Another good starting point is regional and local magazines, which use a tremendous amount of freelance material.

Any would-be author should pick up a copy of *Writer's Digest* or *The Writer*. Both are monthly magazines devoted to the business of freelancing. *Writer's Market*, published yearly, is available in most libraries. Even if you have no writing aspirations, you will find it fascinating. It lists more than 5,000 markets for freelancers. Editors describe the exact formula for their magazine, as in 5.9. These descriptions are often interesting, amusing, and even shocking to the uninitiated.

Unfortunately, there is much more to freelance writing than sending in a story and waiting for the check. Editors are highly selective about what they buy. Big-name magazines may receive more than 100,000 unsolicited manuscripts every year. That's an average of almost 300 a day! This year fewer than 1,000 writers will have their work published in mass-circulation magazines. About 30,000 will be rejected. Only a few hundred will be able to live solely on their freelancing incomes.

The prices that magazines pay for their articles make up only a small fraction of their total production costs. Acceptance of an article is only the beginning. Editors carefully read the stories, altering them to conform to the magazine's style. Graphic designers and photographers supply artwork. Art directors choose typefaces and draw up layouts.

Writers are often unhappy with these processes, since they so vitally affect the finished product. But unless you are Truman Capote or Kurt Vonnegut, Jr., you have very little control over the story as it finally appears. In general, it is very difficult to keep the editor's blue pencil still. Yet in all fairness, the editor is often in a much better position to know what will appeal to the readers. Often, writers are too personally involved with their material and feel that each word is inviolable. Good editing is essential to the finished product.

5.9

Writer's Market: A Peek behind the Editor's Desk

For over half a century, *Writer's Market* has provided descriptions of magazine formulas for the freelance writer in the editor's own words. Some examples:

Bronze Thrills, 1220 Harding St., Ft. Worth TX 76102. Editor: Mrs. Edna K. Turner. Monthly magazine; 82 pages. Estab. 1957. Circ. 80,000. Buys all rights. Buys 60 mss/year. Pays on acceptance. Sample copy 50¢; free writer's guidelines. Reports in 90 days. . . .

Fiction: All material must relate to blacks. Romance or confession; black-oriented. Particularly interested in occult themes or those concerned with UFOs or mental illness. Length: 4,000–6,000 words. Pays $30.

Compressed Air, 253 E. Washington Ave., Washington, NJ 07882. Editor: Charles Beardsley. 50% freelance written. Emphasizes "the application of energy technologies for middle and upper management personnel in all industries." Monthly magazine; 48 pages. Estab. 1896. Circ. 150,000. Buys all rights. . . .

Nonfiction: "Articles must be reviewed by experts in the field." How-to (save costs with air power); and historical (engineering). No solar or wind power stories. Query with clips of previously published work. Pays negotiable fee.

American Blade. Beinfeld Publishing, Inc., 12767 Saticoy St., North Hollywood CA 91605. (213) 982-3700. Editor: Wallace Beinfeld. For knife enthusiasts who want to know as much as possible about quality knives and edge weapons. Bimonthly magazine; 52 pages. Estab. 1972. Circ. 15,000. Pays on publication. Buys all rights. . . . Previously published submissions OK. . . . Sample copy $1.50.

Nonfiction: Historical (on knives and weapons); how-to; interview (knifemakers); new product; nostalgia; personal experience; photo feature; profile and technical. Buys 6 mss/issue. Query. Length: 1,000–2,000 words. Pays 5¢/word.

Intimate Story, 2 Park Ave., New York NY 10016. Editor: Janet Wandel. 95% freelance written. For women 14–70 years old; small minority of readership composed of men; blue-collar. Monthly magazine; 74 pages. Estab. 1948. Circ. 170,000. Buys all rights. No byline. Buys about 100 mss/year. Pays shortly before publication. Rarely sends sample copies. No photocopied or simultaneous submissions. . . .

Fiction: "Sex-oriented and human interest stories; all types of fictional confession stories. Always first person; always enough dialogue. Our stories are within the realm of the believable." No stories with the theme of hopelessness or depressing situations. Most titles are house-generated. Length: 2,000–7,000 words. Pays 3¢/word; $160 maximum.

Though most of its space is devoted to magazines, *Writer's Market* also lists greeting card companies that buy lines of verse, along with poetry publications, regional newspapers, book publishers, and foreign markets.

ISSUES AND ANSWERS:
PROFESSIONAL PRINT—
THE CURIOUS
COLLECTIVE

Since editors, writers, and others all work on magazine stories, what we read is the result of a collective, or collaborative, effort. Yet reading is something we do alone. You can't simultaneously share a magazine with someone else the way you can share a film or a television program. Often the most successful stories are those in which the reader vicariously shares the writer's personal experiences. Yet this one-to-one communication is really a myth. Even the greatest writers have editors who offer suggestions and make changes.

All of the print we consume daily is edited, rewritten, and recycled many times before it reaches us. Take this book, for example. It may be different from other texts you've read because I am speaking directly to you, just as I would if you were in my office. I'm sharing personal experiences with you and hoping they will help you recall your own media experiences. Yet despite all of this, the words you are reading now are not all mine. Some belong to my editors, others to colleagues who have read earlier drafts and offered suggestions; students have read many chapters and suggested that I add or delete material. In short, virtually all books, magazines, and newspapers are written "by committee," even though they are perceived as being written by individuals.

Time magazine has used this one-to-one illusion to its advantage for years. From the beginning it presented the news as if it were written *by* one person *for* one person. For years, *Time* staffers never received a byline. Recently that policy has changed, and bylines are now permitted on some stories. *Time*'s basic formula remains the same, however, and it is an obvious success.

True-confession stories are almost always written in the first-person singular to emphasize the emotional impact of a "this-happened-to-me" experience. On the other hand, the "Talk of the Town" section of *The New Yorker* is always written with a collective "we," even when it is obviously the experience of a single person: "We went to the dinner and danced with Nancy Reagan," for example, or "We cracked open our oysters and talked with the old curmudgeon."

Academic texts often say, "One needs only to read this," instead of "You need only to read this." The feeling is that "one" will bring about a kind of detachment from the subject. What may result is a detachment from the reader. Curiously, this is often just the opposite of what the writer might be trying to achieve. The purpose of a text should be to get the student involved with subject matter.

This is not to say that all textbooks, magazines, newspapers, and printed material should be written the same way. Authors must make decisions based on what they think is best in a given situation. Still, decisions made on the basis of tradition alone are often blind to the real needs of the reader. The consequence is poor communication.

QUERIES AND CONCEPTS

1 What does your favorite magazine supply you with that you can't find anywhere else? Borrow a copy of *Writer's Market* and look up the listing for that magazine. Do you fit the editor's description of a typical reader?

2 In the library there are bound editions of many magazines like *Look* and *Liberty* that have quit publishing except for occasional special editions. Pick one and read a few issues. Venture some guesses as to why it failed.

3 Is *Playboy* a legitimate magazine or still a "skin" mag? Does your local library carry it? Does your school library carry it? Should it?

4 Do you have any special-interest magazines at home? If not, pick one at random off the newsstands and do a brief analysis of what you think the audience might be like. Then check your version against the one in *Writer's Market*.

5 Pick up the latest copy of *Reader's Digest* and select an article that interests you. Now go to the library to read the original version (most *Digest* articles are severely edited). What parts were omitted and why? Does this say anything about what the *Reader's Digest* subscriber is looking for?

6 Which of the top ten magazines in 5.1 does your school library subscribe to? Write a letter asking them to subscribe to one they now overlook. Justify your choice.

READINGS AND REFERENCES

The Mass Menagerie

John C. Merrill
Ralph L. Lowenstein
Media, Messages and Men: New Perspectives in Communication. New York: David McKay, 1971.
   A text on the changing relationships between media, messages, and audience. See Section One, "Media: A New Look at Changing Roles." Particularly effective regarding models and theoretical approaches to media specialization trends.

History: The Good Old Days

Theodore Peterson
Magazines in the Twentieth Century, 2d ed. Urbana: University of Illinois Press, 1964.
   A good comprehensive look at magazines from the beginning to the 1960s. Many stories about colorful early publishers; also sections on advertising and the expanding magazine marketplace. Excellent index.

John Tebbel
The American Magazine: A Compact History. New York: Hawthorn Books, 1969.

This is history in a hurry, but it probably has all the information you need. The author divides the development of American magazines into four historical periods and explores each in depth. Includes a useful suggested reading list and index.

**These Days:
Magazines Since 1950**

Roland E. Wolseley
The Changing Magazine: Trends in Readership and Management. New York: Hastings House, 1973.

The emphasis here is on problems faced by modern magazine publishers. There are also detailed accounts of the rise and fall of some of the magazines that folded after World War II. Some predictions for the future and a good supplementary reading list. One drawback: Magazines are changing so rapidly that this book is rapidly becoming out of date. For more current information, check the *Readers' Guide to Periodical Literature.*

**Specialization and
Marketing Trends**

James L. Ford
Magazines for Millions: The Story of Specialized Publications. Carbondale: Southern Illinois University Press, 1969.

Magazines for Millions is an entertaining and in-depth look at all the specialized publications in the menagerie marketplace. Separate chapters for farm publications, associations, and industry and labor publications—you name it. No bibliography; meager index.

The best single source for up-to-the-minute information on magazine marketing, advertising, and readership trends is *Magazine: A Newsletter of Research.* It is published monthly by the Magazine Publishers Association, 575 Lexington Avenue, New York, N.Y. 10022. Back issues are available. Recently, such topics as "Dimensions of a Magazine and its Readers" and "Target Marketing in 1980's" have been covered. Chock full of interesting statistical information.

Magazine Industry Market Place (annual, R. R. Bowker Co.) can be found in the reference room of most libraries. *MIMP*, as it is known in the trade, lists all magazines published in the U.S. by subject matter and type of publication. In addition, you'll find information on magazine organizations, awards, photography, artists and art services, printing services, and more.

Writing for Magazines

Bernadine Clark, ed.
Writer's Market. Cincinnati: Writer's Digest, annual.

**Issues and Answers:
Professional Print—The
Curious Collective**

Robert T. Elson
Time Inc.: The Intimate History of a Publishing Enterprise 1923–1941. New York: Atheneum, 1968.
The World of Time Inc.: The Intimate History of a Publishing Enterprise 1941–1960. New York: Atheneum, 1973.

Elson draws heavily on the *Time* success formula to explain the most popular news magazine of the 20th century. Includes a lot of background material on the founders of *Time.* Comprehensive index.

James Thurber
The Years with Ross. Boston: Little, Brown, 1959.

James Thurber, one of America's most renowned humorists, recalls his years with *The New Yorker* and its famous editor, Harold W. Ross. Until his death in 1951, Ross dominated the magazine. Thurber's insights into that particular "curious collective" are entertaining as well as informative.

PART TWO
Electronic Media:
Edison Came to Stay

IMAGINE A WORLD WITHOUT ELECTRICITY. NO LIGHTS. NO electric ovens. No TV. No stereo. Electric circuitry is more than a convenience; it has re-created our environment and radically altered our life-styles. When the lights went out in New York City in 1965, there were thousands of incidents of vandalism and looting. Electricity seems to have become part of that thin veneer of civilization that keeps some of us from reverting to our primal selves. From the duplicating machine to the coffeepot, we have come to rely on electricity in virtually every facet of our day-to-day activities.

Electric information is not print in electric form but a brand-new kind of information we are only beginning to understand. In an instant we find out what is happening in the Mideast or what the weather will be like this afternoon. We are plugged into a giant information network that is all-encompassing and all-pervasive.

In Part Two, one chapter is devoted to radio and one to film. We do not often think of film as an "electronic medium," but films do rely on electricity to operate— projectors are not the "magic lanterns" they once were. More important, both film and television have much in common in their use of visual imagery and their consequences in our mass-mediated environment.

The discussion of television is divided into two chapters: one for the structure of TV in America, and another for programming. I have devoted a relatively large amount of space to analyzing prime-time commercial television, with the hope that it will help you become a more critical consumer.

Chapter 7 is devoted exclusively to the phonograph and the development of American popular music—an area ignored in other texts. Like television, popular music is a part of our lives whether we listen or not. So many people *are* listening that we cannot help being affected.

Just as Gutenberg is not responsible for all that has happened since the invention of movable type, Edison cannot be held responsible for all the developments since the light bulb and the phonograph. But he really started something. In that sense, Edison is here to stay.

6

Radio:
The Magic Medium

THE SUMMER I LEFT SAN FRANCISCO I WAS DETERMINED TO make a fresh start and leave all of the Haight-Ashbury craziness behind. I enrolled as a journalism major at California State University in Fullerton. An engineer in a broadcast journalism course tipped me to a job at KYMS, the local "progressive" station. There was an opening for a copywriter. The next morning I was at their door. The station manager was playing the guitar as I entered his office: "Oh—you're the guy about the copywriting job. Got any experience?"

"Sure, I've written a novel, and a lot of poems and short stories. I'm a journalism major and . . ."

He interrupted me. "Is this the easiest job you ever got?"

I gulped—I was actually in radio.

The salary of $250 a month wasn't much, but the job was supposedly only part time. Before long I was working 10 to 12 hours a day and juggling classes in between. The only thing I could think about was getting on the air. The thought dominated my mind night and day—I practiced in the car, in bed before I went to sleep at night: "This is *Edward Jay* on KYMS-FM . . . *This* is Edward Jay on KYMS-FM . . . This *is* Edward Jay . . ."

Finally, the big break came: We had been scheduled to go off the air for maintenance between midnight and five, but the engineer was busy; since nobody else was available, did I want to give it a try? I'd practiced for six months in the production room, but this was the real thing—on the air. Thousands (well, maybe dozens) of people would be listening, and I would be sailing them away on a magic carpet of music, *my* music.

The last thing I needed to worry about was falling asleep. I was so wired all night that I couldn't stop: push a cart here—cue a record there—don't forget the ID on the half hour—not too close to the mike—answer the phone—somebody wants to hear Cream—somebody wants to hear Neil Young—Grateful Dead—Jefferson Airplane—Rolling Stones. . . .

Radio affects most people intimately, person to person, offering a world of unspoken communication between writer-speaker and listener. . . .
MARSHALL McLUHAN

By the time morning came, I was both exhausted and jubilant. I don't think there is any way to describe that incredible night. I've done thousands of radio shows since then, but I can recall that one for you record by record, mistake by mistake. Radio is that kind of thing—it's magic.

That adrenalin rush still surges today when I go into a radio studio to cut a commercial or do an air shift. There is so much to do, so much to remember; and in the true McLuhan spirit, everything happens all at once, all the time, because sound surrounds you. You see only what's in front of you, but you hear all around you. Of course, the disc jockeys are only a small part of what makes radio work, but they *are* radio for the listener. The deejay represents that real-life link with radio, the magic medium.

PIONEERS AND PROGRAMMERS

Several 19th-century inventors paved the way, but credit for the invention of radio is generally given to Lee de Forest (see 6.1 and 6.2). In 1906 he invented a special grid that, when inserted into a vacuum tube, enabled it to function as an amplifier. This formed the basis for the amplification needed to make voice transmission possible via "wireless." The tube itself was the product of the work of Thomas Edison and British inventor John Ambrose Fleming. (Of course none of this would have been possible had not Guglielmo Marconi successfully sent "wireless" dot and dash signals across the Atlantic Ocean in 1901.)

Surprisingly, there was little interest in radio as a commercial vehicle at first. Most early broadcasters were hobbyists who built their own equipment. When Congress finally passed some broadcast regulations in 1912, it

was to keep private broadcasters from interfering with government communication channels. The American Marconi Company set up several huge sending and receiving stations and successfully transmitted wireless signals across the Atlantic. By the time World War I came along, wireless was well established, and it played an important part in the American victory.

In 1919, after a long series of costly court battles to protect its patents, American Marconi was forced to merge with the new Radio Corporation of America (RCA). This gave RCA dominance in the infant industry. Today RCA is one of the world's largest electronics companies and owns broadcast stations in most of the nation's top markets, along with a publishing house and a record company.

In 1920, Westinghouse obtained a license to broadcast, and its KDKA went on the air in Pittsburgh. KDKA offered the listener regularly scheduled programs. During that first year, it broadcast the Harding-Cox election results. Soon many people began to show interest in the new medium; yet to many more, radio still seemed like a fad, and almost everyone agreed that if there was any money to be made in radio, it was in the sale of radio sets.

American Telephone and Telegraph (AT&T) had a better idea. When AT&T opened its radio station WEAF in New York in the summer of 1922, someone decided that radio was really an extension of the telephone. Since AT&T charged for telephone calls, why not charge people to talk on the radio? A Long Island real estate firm bought ten minutes to tell listeners about available properties, and the response was overwhelming. Radio advertising was born. By the end of the decade, WEAF was grossing almost $1 million a year in "toll charges." It didn't take other stations long to get the message. Soon the airwaves were flooded with a barrage of advertisements for everything from gasoline to hair oil. It's been that way ever since.

At about the same time, AT&T began experimentally to link up stations for simultaneous broadcasting. Suddenly a *network* was possible. This had a tremendous impact on advertising practices and on the listening habits of Americans. More important, it paved the way for the coast-to-coast broadcasting that followed.

THE GOLDEN AGE OF RADIO (1926–1948)

In 1922 David Sarnoff of RCA (see 6.3) wrote a memo to his staff arguing that the novelty of radio was wearing off; to convince people to keep buying radio sets, better programs would have to be offered. Sarnoff's idea was a revolutionary one. Why not a "specialized organization with a competent staff capable of meeting the task of entertaining the nation"?

In 1926 RCA formed the National Broadcasting Company (NBC) "to provide the best programs available for broadcasting in the United States." It was so successful that NBC formed a second network a year later to accommodate increasing demand. The two networks were identified by the color of pens used to trace their paths in stockholders' meetings, the *red* and *blue* networks. Initially they linked only the Midwest and the Eastern Seaboard, but by the end of 1927 NBC had leased a transcontinental wire to bring its programs to the West Coast. Simultaneous coast-to-coast broadcasting was a reality.

Young Bill Paley, the 26-year-old heir to the Congress Cigar Company, had been fascinated by the way radio advertising had boosted his father's cigar business. In 1928

6.1

Lee de Forest, the father of radio. He lived long enough to see his cultural vision for the medium replaced by the commercial system we have today.

he bought a 16-station "network" that then dared to challenge the mighty NBC. His United Independent Broadcasters eventually became the Columbia Broadcasting System (CBS). Despite Paley's efforts during the 1920s and 1930s, NBC's two networks aired the most popular radio shows. During that time, a number of other small networks tried to challenge NBC's dominance, but none was entirely successful. After CBS, the Mutual Broadcasting System probably came closest, thanks largely to several popular shows, including *The Lone Ranger.*

6.2

Time Line: The History of American Radio

GUGLIELMO MARCONI

1901 Marconi is successful in sending "wireless" signals across the Atlantic Ocean.

1906 Lee de Forest adds his "audion" grid, which makes the vacuum tube function as an amplifier, thus making voice transmission possible over wireless.

1919 Radio Corporation of America (RCA) is formed.

1920 Westinghouse obtains a license for KDKA, Pittsburgh, the first radio station to offer continuous, regularly scheduled programs. KDKA covers the presidential election.

1922 WEAF, New York, begins selling air time to advertisers, opening the door for advertiser-supported electronic media.

1925 President Coolidge's inauguration is heard coast to coast through a 21-station hookup.

1926 AT&T sells out its radio interest; NBC eventually gains control.

1927 The Radio Act of 1927 is passed, and the Federal Radio Commission (FRC) is established.

1927 The United Independent Broadcasters radio network, later named CBS, airs its first broadcast; it is heard from Boston to St. Louis.

1930 *Amos 'n' Andy,* first heard in 1928, is the first successful radio situation comedy.

1930 Edwin Armstrong, the father of FM radio, applies for patents for "frequency modulation," and a new kind of radio service is born.

1931 The FRC refuses to renew the license of Milford, Kansas' KFKB, citing dishonest programming as the reason.

1932 Al Jarvis's *Make-Believe Ballroom* on KFWB, Los Angeles, becomes the first successful dee-jay show.

1933 President Franklin D. Roosevelt begins his radio fireside chats, talking directly to the American people.

1934 The Communications Act of 1934 includes provisions for a

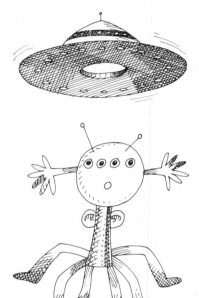

new seven-member Federal Communications Commission (FCC) to regulate radio, television, and telephone communication.

1938 Orson Welles's fictional *War of the Worlds* creates panic among thousands of radio listeners, and a government investigation follows.

1939 First experimental FM station goes on the air in New Jersey.

1940 A federal court of appeals rules that records purchased by radio stations may be played on the air with no prior consent from record companies or artists.

1940 Edward R. Murrow brings the war in Europe to radio listeners in America.

1943 NBC sells its second network; this eventually becomes ABC, the third major network.

1945 The FCC encourages the development of television, to the detriment of FM radio.

1948 Radio's biggest money year; from here on television begins to take a larger share of advertising revenues.

1949 Todd Storz buys Omaha's ailing KOWH and develops the first "Top-40" radio format.

1949 The FCC allows licensees to present editorials as part of regular programming and requires time for opposing views.

1951 Hundreds of radio stations switch to the deejay format and scramble to make up for lost revenues as network feeds diminish.

1955 Bill Haley and the Comets' "Rock around the Clock" becomes the first rock-and-roll hit to make it to number one. The rock era of radio begins.

1959 With the payola scandal uncovered, deejays admit receiving money to "plug" certain records. The rise of the program director follows.

1966 KSAN-FM in San Francisco and KPPC-FM in Los Angeles become the first "underground" FM stations, playing album cuts. Deejays are again given power to select music.

1970 The FCC issues a statement warning that broadcasters are liable for obscene or drug-related lyrics in songs they air.

1970s ABC radio successfully breaks into various "networks" with news, information, and entertainment designed for specialized audiences.

1972 All-news formats go on the air in New York, Washington, and Los Angeles.

1975 Don Imus, controversial and often abusive New York deejay, snares top ratings in the nation's most competitive radio market.

1976 C. W. McCall's hit single "Convoy" celebrates the new era of citizens' band (CB) radio. The FCC opens up 17 new CB channels, and more than 20 million Americans are CB users.

1978 Pressure for a new Communications Act mounts in Congress, but most broadcasters are reluctant.

1980 The FCC creates a furor when it proposes to restructure the AM and FM bands and allow many new stations on the air.

1981 The FCC "deregulates" radio, allowing stations to discontinue public-service programming and exceed 18 commercial minutes per hour if they choose.

1982 More and more AM stations switch to talk as FM dominates music programming.

1984 MTV (Music Television) plays an increasingly larger role in determining FM music playlists.

6.3
David Sarnoff Broadcasts the Disaster of the Decade

On April 14, 1912, young David Sarnoff, an employee of American Marconi, was at his New York station casually listening to the flood of dots and dashes that made up radio messages. Suddenly a dim message, barely audible through the static, startled him. It was coming from the S.S. *Olympic* some 1,400 miles away: "S.S. *Titanic* ran into iceberg, sinking fast."

The *Titanic* was the pride of British shipbuilders, who thought her unsinkable. This made the news all the more amazing, and word of the disaster spread quickly. Many amateur radio transmitters were soon trying to make contact with the sinking ship. To avoid jamming the airwaves and to keep interference to a minimum, President Taft ordered them shut down except for one. David Sarnoff remained on the air.

For three days and nights he received and transmitted messages. There was little time for food or sleep. The first reports included names of survivors.

Later came the long list of casualties. Sarnoff's wireless became the nation's information link with the disaster of the decade.

It was also electronic media's first scoop. Newspapers took their information directly from radio. Many years later Sarnoff recalled, "The *Titanic* disaster brought radio to the front . . . and incidentally me." The 21-year-old who was there when the importance of wireless was first dramatized to the nation went on to become the driving force behind RCA and the National Broadcasting Company.

NBC's greatest hit in the early days was *Amos 'n' Andy*. It was a situation comedy of sorts, featuring the adventures of a group of black workers, one of whom owned the "Fresh-Air Taxicab Company." The show was loaded with black stereotypes. Ironically, the voices of Amos and Andy were those of two white men.

Probably the most popular genres of radio entertainment during the golden age were the mystery and action-adventure series. Among the most successful were *Gangbusters, Calling All Cars, Ellery Queen, The Fat Man, Sam Spade, The FBI in Peace and War*, and *The Green Hornet*. The action-adventure format has been carried on by TV shows like *The A Team* and *Magnum, P.I.*

Like daytime TV today, daytime radio had its soap operas, including *Our Gal Sunday, The Romance of Helen Trent*, and *Pepper Young's Family*. For the kids there were *Jack Armstrong, the All-American Boy; Superman; Uncle Don;* and, of course, *The Lone Ranger*. There were quiz and talk shows as well. If all of these formats sound familiar, it's because television borrowed so heavily from radio. The names have changed, but the genres of television and radio programs are almost identical. Some critics contend that television has supplied very few new ideas in broadcast entertainment.

But radio in the golden age was full of new ideas. It was the magic medium, and everybody loved it. Listeners from coast to coast could hear symphonic music (and fill in the visual picture with their imagination) from the great concert halls in Boston, or they could be transported to the Grand Ballroom at the Waldorf-Astoria Hotel in New York City, where the big bands performed. For those who lived in rural America, radio provided a link with the world outside. Radio brought

6.4

President Franklin Delano Roosevelt spoke on the air often to bring his message to the people.

everyone into the cultural and social mainstream of America.

Of course, entertainment was not the only way radio served the American people. It continued to be what it had been since the *Titanic* disaster: a way to keep people informed. President Franklin Roosevelt made the most of the medium in the early 1930s, speaking directly to his constituents and urging them to support his new and controversial programs (see 6.4). His "fireside chats" gathered most Americans around the radio.

The significance of radio as an arbiter of the national mood was brought home to many in 1938 when the *Mercury Theater on the Air* aired their anxiety-provoking "War of the Worlds" production (see 6.5).

Radio also made Americans acutely aware of current events in Europe in the late 1930s and early 1940s. Broadcasters like Eric Sevareid and Edward R. Murrow were on the scene, bringing listeners the sounds of war as they actually happened. Murrow's reports from London during the bombing were the ultimate in believability—bombs exploded in the background as he reported the latest war news. Those pre–Pearl Harbor broadcasts by Murrow prepared Americans for the war to come. Sentiment shifted rapidly from neutrality to a full commitment to England by 1941. Somehow, the war did not seem very far away, and radio was the reason.

In 1943, NBC's reign as king of network radio suffered a serious blow when the FCC decided to ban the operation of two networks by one company. NBC sold its blue network for $7 million to Edward Noble, who renamed it the American Broadcasting Company.

NBC radio stars began to defect to CBS in the 1940s, lured away by Bill Paley's checkbook. The CBS president offered big-money contracts to Jack Benny, George Burns and

6.5
War of the Worlds and World War

It was a rainy night over most of America, October 30, 1938. In Europe, Hitler was invading Czechoslovakia and was turning his eyes toward Poland. There was a definite tension in the air. Millions of Americans tuned in their radios to CBS's *Mercury Theater on the Air*. Instead, there was a late news bulletin: Aliens had landed in New Jersey—America was being invaded by men from Mars! Thousands of calls poured in to newspapers and radio stations—was it true? Were there really men from Mars? Army personnel were called back to their bases—this could be serious.

Orson Welles's production of H. G. Wells's *War of the Worlds*

set off a genuine panic. There were traffic jams near the "landing site," and many people reported spotting the aliens. Public reaction was overwhelming. Some listeners had tuned in late (Edgar Bergen's show on another network had far more listeners), which added to the confusion. Welles attempted to avert disaster by broadcasting repeated warnings that this fictional radio play was not to be taken seriously; it was only *entertainment*.

That broadcast has been called the most famous of all radio programs, and perhaps it was. It is the one that had the greatest *immediate* impact on its listeners. The FCC investigated, and new regulations were passed: There would be no more "fictional" news bulletins.

In a larger context, *War of the Worlds* demonstrated the

awesome power of radio. No newspaper or magazine had the ability to evoke such immediate emotional response. Radio was an infant medium, but many people began to wonder—this could be more than just an "entertainment" device after all. . . .

Gracie Allen, Ozzie and Harriet Nelson, Red Skelton, Bing Crosby, and others. This helped establish CBS as the top network in the late 1940s and gave it a nucleus of talent for its new television network.

THE BIG CHANGE: RADIO AFTER TELEVISION

When television arrived, comedienne Gracie Allen wryly observed that "it seems like nobody watches radio anymore." Many new

TV stations were put on the air by owners of newspapers and of lucrative radio stations. Radio lost a tremendous amount of revenue to the newer broadcast medium. But in a sense, radio had the last laugh. Almost everything that appeared on television had already been done on radio.

Just as many think that the "good old days" of magazines are gone forever, some contend that radio will never be what it was during the golden age. In a way, they're right. Radio will never be what it was, but it will continue to be what it is, and that is constantly changing. Radio has not really become better or worse since television, but it has undergone a tremendous change in content.

By the mid-1950s, television was using many radio programs and radio stars. An industry-wide panic took hold in radio. In their heyday, national radio networks provided programs from 9:00 A.M. to 11:00 P.M. Local stations simply pulled the switch and raked in the profits. When the networks offerings declined, the locals looked for the least expensive format that would allow them to stay on the air and sell advertising time. The day of the deejay had arrived.

Of course, music had been played on radio since the beginning, and as early as 1932, Los Angeles radio personality Al Jarvis began playing a few records from a tiny studio at KFWB that he called "The World's Largest Make-Believe Ballroom." In New York, Martin Block picked up the idea three years later and made believers of his skeptical bosses at WNEW by arranging sponsorship for the show himself. The program proved successful, but there were problems. Performers fought airing of their songs on radio, fearing it would dilute the product and make record purchases unnecessary. In 1940, however, a federal appeals court ruled that broadcasters who had bought a record could play it on the air without obtaining prior permission from the artist.

The idea of mixing records, chatter, and commercials was just what radio stations needed in the early 1950s. Before long, the local disc-jockey format had replaced network programs as the most common radio commodity.

During the mid-1950s, the transistor reduced the size and price of the portable radio. Now it was truly a medium that "goes where you go." What's more, Americans *were* on the go. A record number of automobiles were sold during the period, and most of them were equipped with radios. The most popular deejays appeared in "drive time" from 6:00 A.M. to 9:00 A.M. and from 3:00 P.M. to 6:00 P.M., keeping commuters company to and from work. Drive time became radio's prime time and helped give the medium a much-needed financial boost. The deejays—colorful, provocative, and eccentric—were largely responsible for keeping radio alive.

MEET THE DEEJAY

Though I have had professional experience in many areas of mass media, it is my years as a Los Angeles deejay that seem to provoke the most questions from students. What are deejays really like?

Real-life deejays are often the proud possessors of giant egos (see 6.6). Most of the male deejays I've known were five or six inches shorter than the norm and had three things in common. They were generally insecure, usually divorced, and almost always hyperactive.

One Los Angeles disc jockey refuses to take a vacation. He works 52 weeks a year because each of his last three vacations cost him his job. Program directors slotted in a newer, younger, and lower-paid deejay in his place. When listeners liked the new voice, the old one was off to the unemployment line. Being on the air is a risky business, because there is always someone willing to do your job for less, or even for nothing. Spinning records is a coveted position, and this does not encourage job security.

One reason disc jockeys are often divorced is that many stations are swarming with "groupies." The deejay, whether male or female, is likely to be accosted by these warm and loving creatures at any moment. The groupie is usually young and is always caught up in the magic of the music and the people who play it on the radio.

Guest Essay by Huber Ellingsworth

Entertainment Radio in the 1950s: More Than an Afterglow of the Golden Age

While many radio stations "bailed out" of entertainment programming and got into music via the deejay after TV, there were a number of network radio offerings in the 1950s that carried on the golden-age tradition. Huber Ellingsworth feels that the golden age and the modern format systems were not as incompatible as some would have us believe. Dr. Ellingsworth is currently a professor of communication at the University of Tulsa.

The decade of 1950–1960 was unique in American broadcasting because it offered the public a choice between network entertainment programming on radio and television. There was in no sense a fair competition for audiences, because the networks had already announced that they would close down entertainment radio as soon as possible, and they undertook extensive print advertising to lure listeners to the new visual medium. New radio programs were not publicized and promoted, and it became increasingly difficult to find program schedules. But a determined group of network radio executives, producers, advertisers, and listeners kept "foreground radio" alive until Black Thursday (Thanksgiving Day, 1960), when the last programs were arbitrarily terminated amid a storm of protest.

In the interim, networks offered full programming that included many new programs of remarkable quality, variety, and originality which supplemented long-running series continued from the so-called Golden Age (1926–1948). The new burst of creativity came about for a variety of reasons. The development of editable audio tape, new sophistication in sound mixing and dubbing, the loosening of artistic control

by national sponsors plus more local sponsorship, and the change from a mass one-medium audience to smaller, more discerning groups of listeners composed mostly of adults all combined to generate opportunities never before available. So entertainment radio reached its maturity at the wrong time, for many of the wrong reasons.

The genres of the adult Western and the police detective show were explored, and became the basis for later

My father did a radio show in Portland, Oregon, during the late 1930s, and I asked him if there were groupies even then. He confirmed that there were, smiled quietly and got a faraway look in his eyes. Finally he added that most of them "wanted to be vocalists with a band" but would settle for a love affair with a disc jockey.

Hyperactivity, the third professional trait, is a necessity. Deejays must be able to play a cart (a tape cartridge with a commercial or prerecorded message), cue up a record, give the time and temperature, and answer the phone—all at the same time. They must do it smoothly, so that the listener never knows how hectic things really are. As far as the

exploitation in television. Certainly the best adult Western, and perhaps the most artistically superior radio series ever produced, was *Gunsmoke.* Marshal Dillon (William Conrad) stayed alive by shooting first and talking later. And when he rode into Dodge after days on the trail and growled, "Where's Kitty?", listeners knew why he was asking. Kitty (Georgia Ellis) ran a tough saloon, the Long Branch, with rooms upstairs definitely not operated by Sheraton. Life was hard and violent and people died of wounds, starvation, freezing, and childbirth, sometimes aided by hard-drinking Doc Adams. A later TV version of this program portrayed Dillon as a gun-toting frontier psychiatrist who brought order and mental health to the snow-capped mountain region of central Kansas. The TV Dillon hung out at the Long Branch YMCA, which inexplicably served liquor but was kept respectable by housemother Miss Kitty.

The long tradition of radio drama was continued and enhanced by a number of BBC imports, including Shakespeare plays and a Sherlock Holmes series. Documentaries and public-service programs included *Capitol Cloakroom, Meet the Press,* and an ambitious series of hour-long *Biographies in Sound.* Light entertainment came from *What's My Line, College Quiz Bowl,* and Groucho Marx's *You Bet Your Life.* There was news analysis by Edward R. Murrow, Howard K. Smith, and Lowell Thomas.

Comedy, one of the brightest spots, was generated by Bob and Ray, who were heard throughout the decade on NBC, CBS, and Mutual. *The Goon Show,* a BBC import with Peter Sellers, Terry-Thomas, and Spike Milligan, was carried on NBC, as well as an occasional Stan Freberg special.

The sharpest contrast with current TV and radio programming philosophy was the richness of programming for the classical-music audience. To counter NBC's live broadcasts of the New York Philharmonic, CBS created its own symphony orchestra, while ABC carried the Metropolitan Opera performances live.

Perhaps the fullest realization of entertainment radio's unique capabilities was in NBC's weekend *Monitor,* which originally aired in 1954. It was an easy mix of live and recorded music, comedy, reviews, interviews, commentary, news, and weather (sultry-voiced Miss Monitor always began with "In Atlanta, the temperature is . . ."). Mike Wallace was one of several New York anchors, and there were segments from six major cities. Comedy was the chief attraction, based around Bob and Ray, with sketches by Bob Newhart, Mike Nichols and Elaine May, Bill Cosby, Stan Freberg, and others. It did require listening, but it was easy listening; stations and listeners could drop in and out.

For ten years listeners had a choice, and enough of them chose radio that it was still producing a tidy financial profit at the end. Some of what it supplied has never been replaced, and American society is the poorer for it.

---

listeners know, the deejay is listening to the music right along with them. TV viewers of *WKRP in Cincinnati* were given a fairly accurate picture of how hectic things can get in the control room.

In the early 1950s, disc jockeys programmed their own shows, selecting the records and planning whatever additional material they wanted. More recently, the program director has taken over, dictating the content of the show right down to the last supposed ad-lib. The rise of the program director came in response to the payola scandal of the late 1950s. Once record companies discovered that air play boosted record sales, there was no stopping them. Disc jockeys would receive

6.6

Imus in the Morning

Which New York deejay had as his regular guest the Reverend Dr. Billy Sol Hargis, who sells "angel-hair cloaks" for the "long trip to heaven"? Whose guests have included Judge Hangin, who states flatly that police brutality is the "fun part" of law enforcement, and Ronald American, who is "110 percent American" and promises to rise and walk from his wheelchair if elected President?

If you have ever spent any time in New York City, you know that this description fits only one air personality, the sometimes foul-mouthed, always controversial Don Imus, morning deejay for WNBC. John Donald Imus, Jr., started at KUTY in Palmdale, California, and was fired from his next job at KJOY in Stockton for running an Eldridge Cleaver look-alike con-

test. Somehow within a year Imus was in the crucial "morning drive" slot for the network-owned WNBC in the nation's top radio market, loving every minute of it. Imus's usual patter included racial slurs, which he insisted were "all in good fun." He thought nothing of spending a few moments talking with his engineer during the middle of a live commercial or criticizing his bosses on the air.

Often Imus could be heard laughing through a newscast or putting down his fellow deejays. All these antics violate every known code of conduct for a deejay, but through it all "Imus's Army" of listeners remained faithful. By 1975 he had more listeners than any other deejay in New York. Yet success was fleeting. WNBC let him go in 1978 after a fall in the ratings. Radio listeners and radio executives seem to be a fickle lot.

But the big executives who hire the lesser executives are also fickle. Those who engi-

neered Imus's demise were eventually fired and replaced by others who wanted him back. By 1980 he was back in the morning-drive slot at WNBC, and at least one ratings service had WNBC back to number two in the market. Hence WNBC's slogan became, "We're the next one." Don Imus might disagree; however, one has the feeling that he knew he was the best all along!

cases of liquor, free passes to concerts and films, and finally lump cash sums to "promote" a song by giving it air time. The net result was a government investigation in 1959. There followed a brief rift in the public's love affair with the deejay.

But the 1960s saw little payola. Is the payola problem solved forever? Probably not. One record industry executive admitted privately to me, "It's a lot cheaper to get to one program director than to get to half a dozen jocks."

"Drug-ola"—the exchange of drugs for preferential treatment of a song—is not unknown in major markets.

The authoritarian rule of the program director was challenged briefly by the appearance of the "underground" FM stations in the late 1960s. These stations played longer album cuts instead of singles, and control by a program director did not fit with their "loose and free" image. For a short time, these disc jockeys were given back the freedom to select the songs they aired. The program director's role was limited to riding herd on the often erratic deejays, who would sometimes forget a commercial or swear on the air. The commercial success of some underground formats led to the similar but slicker and more organized "progressive" stations, which reinstituted the program director's power to select the music.

Of course, all markets are different. At many small stations the deejay may pick all the music, and there may not even be a program director. But even this is changing as small-market owners find that using prerecorded syndicated shows is cheaper than hiring live deejays. Deejays, themselves a product of a big change, are finding that recent changes in radio technology are drastically altering their role in radio programming.

THE PEOPLE YOU NEVER HEAR

To most listeners the radio world may consist of the disc jockey, the newsperson, and the commentator; but the real world of radio is quite different. The on-the-air people may represent only about 10 percent to 15 percent of the total staff of most stations. In metro markets they may make up less than 10 percent. Who are the rest of the people?

Management personnel are at the top of the ladder. Each station has an owner or owners and a general manager (GM), who supervises all station activities. The GM's word is law. Under the GM are the heads of the major departments.

Programming is the first department you might think of. The program director (PD) keeps track of air personnel, schedules shifts, and settles disputes involving the on-the-air staff. It is the PD's job to make sure that air personalities are slotted in at the proper times to elicit maximum audience response. If the ratings for the entire station are poor, the PD is likely to go.

Sales is often the most financially rewarding of all station jobs. Usually sales people have a guaranteed minimum salary of only a few hundred dollars per month, but they make up the difference by selling air time on commission. If they don't sell, they don't eat. There is usually a sales director or sales manager in charge who reports directly to the GM. In major markets there may be a few highly paid stars on the air, but at most stations it is the sales people who take home the most money.

Traffic is the department least known to the average radio listener. The traffic staff must schedule all the commercials. Station policy usually dictates a fixed number each hour, and competing products must not be placed back to back. It wouldn't be a good business practice to have a spot that urged you to "buy a Chevrolet today" played after one that told you "Ford has a better idea!" Traffic people devise the program logs, minute-by-minute records of all commercials and other non-music materials. Air staff and engineers follow these logs exactly.

Engineering people are usually found poking around with screwdrivers and soldering irons, repairing broken station equipment. Again, there is usually a chief engineer who reports directly to the GM. Engineers keep the station running well, and they can often be heard mumbling that nobody notices them "until something goes wrong" (see 6.7).

The *production* department is vital to the overall "sound" of the station. Copywriters and "talent" people produce the jingles, IDs, promos, and, most important, commercials. A salesperson will sell time to a local merchant and then order a spot for production. A copywriter works with information supplied by the salesperson. The "talent" goes into the studio and reads the spot. At a larger

6.7

Many major-market radio stations use facilities such as these at San Francisco's KSFO. The engineer (left) plays the records, turns the mike on and off, and runs and logs all commercials and other materials. The deejay (right) simply talks to the audience and delivers the inevitable "live" commercials from a copy book in front of him. Smaller stations use a combo setup in which the deejay is expected to do it all. The combo studio features turntables, mike, and other broadcast apparatus in one location for the convenience of the deejay.

station there is an engineer who works exclusively in production (see 6.8). At a smaller station the copywriter, talent, and engineer may be one person. At a very small station, that same person may do the selling as well.

Large metro stations have separate departments for editorials, publicity or promotion, public relations, and so on. Still, most of the 8,000 radio stations in America have fewer than 50 employees—and there never seem to be enough people to get all the work done.

As with other media outlets, the environment of most radio stations is frantic and chaotic. From morning to night everyone is on the go, typing up commercials and getting things on the air at the last minute. Coffee makes the American way of radio work; I've never been in a radio station that didn't have a gigantic coffeepot that needed constant

refilling. Chaos just seems to be the nature of the medium. Almost everyone who works in radio complains about it, but no one would really have it any other way.

In direct contrast to this are the new "automated" stations where all music and talk are taped ahead of time and selected by a computer. The atmosphere in the automated stations is more like that of a library or a museum.

MUSIC FORMATS

In previous chapters, we have seen that each mass medium presents a constructed mediated reality that is quite different from real-life experience. The particular CMR is the reason we are attracted to a particular medium. Like all media, radio has its own unique CMR

6.8
Bob Keyker, KFWB production engineer, working in the master control room of the Los Angeles station.

especially designed to reach and hold the mass audience. For most radio stations, music makes up the bulk of that CMR.

While no two radio stations are exactly alike, there are a number of basic formulas. These formulas, or *formats*, involve a specific blend of certain types of music and talk designed to attract the largest possible audience to the station. Radio formats are not permanent things but are constantly shifting as audience needs evolve.

Because of the constraints on its programming, commercial radio is seldom at the forefront of musical trends. It always takes some time for new styles to catch on with the mass audience. When they do, you can be sure that some innovative radio programmers somewhere will find a way to fit them into current programming. For example, disco music was quite popular in the mid-1970s, but it took

several years before disco formats began to appear. Ironically, by the time "all-disco" radio had gotten under way, the disco craze had cooled. Today there are only a handful of disco stations left.

A more current example involves the impact of punk and new-wave music on the radio scene. Punk pioneers like the Sex Pistols and the Ramones were played little if at all by established rock stations in the mid- and late 1970s. In fact, as late as 1982 there was still some resistance to the "new music" in mainstream rock formats.

Sometimes commercial stations can follow the lead of college stations in these areas. KUSF-FM, the station licensed to the University of San Francisco, offered punk and new wave music in the late 1970s. By 1982 a new wave format had emerged and a relatively large and loyal audience along with it.

Not until then did the city's commercial KQAK adopt a similar format, and soon several other commercial rock stations began adding more new music to their play lists.

However, it was the tremendous success of rock videos—coupled with increased record sales by new-wave groups (such as the Clash, whose *Combat Rock* was one of the best-selling albums of 1983)—that forced virtually all rock stations to include some new wave on their playlists. Again, radio was slow to respond to obvious shifts in the public's musical tastes.

Nevertheless, the basic formats of radio cover a wide spectrum of listener needs and tastes. Some, like classical, are tried and true and have been around since the beginning of broadcasting. Others, like adult contemporary, are relatively new and experimental. Yet in each case, the idea remains to get and hold as many listeners as possible, particularly those with desirable *demographics*, or audience characteristics. Top 40, album-oriented rock, middle of the road, adult contemporary, country and western, and "beautiful music" are the major formats achieving success in today's competitive radio marketplace.

Top 40

Top 40, hit parade, boss hits—by any name, this format continues to figure in many major markets. Once the undisputed king of radio formats, Top 40 has lost its luster in recent years due primarily to heavy competition with album-oriented rock (AOR) and adult contemporary. Top 40 emerged during the 1950s when programmers called record stores to find out what the public was buying; then they mirrored public taste by playing those same songs over and over. Today Top-40 radio has become Top 20 or Top 25 at many stations. The same few records receive repeated air play while thousands of others are ignored.

There are a few giants in this genre. Bill Drake's success came in the early 1960s with KHJ, a Los Angeles Top-40 station. While sitting around his pool at Malibu Beach, he picked the songs that were to be played on his station. His method was simple—play only the very top singles and play them more often than anyone else.

Another giant is Casey Kasem, who helped form Watermark Productions to begin his syndicated *American Top 40* (see 6.9). Kasem gets his hits from the number one authority in the industry, *Billboard* magazine. Every week he "counts 'em down in order" to thousands of listeners in hundreds of cities from New York to Newberg, Oregon. *American Top 40* can also be heard in Europe and Asia. Kasem's trademark is airing little-known facts about the group or star:

A certain singer sold his guitar and then decided he had to get it back and spent three weeks wandering around the streets of Columbus, Ohio, until one day, tired and discouraged, he stopped in Winchell's to have a doughnut and there, lo and behold, was the man to whom he had sold it! He went on to form a new singing group and this week they have the number one song on *American Top 40*. Who is it? . . . Well, we'll find out right after this message. . . .

Album-Oriented Rock

Album-oriented rock got its start in the 1960s when it became evident that a lot of rock enthusiasts were tired of the constraints posed by Top 40. Rebellious deejays contended that innovative rock music was not getting on the air because songs were often too long or too controversial to fit into the tight Top 40 format.

The founding father of AOR is generally acknowledged to be Tom "Big Daddy" Donahue, a dissatisfied Top-40 deejay who left a successful job at San Francisco's KYA to start a new kind of radio, first at that city's KMPX-

6.9
Casey Kasem: King of the Deejays

Whose is the most familiar voice in America today? Is it the President's, a popular singer's, a famous actress's? The correct answer is "none of the above." The most recognizable voice is probably that of Casey Kasem, host of the syndicated radio program *American Top 40*. In addition, you'll hear Kasem narrating about 300 radio and TV commercials each year, touting everything from Shasta Cola to Heinz ketchup. Thus it is not unusual for some of us to hear the pear-shaped tones of Kasem a dozen or more times a day.

The man behind the voice is a 51-year-old former Los Angeles deejay who makes about half a million dollars every year by spending 10 to 15 hours each week in a recording studio. Kasem grew up in the Detroit area and got his start working in a number of radio serials in the 1940s. He came up with the idea for *American Top 40* in 1970. He has a wife and three beautiful children and appears to have all that any deejay could want.

Alas, it is not enough. In an interview with *People* magazine, Kasem revealed that what he really wants is to become a successful actor. He has gotten some small parts in "B" films and made-for-TV movies, but as yet he's been less than successful in his attempts to make the Kasem face as familiar as

the Kasem voice. Ironically, he does not listen to music much at home, admitting candidly that "I'd rather read magazines or watch TV." Pretty strange talk from the man whose voice is synonymous with popular music across America and around the world.

FM and later at KSAN-FM. Donahue and his irrepressible rebel deejays would play anything on the air that struck their fancy. In the early days, it was not unusual to hear a 15-minute live recording of the Grateful Dead sandwiched between an esoteric sitar piece by Ravi Shankar and a song by the Jefferson Airplane praising the merits of an illegal drug. Because the music and the deejays' "rap" often centered on counterculture themes, the format was initially dubbed "underground radio."

Most stations using this format were found on the FM dial. Also called "progressive" radio for a time, the form evolved into AOR in the 1970s. Many AOR stations still feature heavy-duty rock, but as the counterculture aged, their musical tastes mellowed. Thus "mellow rock," a derivative of AOR, began making inroads in the mid-1970s. Mellow-rock stations feature music from the softer side of the rock spectrum by artists like Boz Scaggs, the Beatles, James Taylor, and Carly Simon.

Middle of the Road

MOR radio began as "chicken rock" in the 1950s. Stations afraid of playing the hard-driving sounds of artists like Elvis Presley would lean toward the softer love ballads of contemporary artists and blend them with songs by the standard crooners like Bing Crosby and Frank Sinatra. As MOR evolved, the idea was to get some young listeners without alienating the older crowd who found the more raucous rock tunes unacceptable. Unlike Top-40 deejays, MOR personalities feature a continual patter between songs in an effort to entertain the audience with their words as well as the music.

Adult Contemporary

Adult contemporary is really a blend of MOR and AOR programming. In the 1970s, MOR programmers found their audience growing older and thus less desirable to many advertisers. They spiced up their playlist with soft-rock songs, particularly those that had been popular in the late 1960s and early 1970s, in an attempt to reach the 18- to 34-year-old audience. Most major markets have several stations that call themselves adult contemporary.

Country and Western

Next to rock, the C&W format is probably the most commercially successful. More than 50 percent of all popular-music radio stations play some country music. Every major metropolitan market has at least one C&W station. C&W is common in the rural western states. In the Deep South, it competes with Top 40 for the highest ratings.

For years, it was easy to separate country music from Top 40, but the recent country influence on rock groups has made the distinction less clear. In addition, many country singers have found success on the Top-40 charts. The result has been an introduction to country music for many listeners. Several stations now follow a "pop-corn" formula, alternating country and rock hits, hoping to attract listeners from both camps.

Beautiful Music

Originally called "easy listening" or "good music" by its fans, beautiful music is one of the most popular of today's radio formats. The music of artists like Henry Mancini and Mantovani forms the basis for this format, but more adventurous beautiful-music stations may occasionally program a soft vocal track by the Carpenters or Neil Diamond. This trend has become more noticeable of late, because beautiful music, like MOR, appeals to an audience that is growing older (see 6.10).

The secret of the success of beautiful music lies in the nature of radio itself. Often, radio is something we listen to while we're doing something else. It provides a sound backdrop for our daily activities. Beautiful-music programming is perfectly suited to this background function.

Beautiful-music fans see their stations as an oasis from the frantic "noise" of the other stations. The announcers display little emotion or personality, but simply and softly announce the songs. News and commercials (when possible) are done in the same soft-spoken way. The idea is never to violate the listener's trust by starting to sound like "those other stations." Beautiful-music formats are usually automated or prerecorded, with the computer selecting the songs according to a formula (three instrumentals, one vocal, two commercials, and so on).

The competition among beautiful-music stations is fiercer than the name might suggest. Although their fans are often as devoted to their stations as AOR listeners are, they tend to be less tolerant of commercials. Typically, a new beautiful-music station will enter a market with few sponsors. As the ratings grow, so does the number of commercials. Soon the listeners are tuning elsewhere.

The more conservative strains of beautiful music are often piped into dentists' and doctors' offices. Sometimes these offices pay to receive a closed-circuit broadcast of such music, such as the one called Muzak. The Muzak format is the easy listener's dream— no commercials, no disk jockey, no interrup-

■ *PROGRAMMING*

ALWAYS BEAUTIFUL MUSIC
... IS BRIGHTER, MORE CONTEMPORARY, AND
PROGRAMMED FOR THE LISTENER WHO WANTS TO TURN
UP THE VOLUME AND REALLY LISTEN TO THE RADIO!
SELECTIONS INCLUDE FAMILIAR ARTISTS AND
ARRANGEMENTS EXCLUSIVELY FOR
OUR LISTENERS.

FULL STEREOPHONIC SOUND
... THE ADDED DIMENSION 24 HOURS A
DAY.

COMMERCIAL IMPACT
... A LIMITED NUMBER OF COMMERCIALS PER
HOUR MEANS YOUR ADVERTISING MESSAGE STANDS OUT
AND WILL BE REMEMBERED.

WASHINGTON CORRESPONDENTS
... KOIT IS THE BAY AREA'S ONLY STATION OF ITS KIND
WITH A WASHINGTON CORRESPONDENT. U.P.I. AND A.P.
AUDIO SERVICES AND ACCESS TO THE NATION-
AL WEATHER SERVICE ARE IMPORTANT EXTRAS
IN MAKING KOIT NEWS MORE INTERESTING
WITH GREATER DEPTH.

HOME TEAM SCOREBOARD
... A UNIQUE FEATURE THAT KEEPS LOCAL
SPORTS BUFFS UP TO DATE ON THE FATES
AND FORTUNES OF OUR BAY AREA TEAMS AND
SPORTS PERSONALITIES.

GIANT SIGNAL
... ONE OF THE MOST POWERFUL IN THE
BAY AREA, AT 1410 FEET ABOVE
AVERAGE TERRAIN. FROM ATOP
HISTORIC MT. SUTRO, KOIT
BEAMS ITS SIGNAL TO THE
NINE BAY AREA COUNTIES ...
AND BEYOND!

THAT'S WHY KOIT HAS
THE PERFECT SOUND DESIGNED
FOR LISTENER INVOLVEMENT.

KOIT FM 96

TRANSAMERICA PYRAMID · 600 MONTGOMERY ST. · SAN FRANCISCO, CA 94111 · 415 · 434 · 0965

A Bonneville Station

6.10
This programming promotion sheet for San Francisco's KOIT touts the typical advantages of a "beautiful-music" format. Beautiful music's appeal to older, better-educated, and more affluent listeners has helped it become one of radio's most successful formats.

tions, just music. Critics contend that Muzak isn't music at all, but simply a pleasant, mindless noise.

Jazz

In a few urban markets, the jazz format receives a comfortable chunk of the ratings. Jazz stations were once quite popular, but enthusiasm dwindled in the 1960s. Those fans that remained were hard-core, however, and went to great lengths to find a station that offered what they wanted. Now there is some indication that young people are becoming interested in jazz again. Pop performers like Joni Mitchell combine traditional and experimental jazz sounds with rock.

Ethnic

Ethnic stations are so labeled because their programming tends to be targeted largely for one ethnic group. Soul stations appeal predominantly to blacks, though they are often owned and listened to by nonblacks. "Wolf-man Jack" got his start on XERB, a Mexican station that programmed for black and Mexican-American audiences in California. His gravel voice and "soul talk" had most listeners convinced he was black, until he began making television appearances.

Other ethnic stations offer programs in foreign languages. Of these, the Spanish-speaking stations are most numerous, particularly in New York City and the Southwest.

Classical

The commercial classical station, once a firmly established format, is now virtually extinct. There are about 25 full-time commercial classical stations today, down from more than 50 in 1965. Classical music may be alive and well, but teaming it with the financial realities of commercial radio seems an impossible task. Often classical stations are subsidized by listeners or survive because a wealthy owner writes off station losses at income-tax time.

Classical fans now find themselves drawn primarily to noncommercial stations found between 88 and 92 on the FM dial. Many noncommercial stations offer classical music along with other fine-arts programming.

Big Band

One solution for some struggling AM stations has been to switch to a nostalgia–big band format. Such a format appeals to older demographic groups, of course, but often will entice some listeners who would not otherwise listen to music radio.

New Music/Rock of the '80s

The newest and most innovative of all rock formats is *new music*, generally found on FM.

The distinctions between these and AOR stations are sometimes difficult to discern. However, the emergence of punk, new-wave, and new-music songs in the late 1970s and early 1980s generated a tremendous interest and enthusiasm for rock that had not been seen since the 1960s (see Chapter 7). A few stations, mostly in major markets, responded to this interest by featuring what they call "new music" exclusively. KQAK in San Francisco calls their format "Rock of the '80s" and features only what they consider to be innovative contemporary songs. Their playlist includes mainstream groups such as the Police, as well as more esoteric music by groups like R.E.M.

Noting the connection between experimental music of the 1980s and the more innovative music of the 1960s by groups like the Doors and the Jimi Hendrix Experience, Lee Abrams, a renowned radio consultant, created his "Superstars II" format. Currently syndicated around the country, this format capitalizes on both new-music trends and the desirability of reaching the older listeners who identify with the 1960s. Listeners hear everything from Eurythmics to Neil Young.

These are the basic music formats that make up the constructed mediated reality of radio today. Many stations offer a combination of two or more formats. Often program directors claim their sound is a significant variation from established norms in order to convince advertisers that they are offering something unique. But in truth, most stations stay pretty well within the boundaries of established formats. These boundaries, initially set up in the 1950s, have spelled success for many stations. While station programmers always think they should be allowed to experiment, station owners are usually more concerned with the bottom line. If the station is making money, let's keep it the way it is; if it's not, *then* we can talk about change.

According to *Broadcasting* magazine, more commercial music stations report losses than profits each year, but those figures can be misleading. Owners often pay excessive salaries to themselves or their top executives to avoid heavy profit taxes at the end of the year. Actually, as soon as a station is a real money-loser, it will change formats, go up for sale, or both.

NEWS AND NEWS-TALK: THE INFORMATION EXCHANGE

In many markets, the most popular stations carry no music at all. These are the all-news and news-talk formats, which offer an uninterrupted flow of information to the listener. In 1961 Gordon McLendon, a pioneer of Top-40 radio in the 1950s, came up with another winning idea. He signed on as program consultant for XTRA, a station that was just across the Mexican border from California but could be heard plainly in the competitive Los Angeles market. Under his guidance, XTRA became the first all-news radio station, giving Los Angeles commuters and others an up-to-the-minute account of what was going on in international and national affairs. XTRA's early coverage was limited mostly to wire-service copy, since it had no budget for local reporters. But before long, the success of XTRA had sparked competition, and there were a number of all-news stations on the air in most major markets.

All-news programming has some unusual implications. Traditionally, programmers hope to persuade the listener to tune to their station and stay with it. All-news asks only that you tune in every once in a while to get an idea of what's going on in the world. Successful KFWB in Los Angeles typifies this philosophy with its slogan "Give us 20 minutes, and we'll give you the world."

The startling success of all-news radio has been attributed to a number of things. In part, the competition from stereo-equipped FM stations has left AM music stations looking for alternatives. What's more, it appears that the more information we get, the more we want. There seems to be an increasingly large audience that needs to feel it is in tune with up-to-the-minute events (hence the proliferation of TV "news breaks").

Most all-news stations draw their largest audience during crucial drive-time hours in the mornings and late afternoons. In the early 1970s, some began to experiment with attempts to attract the predominantly female daytime audience with cooking shows and other "feature items" designed to appeal primarily to women. The all-news format was also a logical home for weekend and evening coverage of major sporting events, which draw a primarily male audience.

Many all-news stations soon found that audiences wanted to be entertained as well as informed, to have the news explained and discussed as well as reported. Two-way talk shows address these needs, while providing listeners with a vehicle for sounding off about political and social events. So successful was the marriage of news and two-way talk that a new hybrid, *news-talk*, was born. News-talk stations are now number one in the ratings in many major markets. Syndicated news-talk programs such as the Larry King Show have also found listeners, even during the early morning hours. In addition, many music stations, particularly those on AM, now offer substantial portions of news and especially news-talk in an effort to bolster sagging ratings.

Meanwhile, news-talk has gone through several evolutions. Originally designed to give listeners a chance to air their opinions about the news topics of the day, the format now includes discussions of subjects like medicine and health, human-interest stories, famous people and show-business personalities. ABC-FM radio affiliates now feature "Soap Talk" twice every weekday; meanwhile programs such as "Sextalk," frank discussions of sex-related matters between psychologists/sex therapists and listeners, have become increasingly accepted. Perhaps the most popular of these shows are found in New York, where Dr. Judith Kuriansky is WABC's resident therapist and Dr. Ruth Westheimer can be heard Sunday nights on WYNY. Kuriansky reports that she receives as many as 600 calls each night from listeners with a wide range of sexual problems they want to discuss on the air.

A 1983 poll by NBC Radio News indicates that over 80 percent of the listeners questioned would prefer more news and news-talk information about medicine and health, while 70 percent wanted more programs centering on human-interest topics. About 60 percent of the listeners requested that less material be aired on political and show-business personalities.

THE NUMBERS GAME: RATINGS AND RADIO

Most of you have probably heard of the famous Nielsen ratings, the audience estimates that determine whether your favorite TV show lives or dies (see Chapter 8). In radio, the equivalent of the Nielsens is the Arbitron "book." While several smaller companies, such as Media Statistics, Inc. (Mediastat), and RAM Research, compete with Arbitron, it is the Arbitron ratings that generally determine how a commercial radio station is doing in its unrelenting quest for listeners (see 6.11).

An Arbitron book can run to 300 pages or more. It is filled with literally thousands of numbers estimating how many, and what kind of, listeners are tuned in to a given station at a specific time of day. Major markets are

served with up to four Arbitron books each year, while smaller markets might be surveyed only once a year.

Basically, the Arbitron book acts as a guide for advertisers, who want to know which stations can offer the greatest potential audience for their product or service. As with magazine readers (see Chapter 5), "demos," or demographic breakdowns of listeners, provide valuable data. For example, if you are selling a women's shampoo, you want to buy time on a station with a large audience of women, and you want to make sure your spot is aired at a time of day when it will reach the maximum number of them.

Another important demo involves the age characteristics of a station's audience. Advertisers found long ago that if a station's listeners are too young (12 to 17), they do not have the kind of ready cash available to invest in a new sports car. Of course, soft-drink manufacturers and record stores may want to reach exactly this audience. On the other hand, a station that attracts mainly listeners 35 and above is at a disadvantage, since people of this age group can be more easily and economically reached through television. Hence, it is the 18-to-34-year-old age group that is most desirable for many advertisers, and many formats such as AOR and adult contemporary are geared to reach precisely this group.

The Arbitron book delivers data in two broad categories, called *quarter-hour estimates* and *cume estimates*. Quarter-hour figures indicate how many people are listening at any given moment (for example, between 8:00 and 9:00 Sunday morning), while cume (cumulative) estimates indicate the total number of people who have tuned in during a specific period (for example, on Saturdays and Sundays from 6:00 A.M. to midnight).

Armed with such a diversity of information, it is not unusual for half a dozen stations to claim that they are number one in a mar-

6.11

A Rating or a Share?

Most of the confusion people have about radio and television ratings arises from the difference between a rating and a share. These two numbers dominate discussion of the ratings race in both media. Actually, it's quite simple. A *rating* represents a percentage of an entire population. Let's say a radio station has a rating of 3.0. That means three out of every hundred persons who live in that market were listening to that station during the period described. A *share* represents a percentage of the population in question *that had their radios on* during the period in question. Let's say that one quarter of the population had their radios turned on. The station with a 3.0 rating would have a 12.0 share, since 12 of every 100 persons who had their radios turned on were listening to our mythical station.

Share numbers are always larger than ratings because there is never a time when everyone in a given population has his or her radio turned on. Were that to happen sometime, the two numbers would be equal.

ket. There are many ways to interpret the book, and naturally station salespeople want their station to be put in the best possible light.

The biggest complaint about Arbitron—and indeed about all ratings services—is that it can only tell us what people are listening to, not what they really want to hear. Thus commercial programmers are a bit like the dog that is chasing its tail. They know where listeners have been and maybe even where they are now, but not where they would like to go.

The pressures of our commercial system, with the all-important ratings books, probably contribute to the tendency of commercial stations to program more of the same, a tendency many critics find disturbing.

EDUCATIONAL AND PUBLIC RADIO

Away from the din of the marketplace and the ratings wars, educational and public radio stations provide alternative programming for those weary of the commercial stations. The first educational station is generally acknowledged to have been WHA, licensed to the University of Wisconsin at Madison. Under the designation 9XM, it began experimental broadcasts in 1917. The early educational stations were the first step toward the kind of radio that de Forest had envisioned, one that could educate and illuminate the general public.

However, it was not easy going for educational radio in the early years. According to *Educational Telecommunication*, by Donald N. Wood and Donald G. Wylie, "By the mid-1920s only half of the educational institutions that held broadcast licenses actually had stations on the air." While many institutions were quick to obtain licenses, convincing college and university administrators to pay for such stations was another matter. Funding has continued to be a problem for virtually all noncommercial stations (see 6.12).

In 1934 the National Association of Educational Broadcasters (NAEB) was formed. This association included not only those educational institutions that had their own studios but also those that used existing commercial facilities. The NAEB has continued

6.12

Kristie Fujiwara, development director of KANG radio, licensed to Pacific Union College in Angwin, California, fills out a programming form while another employee locates an audio cartridge to be used on the air. Fujiwara describes the rather cramped facilities of KANG as "small but adequate." Space and equipment shortages and other problems related to funding are all part of the daily rigors of noncommercial radio.

to be a strong voice for educational broadcasting through the years.

As late as 1948 there were only 50 on-air radio stations licensed to colleges and universities. Today there are about 130 such stations. In addition to offering the community fine-arts and educational programming, these facilities provide an excellent opportunity for students enrolled in broadcasting courses. Many of today's most successful radio entertainers and executives got their first break and valuable experience in educational radio.

Since the 1960s, most educational radio stations have relied heavily on government funds. In 1967 the Corporation for Public Broadcasting (CPB) was formed. This non-profit corporation is in charge of dispersing government funds to various noncommercial stations. In part, the CPB helped establish the first noncommercial radio network. National Public Radio (NPR) was formed in 1971, and by 1976 it boasted 160 affiliates.

NPR produces and distributes radio programs to member stations. Among the most popular is *All Things Considered*, a news and feature program that examines in depth stories that most commercial stations might handle in a few seconds.

When the term *public* was chosen for National Public Radio, an important distinction was being made. Many broadcasters felt it was necessary to recognize that "educational" radio was only a part of the noncommercial picture. Indeed, a large number of noncommercial radio stations are licensed to private foundations rather than educational institutions.

The idea behind public broadcasting is that these stations not only educate but also offer programming not available on their commercial counterparts. For example, as we have noted, the classical-music format survives largely on noncommercial stations. Virtually all noncommercial stations can be found between 88 and 92 megahertz on the FM dial. The FCC has reserved this space exclusively for such stations.

Despite the excellent record that educational and public stations have established, their very existence seemed jeopardized in 1981 when the Reagan administration announced plans for phasing out the CPB. If this vital source of funding were lost, the future would be bleak for many noncommercial stations.

When considering the budgets for 1985 and 1986, for example, the administration proposed cutting the $130 million annual CPB budget to $85 million. Meanwhile, National Public Radio was having financial problems of its own. In 1983 President Frank Mankiewicz resigned after disclosure of significant debt problems for the network. Temporary chief operating officer Ronald Bornstein then negotiated a $9 million loan from the CPB to keep the troubled network afloat, at least through 1984.

The CPB cuts were part of the "marketplace" philosophy that seemed to dominate the politics of this period. According to *Broadcasting* magazine, the Reagan administration felt that "stations should generate revenue by soliciting contributions from the public and corporations. If the stations can find enough support in the marketplace, they'll survive. If the marketplace won't support them, obviously some stations will die."

"THAT OTHER BAND": FM RADIO

The concept of FM was developed by Edwin Armstrong. He first applied for patents for this new type of radio service in 1930. FM, or *frequency modulation*, was more than just another radio band. In fact, it was a whole new way of broadcasting, one that eliminated the static and interference so common on the AM dial.

When he had a working model, Armstrong approached RCA's Sarnoff, an old friend, and offered to let RCA develop it. Though Sarnoff was properly impressed, it soon became evident that RCA was not about to introduce an entirely new radio service when the old one was paying off so well. Eventually, friction between Armstrong and Sarnoff over the future of FM increased, and in time they became bitter enemies. Armstrong took his idea to others, and with some financial backing in 1939 his W2XMN in Alpine, New Jersey, became the first successful FM station.

Just as it appeared that FM would finally get off the ground, along came World War II, and development of the medium stalled. After the war, the FCC decreed that FM broadcasting would have to move to another part of the spectrum, thus making all existing FM receivers obsolete. Adding insult to injury, the commission also ruled that part of the FM band would now be allocated for TV sound.

In 1964 the FCC, bowing to pressure from UHF (ultrahigh frequency) television stations, forced manufacturers of TV sets to include both VHF (very high frequency) and UHF capability on all sets sold in this country. Naturally, FM radio stations were anxious for the same sort of boost, but it never came. For years FM floundered while TV boomed. Finally in the 1960s the underground movement in radio found a home on FM. By then it was getting increasingly less costly to own an FM set, and soon they became commonplace in homes and cars all over the country.

Today, FM revenues exceed those of AM, and it is not unusual for FM outlets in most major markets to be among the most popular stations. Once upon a time, prosperous AM stations bought money-losing FM outlets just to hedge their bets, much as they had purchased TV stations. Now the reverse is true in many cases. Edwin Armstrong's vision of FM as a superior alternative to AM has finally come true. Unfortunately, he did not live to see it happen. In 1954, a broken and bitter man, he jumped to his death from the 13th floor of his apartment house overlooking New York's East River.

WHITHER RADIO?

From early experimental stations run by devoted amateurs to the computerized programming of today, radio has undergone a number of metamorphoses. It is a tremendously fluid medium, able to adapt immediately to the desires and needs of its audience. In the 1950s, when television was stealing radio stars and programs, radio rediscovered music programs, and business boomed.

Whether AM or FM, commercial or noncommercial, most radio stations fight to survive in today's crowded mass-media marketplace. Mark Twain once quipped, "The reports of my death are greatly exaggerated." The same is true of radio. The death of radio was predicted at the end of the golden age in the late 1940s, when rock music took over in the 1950s, and in the wake of extensive commercialization in the 1960s and 1970s. But like the famous watch, radio seems to be able to "take a licking and keep on ticking."

There are now more than 8,000 radio stations in America, which continue to offer a great diversity of information. Radio ad revenues are currently over $3 billion yearly. There are over 440 million radios in America—about two for every man, woman, and child in the country. Radio offers many music formats as well as all-news and all-talk stations. Radio futurists envision the day when some stations will be all-sports or even all-weather. Every indication seems to be that radio is destined to grow and to continue to serve its diverse audience in the years ahead.

ISSUES AND ANSWERS:
REGULATION OF RADIO—
THE ZIGZAG TRAIL

We have seen how many ways radio has changed over the years. This has posed a problem for those who are charged with regulating the medium. By 1927 there were more than 700 private radio stations in operation. Until that time, licensing procedures had been rather loose, and stations could go on and off the air at will. This was detrimental to both listeners and other stations, so Congress passed the Radio Act of 1927. It created a five-person Federal Radio Commission (FRC) to oversee licensing of radio stations. Each station was given permission to broadcast for three years and was assigned a specific frequency.

Almost everyone agreed that some form of regulation was needed at that time. Stations were springing up at an astounding rate, and signals were interfering with one another. In many populated areas, the poor befuddled listener could pick up little more than a mumbled cacophony.

The act established a policy that no one had a "right" to broadcast in the same way that there is a "right" to print. While the supply of paper and ink may seem unlimited (though we know today that this is not the case), the airwaves contain only a certain number of channels. These channels cannot belong in perpetuity to any individual; like some lands and minerals, they are a national resource that must be operated in the "public interest, convenience, or necessity." This clearly established the FRC's power to make decisions about who could and who could not broadcast. These laws remain today, despite technological innovations like cable and the laser, which may mean that there will be an unlimited number of channels available.

The FRC decided to include the quality of programming as one criterion in making license decisions. Though this was not always a major determinant, some licenses were awarded to those who promised the highest-quality programs.

"Aha!" you exclaim. "Then what happened to radio? Why don't we have better programs?" The problem is, what is "quality" programming for you may not be "quality" for someone else. Some people would like to banish Top-40 music from the face of the earth. Others couldn't live without it. The FRC didn't help much; it never actually defined "quality." In fact, we still don't have a real working definition for it, and perhaps we never will.

An important precedent was set in 1931 when the FRC refused to renew the license of KFKB in Milford, Kansas. The station had been selling patent medicine over the air, and phony "doctors" had been telling would-be patients about "miracle" cures. KFKB took the FRC to court, contending that it had the right to broadcast anything it liked and that the FRC could not restrict the content of radio programs. KFKB lost the case. The courts ruled that the "public interest, convenience, or necessity" clause gives the FRC the right to control certain kinds of programs.

A few years later Congress passed the Communications Act of 1934, which included provisions for telephone, telegraph, and television as well as radio. To administer this, the seven-person FCC replaced the FRC. The FCC commissioners have seven-year terms. Each year one retires and a new one is appointed by the President. FCC decisions are often split, since FCC commissioners reflect the political philosophy of their party. These appointments are among the most important a President can make, because an FCC commissioner has the potential to influence every piece of information we receive from radio and television.

However, that potential is seldom realized. Traditionally, FCC commissioners exercise little power over broadcasters. Almost 60,000 applications for broadcast licenses and license renewals have been reviewed since 1954. Only about 100 applicants have ever been rejected or given less than a complete renewal. Of these, just a handful have been revoked entirely.

Why is the FCC so reluctant to act? One reason is that the commissioners are under tremendous pressure from the media industry. Another reason is that radio stations do their best to behave themselves. Owning a TV station has been a called a "license to print money," and ownership of most radio stations is also usually quite lucrative. Obviously nobody wants to lose such a valuable license. Licensees do everything they can to ensure that the FCC will not be displeased, and this often means going along with every FCC whim.

This can be both good and bad for the public. The FCC, as an agent of the government and the people, can ensure that phony patent medicines are not sold over the air. But the seven FCC commissioners, who are often advanced in years and sometimes out of step with the tastes of the general public, can also heavily influence programming. Broadcasters often overreact to FCC "suggestions" and bend over backward to provide dull, noncontroversial content. For example, during the early 1970s when the FCC attempted to crack down on stations playing songs with drug-related lyrics, Peter, Paul and Mary's "Puff the Magic Dragon" was banned on many stations. Station owners thought "Puff" might be about marijuana, and they weren't taking any chances.

At about the same time, Los Angeles deejay Bill Balance was pioneering a new kind of radio talk show. His *Feminine Forum* invited female listeners to call in and talk about their most intimate sexual problems. Immediately popular, *Feminine Forum* and its imitators spread to every major radio market. The FCC soon made it clear that there might be an obscenity action if the content was not moderated. Balance was issued a set of guidelines by his bosses, and the more extreme topics were deleted. He complained on the air that his freedom of speech was being violated, but to no avail. No matter how popular the show, the station simply did not want to risk a run-in with the FCC.

In a 1975 case, the FCC placed a sanction against WBAI-FM in New York for airing a George Carlin monologue that contained a number of four-letter words. Previous court decisions had ruled that it was not the commission's place to set obscenity standards for broadcasters, but this didn't seem to deter the FCC. In 1978, the U.S. Supreme Court upheld the FCC action in the WBAI case.

In all of these cases it can be argued that the FCC has set standards for broadcasters that may not be in the best interests of listeners. Perhaps the FCC has outlived its usefulness. It may be that a review of the entire Communications Act of 1934 is needed. In 1934, there was no network television or cable TV. Radio stations were all network-affiliated, and most recordings were not permitted on the air. The FCC has tried to adjust to the tremendous changes since then by reversing a decision here and patching up a problem there. As a result, no one is happy.

Commissioners require each licensee to submit mounds of paper, including programming logs, replies to any license challenges, copies of listener complaints, community ascertainment studies, and much more. Some of these are necessary and proper; some are a waste of time. There are so many hundreds of rules and amended rules that broadcasters are running in circles trying to comply. Meanwhile, the public is dissatisfied with the lack of quality and diversity in the programs it receives.

Occasionally, the commission moves to try to increase diversity. In 1980, it announced that it was looking into the possibility of major alterations in the FM band. Basically, the technical refinements of recent years mean that there is less chance for one station to interfere with the signals of another nearby station. Since the basic allocation decisions were made more than 50 years ago, a change might be possible. By requiring power and antenna alterations in some existing stations, new laws could open up the airwaves for many (some say 100 or more) new FM stations.

At the same time, some commission actions seem destined to reduce the availability of certain kinds of information on radio. In 1981 the FCC voted six to one to "deregulate" radio. Detailed program logs would no longer have to be kept. Before 1981, the FCC had stated flatly that no station should carry in excess of 18 minutes of commercials per hour. That restriction has now been lifted. Nonentertainment functions of commercial radio stations are now to be governed by "marketplace forces." This means a reduction of public-affairs programming at most commercial stations.

As you can see, the FCC has followed a zigzag trail with respect to the regulation of radio and the encouragement of diverse points of view. At some point the commission will have to come to grips with a whole new approach to the medium. A complete overhaul of the Communications Act of 1934 would be a good start. Ideally, the new act would incorporate a realistic view of contemporary public tastes and modern station practices. It might not solve all of the problems facing the medium today, but it would be a beginning.

QUERIES AND CONCEPTS

1 Rock videos have had a tremendous impact on rock radio programming in the mid-1980s. Can you think of at least five ways our *perception* of music (PMR) might change as a result of *seeing* songs on TV rather than hearing them on the radio? How might buying patterns change? How about our awareness of the song itself? The singer(s)?

2 How much impact has the "new music" had on your local stations? What is the percentage of new vs. traditional rock on your local rock outlets?

3 Interview a selected audience of people older than 50 about radio's golden age. Design a questionnaire to measure their attitudes about how early radio programs compare with today's TV and radio programs.

4 Pick an hour of the day when you are usually free. Listen to a different disc jockey each day for three days in a row. How do they differ? Are there any differences in music? What kind of audience might each be appealing to?

5 Identify the top five radio stations in your market. Write a two-paragraph description of the format each uses.

6 Come up with your own list of *must* items for "quality" radio programs. Compare with others in the class. Are there any items that *everyone* considers essential for "quality"?

READINGS AND REFERENCES

Pioneers and Programmers

Erik Barnouw
A History of Broadcasting in the United States, 3 vols. *A Tower in Babel: To 1933.* New York: Oxford University Press, 1966. *The Golden Web: 1933 to 1953.* New York: Oxford University Press, 1968.

Easily the most comprehensive and often-quoted historical account of the rise of radio in North America from an amateur toy to a dynamic social institution. The first two books in this trilogy are tough going in places but full of radio lore and legend that keep the reader interested. A definitive bibliography and index.

Christopher H. Sterling
John M. Kittross
Stay Tuned. Belmont, Calif.: Wadsworth, 1978.

> Offers a chronological look at the development and evolution of radio and television in America. Covers all important aspects of broadcast history; topical and up to date. Interesting narrative bibliographies at the ends of chapters; excellent index.

The Golden Age of Radio (1926–1948)

Frank Buxton
Bill Owen
The Big Broadcast: 1920–1950. New York: Viking Press, 1972.

> A catalog of programs and stars from radio's golden age, complete with a short synopsis of each program.

Irving Settel
A Pictorial History of Radio. New York: Grosset & Dunlap, 1967.

> An entertaining visual exploration into the people who made radio during the early years. It is a profusely illustrated and informative text. Radio's history is neatly broken down decade by decade. A must for old-time-radio buffs, the book includes particularly thorough coverage of the 1930s and 1940s. Useful index.

Glenhall Taylor
Before Television: The Radio Years. Cranbury, N.J.: A. S. Barnes, 1979.

> A good account of entertainment radio during the golden years. The emphasis is on the great network giants who made a name for themselves in the era. Lots of pictures.

Alexander Kendrick
Prime Time: The Life of Edward R. Murrow. New York: Avon Books, 1970.

> This biography features an excellent account of the war years and the part that radio played. See especially Chapters 5 and 6, "Hello America . . . Hitler Is Here" and "London Is Burning, London Is Burning."

The Big Change: Radio After Television; Meet the Deejay; The People You Never Hear

Broadcasting Yearbook. Washington, D.C.: Broadcasting Publications, Inc., published annually.

> This is the primary reference book for professional broadcasters. Statistics of every conceivable kind are found here, including ownership and other information for every radio and TV station in the country. Available in most libraries.

Joseph S. Johnson
Kenneth K. Jones
Modern Radio Station Practices, 2d ed. Belmont, Calif.: Wadsworth, 1978.

> Not the most exciting text you'll ever read, but one that covers every department of the radio station and what makes it work. Some interesting material in the "Station Profiles" section. The only one of its kind, this thorough book includes chapters on radio production, equipment, programming, news, and other topics.

Music Formats; News and News-Talk; The Information Exchange

Edd Routt
James B. McGrath
Fredric A. Weiss
The Radio Format Conundrum. New

York: Hastings House, 1978.

This is the only book I know of that accurately details radio programming format by format. The authors offer interviews with a number of notable programmers and include a good analysis of each of the major format types. A bit dated already (beautiful music is referred to as "good music," for example), but well worth reading. A much needed contribution.

The best bet for students interested in the latest in the format wars is to check *Broadcasting*. Other sources are the *Readers' Guide to Periodical Literature* and the *Popular Periodicals Index* under "radio." *Rolling Stone* is the best single source for up-to-the-minute news of rock. *Billboard* supplies charts for classical, country and western, rock, beautiful music, and other formats, plus industry news.

John R. Bittner
Denise A. Bittner
Radio Journalism. Englewood Cliffs, N.J.: Prentice-Hall, 1977.

This text is the first comprehensive effort designed for radio classes. There is a chapter on news sources and covering radio news as well as chapters on writing, production, and programming. See especially Chapter 10, "Landing a Job," if you're interested in breaking into radio news.

Claude Hall
Barbara Hall
This Business of Radio Programming.
New York: Watson-Guptill Publications, Inc., 1977.

An excellent appraisal of the various radio formats and how they work throughout the world. This audience-oriented inside look at the world of radio programming is a must for any serious radio student.

John Hasling
Fundamentals of Radio Broadcasting.
New York: McGraw-Hill, 1980.

The author has done a good job of covering a number of radio-related areas, including careers in radio, history and regulation, licensing, promotion, sales, and economics.

Edward Jay Whetmore
The Magic Medium: An Introduction to Radio in America. Belmont, Calif.: Wadsworth, 1981.

This text covers all the major aspects of radio. It includes chapters on history, contemporary programming, popular music, ratings and research, employment opportunities, production and evaluation, and the future of radio. An obvious favorite.

**Issues and Answers:
Regulation of Radio—
The Zigzag Trail**

Sydney Head and Christopher Sterling's *Broadcasting in America* (New York: Houghton Mifflin, 1982) covers a number of pivotal FCC rulings on the legal implications involved in censorship of broadcast media. For more detailed accounts, see Nelson and Teeter's *Law of Mass Communication* (Mineola, N.Y.: Foundation Press, 1981) or Howard Simon and Joseph A. Califano's *The Media and the Law* (New York: Praeger, 1976). The very latest issues in broadcast regulation are followed intently by *Broadcasting* magazine, which is a favorite of station owners and employees alike.

The Sound of Music

I WAS DRIVING HOME AFTER DINNER ON THAT DECEMBER evening in 1980. Many of us remember exactly where we were when we first heard John Lennon had been shot to death in New York City. There was an outpouring of grief in America similar to that experienced when John F. Kennedy was assassinated in 1963. There was indeed something special about John Lennon.

Hundreds of radio and TV stations throughout the country honored his wife Yoko Ono's request for ten minutes of silence. Newspapers and magazines ran extensive stories about the shooting and the massive public outcry that followed. Lennon's death served to remind us once again of the power of popular music. It reminded us how intimately we come to regard those who play and sing it as our friends. And it reminded us of how our deep involvement with them is made possible by the process of mass communication.

Popular music is a global language that leaves a personal and permanent impression. With little effort you can probably think of many songs that have a very special meaning for you. One represents a summer romance. Another reminds you of someone far away. Perhaps there's a song you still can't listen to because you have associated it with an unpleasant experience.

Records represent a mediated reality we can enjoy alone or with others. They seem to grow and take on new depth as we become more familiar with them. When we share that experience, we seem to enjoy it even more. There is a special feeling in playing a favorite album for someone who is hearing it for the first time. You want so much for that person to enjoy it, to hear what you hear and experience what you feel.

If live concerts are like motion pictures, records are like still photos that we can return to time and time again. We may join Fleetwood Mac or Billy Joel at any time, simply by putting a needle on a piece of vinyl. Records are literally a "record" of our important thoughts and feelings.

The effect that pop music has on society is incredible. . . . If everyone that was thinking in pop music terms were to stand end to end, they'd go around the world ten times. . . . Pop music is basically big. It concerns far more than 20-year-olds. It's lasted too long. It concerns everybody now.

PETER TOWNSHEND

Scientific American, Dec. 22, 1877

7.1

Edison's original phonograph.

For those that have grown up after World War II, popular music seems to have a very special meaning. Many of this generation's heroes—Elvis Presley, Bob Dylan, the Beatles, Janis Joplin, Joni Mitchell, Neil Young, David Bowie, to name a few—are recording artists. Their lyrics convey eternal truths and cultural clichés. The beat matches the audience's feelings about their lives.

"And the beat goes on."

THE FABULOUS PHONOGRAPH

In 1877 Thomas Edison's carbon transmitter had greatly improved Alexander Graham Bell's telephone and given the young Edison ample funds to experiment with a "talking machine." Edison's talking machine used a metal cylinder with a spiral groove (helix) impressed on it (see 7.1). A piece of tin foil—the record—was wrapped around the cylinder. The first words ever recorded were "Mary had a little lamb." When Edison played them back, he recognized his own voice and it startled him (see 7.2).

No time was lost exploiting this marvelous new invention. By 1878, the Edison Speaking Phonograph Company was formed to conduct exhibitions of this new device all over the country. As a curiosity, the phonograph was a success. In June 1878, Edison predicted ten uses of the phonograph that would benefit humanity. These predictions proved remarkably accurate:

1. Letter writing and all kinds of dictation without the aid of the stenographer.

2. Phonographic books, which will speak to blind people without effort on their part.

3. The teaching of elocution.

4. Reproduction of music.

5. The "Family Record"—a register of sayings, reminiscences, etc., by members of a family in their own voices, and of the last words of dying persons.

6. Music-boxes and toys.

7. Clocks that should announce in articulate speech the time for going home, going to meals, etc.

8. The preservation of languages by exact reproduction of the manner of pronouncing.

9. Educational purposes, such as preserving the explanations made by a teacher, so that the pupil can refer to them at any moment, and spelling or other lessons placed upon the phonograph for convenience in committing to memory.

10. Connection with the telephone, so as to make that instrument an auxiliary in the transmission of permanent and invaluable records, instead of being the recipient of momentary and fleeting communication.

7.2

Thomas Edison and an early phonograph.

By the turn of the century, home phonographs were being marketed with great enthusiasm. They were crude by today's standards, with large hornlike protrusions to amplify the sounds. Still, the early cylinder records contained some great music, and the well-to-do family had to have one. Prices started at $25. There were no plug-in models, of course; all phonographs had to be wound up by hand.

Enrico Caruso, a famous opera singer at the turn of the century, lent prestige to the new invention by allowing his performances to be recorded. These recordings were enormously successful. In the two decades following his first recording session in 1902, Caruso earned more than $2 million from record sales.

The Victor Talking Machine Company developed and promoted the flat disc (forerunner of today's record), which eventually made the cylinder obsolete. At first cylinders were of far superior quality, but the disc was more portable and easier to use. Were it not for the rise of the disc, today's radio announcers would be cylinder jockeys!

After World War I some of the early Edison patents ran out, and the record field became more competitive. There were more than 200 phonograph manufacturers by 1920, up from just 18 before the war. The heyday of the phonograph record had begun, and that heyday coincided with what was known as "the jazz age." Jazz was really the first popular music to gain status with the aid of the medium. The record industry boomed; 100 million records were sold in 1927.

An important technological barrier was overcome in 1931 when Leopold Stokowski's Philadelphia Orchestra recorded Beethoven's entire Fifth Symphony on a single record without a break. Music fans could look forward to the day when their favorite operas and symphonies would no longer be cut up to fit on four-minute records.

But the Depression and the rise of radio's popularity in the 1930s seemed to cripple the growing phonograph industry. By 1932, record sales had dropped to 6 million, and magazine writers wrote of the "rise and fall of the phonograph." Record collectors were akin to antique dealers. Few people thought there was a future in the phonograph record.

POPULAR MUSIC IN THE 1940s

In 1939, big-band leader Harry James went to the Rustic Cabin in Teaneck, New Jersey, and happened to hear a new singer. James liked what he heard and hired Francis Albert Sinatra to sing with his band for $75 a week. Within a year Sinatra had left and signed with Tommy Dorsey's orchestra. He was described by one critic as "a skinny kid—not much to look at—but he really had a sound."

By 1943 Sinatra was the most familiar vocalist in America. His national fame came when thousands of "bobby soxers" mobbed New York's Paramount Theatre to see him. His was dubbed "the voice that thrills millions." Fans were actually screaming and passing out during Sinatra's performances. No one had ever seen anything like it. But not everyone could be in New York or afford to see the singer in person. Record prices had dropped, and mass production kept them down to about a dollar each, so now the whole country began listening to Sinatra on their phonographs.

There had been other popular recording vocalists, among them Al Jolson and Rudy Vallee. But Vallee had been the "megaphone man," while Sinatra's intimate style seemed more suited to the microphone. He was exclusively the product of a new technology, a new electric sound.

Not too much is made of it now, but Sinatra was also a social hero to young people of his day. He made a documentary film attacking racial prejudice even though his business managers warned him it could cost him the support of some influential newspaper columnists. The film alienated some critics but

won the hearts of young people everywhere. Sinatra didn't need the newspapers, the magazines, or even the radio. His records were instant hits.

Bobby soxers and other young people took over the record market. Record promoters discovered that most record buyers were in their teens. These new record buyers were not as interested in *songs* as they were in *singers*. "Do you have the latest Sinatra record?" became the request at the record store. It had never been like that before.

During the 1940s a number of popular vocalists enjoyed success, including Frankie Laine, Perry Como, Mel Tormé, Dick Haymes, Vic Damone, Peggy Lee, Doris Day, Jo Stafford, and Dinah Shore. The songs were ballads, love songs mostly. Boy meets girl, boy falls in love with girl, boy can't live without girl, and on and on. But you could always understand the words, and most lyrics seemed to make sense.

THE BIRTH OF ROCK

In some ways, the origin of rock and roll can be traced to a rivalry between two organizations in the music industry: ASCAP and BMI. The American Society of Composers, Authors, and Publishers was formed in 1914 to guarantee that its members received a fee for the playing of their songs. ASCAP's right to collect this fee from the radio stations stood one court test after another. ASCAP charged each station a blanket amount to use its material. In 1941 it announced a 100 percent fee increase. Radio stations refused to go along, and as a result all songs protected by ASCAP were taken off the air. This included the work of many of the popular songwriters of the time and left stations with very little music. The dispute was settled, at least temporarily, toward the end of 1941, but by that time radio stations had begun to rely on music provided by a new guild of composers.

Broadcast Music, Incorporated (BMI) was formed to scout for fresh talent who could provide radio stations with music. This became increasingly important as more stations switched to the deejay format. BMI was looking for a new sound. The sound they found was rock and roll. By the mid-1950s BMI was a powerful force, and so was the new sound.

In 1956 the antitrust subcommittee of the House Judiciary Committee investigated BMI's domination of the recording industry. Songwriter Billy Rose, an ASCAP member, outlined BMI's role in the rise of rock and roll:

Not only are most of the BMI songs junk, but in many cases they are obscene junk pretty much on a level with dirty comic magazines. . . . It is the current climate on radio and TV which makes Elvis Presley and his animal posturings possible. . . .

When ASCAP's songwriters were permitted to be heard, Al Jolson, Nora Bayes, and Eddie Cantor were all big salesmen of songs. Today it is a set of untalented twitchers and twisters whose appeal is largely to the zootsuiter and the juvenile delinquent.

But of course there was much more to it than that. Rock and roll had come at a time when young people were finding it difficult to relate to the likes of Doris Day and Patti Page. There had been too many "adult" bands and too many tired crooners. Youth now wanted a sound of its own—something new, different, and vital.

Rock was actually a blend of country music and the rhythm and blues (R&B) that was popular among black people during the early 1950s. But record producers suspected that national white audiences would never idolize a black popular singer, no matter now much they liked the R&B beat.

Sam Phillips, the lawyer and former disc jockey who formed Sun Records in the early 1950s, was a tireless researcher. He drove all over the South looking for new talent and promoting his records. "What I need," he said unabashedly, "is a white boy who can sing colored." In 1954 he found him. Elvis Presley recorded "That's Alright Mama," and the song enjoyed moderate success on the country music charts. Within two years, Presley became the Sinatra of the 1950s, and by the end of the decade the older generation was explaining to the young that Sinatra had been the Elvis Presley of the 1940s.

The father of rock and roll was Cleveland deejay Alan Freed, who had started mixing R&B songs with Al Martino and Frank Sinatra records as early as 1951 on WJW. It was he who coined the term *rock and roll* to make R&B palatable to his white audience. In 1954 Freed moved to WINS in New York, where his *Moondog's Rock and Roll Party* was an instant success. WINS was soon the number one station in New York. Freed helped introduce Bill Haley's "Rock around the Clock," the first rock-and-roll single to reach the top of the charts.

Blackboard Jungle, a film about juvenile delinquency, featured "Rock around the Clock" as part of the soundtrack. The pulsating, uninhibited new sound was linked with restless, rebellious youth. Young people flocked to that film and others like it. Radio, movies, and print media all contributed to the rise of rock and roll as the dominant form of popular music.

"Rock around the Clock" was the best-selling song of 1955. In 1956 Elvis Presley had 5 of the year's 16 best sellers, including the number one and number two records: "Don't Be Cruel" and "Heartbreak Hotel." Dick Clark's TV show *American Bandstand* sent the latest songs out to millions of America's teenagers. Many artists like Frankie Avalon,

Fabian, Paul Anka, Bobby Darin, and Bobby Rydell used the dance show as a stepping-stone in their careers. Every one of them was a teenage idol in the mold of Sinatra and Presley; all made millions of dollars and were worshiped everywhere they went. But none surpassed Presley; he remained "The King." Though he died in 1977, his music and the impact it had on American youth will be felt for decades to come.

Another change during the 1950s was the disappearance of the 78-rpm discs that had taken over from Edison's cylinders. The 78s were too large and too breakable, so they were replaced by the smaller, more durable 45-rpm records. Teenagers could pick up a couple of dozen of these and take them to a "sock hop." This helped records to become an important part of the youth culture.

Despite the anguished pleas of the older generation and of songwriters like Billy Rose, rock and roll was here to stay. Danny and the Juniors, a popular rock group, sang it this way in 1958:

> Rock and roll is here to stay
> I'll dig it to the end.
> It'll go down in history,
> Just you wait, my friend.
> I don't care what people say
> Rock and roll is here to stay.

THE BRITISH
ARE COMING!

By 1964 rock music had topped the charts for almost a decade, solidifying its position as the most important "new sound" in popular music. But was it still new? How long would American youth stay enchanted with the same old rock and roll?

If the fickle pop audience was looking for something new, they found it in the Liverpool sound. The Beatles led the "British invasion"

of American popular music. On April 4, 1964, the top five singles in the nation were (from Rohde, 1970):

1. "Twist and Shout"   The Beatles
2. "Can't Buy Me Love"   The Beatles
3. "Please Please Me"   The Beatles
4. "She Loves You"   The Beatles
5. "I Want to Hold Your Hand" The Beatles

No musical artists had ever so dominated the hit parade. Dressed in Edwardian suits and sporting similar mop haircuts, the "fab four" stirred up tremendous excitement among America's teens (see 7.3). Ed Sullivan featured them on his Sunday night TV variety show just as he had featured Presley the decade before.

Why the sudden Beatlemania? Perhaps rock fans needed new love objects or idols, or maybe it was the appeal of a "foreign" culture. The older generation greeted the Beatles with the same hostility they had earlier shown toward Presley. Fundamentalist preachers urged their congregations to burn Beatle records; they considered the new music a sacrilege. But Beatle fans were too engrossed in the sound to worry.

The first Beatle tours in America brought back memories of Presley and Sinatra. Young women screamed, mobbed the stage, and fainted at the sight of the Liverpool quartet. Young men adopted Beatle haircuts. But the Beatles were not the only British invaders. Herman's Hermits, the Dave Clark Five, and Peter and Gordon all had Top-10 hits that year.

I call the period from the birth of rock in 1955 to the end of 1964 the Age of Innocence, because on the whole rock music was just plain fun. The conflicts addressed in rock lyrics were not the conflicts of the world but those between boy and girl, those simple yet sometimes intense moments filled with love and anxiety, often in equal measure.

7.3

Masters of the Mersey Beat

It all began in a strip joint in Germany in 1962. Brian Epstein, a London music promoter, found four young men playing there. Their music was just loud enough to be heard over the din. "Their act was ragged, their clothes were a mess," he said. "And yet I sensed at once that something was there."

That something was called the "Mersey Beat" (named after the Mersey River in Liverpool), a new sound that was sweeping Britain. The American press found the Beatles curious. *Newsweek* said, "The sound of their music is one of the most persistent noises heard over England since the air raid sirens were dismantled. . . . Beatle music is high pitched, loud beyond reason, and stupefyingly repetitive. . . ."

Time predicted flatly that the Beatles stood little chance of making it with the American audience:

"Though Americans may find the Beatles achingly familiar (their songs consist mainly of Yeh! screamed to the accompaniment of three guitars and a thunderous drum) they are apparently irresistible to the English."

Irresistible indeed. "Beatlemania" was already part of the English vocabulary in 1963 . . . and that was only the beginning.

THE ROCK RENAISSANCE

At the end of 1964, one fan magazine held a contest among readers to decide which of the new British groups would be around ten years later. The readers voted for the Beatles, who barely won over the Dave Clark Five. That seems absurd now, but one of the reasons the Dave Clark Five were not able to sustain their initial fanatic following was because their music remained the same. The Beatles, on the other hand, dared to change. They saw that rock was growing up, and they grew with it. Even if the Beatles didn't last ten years as a group (they disbanded in 1970), Paul, George, and Ringo are still performing. And they haven't stopped changing.

When I moved to southern California in the summer of 1965, I tuned in Top-40 radio and heard a new kind of rock lyric. Rock artists were attempting to go beyond traditional clichés to actually communicate something meaningful with their songs. The Rolling Stones sang of social discontent and alienation in "I Can't Get No Satisfaction." The Byrds' "Mr. Tambourine Man" (written by Bob Dylan) was a strange lyrical journey with heavy spiritual overtones. Barry McGuire's "Eve of Destruction" was an angry protest ballad that urged the young audience to:

> Look at all the hate
> There is in Red China,
> Then take a look around, to Selma,
>   Alabama.
> You may leave here for four days in space
> But when you return it's the same old
>   place. . . .

In September, Dylan's "Like a Rolling Stone" became the number one song. It was an extraordinary, long, and cryptic song, and understanding the lyrics meant trying to put together the pieces of a mysterious puzzle. Dylan, a wandering poet from Hibbing, Minnesota, by way of New York's Greenwich Village, clearly had a message that was unlike any other in pop music.

In the next year, Simon and Garfunkel's songs of quiet social protest and personal bitterness also hit the top of the charts. The Beatles joined this movement with their *Revolver* album. One song urged listeners to "turn off your mind, relax, and float downstream." In 1967 the Jefferson Airplane's *Surrealistic Pillow* pointed the way toward San Francisco. Haight-Ashbury was the gathering place for a generation looking for a better way. Scott McKenzie sang, "If you're going to San Francisco, be sure to wear some flowers in your hair." Eric Burdon and the Animals advertised those "warm San Francisco nights."

This was the Rock Renaissance. During the period from 1965 to 1970, rock came of age. Lyrics dealt with the grim realities of war, hatred, racism, and the infinite complexities of interpersonal relationships. To be sure, the simplistic lyric of old was still around, but all over the country people began to take rock seriously for the first time. Perhaps the new music had something to say after all.

THE DIFFUSION OF ROCK

Of course, if anyone actually counted on rock to solve the world's problems, they were in for a big disappointment. Despite antiwar protest ballads of the 1960s, the war in Vietnam continued into the 1970s. And as rock continued to develop, it didn't stay preoccupied with complex social problems. Even the great crusader, Dylan, brought out an album of simple country ballads aptly entitled *Nashville Skyline*.

The early 1970s saw a trend toward a gentler rock style, with musicians like James Taylor, Gordon Lightfoot, and Crosby, Stills, Nash, and Young becoming big stars. Their music was often soft and melodic, and the words were simple, soothing. The success of Joni Mitchell, Carly Simon, Carole King, and Linda Ronstadt in the 1970s gave women more voice in popular music than they had had since the 1940s (see 7.4). These women rode the crest of the softer rock, which purists claimed was not rock at all but some sort of new folk music set to an electric beat.

Not all the music that came from female artists was on the soft side, however. Artists like Grace Slick (with the Jefferson Starship as well as in solo efforts) and Heart carried on with straight-ahead rock and roll, often with a hard edge.

"Soft rock" had hardly arrived when Alice Cooper, Kiss, and David Bowie appeared on the scene. Cooper's favorite stage antics included cutting off the heads of live chick-

7.4
Singer-songwriter Carly Simon's writing, talent, and sheer sensual appeal helped make her one of the most successful women in rock's diffusion era of the 1970s. During the 1980s, successful female artists like Stevie Nicks carried on the tradition.

ens, something that did not endear him to critics who had decided that rock had grown up. But the success of these groups points out that rock is flexible enough to offer something for everyone in the pop audience. If rock gets a little too staid, there is always a new group to turn it on its ear.

The mid-1970s brought disco, perhaps the antithesis of the lyrically complex music of the 1960s. Disco was listened to strictly for the beat. Disco music revived dancing, which had been very popular during the early 1960s, when the Twist, the Fly, and the Loco-motion were the rage. One enthusiast reported turning down a college basketball scholarship to continue his daily ritual of sleeping all day and dancing all night. "I'd rather disco," he said. "If it wasn't for the music, I wouldn't want to be in the world."

There was no real unifying rock trend in the 1970s. Those who had gyrated to "Rock around the Clock" were now in their 30s or 40s. Many of them preferred to sink nostalgically back into the "good old" rock and roll of the 1950s, and that too enjoyed a revival.

From the soul blues of Stevie Wonder to the urban blues of Paul Simon, the 1970s brought rock enough for everyone. As the rock audience has grown in number, its needs have diversified. In the best traditions of commercial mass media, there was a rock product to fit every need.

NEW MUSIC AND THE 1980s

A fourth era of rock and roll burst onto the scene on the heels of disco in the late 1970s. Though it has already been through a number of changes and has been labeled everything from punk to new wave to techno pop, we'll refer to it here simply as *new music*.

The first successful punk group is generally acknowledged to have been the Sex Pistols, an erratic and uninhibited group from England. Their first (and only) American tour was hailed as a breakthrough by many critics. On the heels of punk came the slightly more melodic and far more accessible new-wave artists like Elvis Costello, the Ramones (see 7.5), Tom Petty and the Heartbreakers, and the Clash. Mainstream artists like Linda Ronstadt and Billy Joel were soon releasing new wave–like albums, though Joel pointed out in one song that, no matter what the trend, "It's still rock and roll to me."

The early 1980s brought a flood of new music. While new music is still too recent to be categorized and identified in any meaningful way, there are some clear trends that have emerged.

The term *techno-pop* has been generally associated with groups that incorporate a new-music sound but seem to be more accessible to the average listener. Their music tends to be more content-oriented, with lyrics that are fairly recognizable to the mass audience. Among these are Culture Club, Duran Duran, Human League, Men at Work, A Flock of Seagulls, and especially the Police.

A number of new-music bands, less in the mainstream, have developed a cult following. These groups tend to be more form-oriented, with nontraditional lyrics and a heavy dose of computerized effects. Among those heard most often are the Fixx, U2, the Cure, R.E.M., and Berlin.

Of course, assigning any group to a specific category can be risky business. The pop-music scene goes through so many changes that today's artsy cult band might be tomorrow's mainstream idols. Duran Duran was generally regarded as a cult band until "Hungry Like a Wolf" became a rock-video classic. Now they are considered to have wide audience appeal. The Police developed a cult following

for several years and had a couple of radio successes, but their 1983 LP *Synchronicity* put them square in the mainstream. Today Police fans are found in all demographic categories.

Of interest also is the work of Thomas Dolby, a synthesizer expert whose songs enjoy wide appeal but still seem to be on the cutting edge of what the new music is about. Perhaps more than anyone's, Dolby's music tends to reflect a combination of esoteric lyrics and newly created musical forms. Any analysis of the impact of the new music would not be complete without considering the marriage of the computer/synthesizer and more traditional instruments.

Laurie Anderson is an artist/performer who experiments with various musical forms, breath techniques, and studio effects. Much of her work seems to be marked by a sense of satire and humor.

Where the new music goes from here is anybody's guess. Clearly it is the freshest, most innovative trend in rock and roll since the 1960s. Some have even credited the new music and rock videos with saving the sagging record industry, but perhaps they overstate their case. The record industry, like many American industries, experienced an economic decline during the late 1970s. Home taping and the lack of creative music that excited the consumer were generally given as the reasons for that decline, along with the general economic climate. Home taping has continued to be a problem for the industry, with no solution in sight. No amount of fresh music can solve that problem.

It will be interesting to see what direction the new music takes in the next five years. From an economic and creative perspective, it has given the record industry a much-needed boost. Whatever happens, it will have left an indelible mark on the evolution of popular music.

7.5
The Ramones were among the first of the new-wave artists to receive radio air play and produce a hit album.

ROCK AND ROTE: THE THEMES OF ROCK MUSIC

To a generation raised in the golden age of radio, rock remains a mystery. What is it all about? How does it work? Dylan's words "You know something is happening here but you don't know what it is, do you, Mr. Jones?" come to mind. I vividly recall my father's description of his first brush with rock. Though he was a professional musician most of his life, the music of the 1950s baffled him; he dubbed it "pots and pans . . . because it sounds like pots and pans banging together." After that I could expect to hear, "Edward, turn down the pots and pans!" whenever my radio was at top volume.

When critics complain that rock and roll "all sounds the same," they mean the *form* sounds the same. To the untrained or uninterested ear, all rock songs do sound very similar. This makes examination of content even more important, since the lyrics contain a rich diversity of ideas that parallel the social and emotional concerns of the youth culture. These are similar to patterns emerging in other media. The themes of rock lyrics can also be found in magazine advertisements, the great Shakespeare plays, and popular American novels.

Rock lyrics are learned by rote—that is, through repetition. Lyrics that may be barely recognizable the first time around usually become quite clear by the 10th, 20th, or 200th time. Both AM and FM rock stations tend to play relatively few songs, most of them by just a handful of superstars. That way we hear the same songs over and over again, and we can't help learning the words. Millions of Americans share the same words and ideas simultaneously.

Though rock from the Age of Innocence is defended by some, both the musical form and

Guest Essay by Deborah Gordon

The Image of Women in Contemporary Music

Deborah Gordon is a graduate of the American Studies program at the University of Maryland, where she helped teach a course about popular music in American culture. Here she reviews the status of women in the industry and the images of women most often found in the lyrics to popular songs.

The history of popular music has been, and continues to be, dominated by men singing about men's lives. The overwhelming majority of the writers, producers, and executives in the music industry are men. Because of this, much of popular music has either distorted women's life experiences or omitted a female perspective on those experiences.

Early rock-and-roll themes of romantic love presented images of women like that of "Earth Angel." "Earth angels" derived their power and influence over men's lives through their sexuality and femininity. Those women who failed to meet the feminine standards set in the music were made to feel inadequate. Those who did fit the image were viewed as sex objects, as portrayed in the lyrics of songs like "What is Love?" The answer? Someone who "sways with a wiggle when she walks."

The early 1960s saw a continuance of traditional sex roles. The sex double standard could be seen in the double messages of Dion's hits "Runaround Sue" and "The Wanderer." Dion warned, "Keep away from Runaround Sue" but glorified himself as the "type of guy who'll never settle down." If you were a female and "ran around," you were wicked— someone to be avoided, but if you were a male who did the same, you were popular.

Female singers in the early 1960s made hits by singing songs idolizing men. The central message of Connie Francis's "Where the Boys Are" was the same as that of the fairy tale *Sleeping Beauty*. She sang of a boy somewhere waiting to find her, and she pledged, "Till he finds me I'll be waiting patiently." Like the passive Sleeping Beauty, the woman of this song is seen as dreaming and waiting for a man to give her life. Little Peggy March sang "I Will Follow Him," which was one of the few active interests a young woman could pursue. Like the images of women and men from Stone Age myths, Joanie Sommers begged Johnny to get angry and "give me the biggest lecture I've ever had." She claimed that she wanted "a brave man . . . a cave man."

The Beatles sang traditional themes of boy meets girl, boy gets girl, and boy gets hurt by girl. Females were portrayed as teases in songs like "Day Tripper," in which they sang, "She's a big teaser." Much of the early Beatles music was filled with images of men and women in traditional sex roles. Boys were active and girls were passive, as seen in the lyrics of songs like "I Saw Her Standing There" and "I Should Have Known Better."

When the second wave of the British invasion hit America, the Rolling Stones challenged the Beatles as the most popular musical group in the country. The Stones' music expressed more blatant hostility and contempt toward women than the earlier British music. Mick Jagger sang "Under My Thumb" about a girl "who does just what she's told." In "Time Is on My Side," the Stones mocked the dependence of a woman, telling her she'd come running back "like you did so many times before, to me."

Along with the more overt objectification of women, violence against women appeared more and more frequently in the music of the late 1960s and the 1970s. In the Rolling Stones' version of "Midnight Rambler," Albert De Salvo, the notorious Boston Strangler who killed a number of women, is celebrated as a hero.

Despite the generally negative images of women in popular music during this period, some songs achieving popularity suggested that women's roles were in a state of transition. In the early 1960s when female singers were worshiping "Johnny Angel" and "The Leader of the Pack," Lesley Gore sang "You Don't Own Me," in which she told a man not to tell her what to do or say. In "Different Drum," Linda Ronstadt sang that she was "not in the market for a boy who wants to love only me," and Aretha Franklin asked for "respect" for herself. The rigid sex roles of the 1950s, with women seen as appendages of men without identities of their own, were directly challenged in songs like these.

Some popular music has reflected the growing consciousness of feminism. Helen Reddy's "I Am Woman" was perhaps the song most widely associated with the women's movement of the 1970s. In it Reddy sang, "I am woman, hear me roar in numbers too big to ignore," proclaiming that women were determined to change their position within the culture.

Carly Simon's "You're So Vain" portrayed a man's narcissism with bitterness and anger. Loretta Lynn sang "The Pill," a hit on country and western charts, in which she told her husband, "There's gonna be some changes made right here on Nurs'ry Hill." Women were less inclined to subordinate their own needs to those of men, and they protested more

about poor treatment they received from men.

By 1975 a new genre of music was offering an alternative to popular music for feminist listeners. "Women's," or "feminist," music was part of a larger consciousness within the feminist movement, which produced creative expressions of women's experiences as well as the social problems they faced.

As part of the sexual revolution of the 1960s, another image of women in popular music became that of a sex bomb, who projected liberation through good sex. Donna Summer's "Love to Love You Baby" aimed moans and groans, imitating sexual excitement, at the male listener. But it covertly spoke to women, reinforcing their role as sex object.

The 1970s brought an ever-increasing amount of violence aimed at women in the music of punk-rock groups like the Ramones, who sang "You're Gonna Kill That Girl."

With an antifeminist backlash emerging, feminists began mobilizing against the music industry. They protested against what they felt were violent and pornographic images of women on album covers and promotional materials. In Los Angeles, feminists protested against an advertising billboard for the Rolling Stones' album "Black and Blue." On the billboard was a picture of a woman beaten and tied up; the caption read "I'm black and blue from the Rolling Stones,

and I love it." Those protesting the billboard attempted to get it taken down through legal channels; when those efforts didn't work, they painted across it, "This is a crime against women." The billboard was then taken down.

In November 1979, feminists won a victory over Warner/Atlantic/Elektra/Asylum Records, which they had been boycotting and protesting against for two and a half years. The record company issued a statement saying that it opposed violence against women or men depicted on album covers and promotional materials. Of course, sometimes an individual artist or group may have final control over album-cover design, so it is not easy to say what kind of impact this statement will actually have. Still, it is significant that there was enough pressure by feminists to move the company to respond.

The different messages of a number of genres of music do not give us a simple, clear-cut picture of what future images of women will be. There is ambiguity in cultural definitions of male-female relationships and changing sex roles and politics. On the one hand, there is a growing amount of violence against women depicted in punk rock and new wave. On the other hand, the 1970s brought a growing number of female musicians who portrayed images of women that show human complexity and a break with traditional beliefs. The ambiguity of the 1970s suggests that the 1980s may prove to be a turning point for women and their relationship with the media. Feminist recording companies and businesses like Olivia Records face an economic situation that may not allow them to continue operating as autonomous structures countering the larger recording companies. The survival of alternative music for feminist listeners may be threatened in the 1980s. Thus what the image of women in popular music becomes during the rest of this decade remains to be seen.

Used with permission of Deborah Gordon.

---

the content were often pretty elementary. Songs fell into predictable categories. Lyrics tended to repeat phrases such as "I love my baby," "I lost my baby," "I need my baby," or, later, "My baby got run over by a train."

Love

Rock has grown up since the 1950s, and examination of its content yields some interesting patterns. These patterns help unravel what rock is about. Many rock songs still revolve around love. But then, *all* songs do. What else have we been singing about since the beginning of civilization?

The joys of discovering that someone cares about you and that you feel the same way (Paul McCartney's "Maybe I'm Amazed"); someone special who's left (Hall and Oates's "She's Gone"); love affairs gone wrong (Paul Simon's "April Come She Will," "Dangling Conversation," and "50 Ways to Leave Your Lover"). Simon is of particular interest, since his lyrics use traditional literary tools like allegory and metaphor. He weaves these carefully into the music to give it a depth that is rarely matched in rock music.

But in recent years rock has begun to offer some new views on the subject of love. David Crosby's "Triad" suggests to two women who love him, "Why can't we go on as three?" Another topic frequently discussed in rock lyrics is homosexuality. Lou Reed's "Walk on the Wild Side" paints a graphic picture of the transvestite jungle of New York City. The Kinks' "Lola" tells the story of a guy who took home a gal and found out she was really another guy. In a touch of naiveté he notes that it's a "mixed-up, jumbled-up, shook-up world." More recently, Rod Stewart sang of "Georgie," his homosexual friend, while a new-wave group called the Vapors released a single called "Turning Japanese," which extols the virtues of masturbation.

Social Issues

The lyrics of Bob Dylan, one of the first rock poets, were complex where others had been simple, mysterious where others had been transparent, socially significant where others had been narcissistic. Many of the Dylan songs from the mid-1960s were scathing indictments of society. They had something to say about war ("Blowin' in the Wind," "A Hard Rain's Gonna Fall," "Talking World War III Blues") and racial injustice ("Oxford Town"). Dylan's intensely personal and politically charged lyrics, coupled with his unwillingness to be packaged, promoted, or even interviewed, seemed to contribute to his success.

A concern for the environment is evident in the hundreds of rock and country and western songs that offer an escape from the city ("Goin' up the Country," "Thank God I'm a Country Boy," "Rocky Mountain High").

The new-music era has been characterized by lyrics which point up a number of social concerns. The deceptively simple lyrics of the Clash, for example, are clearly about the freedom of the individual in society. Neil Young's 1983 *Trans* LP is a dissertation on what might happen to human beings in the computer age. In fact, the heavy use of synthesizers and computer techniques in recording many new-music songs seems to represent an attempt to bring together the computerized reality of the 1980s and the artistry and aesthetics that have always been associated with music and all things musical.

The Artist and Society

Don McLean's "Vincent" describes the tortured world of Vincent van Gogh, and Joni Mitchell's "Judgment of the Moon and Stars," subtitled "Ludwig's Tune," was a portrait of the agony Beethoven felt as he was going deaf, losing the ability to hear the very music that was making him famous.

In developing the theme of the artist's alienation, rock artists often describe their own situation. Hence, we have rock songs that describe what it's like to be a rock star or a would-be star. That star is a product of the jet age, often doing concerts all over the world in the same month. There are moments of

loneliness ("Holiday Inn," "Come Monday," "Goodbye Again") and ever-present groupies ("String Man," "Guitar Man," "Blonde in the Bleachers"). In an age when artists are bought and sold in a maze of record contracts and highly promoted concert dates, they sometimes feel like prisoners of the system. Joni Mitchell's "For Free" laments the plight of a musician who couldn't attract an audience because "they knew he'd never been on their TV so they passed his music by." James Taylor tells an unbelieving patron in a café, "Hey, mister, that's me up on the jukebox."

COUNTRY AND WESTERN MUSIC

Though rock has been the most listened-to popular music of the last two decades, that period has also brought an amazing growth in country and western (C&W) music. In 1961, only 81 radio stations were playing C&W, but by 1980 there were more than 1,000 full-time country stations and 1,500 more stations that played at least three hours of C&W daily. On the West Coast, two radio legends—KHJ in Los Angeles and KSAN-FM, San Francisco's first underground rock station—both switched to country in 1980. Although KHJ recently returned to rock, country fans say that their music is more popular than jazz, soul, and classical, and sales figures back them up.

Nashville, home of the "Grand Ole Opry" and center of the country-music business, now boasts the most sophisticated recording studios in the country. More songs are now recorded in Nashville than in New York City, Los Angeles, and Detroit combined. In fact, over *half* of all the music recorded in America is recorded in Nashville. Robert Altman's film *Nashville*, an overwhelming critical success in the mid-1970s, familiarized many with the city and its music.

7.6
Jim Bouton and the Ultimate C&W Song

Since its release in 1970, *Ball Four* has become one of the best-selling sports books ever written. It's a diary, an intimate glimpse into the locker-room world of the professional athlete. There we find that country and western music holds sway. When Bouton objects and insists on equal time for rock, he and fellow pitcher Larry Dierker write the ultimate country and western song. Bouton reveals: "It took us about two innings. . . ."

I want my baby back again,
She done left town with my best
    friend,
And now I lie here all alone,
I'm just a-waitin' by the phone.
Her lips were sweet as summer
    wine,
And when I held her hand in
    mine,
I thought she'd never be untrue,
But now she's broke my heart in
    two.
The mailman let me down
    today,
And so I made that mother pay,
And now I'm locked in this old
    jail,
And my dog died and there's no
    bail.
My teardrops fall like pouring
    rain,
The bottle doesn't ease my
    pain,
And no one gives a hoot for me
Since Billy Joe took my Marie
And ran away to Tennessee.
I wish I had someone to tell
'Bout how I'm locked up in this
    cell,
And all my kinfolk dead and
    gone
But with the Lord I'll carry on.

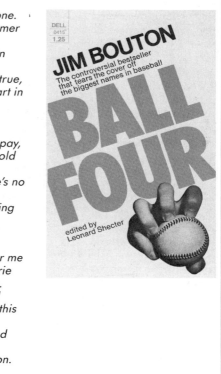

DELL
0415
1.25

JIM BOUTON
The controversial bestseller
that tears the cover off
the biggest names in baseball

BALL FOUR

edited by
Leonard Shecter

Issues and Answers

Guest Essay by Don Weller

"And the Hits Just Keep on Comin' "

Don Weller has been associated with rock music much of his life. He has taught college courses in rock via radio and is currently a rock critic for the Honolulu Star Bulletin. *In addition, he teaches in the Communication Department at the University of Hawaii.*

"AND THE HITS JUST KEEP ON COMIN'." Those words. How many times have they made their way into your brain? Have you ever wondered just *how* those hits keep on comin'? Have you ever thought about having your very own hit single on the charts—making your own living-room (basement?) tape, sending it to a record company, and ZAP! . . . instant stardom? Most of you know one basic thing about the record industry and landing a hit record: It isn't easy or simple.

The process involves *gatekeepers,* organizations and individuals whose job it is to let a few items into the big spotlight while blocking out the others. As rock critic R. Serge Denisoff aptly puts it, "Gatekeepers in the music industry are the Berlin Wall between the manufacturer and the audience." They are hurdles, barriers, and fences, and musicians who want to see their record rise on the charts have to overcome them.

It is not unusual to find 100 LPs released *in any given week,* and hundreds more 45-rpm singles. Only a very tiny minority of them will ever be blessed with radio air play, press reviews, or jukebox inclusion. Question: Who's Mr. Big, who determines which ones get to the turntables, jukeboxes, and magazines? Answer: There's no *one* Mr. Big, but rather a *number* of influential people in a *number* of organizations who make those decisions. Together with mass audience response in target geographic areas, their decisions determine which songs are hits and which are flops.

The next step involves your imagination. Picture a game board. On the board near the top is the winner's circle—the gold record—the hit single— the hit album. There are a number of paths leading to that circle, and each one has a different width. The wider the path the greater the influence of that path in getting the record to the winner's circle.

One of the widest paths is labeled "trade papers." Trade magazines and newspapers (like *Billboard* and *Cashbox*) are subscribed to by record company personnel, disc jockeys, and record reviewers to keep up with "industry happenings." In addition, they provide up-to-the-minute lists of "hot" songs. In *Billboard* there is a page called "*Billboard*'s Singles Radio Action: Playlist Top Add Ons/Playlist Prime Movers/Regional and National Breakouts." It is from here that program directors learn who is playing what and where. Armed with this information they decide what to add to their own small "playlist," or list of records receiving air play.

Artists can get their product to the gatekeepers via print media by receiving favorable reviews from critics in magazines like *Rolling Stone.* In addition, most metropolitan daily papers now have at least one staffer who turns in regular record reviews. Each record company has a publicity or public affairs department whose job it is to make sure that free promotional copies of their product are provided to the reviewers. This free service makes the reviewers a rather "elitist" group, to be sure, and they tend to become a little jaded. Along with the albums comes a plethora of other goodies—biographies, stickers, 8 × 10 glossy pictures, buttons, personalized T-shirts, personalized matches, you name it. The goal is simple: to get the album public attention, preferably with a favorable review.

The music industry is overstaffed with people and overstuffed with record products. There is much more expensively recorded music than the fickle public could ever consume. What happens when that public trots off to their local record store to pick up an album? The store owner may be still another gatekeeper. Chain-store czars may agree to cut the prices of certain albums for a time. There are extra displays, provided by the record company, of course, that can increase the sale of an album. Usually, record store owners are not concerned so much with what they sell, just as long as they sell something.

So the next time you hear a strung-out, caffeine-soaked boss deejay wail "AND THE HITS JUST KEEP ON COMIN'"—remember only a few of the hundreds of records released today will ever sell very many copies. That leaves a lot of wasted polyvinyl chloride lying around in the bins at supermarkets and swap meets!

FOR WEEK ENDING JULY 16, 1983

58

Billboard HOT 100

Copyright 1983, Billboard Publications, Inc. No part of this publication may be reproduced, stored in a retrieval system, or transmitted, in any form or by any means, electronic, mechanical, photocopying, recording, or otherwise, without the prior written permission of the publisher.

This Week	Last Week	Wks. on Chart	TITLE—Artist (Producer) Writer, Label & Number (Distributing Label)	
☆1	1	7	EVERY BREATH YOU TAKE—The Police (Hugh Padgham, The Police), Sting; A&M 2542 (WEEKS AT #1: 2)	HL
2	2	14	ELECTRIC AVENUE—Eddy Grant (E. Grant), E. Grant; Portrait/Ice 37-03793 (Epic)	
3	3	16	FLASHDANCE . . . WHAT A FEELING—Irene Cara ● (Giorgio Moroder), K. Forsey, I. Cara, G. Moroder; Casablanca 811440-7 (PolyGram)	CHA/HL
★4	4	14	NEVER GONNA LET YOU GO—Sergio Mendes (Sergio Mendes), B. Mann, C. Weil; A&M 2540	CLM
★5	6	8	WANNA BE STARTIN' SOMETHING—Michael Jackson (Quincy Jones), M. Jackson; Epic 34-03914	WBM
★6	8	11	COME DANCING—The Kinks (Ray Davies), R. Davies; Arista 1054	
7	5	13	TOO SHY—Kajagoogoo (Colin Thurston, Nick Rhodes), Limahl, N. Beggs Kajagoogoo; EMI-America 8161	HL
★8	10	11	OUR HOUSE—Madness (Clive Langer, Alan Winstanley), C. Smyth, C. Foreman; Geffen 7-29668 (Warner Bros.)	WBM
★9	13	7	IS THERE SOMETHING I SHOULD KNOW—Duran Duran (Ian Little, Duran Duran), Duran Duran; Capitol 5233	CHA/HL
10	7	14	TIME—Culture Club (Steve Levine), R. Hay, J. Moss, M. Craig; Virgin/Epic 34-03796	CHA/HL
★11	14	7	STAND BACK—Stevie Nicks (Jimmy Iovine), S. Nicks; Modern 7-99863 (Atco)	WBM
12	12	11	I'M STILL STANDING—Elton John (Chris Thomas), E. John, B. Taupin; Geffen 7-29639 (Warner Bros.)	CHA/HL
★13	15	7	1999—Prince (Prince) Prince; Warner Bros. 7-29896	CPP
★14	18	8	SHE WORKS HARD FOR THE MONEY—Donna Summer (Michael Omartian), D. Summer, M. Omartian; Mercury 812370-7 (PolyGram)	
★15	20	10	SWEET DREAMS—Eurythmics (David A. Stewart), Lennox, Stewart; RCA 13533	
★16	19	8	BABY JANE—Rod Stewart (Rod Stewart, Tom Dowd), Stewart, Davis; Warner Bros. 7-29608	
★17	17	13	ALL THIS LOVE—Debarge (Iris Gordy, Eldra Debarge), E. Debarge; Gordy 1660 (Motown)	CPP
18	9	12	DON'T LET IT END—Styx (Styx), D. DeYoung; A&M 2543	CPP/ALM
★19	25	7	MANIAC—Michael Sembello (Phil Ramone, Michael Sembello), M. Sembello, D. Matkosky; Casablanca 812516-7 (PolyGram)	CHA/HL
★20	22	6	CUTS LIKE A KNIFE—Bryan Adams (Bryan Adams, Bob Clearmountain), B. Adams, J. Vallance; A&M 2553	CPP/ALM
★21	23	6	HOT GIRLS IN LOVE—Loverboy (Bruce Fairbairn, Paul Dean), P. Dean, B. Fairbairn; Columbia 38-03941	CLM/APB
22	11	12	FAMILY MAN—Daryl Hall & John Oates (Daryl Hall & John Oates), M. Oldfield, T. Cross, R. Fenn, M. Frye, M. Reilly, M. Pert; RCA 13507	CHA/HL
23	16	15	SHE'S A BEAUTY—The Tubes (David Foster), Lukather, Foster, Waybill; Capitol 5217	CPP
★24	28	8	(KEEP FEELING) FASCINATION—The Human League (Martin Rushent, Human League), Oakley, Callis; A&M 2547	CHA/HL
★25	32	3	IT'S A MISTAKE—Men At Work (Peter Mclan), C. Hay; Columbia 38-03959	CLM/APB
26	26	10	WISHING—A Flock Of Seagulls (Mike Howlett), M. Score, A. Score, F. Maudsley, P. Reynolds; Jive/ Arista 2006	HL
★27	29	5	TAKE ME TO HEART—Quarterflash (John Boylan), M. Ross; Geffen 7-29603 (Warner Bros.)	WBM
★28	30	8	SAVED BY ZERO—The Fixx (Rupert Hine), Curnin, Woods, West-Oram, Greenall, Agies; MCA 52213	CPP
★29	34	6	ROCK OF AGES—Def Leppard (Robert John "Mutt" Lange), Clark, Lange, Elliott; Mercury 812604-7 (PolyGram)	CLM
★30	39	4	ROCK 'N' ROLL IS KING—ELO (Jeff Lynne), J. Lynne; Jet 4-03964 (Epic)	CLM/APB
★31	38	7	CHINA GIRL—David Bowie (David Bowie, Nile Rodgers), D. Bowie, I. Pop; EMI-America 8165	WBM/HL
★32	35	7	STOP IN THE NAME OF LOVE—The Hollies (The Hollies, Graham Nash, Stanley Johnson, Paul Bliss), Holland, Dozier, Holland; Atlantic 7-89819	CPP
33	24	21	BEAT IT—Michael Jackson ● (Quincy Jones), M. Jackson; Epic 34-03759	WBM
34	21	14	AFFAIR OF THE HEART—Rick Springfield (Rick Springfield, Bill Drescher), R. Springfield, B. Tosti, D. Tate; RCA 13497	CLM
★35	48	3	I'LL TUMBLE 4 YA—Culture Club (Steve Levine), R. Hay, J. Moss, M. Craig, G. O'Dowd; Virgin/Epic 34-03912	CHA/HL
36	27	8	ROLL ME AWAY—Bob Seger And The Bullet Band (Jimmy Iovine), B. Seger; Capitol 5235	WBM
37	33	19	ALWAYS SOMETHING THERE TO REMIND ME—Naked Eyes (Tony Mansfield), B. Bacharach, H. David; EMI-America 8155	CHA/HL
★38	44	5	THE BORDER—America (Russ Ballard), R. Ballard, D. Bunnell; Capitol 5236	
★39	43	9	THE SALT IN MY TEARS—Martin Briley (Peter Coleman), M. Briley; Mercury 812165-7 (PolyGram)	CLM
★40	59	2	LAWYERS IN LOVE—Jackson Browne (Jackson Browne, Greg Ladanyi), J. Browne; Asylum 7-69826 (Elektra)	WBM
41	36	9	WHITE WEDDING—Billy Idol (Keith Forsey), B. Idol; Chrysalis 4-42697	CLM
★42	51	4	PUTTIN' ON THE RITZ—Taco (David Parker), Berlin; RCA 13574	
★43	50	4	PIECES OF ICE—Diana Ross (Gary Katz), M. Jordan, J. Capek; RCA 13549	CLM/WBM
★44	46	10	SLIPPING AWAY—Dave Edmunds (Jeff Lynne), J. Lynne; Columbia 38-03877	CLM/APB
45	31	17	LET'S DANCE—David Bowie ● (David Bowie, Nile Rodgers), D. Bowie; EMI-America 8158	HL
★46	62	2	AFTER THE FALL—Journey (Mike Stone, Kevin Elson), S. Perry, J. Cain; Columbia 38-04004	CPP
47	40	16	TRY AGAIN—Champaign (G. Massenburg), D. Walden, R. Maffit, M. Day; Columbia 38-03563	CPP
★48	52	4	WAR GAMES—Crosby, Stills & Nash (Stephen Stills, Graham Nash, Stanley Johnston), S. Stills; Atlantic 7-89812	WBM
49	45	10	HOW DO YOU KEEP THE MUSIC PLAYING—James Ingram with Patti Austin (Quincy Jones, Johnny Mandel), M. Legrand, A.&M. Bergman; Qwest 7-29618 (Warner Bros.)	WBM
★50	55	4	IT'S INEVITABLE—Charlie (Kevin Beamish, Terry Thomas), T. Thomas; Mirage 7-99862 (Atco)	
★51	56	5	MIDNIGHT BLUE—Louise Tucker (Tim Smit, Charlie Skarbek), Beethoven, Smit, Skarbeck; Arista 1-9022	CPP
★52	54	6	SPACE AGE WHIZ KID—Joe Walsh (Bill Szymczyk), J. Walsh, J. Vitale; Full Moon/Warner Bros. 7-29611	
53	53	7	CHINA—Red Rockers (David Kahne), D. Hill, J. Griffith, J. Singletary; Columbia 38-03786	WBM
★54	57	5	JUICY FRUIT—Mtume (J. Mtume), J. Mtume; Epic 34-03578	
★55	70	2	HUMAN TOUCH—Rick Springfield (Rick Springfield, Bill Drescher), R. Springfield; RCA 13576	CLM
★56	60	3	ALL TIME HIGH—Rita Coolidge (John Barry), J. Barry, T. Rice; A&M 2551	B-3/CPP
★57	68	2	FAKE FRIENDS—Joan Jett and the Blackhearts (J. Jett, R. Cordell, K. Laguna), J. Jett, K. Lajuna; Blackheart/MCA 52240	
58	58	8	THE METRO—Berlin (Daniel R. Van Patten), J. Crawford; Geffen 7-29638 (Warner Bros.)	WBM
59	37	14	FAITHFULLY—Journey (Mike Stone, Kevin Elson), J. Cain; Columbia 38-03840	CPP
★60	67	4	DEAD GIVEAWAY—Shalamar (L.F. Sylvers, III), J. Gallo, M. Dare, L.F. Sylvers, III; Solar 7-69819 (Elektra)	CPP
★61	64	5	STAND BY—Roman Holiday (Peter Collins), S. Lambert, R. Lambert; Jive/Arista 1-9036	
★62	69	4	THE SAFETY DANCE—Men Without Hats (Marc Durand), Ivan; Backstreet 52232 (MCA)	
★63	74	3	HOW AM I SUPPOSED TO LIVE WITHOUT YOU—Laura Branigan (Jack White), M. Bolton, D. James; Atlantic 7-89805	
64	41	9	THE WOMAN IN YOU—The Bee Gees (Barry Gibb, Robin Gibb, Maurice Gibb, Karl Richardson, Albhy Galuten), B. Gibb, R. Gibb, M. Gibb; RSO 813173-7 (PolyGram)	CHA/HL
65	47	11	WE TWO—Little River Band (Little River Band, Ernie Rose), G. Goble; Capitol 5231	HL
★66	77	3	EWOK CELEBRATION—Meco (Meco Monardo, Lance Quinn, Tony Bongiovi), J. Williams, B. Burtt, J. Williams; Arista 1-9045	WBM
67	42	12	DON'T PAY THE FERRYMAN—Chris Deburgh (Rupert Hine), C. Deburgh; A&M 2511	CPP/ALM
★68	72	5	HOLD ME 'TIL THE MORNIN' COMES—Paul Anka (Denny Diante), P. Anka, D. Foster; Columbia 38-03897	HL
★69	78	3	DO YOU COMPUTE—Donnie Iris (Mark Avsec), Avsec, Ierace; MCA 52230	
★70	73	3	BLAME IT ON LOVE—Smokey Robinson & Barbara Mitchell (George Tobin), D. Deluca, T. Munda; Tamla 1684 (Motown)	CPP
★71	NEW ENTRY		PROMISES, PROMISES—Naked Eyes (Tony Mansfield), P. Bryne, R. Fisher; EMI-America 8170	CPP
72	49	15	OVERKILL—Men At Work (Peter Mclan), C. Hay; Columbia 38-03795	CLM/APB
73	61	21	LITTLE RED CORVETTE—Prince (Prince), Prince; Warner Bros. 7-29746	CPP
74	63	15	MY LOVE—Lionel Richie (Lionel Richie, James Anthony Carmichael), L. Richie; Motown 1677	CLM
★75	NEW ENTRY		TOTAL ECLIPSE OF THE HEART—Bonnie Tyler (Jim Steinman), J. Steinman; Columbia 38-03906	
76	65	8	I.O.U.—Lee Greenwood (J. Crutchfield), K. Chater, A. Roberts; MCA 51299	MCA/HL
77	79	5	BOOGIE DOWN—Jarreau (Jay Graydon), A. Jarreau, M. Omartian; Warner Bros. 7-29624	CPP
★78	83	3	WEST COAST SUMMER NIGHTS—Tony Carey (Peter Hauke), T. Carey; Rocshire 95037	
79	71	6	SOLID ROCK—Goanna (Trevor Lucas), S. Howard; Atco 7-99895	
★80	89	2	TONIGHT I CELEBRATE MY LOVE—Peabo Bryson/Roberta Flack (M. Masser), M. Masser, G. Goffin; Capitol 5242	CPP/ALM
★81	87	2	WHO'S BEHIND THE DOOR?—Zebra (Jack Douglas), R. Jackson; Atlantic 7-89821	
82	85	3	WAITING FOR YOUR LOVE—Toto (Toto), B. Kimball, D. Patch; Columbia 38-03981	WBM
83	86	3	SHY BOY—Bananarama (Tony Swain, Steve Jolley), T. Swain, S. Jolley; London 810-112-7 (PolyGram)	
84	66	12	THAT'S LOVE—Jim Capaldi (Steve Winwood), J. Capaldi; Atlantic 7-89849	WMB
★85	95	2	JOHNNY B. GOODE—Peter Tosh (Chris Kimsey, Peter Tosh), C. Berry; EMI-America 8159	CLM
86	82	5	YOU ARE IN MY SYSTEM—Robert Palmer (Robert Palmer), D. Frank; Island 7-99866 (Atco)	WBM
★87	NEW ENTRY		TIL YOU AND YOUR LOVER ARE LOVERS AGAIN—Engelbert Humperdinck (Even Stevens), J. Buckingham, H. Gray; Epic 34-03817	WBM/CPP
★88	NEW ENTRY		LEGAL TENDER—The B-52's (Steven Stanley), B-52's, R. Waldrop; Warner Bros. 7-29579	WBM
★89	NEW ENTRY		DON'T YOU GET SO MAD—Jeffrey Osborne (George Duke), J. Osborne, M. Sembello, D. Freeman; A&M 2561	CPP
★90	NEW ENTRY		DON'T CHANGE—Inxs (Mark Opitz), Inxs; Atco 7-99874	
91	80	11	CANDY GIRL—New Edition (M. Starr, M. Jonzun), M. Starr, M. Jonzun; Streetwise 2208	
92	76	22	SHE BLINDED ME WITH SCIENCE—Thomas Dolby (Tim Friese-Greene, T. Dolby); T. Dolby, J. Kerr; Capitol 5204	CLM
93	81	9	SAVE THE OVERTIME FOR ME—Gladys Knight & The Pips (L.F. Sylvers, III, E. Sylvers), R. Smith, J. Gallo, B. Knight, G. Knight, S.L. Dees; Columbia 38-03761	CPP/ALM
94	90	5	DON'T MAKE ME DO IT—Patrick Simmons (John Ryan), H. Lewis & The News; Elektra 7-69817	
★95	NEW ENTRY		WHEN YOU WERE MINE—Mitch Ryder (Little Bastard), Prince; Riva 213 (PolyGram)	
96	92	3	NIGHT PULSE—Double Image (Bob Gaudio), P. Bolen, G. Katona, B. Butler; Curb 4-03942 (CBS)	
97	75	5	EUROPA AND THE PIRATE TWINS—Thomas Dolby (Thomas Morgan Dolby Robertson), T. Dolby; Capitol 5238	CLM
98	96	10	INSIDE LOVE—George Benson (Arif Mardin, Kashif), Kashif; Warner Bros. 7-29649	MCA
99	84	19	STRAIGHT FROM THE HEART—Bryan Adams (Bryan Adams, Bob Clearmountain), Adams, Kagna; A&M 2536	CPP/ALM
100	91	11	THE CLOSER YOU GET—Alabama (Harold Shedd, Alabama), J.P. Pennington, M. Gray; RCA 13524	CPP/ALM

★ Bullets are awarded to those products demonstrating the greatest airplay and sales gains this week (Prime Movers). ● Recording Industry Assn. of America seal for sales of 1,000,000 units (seal indicated by dot). ▲ Recording Industry Assn. of America seal for sales of 2,000,000 units (seal indicated by triangle).

Sheet music suppliers are confined to piano/vocal sheet music copies and do not purport to represent mixed publications distribution. ABP = April Blackwood Pub.; ALM = Almo Publications; B-M = Belwin Miss; B-3 = Big Three Pub.; BP = Bradley Pub.; CHA = Chappell Music; CLM = Cherry lane Music Co.; CPI = Cimino Pub.; CPP = Columbia Pictures Pub.; CRIT/JG = Criteron/Joe Goldfeder; HAN = Hansen Pub.; HL = Hal Leonard; IMM = Ivan Mogull Music; MCA = MCA Music; PSP = Peer Southern Pub.; PLY = Plymouth Music; WBM = Warner Bros. Music

HOT 100 A-Z–(Publisher-Licensee)

Affair Of The Heart (Vogue/Welk, BMI/Bibo, ASCAP) 34
After The Fall (Twist and Shout/Weed High Nightmare/Colgems-EMI, ASCAP) 46
All This Love (Jobete, ASCAP) 17
All Time High (Blackwood, BMI) 56
Always Something There To Remind Me (Intersong/Blue Seas/Jac, ASCAP) 37
Baby Jane (Rod Stewart/Anteater, ASCAP) 16
Beat It (Mijac, BMI) 33
Blame It On Love (Chardax, BMI) 70
Boogie Down (Al Jarreau, BMI/See This House, ASCAP) 77
Border (April/Russell Ballard/Poison Oak, ASCAP) 38
Candy Girl (Boston International, ASCAP/Streetsounds, BMI) 91
China (Very Safe/Dead Heroes/Bug/See Squared, BMI) 53
China Girl (Jones/Bug/James Osterberg/Fleur, ASCAP/BMI) 31
Closer You Get (Irving/Down 'N Dixie/Chinnichap/Careers, BMI) 100
Come Dancing (Davray, PRS) 6
Cuts Like A Knife (Irving/Adams/Calypso Toonz, BMI) 20
Dead Giveaway (Spectrum VII, L.F.S. III, ASCAP) 60
Do You Compute (Bema, ASCAP) 69
Don't Change (Browning, BMI) 90
Don't Let It End (Stygian Songs/Almo, ASCAP) 18
Don't Make Me Do It (April/Russell Ballard/Poison Oak, ASCAP/Hulex/Red Admiral, BMI) 94
Don't Pay The Ferryman (Rondor/London/Irving, BMI) 67
Don't You Get So Mad (Almo/March 9/Gravity Raincoat/WB, ASCAP/Haymaker/Warner Tamerlane, BMI) 89
Electric Avenue (Greenheart, ASCAP) 2
Europa & The Pirate Twins (Participation, ASCAP) 97
Every Breath You Take (Magnetic/Reggatta/Illegal, BMI) 1
Ewok Celebration (Warner Tamerlane/Bantha, BMI) 66
Faithfully (Twist and Shout/Weed High Nightmare/Colgems EMI, ASCAP) 59
Fake Friends (Jett Pack, BMI) 57
Family Man (Virgin/Chappell/Josef Weinberger, PRS/TBP/April, ASCAP) 22
Flashdance . . . What A Feeling (Chappell/Famous/GMPC/Alcor, ASCAP) 3
Hold Me 'Til The Mornin' Comes (Squwanko/Foster Frees, BMI) 68
Hot Girls In Love (Dean of Music/Blackwood, BMI) 21
How Am I Supposed To Live Without You (April/Is Hot, ASCAP/Blackwood, BMI) 63
How Do You Keep The Music Playing (WB/ASCAP) 49
Human Touch (Vogue/Welk, BMI) 55
I.O.U. (Vogue/Welk/Chriswald/Hopi/MCA, BMI/ASCAP) 76
I'll Tumble 4 Ya (Virgin/Chappell, ASCAP) 35
I'm Still Standing (Intersong, ASCAP) 12
Inside Love (Music Corporation of America/Kashif, BMI) 98
Is There Something I Should Know (Tritec) 9
It's A Mistake (April, ASCAP) 25
It's Inevitable (T.J.T./Crumpet, ASCAP) 50
Johnny B. Goode (Arc, BMI) 85
Juicy Fruit (Mtume, BMI) 54
(Keep Feeling) Fascination (Virgin/Chappell/Sound Diagrams/WB, ASCAP) 24
Lawyers In Love (Night Kitchen, ASCAP) 40
Legal Tender (Bootant/Island, BMI) 88
Let's Dance (Jones, ASCAP) 45
Little Red Corvette (Controversy, ASCAP) 73
Maniac (Intersong/Famous/Warner Bros., ASCAP) 19
Metro (Berlin Era, BMI) 58
Midnight Blue (Chartel/Arista, ASCAP) 51
My Love (Brockman, ASCAP) 74
Never Gonna Let You Go (ATV/Mann and Weil, BMI) 4
Night Pulse (See No Evil/Keeper, ASCAP) 96
1999 (Controversy, ASCAP) 13
Our House (Nutty Sounds/WB, ASCAP) 8
Overkill (April, ASCAP) 72
Pieces Of Ice (WB/Jamm/Bibo/Welk, ASCAP) 43
Promises, Promises (Rondor, ASCAP) 71
Puttin' On The Ritz (UFA) 42
Rock 'N' Roll Is King (April, ASCAP) 30
Rock Of Ages (Zomba, BMI) 29
Roll Me Away (Gear, ASCAP) 36
Safety Dance (Off Backstreets/Les Editions Chapeau, BMI) 62
Salt In My Tears (Rare Blue/Miserable Melodies, ASCAP) 39
Save The Overtime For Me (Richer/Chappell/Bub's, ASCAP/Jim Ken/Irving/Ljesrika, BMI) 93
Saved By Zero (Colgems EMI, ASCAP) 28
She Blinded Me With Science (Participation, ASCAP) 92
She Works Hard For The Money (Sweet Summer/See This House, ASCAP) 14
She's A Beauty (Foster Frees/Rehtakul Veets/Decomposition/Boone's Tunes, BMI/ASCAP) 23
Shy Boy (MCA, ASCAP) 83
Slipping Away (April, ASCAP) 44
Solid Rock (Uluru, APRA) 79
Space Age Whiz Kid (Wow & Glutter/Marinara, BMI) 52
Stand Back (Welsh Witch, BMI) 11
Stand By (Zomba, BMI) 61
Stop In The Name Of Love (Stone Agate, BMI) 32
Straight From The Heart (Irving/Adams Communications, BMI) 99
Sweet Dreams (Sunbury) 15
Take Me To Heart (Narrow Dude/Bonnie Bee/Good/WB, ASCAP) 27
That's Love (Warner Bros., ASCAP) 84
Til You And Your Lover Are Lovers Again (Warner House Of Music/Pullman/Warner Tamerlane/Daticabo, BMI) 87
Time (Virgin/Chappell, ASCAP) 10
Tonight I Celebrate My Love (Almo/Prince Street/Screen Gems EMI, ASCAP/BMI) 80
Too Shy (Tritec) 7
Total Eclipse Of The Heart (Lost Boys, BMI) 75
Try Again (Walkin, BMI) 47
Waiting For Your Love (E Balastin'/Hudmar, ASCAP) 82
Wanna Be Startin' Somethin' (Mijac/Warner Tamerlane, BMI) 5
War Games (Gold Hill, ASCAP) 48
We Two (Screen Gems-EMI, BMI) 65
West Coast Summer Nights (Not Listed) 78
When You Were Mine (Encirp, BMI) 95
White Wedding (Rare Blue/Bonerdol, ASCAP) 41
Who's Behind The Door? (Riddy Diddy, ASCAP) 81
Wishing (Zomba, BMI) 26
Woman In You (Gibb Brothers/Unichappell, BMI) 64
You Are In My System (Science Lab/Green Star, ASCAP) 86

Compiled by the Music Popularity Chart Dept. of Billboard from national retail store and one-stop sales reports, and radio airplay reports.

JULY 16, 1983, BILLBOARD

Courtesy: Billboard Publications, Inc. 1983. Used by permission.

The Billboard "Hot 100" are watched closely by artists, record executives, and everyone else in the recording industry.

QUERIES AND CONCEPTS

1 How many songs can you name that mark a special place or time for you? Can you remember the first time you heard them? The last time you heard them?

2 Check *Billboard* for the top ten songs of today. Can any of them be traced logically to the roots of early rock? How do the lyrics compare with those of the 1956–1960 era of the birth of rock? Other eras?

3 Do a content analysis of those same top ten songs. What kinds of issues and emotions do their lyrics deal with? Are they largely interpersonal or political? How many deal exclusively with love relationships?

4 "The most creative era of rock was the coming of the Beatles and the more complex lyrics of Bob Dylan. Since that time, rock has made no major steps forward." Support or refute this statement using today's popular songs as evidence.

5 Country and western and rock have borrowed heavily from each other during the last decade. Which has borrowed the most from the other and why? Back your answer with specific songs and lyrics.

6 Spend an hour listening to your favorite music radio station and keep a list of all the songs played. How many fit into the "new music" category? Other categories?

READINGS AND REFERENCES

The Fabulous Phonograph

Roland Gelatt
The Fabulous Phonograph: 1877–1977, 3d ed. New York: Macmillan, 1977.
    This book covers the development of the record player from Edison to stereo with many personal stories about the men and women who made it happen. Particularly good chapters on the early years.

Popular Music in the 1940s

Ian Whitcomb
After the Ball. New York: Simon & Schuster, 1973.

You may recognize the author's name. He's a former rock star who took to writing about music after his fall from the charts. This is a panorama of popular music "from rag to rock," written in an entertaining style. There are sections on jazz, swing, ragtime, and Tin Pan Alley. Highly recommended.

The Birth of Rock; The British Are Coming!

Carl Belz
The Story of Rock, 2d ed. New York: Oxford University Press, 1972. (Available in paperback from Harper & Row.)
    I prefer this to Charlie Gillett's *The Sound of the City: The Rise of Rock and Roll* (New York: Dutton, 1970),

though both do an admirable job of chronicling the rise of rock from rhythm and blues to the age of the superstars. Belz is the more meticulous writer with his cautious assessment of the contributions of many "sacred cows," including Bill Haley, Chuck Berry, and Elvis Presley. Excellent annotated bibliography.

H. Kandy Rohde, ed.
The Gold of Rock and Roll, 1955–1967. New York: Arbor House, 1970.

> A year-by-year account of *Billboard's* top songs. Included are the Top 10 for each week during the 13 years covered as well as the Top 50 songs (in retail sales) from each year. There are also a brief introduction and some commentary for each year.

The Rock Renaissance

See Alan Aldridge, ed., *The Beatles' Illustrated Lyrics*, 2 vols. (New York: Dell, 1980) and Bob Dylan's *Writings and Drawings* (Westminster, Md.: Knopf, 1973) for the complete works of the two most influential forces on rock in the 1960s.

The Diffusion of Rock;
New Music and the 1980s

Again, things change so rapidly in this area that you are better off going to the *Readers' Guide to Periodical Literature* and *Popular Periodical Index. Rolling Stone* is, again, the number one source. In addition, *Rolling Stone's Illustrated History of Rock and Roll* (New York: Random House, 1981) is the best single source for a panoramic history of rock from the mid-1950s to the early 1980s. Most impor-

tant groups are covered in surprisingly exceptional detail, and the artists' hit records are listed along with their best showing on the charts. A must for every serious rock fan.

Rock and Rote:
The Themes of
Rock Music

Simon Frith
Sound Effects: Youth, Leisure, and the Politics of Rock 'n' Roll. New York: Pantheon Books, 1982.

> Divided into three sections: Rock Meanings (rock roots, rock and mass culture), Rock Production (making music, records, and most important, money), and Rock Consumption (youth, music, sexuality, and leisure). This book is an excellent sociological look at how rock works and why it works. Traces closely the relationship between rock and the mass audience.

Richard Goldstein, ed.
The Poetry of Rock. New York: Bantam Books, 1969.

> A good anthology of significant rock lyrics. This kind of book is rare, since rock artists demand an arm and a leg for reprint rights to lyrics of their songs. It includes some interesting illustrations.

Edward Jay Whetmore
The Magic Medium: An Introduction to Radio in America. Belmont, Calif.: Wadsworth, 1981.

> Two chapters from this text are of particular interest to the student seeking additional information on popular music. Chapter 8 in particular covers the popular-music industry and its relationship to radio programming.

Country and Western Music

"Why Country Music Is Suddenly Big Business," *U.S. News & World Report*, July 29, 1974, pp. 58–60.

Issues and Answers: "And the Hits Just Keep On Comin'"

Theodor W. Adorno
Introduction to the Sociology of Music. New York: Continuum Publishing Co., 1976.

> This collection of philosopher Adorno's lectures on popular music is perhaps the most scathing indictment of the phenomenon published to date. Recently a number of Marxist-oriented scholars of what is called the Frankfurt School have charged rather eloquently that popular music, in fact all popular media, are at least tacitly in league with the capitalist forces that keep "the masses" enslaved. Popular music here is seen to promise "permanent gaiety" yet deliver "inner emptiness."

R. Serge Denisoff
Solid Gold: The Popular Record Industry. New Brunswick, N.J.: Transaction Books, 1981.

> This book is best when describing how the record industry works, how a record becomes a hit, and other processes. Particularly informative regarding the business end, its history and current trends.

Charlie Gillett
Making Tracks: Atlantic Records and the Growth of a Multi-Billion Dollar Industry. New York: Dutton, 1974.

> The author traces the development of Atlantic Records and analyzes its impact on the industry. Using this case-in-point approach, he documents his general statements about industry trends. Recommended reading to those interested in the business.

Geoffrey Stokes
Star-making Machinery: Inside the Business of Rock and Roll. New York: Random House, 1977.

> One critic described this as "simply the best book there is about the business of pop music." At least it is the most concise effort to date. The author concentrates on how the process goes, from artist to record company to consumer, in a refreshing and innovative way. Well indexed.

Television, Part One: Structures and Strategies

8

ON THE EVENING OF NOVEMBER 21, 1980, IN AN ESTIMATED 41.4 million American homes, 83 million viewers had their TV sets tuned to CBS. All these Americans had one common goal: to find out who shot J.R. Ewing, the fictitious villain who dominates Lorimar Productions' *Dallas*. Suspense had been building since the spring of that year, when J.R. finally got what was coming to him in the form of two bullets as he worked late at night in the offices of Ewing Oil.

When all the ratings were in—some three days after viewers had found out that Kristin Shepard, J.R.'s sister-in-law and former mistress, had done the dastardly deed—it was reported that 76 percent, or just over three out of every four Americans who were watching TV during that hour, were tuned in to *Dallas*. That made that episode the most popular regular television event ever. (*Dallas* held that record until the final episode of *M*A*S*H* ran in 1983; see Chapter 9.)

All of this was music to the ears of CBS executives, who had been busily trying to knock off the front-running ABC in the ratings race since the mid-1970s. When we think of TV, we tend to think of our favorite programs, or perhaps those we simply cannot stand. But an important part of the total TV picture involves programming only indirectly. There is a constant war for viewers among the three major networks, independent stations, and dozens of cable suppliers of TV programming. This relentless struggle is as fascinating and frustrating as any *Dallas* episode. The stakes are high, and the twists and turns to the "plot"—that is, the structure and strategies employed—are as difficult to follow as those of any soap opera. For unlike radio, TV was designed as a creature of corporate America right from the beginning.

> Television is one of the most powerful forces man has ever unleashed upon himself. The quality of human life may depend enormously upon our efforts to comprehend and control that force.
>
> NICHOLAS JOHNSON

PIONEERS

The technical devices that make TV possible were developed long before the new medium was "discovered" by society. In 1923 Vladimir Zworykin invented the iconoscope tube (see 8.1). The kinescope came shortly thereafter. These were the technical bases for television as we know it today. Historians usually give credit for the invention of television to Philo Farnsworth, who invented the electric camera, and Allen B. Dumont, who was responsible for the receiving, or "picture," tube. Old-timers will remember the Dumont name; many of the early TV sets were "Dumonts," and once there was even a Dumont Network.

In the beginning, everyone agreed that TV could never replace radio, since radio was the "theater of the imagination." During the late 1930s, experimental broadcasts of major political and sports events began to make more people aware of the tremendous potential of TV. In 1939 a Milwaukee newspaper applied for a *commercial* TV license. Since it was the first such application, the FCC pondered a bit and finally granted it in 1941, along with licenses for nine other stations.

But radio was in its heyday, films were doing better than ever, and Americans had a war to worry about. Only six of the original ten applicants for TV licenses were left in 1945. But at that time the FCC decided that TV was here to stay and allocated band space for 12 VHF, or very high frequency, channels. This move involved cutting back space that had been allotted for FM radio, and it made existing FM receivers obsolete. CBS—which, although experimenting with TV, had invested heavily in new equipment for FM—was badly hurt, and the technical advantage was given to NBC in the new world of television.

In fact, the FCC decision to go primarily with the VHF band helped lead to the domination of television by the networks, since most cities could have only a handful of stations. Had the UHF, or ultra-high frequency, band been utilized as the primary TV broadcast band, each market could have had dozens of channels in just a few years.

By 1948, the FCC was deluged with applications and decided to freeze the granting of licenses until it had more time for study. By the time the freeze was lifted in 1952, one-third of all American families had bought a TV set. Television was enjoying its honeymoon with the American people.

THE GROWTH OF TELEVISION

By the time the freeze was over, most of the country was already involved with Ed Sullivan, Milton Berle, and *I Love Lucy*. The transition from radio to television was brief. Many radio stars fell by the wayside, many switched over to the newer medium, and dozens of new television stars were born overnight. When the freeze ended, there were hundreds of license applications in. By the mid-1960s, there were more than 600 stations on the air, and the number grew to over 1,000 by 1982.

The numbers describing television's hold on the top spot in the media business boggle the mind. According to figures released in 1984 by the A.C. Nielsen Co., America's "television fixation" reached an all time high in 1983 with average daily TV viewing per household surpassing the seven hour mark for the first time. This meant that somewhere in each "average household" a set was turned on for seven hours and two minutes each day, on the average. Over the twenty-four hour broadcast day about 30 percent of all households had at least one set turned on at any given moment. By the time most American children enter kindergarten, they have already spent more hours watching TV than they will spend in college classrooms getting a degree. Those hours come when the child is considerably more open to new impressions and ideas than the average college student. (And information presented on television is designed to keep the "learner" constantly involved and entertained, something I see rarely in college classrooms.)

The FCC set the same evaluation standards for television as it did for radio. Broadcasters were supposed to be broadcasting in the "public interest, convenience, and necessity." Critics are quick to point out that TV stations more often broadcast in their own self-interest. Prime-time programs are aimed at the "lowest common denominator," with the idea that if everyone can understand a show, everyone will watch it. With a large audience come better ratings and more advertising income. Some critics argue that TV programmers should be concerned with quality, and of course they should. The fact is that they aren't (for the most part), and they won't be until it becomes financially rewarding.

Those who criticize these practices forget that the average newspaper is written at an eighth-grade vocabulary level; even the *New York Times* never prints a word that the average high school graduate can't understand. The rationale here is easier to understand if you think of the term *mass medium.* Newspapers, radio, and television are all designed to be consumed by a mass audience, composed of Ph.D.s and high school dropouts. Because of commercial network practices, television cannot cater to only one segment of the audience.

Advertisers are becoming increasingly concerned with the demographics of the mass audience as well as its size. Age, social and ethnic background, and income are factors that determine how receptive a given viewer might be to the sponsor's message.

THE RATINGS WAR

At the heart of the dilemma over the quality of all TV programming is the ratings system currently employed by the three major networks. All three subscribe to the A.C. Nielsen Company's service. Nielsen chooses some 1,700 homes at random to represent all viewers and installs an Audimeter, which automatically records which channel the set is tuned to while it is on. Generally, a Nielsen family or household is so designated for a four-year period. Household members are sworn to secrecy and are not paid. However, Nielsen does pick up half of the TV repair bills during this period. The findings are described in the Nielsen Television Index (NTI).

The NTI provides the fastest possible way for networks and advertisers to know how many households will be reached by a given program. Often information is available in the morning about TV programs that were aired the night before. This is possible because many Audimeters are wired via telephone lines directly to Nielsen headquarters in Florida. Normally the meter is "called" automatically by a computer twice a day to yield tallies of viewer habits.

Of course, the meter cannot tell Nielsen how many people (if any) are watching a given set. To solve this problem the company surveys a *matched sample* of some 2,400 additional homes. Members of these households keep a diary that reveals their viewing habits as well as their demographic characteristics: age, sex, ethnic origin, and other data. Nielsen combines this information with that obtained from the Audimeters for its final NTI reports.

These reports are then used by national advertisers to determine their *CPM*, or *cost per thousand*. (The "M" comes from the Roman numeral designation for 1,000.) CPM is a vital statistic for advertisers, since it allows

8.1

Time Line: The History of American Television

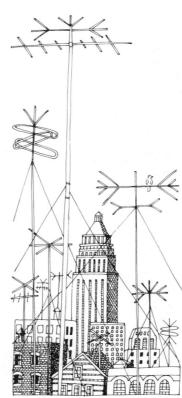

1907 The word *television* is first used in *Scientific American.*

1923 Vladimir Zworykin invents the iconoscope tube.

1927 Philo Farnsworth applies for a patent on an "electronic television system."

1936 Regularly scheduled TV begins in Great Britain.

1939 RCA demonstrates television at the New York World's Fair.

1940 The Journal Company of Milwaukee (now the owner of WTMJ-TV) applies for the first commercial television broadcasting license.

1944 Sponsors begin to buy TV time.

1945 FCC moves FM radio to another place on the band and gives part of the FM band to TV.

1946 First demonstrations of color television are given by CBS and NBC.

1948 FCC freezes granting new TV licenses.

1951 Movie attendance declines in many cities that have TV.

1951 NBC *Today* show begins, and CBS airs *See It Now.*

1953 First noncommercial TV programming, in Houston, Texas.

1954 The Army-McCarthy hearings are shown on TV; Edward R. Murrow challenges McCarthy on *See It Now.*

1955 *The $64,000 Question* begins, the first successful big-money TV quiz show.

1956 The Eisenhower-Stevenson presidential campaign is covered extensively by all networks.

1959 Westerns, including *Gunsmoke, Have Gun, Will Travel, Rifleman, Maverick,* and *Wyatt Earp,* dominate the ratings.

1959 Quiz-show scandals sweep TV, and networks become more responsible for programs. Sponsors have less to say.

1960 Nixon-Kennedy debate is the first of TV's presidential "Great Debates."

1961 FCC Chairman Newton Minow describes TV as a "vast wasteland."

1962 *The Beverly Hillbillies* is the latest rage.

1963 The assassination of John Kennedy brings the nation together in a communal electronic experience.

1966 FCC assumes control over cable television in a precedent-setting decision.

1966 *Bonanza* is the number one prime-time show; it stresses traditional American values.

1968 *Rowan and Martin's Laugh-In* pioneers a new kind of made-for-TV comedy.

1968 The Robert Kennedy and Martin Luther King assassinations and funerals are covered by TV.

1968 Unprecedented viewer protests bring *Star Trek* back for a third season.

1969 CBS cancels *The Smothers Brothers Comedy Hour,* deeming its political satire too controversial.

1969 There is live TV coverage of the first moon landing.

1970 *The Mary Tyler Moore Show* premieres.

1971 *All in the Family* is the first of Norman Lear's controversial but successful sitcoms.

1972 Television is blamed for the death of *Life* magazine.

1973 Televised hearings of the Watergate affair give Americans a chance to see the cast of characters.

1973 *Upstairs, Downstairs* is first aired on PBS.

1974 Televised impeachment hearings of the House Judiciary Committee again focus the nation's attention on Watergate.

1976 The bionic man and woman help push ABC to the top of national prime-time ratings; CBS is second.

1976 Norman Lear airs the controversial *Mary Hartman, Mary Hartman* without network backing by syndicating it to local stations.

1977 *Roots,* a special eight-part ABC made-for-TV movie, becomes the most watched mini-series of all time. Its success prompts dozens of multiple-part "specials" to compete with regular weekly shows.

1978 Controversial programmer Fred Silverman takes over as president of the NBC television network.

1980 An episode of *Dallas* becomes the most-watched show with a 53.3 Nielsen rating and a 76 percent share of the audience.

1981 Fred Silverman is fired as president of NBC television. Former MTM head Grant Tinker is signed to replace him.

1982 After sweeping the Emmy awards, NBC's *Hill Street Blues* becomes one of prime time's top-rated shows.

1983 Mobil creates a temporary network for the showing of *Nicholas Nickleby.*

1984 The three networks face tougher times as research indicates viewers are increasingly attracted to HBO and other non-network offerings.

1984 In a controversial 5–4 decision, the Supreme Court rules that the videotaping of television programs for private use does *not* violate the copyright law.

them to determine how much money they paid to reach each thousand viewers during a particular show. Obviously, the lower the CPM, the better the bargain for the advertiser.

A second service provided by Nielsen is the Nielsen Station Index (NSI), oriented to the local television market. Nielsen divides the country into 220 designated market areas (DMAs). There is a separate NSI for each DMA. Information from viewers in these markets is gathered exclusively via the diary method. Over 90,000 diaries are mailed out annually.

The NSI tells advertisers which TV stations in each local market viewers report they are watching. Thus the NSI includes independent as well as network stations and serves local as well as national advertisers. All of this is very expensive, and about 80 percent of the costs are borne by the stations themselves. Charges are based on the size of the market. It is not unusual for a station in a major market to pay more than $50,000 a year for the service, while stations in small markets may pay as little as $10,000 annually.

Nielsen's main competitor in the TV ratings business is Arbitron, Inc. Arbitron also uses the diary method, surveying more than 200 TV markets a year. Like Nielsen, Arbitron issues regular reports, usually four a year in major markets.

All the networks subscribe to both services, as do most local stations. They often choose the one that reports the best ratings to ballyhoo in their sales literature. While Arbitron is recognized as the leader in radio ratings, it has continually lagged behind Nielsen in TV.

In recent years, Arbitron has begun using meters in some of the major markets in an attempt to topple Nielsen from first place. There is a war even between those who provide the ratings for the ratings war.

RATING THE RATINGS: PROBLEMS AND PARADOXES

A ratings book for a major market is an impressive sight: hundreds of pages crammed with tiny numbers (see 8.2). Viewers are carefully categorized by age, sex, and countless other subdivisions. The temptation for most of us is to believe what is written there. Yet at the back of each book, Arbitron reminds us in small type: *"Remember, ratings are only estimates."* That crucial little reminder is often overlooked by advertisers and stations alike. A number of things can influence ratings and affect their usefulness. First, both Arbitron and Nielsen suggest that any figures they issue can vary by plus or minus 5 percent because of sampling errors. This is because it is not practical for ratings services to survey every TV user in the country. Hence they must choose a *sample* to represent all viewers. Nielsen claims that its sample of 1,700 homes can deliver estimates that do not vary more than plus or minus 5 percent from the actual number of people watching.

Audimeters can tell only whether a set is on. They cannot tell who, if anyone, is watching, why they are watching, or whether they see a specific commercial.

Diaries can give supplemental information that meters cannot, but do they? There is a phenomenon known as viewer fatigue. Viewers might be very good about filling in their diaries for the first few days during the week, but they inevitably lose interest as the week goes on. This problem became so acute that some years ago both services began starting their survey week on Thursday or Friday so that there would be more accurate viewer information during the crucial weekend period.

Certainly there must be some viewers who, knowing that they will be counted as representing thousands of households, cannot resist

8.2

This compilation of figures is from an Arbitron book for Los Angeles. In the 8:30 time slot we see Private Benjamin *and* One Day at a Time *on CBS competing with ABC's* Monday Night Football *and* That's Incredible. *Meanwhile, NBC offered* Little House on the Prairie. *In this book, at least, ABC appeared to be the winner.*

©Arbitron Ratings Company, 1982. Used with permission for educational purposes only.

Weekly Program Estimates — **Time Period Average Estimates**

Arbitron ratings table for Los Angeles, Monday, November 1982 Time Period Averages (TPA-31). Columns include Day and Time, Station, Program; Week-by-Week ADI TV HH Ratings (Wk 1–4); ADI TV HH; ADI TV HH Share/HUT Trends; Metro TV HH; TV HH; and Total Survey Area in thousands for Persons, Women, and Men across various age groups.

LOS ANGELES   TPA-31   MONDAY   NOVEMBER 1982 TIME PERIOD AVERAGES

* SAMPLE BELOW MINIMUM FOR WEEKLY REPORTING
** SHARE/HUT TRENDS NOT AVAILABLE
··· DID NOT ACHIEVE A REPORTABLE WEEKLY RATING
‡ TECHNICAL DIFFICULTY
▲ COMBINED PARENT/SATELLITE
▲ SEE TABLE ON PAGE iv

the temptation to "play God" by reporting that they watched programs that *they think* the rest of the country should be watching, rather than what they actually watched.

Diary participation is another problem. Only about 54 percent of all diaries mailed are returned in usable order. Do the viewing habits of those who do not return their diaries or those who fill them out improperly differ from those who do? Both ratings services contend that they do not, but no one really knows for sure.

Finally, there is the phenomenon known as the "sweep period." These typically occur three times each year, when the ratings taken will determine what the advertising rates will be for that "book." It means that local news shows will be running more sensationalized material and that TV networks will introduce their "blockbuster" films and other specials with high ratings potential. This often means tough decisions for the viewers, since two or three "must-see" movies may run at the same time. Of course this also means that during nonsweep weeks there may be little of inter- on any channel for many viewers.

It's safe to say that ratings should be taken with at least a few large grains of salt. After all, they are only estimates. However, advertising agencies, stations, and networks all tend to treat them as gospel. Until these attitudes change, or until some more accurate and economically feasible ways of gathering ratings appear, we are all stuck with them pretty much the way they are.

THE ECONOMICS OF NETWORK PROGRAMMING

We have seen that the ratings play a major role in determining the financial stability of every TV station. Since advertisers accept the ratings as indications of how many view-

ers will be exposed to their message, networks have no choice but to try to line up the programs that will reach and hold the largest possible audience and thus receive the highest ratings. High ratings guarantee networks that it will be easy to sell out available commercial space and make a profit.

Contrary to popular belief, networks produce very few of their own programs. Most of the time they rely on individual production companies, such as Tandem and Lorimar, to produce the shows they need for prime time. In fact, the FCC has discouraged networks from producing their own shows, for fear they will monopolize broadcasting even more than they already do. Thus the networks buy a product (program), provide the means to distribute that product (local affiliates), and make their money by selling commercial time to national advertisers. If the networks pay too much for a program, or if ratings are low, they cannot hope to make a profit.

Programming costs have skyrocketed in recent years, which has affected all other factors in determining network fortunes. As recently as 1968, the average cost for a 30-minute situation comedy was about $70,000 an episode. Now the networks routinely pay a quarter of a million dollars or more an episode. According to *Broadcasting* magazine, the one-hour show on the 1980 schedule that was cheapest to produce was CBS's own *60 Minutes*, at about $140,000 an episode. Among the most expensive was Spelling/Goldberg Productions' *Charlie's Angels*, at a hefty $750,000 an episode, or approximately $20 million for a 26-week season. Interestingly, many of these shows actually cost more to produce than the network pays. They are "money losers" for their producers during their prime-time network runs. It is only through syndication, when production companies sell reruns to local stations, that profits are realized. Nevertheless, by 1981 the networks were spending about $40 million a week for first-run programming. That comes to a total of about $2 billion every year.

To offset these increased costs, networks have had to charge advertisers steeper rates. It is now routine to pay $100,000 or more to air a 30-second commercial. When the "Who Shot J.R.?" episode of *Dallas* ran in the fall of 1980, the rates were said to be $250,000 for 30 seconds, or a cool $3 million for the six available minutes. CBS topped that figure in the spring of 1983 when advertisers wishing to air their 30-second messages during the final 2½-hour episode of *M*A*S*H* paid an estimated $450,000 apiece.

TV AS MOVIE

One way network executives have tried to cope with increasing series costs is through the use of the "made-for-TV" movies.

TV movies did not become popular until the mid-1960s, when the burgeoning budgets of traditional formats made it cheaper to film a 90- or 120-minute made-for-TV movie than three or four 30-minute shows. The made-for-TV movie usually suffers by comparison with those designed for theaters. TV movies are filmed for 50 percent or less money than their theatrical counterparts, and it shows. Still, some have been outstanding. Made-for-TV movies have treated controversial subjects like homosexuality, rape, incest, drugs, and abortion. There have even been made-for-TV disaster movies. The attitude of their promoters seems to be, Anything theatrical movies can do, we can do cheaper. Despite the low budgets, the mass audience watches made-for-TV movies. Often, a heavily promoted made-for-TV movie will "outrate" other shows offered at the same time.

Though single-event made-for-TV-movies still abound, the 1970s saw the coming of the *mini-series*. In actuality, most mini-series are movies running some 10–18 hours in length.

No theater audience could sit still for such a long time, but by dividing the showing of long films into four or five evenings the networks have been able to generate a unique audience involvement.

The Day After, perhaps the most widely publicized event of this kind, brought kudos and healthy ratings to ABC when it aired late in 1983. A gripping "real life" type account of World War III, the mini-series was surrounded by controversy and received extensive press coverage.

Other popular mini-series "events" have drawn on historical themes or been based on real life events. *Docu-dramas*, as they are sometimes called, combine historical fact and scriptwriter imagination *(Kennedy, Sadat)*.

Actors, actresses, scriptwriters, and other people involved in the creative end of the business generally laud the mini-series. Here is the potential to develop characters in a way not possible in films made for the theater. *Roots*, *Shogun*, and *The Thorn Birds* serve as sterling examples of the potential for high-quality movies in this genre.

MOVIE AS TV

A major source of TV programming is still theatrical films. Each night there is at least one full-length feature film sliced up for commercial TV. The frank nature of many contemporary films has forced the networks to issue audience warnings before they air them. But network censors and the public are both becoming more lenient about what they will tolerate on the air, and many R-rated films arrive on TV with minimal cuts.

At first, only second-rate theater films came to TV, but now the networks bid astounding sums for the right to "premiere" a major motion picture. *TV Guide* reported that NBC paid $5 million for a single airing of *Gone with the Wind* in 1976. NBC lost money, even

"*It's the very beginning of the first part of a sixty-five-part, two-hundred-and-sixty-hour mini-series spread out over twenty-nine months. Want to watch?*"

Drawing by Maslin; © 1983 The New Yorker Magazine, Inc.

though the movie had the largest TV audience ever to that date. Network executives claimed that the "prestige" of being *the* network that showed the film made up the difference. In addition, that huge audience was turned to NBC when the next program aired. The same was true when NBC bought and aired *The Godfather* films in 1977.

The most common viewer complaint is that these movies are cut up so badly that the filmmaker's intent is lost between dog-food and deodorant commercials. *Gone with the Wind*, for example, was 3 hours and 40 minutes long, but it was spread over two nights and interrupted by 78 minutes of station breaks and commercials. This does make a difference; whenever there is transfer of content from one medium to another, there is change. A theatrical movie that appears on TV is no longer a movie—it is television, with all of the limitations that implies.

There are some important reasons TV is not cinema. While television is something we take for granted, a movie is an *event*. When we enter a theater, we *expect* a lot; after all, we paid to get in. The screen is huge; the picture is bright, colorful, and larger than life. TV is different. We may not "plan" to watch it but flip it on when there is nothing else to do. We watch it casually, and if the program is poor, we can always turn it off and do something else . . . like go out to a movie!

But the networks try to accommodate the audience's desire for living-room cinema, announcing films as "major events" and padding introductions by saying, "You are watching the television premiere of a major motion picture: *The Thing That Devoured Toledo*." Many local stations have gone one step further, presenting certain films without commercial interruption. The idea is to sell the time immediately before and after the movie for enough money to make up the difference.

For better or worse, all types of movies are a prime source of television programming. Each of the three major networks feeds its local affiliates about 18 hours of programs a day, 7 days a week, 365 days a year. That comes to about 20,000 hours every year. Sometimes local stations will buy their own prints of certain films, which is why they seem to show the same obscure "B" films over and over again. Movies will probably remain a significant (yet still relatively cheap) source of prime-time programming. What's more, the movie studios are cranking out many made-for-TV films. Without the extra income from TV, they might have gone bankrupt years ago. This is another part of the curious symbiosis between the film and television industries.

NETWORK DECISION MAKERS

For all of the contributions that movies have made to TV programming, it is still the hit series that seems to make or break a network's ratings. Given the economic realities of the business and the incessant pressure from advertisers for high-rated shows, it's no wonder that network programming executives stay up nights trying to decide which of the many proposed new series should appear on the fall schedule.

Former NBC president Fred Silverman, perhaps the most controversial network decision maker in the history of the medium, estimates that in any one season each network receives about 1,200 series submissions. These can range from an outline of a few pages to a completed script. The network will then agree to finance between 120 and 150 completed scripts. Of these, about a third, say 40 to 50, will be made into a *pilot*—a single episode to test on potential audiences. These pilots will then compete for the dozen or so slots that might be available in the network's schedule. Silverman says with some justification, "I don't think there is any more competitiveness anywhere than that involved in getting a show on the air."

The mortality rate of those that do make it is also high. In fact, only about one in ten new shows will be back for a second season. Thus the odds of the original submission's becoming a hit series are in the neighborhood of 1,000 to 1. Yet, as has been pointed out, one hit series can often make the difference between being the number one network and number two. Millions of dollars ride on the outcome.

As a viewer, you may feel that the quality of many new shows—and even some hits—is questionable. How do producers decide what shows to sell to the networks?

In a local ABC newscast in Los Angeles some years ago, producer Aaron Spelling (*Charlie's Angels, Love Boat, Fantasy Island*) revealed that "we try to anticipate what the audience wants to see, and of course we have to anticipate what the networks will buy too. . . ."

Three thousand miles away in New York City, network programming executives are scrambling to try to fill holes in their schedules and to come up with as many hit series as possible. This is not an easy task. Why are there so many mediocre shows? Many blame producers like Spelling; ultimately, however, it comes back to the public. Spelling points out that "you can be a marvelous shoe salesman, but it's the customer that buys the shoes."

To predict public reaction to new pilots, networks have become increasingly involved in audience research. In Los Angeles at an institution known as the Preview House, pilots for new series and freshly made commercials are aired on a regular basis. Volunteers, some of whom are wired to electronic machines that measure physiological reactions indicating emotional response, watch program after program and feed millions of bits of data into a computer. Silverman feels that the industry-wide trend toward more empirical research results in an increase of lowest-common-denominator programs, those that offend no one yet please no one.

Despite this process, someone out there is being offended. According to *TV Guide*, the Reverend Jerry Falwell, whose Moral Majority played a role in the election of Ronald Reagan and other conservatives in 1980, revealed that his organization was turning its attention to television. It has attempted to decide which aspects of TV are unacceptable, "such as bedroom scenes and the use of vulgar language." The group has begun economic boycotts against the sponsors of such "unacceptable" shows by its estimated 21 million followers.

With increasing production costs, the public's continuous clamoring for "quality shows," the threat of economic sanctions by the Moral Majority, and competition from cable outlets as well as the Public Broadcasting Service, the road ahead does not look smooth for commercial television's network decision makers.

PUBLIC TV

During the 1950s there was much excitement about a possible "educational" TV network, one that would provide traditional classes and create a "university of the air." But educators found they could not tape lectures, put them over the air, and interest the audience, even when they offered college credit. The programs were not visually appealing. Content criteria were borrowed from print, and often too much information was crammed into too short a time.

Although the educational-TV idea of the 1950s did not work, public television still exists in the form of noncommercial stations funded by government, corporate, and viewer contributions. In 1970 an alliance known as the Public Broadcasting Service (PBS) was formed.

At first glance it would seem that noncommercial stations have a big advantage over their competitors. After all, they offer programs uninterrupted by hypes for denture adhesives or underarm deodorant. Yet in every major market, noncommercial viewers total less than 5 percent of the audience. Why?

Public TV stations have not succeeded with the mass audience because their programming form does not live up to audience expectations created by the slicker commercial programs. In fact, some public TV programmers have deliberately avoided appearing slick. Smooth acting, professional editing, exact lighting, and perfect timing have become the hallmark of commercial prime-time programming. Some noncommercial outlets have lagged behind and presented "talking heads" (two or three people sitting on stage just talking to one another). For example:

Fade in: Two people are seated in a bare room, discussing the economic implications of the currency exchange rate between the United States and Uganda. The lighting is poor, and shadows cross the faces of both participants. They talk back and forth for what seems like hours. Neither has much professional TV experience, so both sweat nervously. The camera operator can't hold the lens still, and the picture is occasionally out of focus. There are only two cameras, so we change from close-up to long shot to close-up to long shot. Since this is all live, we get every mistake and embarrassing redundancy.

Pretty soon you say, "Hey, let's turn this off and go out to a movie."

Envision the same program as it might be handled by a top commercial television producer:

Fade in: Film of violence in Uganda. Quick cut to violence on the streets of New York City. Suddenly two small green spots appear in the middle of the screen, and as the music builds they get larger and larger—there they are—dollar signs! A relaxed emcee looks straight into the camera; behind him is a revolving set of books, lights, colors, charts, and world map. It whirls by as he says in perfect pear-shaped tones: "Uganda, the United States, and money. What's going on here? We'll find out, right after this message."

You say, "No thanks, I know you have free front-row tickets to the Rolling Stones concert, but I can't go just now. I have to stay and see what's happening between the United States and Uganda."

I exaggerate, of course, but you get the point. Our experiences with commercial TV have shown us that visual form is much more important than story content. *All in the Family* scripts were good, but audience reaction was strongest when those incredible exasperated looks crept across Archie's face. Without his uttering a word, we knew he'd had enough of "the dingbat." The popularity of shows like *Love Boat* and *Fantasy Island* has more to do with scene than with script. *The A Team* did not rise to popularity on the strength of its story line.

Almost any subject can interest the mass audience if the visual form is attractive. The success of *60 Minutes* proved that the mass audience could be drawn to documentary material if it was packaged in a form that met its expectations. And when public TV does air material of professional (commercial?) quality, it is often a success. English imports like *Upstairs, Downstairs* and *Civilisation* had surprisingly strong ratings. *Sesame Street* was a collage of bright colors, clever editing, and professional production techniques. Its form became a model for commercial children's programs.

Of course, such productions are usually more expensive than talking heads. This means that public TV stations must be funded adequately if they are to compete for the mass

audience. But Congress is getting tired of funding a television network that serves so few citizens. If this vicious circle continues, there will be no public television in America, and a great opportunity will have been lost.

Not everyone would agree that public TV has failed. Some contend that noncommercial stations exist to offer an alternative to commercial fare. Even if only one person is watching, they have succeeded. But again, television is a *mass* medium, and the *mass* audience is what it's there for.

All TV is educational. It teaches us cultural norms, speech patterns, and interpersonal strategies. It is possible to teach any social, moral, or political subject via TV if programs are packaged properly. *Sesame Street* and *The Electric Company* are large-scale examples, and their success may finally have shaken the educational-TV establishment awake (see 8.3, 8.4).

UHF AND LPTV

Of the more than 700 commercial TV stations on the air, about 25 percent are UHF, channels 14–83. UHF also accounts for more than half of the 250 noncommercial stations. When the FCC ended the freeze on new licenses in 1952, it added 70 new UHF channels to the 12 existing VHF channels, 2–13. But there were already millions of TV sets in America not equipped to receive the new channels. It wasn't until 1964 that it became mandatory for manufacturers to add UHF. By the late 1970s, some commercial UHF stations were earning a profit, particularly those in smaller cities where they were the only outlet for local TV advertising.

Most UHF stations in major markets have had an uphill battle. Many commercial UHF stations are independent, since they entered the market too late to be affiliated with one

8.3

Judy Graubart's gesture tells young viewers that the "e" is silent in this scene from The Electric Company. *Like* Sesame Street, The Electric Company *uses exciting visual form to teach traditional language content to children.*

of the networks. This means they must pay for the programs they air, which limits them to syndicated shows that ran in network prime time years ago, old movies, and locally produced efforts hardly up to network standards. Ten percent of the TV sets in service are still without UHF, and all sets need a special antenna to receive the higher channels. Given all these drawbacks, most viewers stay with VHF channels.

UHF has one distinct advantage: There is a lot more room for growth. Many predict rapid growth for UHF when cable TV comes of age. Viewing habits could diversify as more channels become available. The pattern would be like radio in the 1950s. Rather than relying on a few mass-audience stations, viewers would seek out those more closely in tune with their own particular tastes and interests. The FCC requires all cable companies

to carry all VHF and UHF stations in a market. Hence cable subscribers can tune in any station with equal ease, and every station's reception is equally clear.

The advent of cable and the refinement of broadcast transmission techniques have induced the FCC to authorize licenses for a large number of new UHF stations. Several minority groups (see 8.5) have been active applicants for these new licenses, but large corporations and other traditional applicants are competing for them as well.

Destined to have an even greater impact on the video scene are low-power television stations (LPTV). By the end of 1983 the FCC had granted licenses to over 200 new LPTV stations and construction permits for another 150. When they first authorized the new service in 1982, the FCC estimated that it was possible to license as many as 4,000 new sta-

8.5
Minorities in the Broadcast Media: A Score Card

Because the broadcast industry holds such a special place in our society, and because broadcast media have such a tremendous influence on the way we perceive reality, concern has been growing about the role that women and minority groups will have in shaping its future. Of course the place where these groups can have the most influence is within the structure of broadcasting itself. Hence many stations and other broadcast employers, with an occasional nudge from the FCC or the federal government, have been making extra efforts to hire women and minority-group members. Here are the results to date and some predictions for the future.

Women started actively seeking media employment in the 1970s. Particularly irked by the hiring of women exclusively as secretaries and receptionists, they demanded that networks and stations recruit women for management positions.

The FCC currently examines the employment practices of virtually every station at license-renewal time, and its "rule by raised eyebrows" routine is having its usual effect. At present, women make up about one-third of the work force at the network headquarters and at network-owned and -operated stations. It's likely that the FCC will soon begin inquiry into the limited role women play in policy and decision making at all three networks.

Currently, women control less than 2 percent of broadcast properties; American Women in Radio and Television (AWRT) is offering seminars for women who want to get involved in broadcast ownership.

In the area of sales, however, things are booming. It is not unusual for a major-market radio station to have more female account executives than males. The reason is quite simple: Stations are finding that men, who make the majority of media-buying decisions, are more likely to buy from a woman than they are from another man.

Women with technical expertise can virtually "write their own ticket," according to one source, because there are so few of them. Thus the prospects in engineering and production will be particularly bright for women in the years ahead.

Blacks have been particularly prominent in the programming side of television in recent years. In the 1960s, Bill Cosby costarred in *I Spy* and thus became the first black continuing character in a network prime-time series. Since then, of course, numerous programs featuring black characters have aired, most of them situation comedies: *The Jeffersons, Good Times, Sanford,* and *Benson,* to name just a few. From a strictly statistical point of view, blacks are overrepresented in prime-time TV. But the crucial question may be *How* are they represented? As one critic noted: "Why is Benson a butler? James Earl Jones a super cop? George Jefferson still a predictable buffoon? Everything is still set in an *Amos 'n' Andy* format."

Hispanics are making their presence increasingly felt in broadcasting. Organized professional groups such as the California Chicano News Media Association have been instrumental in placing an increasing number of Hispanics in broadcasting positions.

Sesame Street is one of a number of television programs that have begun to introduce some Hispanic culture into the mainstream. Chances are that a greater awareness of Chicano and other Hispanic cultures will spur a growth in the number of broadcast positions open for Hispanic job seekers.

Advertisers are just now beginning to realize the tremendous potential in Spanish-language stations operating in such diverse communities as El Paso, New York, and San Francisco. Employment opportunities at such stations are obviously geared toward Hispanics; the important challenge lies in bringing more Hispanics into the traditionally "Anglo" broadcast media, and in giving those already employed the opportunity for upward mobility.

ISSUES AND ANSWERS: WHO'S IN CHARGE HERE?

Eric Sevareid has pointed out: "Until a few years ago every American assumed he possessed an equal and God-given expertise on three things: politics, religion, and the weather. Now a fourth has been added: television." Television, like the weather, is something that everybody talks about but few people do anything about.

It's hard for the average TV consumer to understand how so many poor-quality programs get on the air. It's equally hard to understand how a station pledged to operate in the *public* "interest, convenience, and necessity" can devote so much air time to commercials touting the *private* enterprises of thousands of sponsors. For that matter, a sizable minority of TV's potential audience finds nothing in the medium that interests it, so it watches little or none at all.

But what can the public do about such matters? And isn't the FCC supposed to act as a watchdog and make sure TV stations are programming in the public "interest, convenience, and necessity"? Why isn't the FCC doing its job?

Some of the most salient criticism of network television practices has come from Nicholas Johnson, an FCC commissioner during Lyndon Johnson's administration. His book *How to Talk Back to Your Television Set*, which deals with the whole issue of who controls television, will never *really* be dated as long as broadcast licensing procedures stay the same (see 8.6). And they have changed very little since 1934, when the present system was set up.

As with radio, TV channels have practically become the property of the licensees. Only on the rarest of occasions does the FCC refuse to renew a license, and then only for flagrant violation of broadcast law. More often, "warnings" will be issued, or licenses will be renewed for one year instead of the usual three. Johnson's book points out that there is really no deep, dark conspiracy between the broadcast industry and the agency that is supposed to regulate it. It's much more subtle than that. Over the years, friendships develop; lawyers meet lawyers and go out to dinner. It's just a lot more "pleasant" if licenses are granted as a matter of course, and a lot more practical as well.

License renewals involve mountains of paperwork, and the FCC does not have a large enough staff to review every word or to monitor every program. In addition to the paperwork, the FCC budget must sustain a small core of field engineers whose job it is to make sure stations are not straying from their assigned frequencies and power limits. There is little time to monitor program content; it is enough to worry about outright violations of broadcast law without getting into gray areas like program "quality." The FCC takes the stations' word that "good works" are being done for the community.

Johnson concludes that if the public wants change, it is going to have to invest its own time and energy, do the necessary research, and submit findings to the FCC, the press, and anyone else who will listen. He suggests that though the FCC responds to pressure from the broadcast industry, it also responds to pressure "from anybody." Ralph Nader has shown just how much impact citizens' groups can have. The 1970s was an era when citizen lobbies made significant inroads into corporate America. Many groups have used the courts in their quest, and class-action suits have appeared with greater frequency. Perhaps it is a fantasy to envision

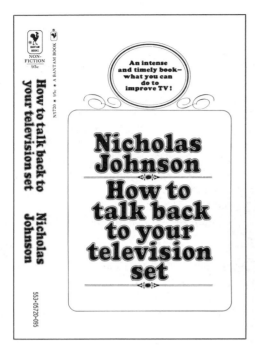

8.6

He has been called everything from the "hostile hippie" to the "citizens' least frightened friend in Washington." He is Nicholas Johnson, author of How to Talk Back to Your Television Set, *one-time FCC commissioner, and still a force to be reckoned with in broadcasting. So critical of the corporate interests controlling broadcasting was Johnson that the industry magazine,* Broadcasting, *called him "a shrill and frequent critic of his elders" and predicted that when his term ended there would be "dancing in the streets." When he left office in 1973, no unusual dancing was seen to take place, but some reported a huge sigh of relief from broadcasters all over the country.*

citizens banding together to sue local stations for presenting inferior programs, but after all, the local station is legally pledged to operate in your "interest, convenience, and necessity." If you feel that it's breaking that pledge or could be doing a lot better, there are ways to bring about change.

Letters to the local station are not thrown away but are carefully filed. You will get a response, particularly if you mail a carbon copy to the FCC, which also keeps all letters it receives. This material is reviewed when the station comes up for license renewal. Be as specific as you can about your complaint; write one letter for each practice or program you find objectionable. Sponsors are particularly sensitive to letters of this type.

Your letters take on increased significance when you have collected data to back your value judgments. Is your local station airing too much advertising? Get out a stopwatch: Just exactly how many minutes of commercials are aired each hour? Is enough time devoted to public-service announcements? What about the balance between news, entertainment, and other types of programs? A quick check of the TV schedule will tell you how many hours a week are devoted to various program types.

Many women's groups brought about change by taking apart the content of the shows themselves. Are minorities fairly represented? Remember that even if a show is piped in by the network, *your local station* is responsible. The FCC does not license networks; it licenses local stations.

Most stations are members of the National Association of Broadcasters (NAB) and as such subscribe to the NAB code, which has rules of conduct governing news and editorial practices and limitations on commercials. Unfortunately, the NAB has no staff to monitor stations, but again you can be of service. It's no secret that many stations operate in direct violation of the code by running excessive amounts of commercials and making few attempts to bring diverse programming to their viewers. If a station is violating the code, the NAB should be notified and the seal of approval withdrawn.

The urgency of such actions seems particularly acute now as the FCC turns its attentions toward the "deregulation" of television. In 1983 the Commission issued a "notice of proposed rulemaking" that would eliminate guidelines that force stations to offer a certain percentage of nonentertainment programming. In addition, the limit on the number of commercials broadcast per hour would be eliminated with the hope that stations would not overload their audiences with commercials because of marketplace constraints.

Many organizations have been formed by citizens determined to improve television offerings. All provide literature and suggestions about what you can do to improve TV.

All of this may sound like a lot of work and bother, and perhaps it is. Still, one letter can sometimes make all the difference. Take heart from the story of John Banzhaf, a lawyer who got tired of seeing all those cigarette commercials on TV in the 1960s. He reasoned that if stations are required to give various political partisans "equal time," why weren't antismoking forces given air time, too?

He challenged all stations indirectly but narrowed his focus to one. He authenticated his claim by monitoring New York's WCBS-TV and citing specific commercials. That one letter, carefully documented, opened the door for a new FCC ruling: Stations had a responsibility to air the "other side" of the smoking question. Millions and millions of dollars' worth of broadcast time was offered to antismoking groups, who produced a series of rather clever ads. Eventually, cigarette commercials were banned from radio and television. And it all started with one letter.

QUERIES AND CONCEPTS

1 Do you feel that the incessant competition between the TV networks helps or hurts the quality of television programs currently offered? Why/why not?

2 Many TV critics contend that the quality of TV programs should be improved. But network programming executives are quick to point out that the ratings offer

solid proof that the public would rather watch *Dynasty* than Shakespeare. Make a list of all of the ways you can think of that the ratings, as they are currently conducted, affect network program decision making. Discuss.

3 Do you have cable TV in your area? How much does it cost per month? What does cable provide that broadcast TV cannot? What percentage of homes in your area have cable? Many cable outlets offer you the chance to produce, direct, and star in your own TV show. Investigate.

4 Compare and contrast a random hour of public TV and an hour of commercial TV.

What could commercial programmers learn from public programmers and vice versa?

5 You have just been awarded an LPTV license for your area. What type of programs do you intend to put on the air? Why?

6 After reading 8.5, do you feel that commercial television employers and programmers are doing enough to encourage minority participation in the broadcast media? If not, can you think of three specific suggestions that might help?

READINGS AND REFERENCES

Note: Many of the books in the Readings and References for Chapter 6 have a section dealing with television. Agee, Ault, and Emery's *Introduction to Mass Communications* (New York: Dodd, Mead, 1970) has a very useful bibliography if you want to focus on the contribution of some specific person.

Pioneers

Erik Barnouw
A History of Broadcasting in the United States, 3 vols. *The Image Empire from 1950.* New York: Oxford University Press, 1970.

This is the third volume of the most quoted historical treatment of the rise of the electronic media. It deals with television as a societal force. There is ample material on the early TV hardware and software pioneers.

Erik Barnouw
Tube of Plenty: The Evolution of American Television. New York: Oxford University Press, 1975.

This is an updated and abridged version of Barnouw's treatment of TV in his historical trilogy. Included are sections on prime time and the rise of the major network corporations and advertising.

The Growth of Television

Laurence Bergreen
Look Now, Pay Later: The Rise of Network Broadcasting. Garden City, N.Y.: Doubleday, 1980.

A highly readable inside view of the rise of network broadcasting in America. The final section, "Signs of Obsolescence," critically examines the prospective role the networks will play in shaping broadcasting's future.

Ron Lackmann
Remember Television. New York: G. P. Putnam's, 1971.

An interesting collection of stars and shows from 1947 to 1958. Highlights include a *New York Times* TV guide from those years, as well as a paragraph or two on all the popular programs of the era. Useful index.

The Ratings War; Rating the Ratings: Problems and Paradoxes

Arbitron is very helpful about supplying students and others with support materials regarding its ratings. Especially useful is the monthly newsletter, *Beyond the Ratings*. Address inquiries to Arbitron Company, Inc., 1350 Avenue of the Americas, New York, NY 10019.

Elizabeth J. Heighton
Don R. Cunningham
Advertising in the Broadcast and Cable Media, 2nd ed. Belmont, Calif.: Wadsworth, 1984.

An excellent primer for those interested in the business side of broadcasting. Ratings and their relationship to buying and selling time in radio, TV, and cable are covered in Section Three.

The Economics of Network Programming; Network Decision Makers

Quotes from Aaron Spelling and others regarding network decision making are from an ABC News *Close-Up*, "Prime Time TV: The Decision Makers," aired September 2, 1974. Copies of the complete script are available through ABC, 7 West 66th Street, New York, NY 10023.

Susan Tyler Eastman
Sydney W. Head
Lewis Klein
Broadcast/Cable Programming: Strategies and Practices, 2d ed. Belmont, Calif.: Wadsworth, 1984.

A solid comprehensive overview of broadcast and cable advertising practices. The text includes sections offering a historical overview, how advertising campaigns are developed, buying and selling time, and social responsibility. Highly recommended for students interested in the subject.

Public TV

Carnegie Commission on Educational Television
Public Television. New York: Harper & Row, 1967.

The Carnegie Commission spent 18 months reviewing the status of public television before issuing this impressive report. Its conclusion ("a well-financed, well-directed educational television system . . . must be brought into being if the American public is to be served") is as convincing now as it was in 1967.

Issues and Answers: Who's in Charge Here?

Nicholas Johnson
How to Talk Back to Your Television Set. New York: Bantam Books, 1970.

This may be the book people look back on in 30 or 40 years and say: "This is where it all began. People actually started taking charge of their own media." A must. In many ways, still as relevant as when it was written a decade and a half ago.

Erwin G. Krasnow
Lawrence D. Longley
Herbert A. Terry
The Politics of Broadcast Regulation, 3d
ed. New York: St. Martin's, 1982.

An excellent political and economic
analysis of the regulation of broadcasting in America. Includes a comprehensive section on early (1976–1980)
efforts to rewrite the Communications
Act. The book is decidedly pro-regula-
tion at a time when the mood of Congress and the FCC is just the opposite.
Includes a superb annotated bibliography of many significant works on
broadcast regulation.

Harry J. Skornia
*Television and Society: An Inquest and
Agenda for Improvement*. New York:
McGraw-Hill, 1965.

Though dated in parts, this is proof
that things change very little in the
world of TV programming. Many a student has become an outraged critic of
modern TV practices after reading it.
There are sections on leadership, regulations, ratings, economics, and effects.
The most cohesive indictment of television ever.

9

Television, Part Two: Patterns and Programs

WHEN NBC ANNOUNCED THAT IT WAS BRINGING BACK JAMES Garner in *Maverick* in the fall of 1981, I was ecstatic, for in many ways it promised to be like living an important part of my life all over again.

Gambling: I have always been preoccupied with cards and the track. I keep coming up with plans to break the bank. (So far the bank is still intact.) It started when I was 14—I'd sneak into the race track (no one under 21 was admitted without a parent) and find kindly old men to place bets for me.

Travel: At 16 I dropped out of high school and drove my old Pontiac thousands of miles, crisscrossing the country like a madman, looking for . . . anything—action, adventure, whatever. There was something glamorous about being "on the road," traveling from town to town.

Work: I had always hated it. Not a day went by when I wasn't up to some scheme, legal or slightly illegal, to beat it. I looked around at everyone doing an eight-hour shift at the sawmill and thought, My God—this isn't for me. A job may be fine temporarily, but I couldn't do it for a living!

I was thinking about all of this one day and wondering how such an antisocial set of values could have evolved, so contradictory to the American spirit. Then I turned on the television set. There was a rerun of an episode from the old *Maverick* series. It had been my favorite when it was first aired in 1957. I can vividly remember my brother and me keeping time on Sunday afternoons by "how many hours it is till *Maverick*." Now that's devotion!

NOW BACK TO *MAVERICK*

James Garner was the antihero of the old West. A hero was virtuous, but Bret Maverick was expedient. A hero was strong,

> **The problem with television is that people must sit and keep their eyes glued on a screen; the average American family hasn't time for it. Therefore, the showmen are convinced that for this reason, if no other, television will never be a serious competitor of broadcasting.**
>
> NEW YORK TIMES, MARCH 19, 1939

stable, and hard-working; Bret abhorred work. He always took the coward's way out; whenever trouble developed, he left town. A home was something he never needed; he just wandered around from place to place meeting beautiful women and playing poker. He always had fine clothes and plenty of money; his was the life of action, adventure, and, above all, leisure.

Suddenly it struck me. My entire life had developed around *Maverick!* All of those inexplicable impulses—it was as if I had been playing out the Maverick role. Even though the new *Maverick* series was canceled after only one season, the lessons that I had learned from Bret Maverick remain lifelong and indelible.

Television has become a vast resource, the ultimate educational device, not because it teaches traditional curricula but because it supplies *roles*. Countless characters parade through our lives each day via TV: priests and politicians, doctors and lawyers, private detectives and public enemies, sex objects and sex offenders. Each character supplies us with bits of information about what his or her role is like. We have personal contact with a few people every day, but television gives us contact with a cast of hundreds. These roles may have a direct impact on how we perceive ourselves and our own roles in our personal day-to-day environment.

TV'S MEDIATED REALITY

To understand the relationships between real life and TV's special brand of mediated reality, we can again use the *cone effect* (see Chapter 1 and 9.1). We know that TV situations are based on real-life experiences. After all, there really was an American West, and there really were men who made a living playing poker there. We also know that the TV version differs considerably from what

actually happened. Bret Maverick never seemed to get very dirty, despite the fact that none of the western streets were paved. I can't remember him ever stepping in any horse manure, yet "authentic" accounts of the West tell us that this was a daily occurrence. In short, the western, and in fact all TV programming, differs considerably from real life. Thus, TV's constructed mediated reality pictures a world that is funnier, sexier, bolder, more violent, and more intense than our own.

This is because those who construct the genres, or categories, of TV programming realize that the perceived mediated reality of the mass audience must contain certain things in order to attract and hold that audience. These things involve gratification of basic real-life needs (see 9.2).

Our lives are made up of many social experiences. Some of those are interpersonal. Our parents and friends all have an influence on the attitudes we develop and the decisions we make. But of tremendous impact are the hundreds of people we have "known" from TV. We carry around their images in our heads, and we can recall them in an instant.

Are you skeptical? Okay, try this. Close your eyes and make your mind a complete blank. Then think "the Fonz." Try it before reading on.

★ ★ ★ ★ ★ ★ ★

What did you see? Yes, it was the Fonz, or rather Henry Winkler, who plays the Fonz. He was wearing his black leather jacket, wasn't he? His hair combed in that familiar style? What's more, he was probably giving the thumbs-up salute. The Fonz is more familiar to you than many people you have met in real life. Who conjures up the clearest picture, the Fonz or, say, your third-grade teacher?

None of us really likes to concede that "the boob tube" affects us. It seems like such a shallow medium; the stories are so simple.

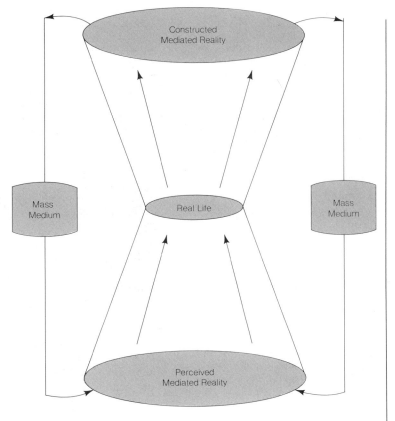

9.1

Here we see the cone effect applied specifically to television. Scriptwriters, newswriters, and others in the industry use real-life experiences and fashion a constructed mediated reality from them. This CMR may take the form of a situation comedy, game show, newscast, or any of TV's other program genres. The final version is distributed through the TV set to the audience, for which it is a perceived mediated reality. This PMR is then taken back and incorporated into the real lives of the audience.

But television is the most powerful and the most influential of all mass media; ignoring it won't make it go away. Ignoring leads to ignorance, and ignorance is always dangerous.

FROM SITCOM TO *STAR TREK*: THE GENRES OF PRIME TIME

I once passed by a Chicago ice cream shop with this sign posted in the window: "31 Flavors—Instant Gratification!!!" The mediated reality of television is the ice cream shop of the imagination. It offers many things to "gratify" us.

Back in the 1960s, broadcast researcher

Stuart Hyde, who teaches at San Francisco State University, came up with a list of various gratifications from watching TV. The list presented in 9.2 differs somewhat from his original, but it can be argued that some of the basic gratifications that were offered by the westerns and variety shows of the 1950s could also be found in the sitcoms and action-adventure series of the 1960s and 1970s and in the successful programs of today. TV fills these needs by presenting various types, or genres, of programming. Each program is aimed at a slightly different set of needs.

This is a different way of looking at the influence of media. Traditional media research centers on how media are changing attitudes and beliefs, while the "uses and gratification"

9.2

31 Possible Gratifications Derived From Watching Television

Vicarious

1. The need for vicarious, but controlled, emotional experience.
2. The desire to live vicariously in a world of significance, intensity, and larger-than-life-size people.
3. The desire to experience, in a guilt-free arena, the extreme emotions of love and hate.
4. The need to confront, in a controlled situation, the horrible and the terrible.
5. The desire to see villains in action.
6. The desire to imagine oneself a hero or heroine.
7. The need to be purged of unpleasant emotions.
8. The need to experience the beautiful and the ugly.

9. The desire to experience vicarious financial reward.
10. The desire to engage in vicarious gambling or risk taking.
11. The desire to vicariously explore dangerous territories and experience totally new situations.

Escapist

12. The need to be distracted from the realities of life.
13. The desire to believe in the miraculous.
14. The desire to return to "the good old days."
15. The desire to be amused.
16. The desire to believe in romantic love.
17. The desire to experience "the happy ending."
18. The need to find outlets for the sex drive in a guilt-free context.

Social

19. The need to have shared experiences with others.
20. The need to share in the suffering of others.

21. The need to feel "informed."
22. The need to see authority figures exalted.
23. The need to see authority figures deflated.
24. The need or desire to feel superior to a societal deviant.
25. The desire to see others make mistakes.

Spiritual and Moral

26. The need to believe that spiritual or moral values are more important than material goods.
27. The need to identify with a deity or a divine plan.
28. The desire to see evil punished and virtue restored.
29. The need to explore taboo subjects with impunity.
30. The need for spiritual cleansing.
31. The need to see order imposed on the world.

Based on course outline, "History and Analysis of the Public Arts," by Stuart W. Hyde.

approach looks instead at how television and other media meet our social and individual needs.

The emphasis is not on a passive audience soaking up information and reacting to mediated reality but instead on an active audience "deliberately using the media to achieve specific goals." The studies that have been produced thus far are based on a "common set of assumptions" about TV and other media:

1. Media use is goal-directed. We use mass media to satisfy specific needs. These needs develop out of our social environment.
2. Receivers (viewers) select the types of media and media content to fulfill their needs. . . . We are able to "bend" the media to our needs more readily than they can overpower us.

3. There are other sources of need satisfaction that must compete with TV and other media, e.g., family, friends, work, leisure.

This research, along with the list of 31 gratifications, helps us understand more completely the complex relationships between audiences and their favorite television programs. In this section we'll take a look at these program genres: sitcom, variety, western, doctor and lawyer shows, action-adventure, and drama. Surprisingly, these six alone account for the vast majority of all successful prime-time programming. It seems likely that the popularity of these various genres reflects the times, since audience needs and gratifications may differ somewhat from one decade to the next. Thus we can talk about the traditional American values evident in the westerns of the 1950s or the need for an escape into the past evident in certain popular sitcoms of the 1970s like *Laverne and Shirley* and *Happy Days*.

Sitcom

Situation comedy has been part of television from the beginning. *I Love Lucy* (1951–61) was one of the first and certainly wins the longevity award. It has probably been recycled more than any other program on TV. Lucille Ball was the first of many "dingbat wives" who became stock characters in sitcoms. Desi Arnaz was the husband and father. He wasn't too bright, but he patiently tried to keep the "situation" from getting out of hand. Of course, it is when the situation gets out of hand that it begins to be funny.

Unlike the durable *I Love Lucy*, most sitcoms don't last long; the average life span is a season or less. Most are based on situations that seem funny at first, but writers soon run out of ideas, and there is always a new show waiting in the wings. In the 1950s, a show was guaranteed a berth for 39 weeks. Now a show is lucky to make it for ten weeks—many are canceled after only six weeks on the air. NBC began something called the "second season" in the mid-1970s to promote the shows replacing the fall failures. With the TV season now less than 25 episodes long, many predict that the "season" concept will soon disappear. Shows will just come and go at will, being replaced as ratings fall.

Cable TV, with its huge capacity for programming, is recycling a number of classic sitcoms from the past, including *Jack Benny* and *Burns and Allen*. A number of independent TV stations air these as well, giving viewers a unique opportunity to study the evolution of the genre.

During the 1970s, TV viewers showed a marked preference for sitcoms; they occupied more prime time during that period than any other genre. Many were the product of the most prolific sitcom producer of them all, Norman Lear. Lear first hit prime-time paydirt with *All in the Family* in 1971. He rapidly launched a string of sitcoms based on the success of Archie Bunker and company, including *Good Times*, *Maude*, and *The Jeffersons*. Most were readily identifiable by the Lear formula: "realistic" dialogue and a tendency toward racial and ethnic controversy. Plots often revolved around sex, drugs, and abortion.

Lear deserves more credit than any other single person for introducing previously taboo subjects to TV shows. In the 1970s, he forced television to grow up, contending that the audience was ready for something a little different. By 1977, there were nine different Lear productions on the air, leading more than one critic to conclude that his "fresh new approach" was no longer fresh.

Nevertheless, his shows revolutionized the genre. Sitcoms had been easy-to-swallow little stories reinforcing traditional American values (for example, the father is the head of household). Lear's explored suicide, unemployment, racism, and women's liberation. Not everyone is enthusiastic, of course; many feel such matters are better examined in a more sober context, such as a documentary. But Lear's commercial success assured him a place on TV.

Another stable of 1970s sitcoms was built by the producers of the highly rated *Mary Tyler Moore Show* (1970–77). Some, like *The Bob Newhart Show* (1972–78), featured all new characters; others, like *Rhoda* and *Phyllis*, were spinoffs from *Mary Tyler Moore*. While these shows were not preoccupied with controversial issues, they did raise the "state of the art" of sitcoms significantly through skillfully constructed plots and carefully written scripts. Audiences appreciated the quality sitcoms and made them among the most successful of the 1970s.

One trend involved scripts with multiple situations. Several subplots would be woven in while the main plot was working itself out. This lent diversity, provided new joke material, and seemed to involve the audience a little more. Sitcom producers of the 1970s were also bent on convincing the audience that their characters had depth. In doing this, they often wrote more complex scripts that allowed a character who had been stereotypically "funny," let's say, to experience a serious situation. During the seasons that *The Mary Tyler Moore Show* headed CBS's Saturday night lineup, the characters developed significantly. Mary grew from a prima donna to a capable working woman. Mr. Grant developed from a no-nonsense boss to an often troubled and sensitive person. In fact, in various episodes the character created by Ed Asner went through a divorce (there was never a reconciliation) and became a borderline alcoholic. Hardly *Father Knows Best!* The character was so strong, it was spun off into

the hour-long drama series *Lou Grant*, which many critics hailed as one of the best new shows of 1977.

The success of shows like *Happy Days* (1974–84) and *Laverne and Shirley* (1976–83) was part of the nostalgia craze. Both were set in the 1950s and originally aimed at the audience that had been in high school during that time. (People in the 25–49 age group are the most desirable audience, since they buy most of the products advertised on TV.) These shows won that audience and much more. Young people turned their stereos off long enough to watch their favorite nostalgia characters, particularly the Fonz.

Happy Days, *Laverne and Shirley*, and *Mork and Mindy* formed a successful trilogy of sitcoms for Garry Marshall, who heads one of TV's most successful production companies. Marshall admits that most of his programs go for the belly laugh rather than social awareness.

The most successful sitcoms of the early 1980s seemed to reflect this belly-laugh philosophy. *The Dukes of Hazzard* was continually rated among the top ten, along with *Three's Company* and *Mork and Mindy*. Only *M*A*S*H* (1972–1983) seemed to be able to draw top ratings while making serious social comment, perhaps because it combined that comment with a lot of visual comedy.

During its eleven-season run, *M*A*S*H* became a national pastime. Widely syndicated, the exploits of Hawkeye and the gang can still be seen up to a half dozen times each day in some major markets.

When the crew of the 4077th at last packed up and returned to the States, the 2½-hour final segment became the highest-rated single episode in the history of the medium, surpassing previous champion *Dallas*.

Many critics felt that *M*A*S*H* added new depth and dimension to the sitcom genre, proving once and for all that there is a place

9.3
*In 1964, Ed Sullivan intro-
duced the most popular rock
and roll group of all time to
an enthusiastic TV audience.*

on commercial network television for intelligent and meaningful humor that appeals to a
diverse audience.

Variety

Variety shows offer something for everybody. Often they may be centered on the personality of a single star or a troop of familiar
faces. Ed Sullivan was the acknowledged king
of the variety format, and his Sunday evening show (1948–71) was top rated for more
than 20 years. Sullivan prided himself on being
a good evaluator of talent and entertainment
trends. It was he who boosted Elvis Presley

to prominence on TV (though Elvis had
appeared on a few TV shows previously).
Later came the Beatles (see 9.3) and dozens
of other rock groups. But that was only a
small part of the story. No matter what your
entertainment tastes, you could find something each week on the Sullivan show. There
were stand-up comics, opera stars, elephant
acts, talking dogs, jugglers and cartoonists.

Sullivan himself was an enigma. Before
working in TV, he had been an entertainment
columnist for a New York newspaper. He had
absolutely no talent as a performer and seldom got involved with his talented guests.
Dozens of comics loved to do imitations of

"It's a variety show. There's something in it for everyone."

Drawing by Frascino; © 1981
The New Yorker Magazine, Inc.

him, often while he watched. It was his very lack of talent that seemed to help him become such a success. He spent very little time in front of the camera, simply introducing the acts and getting out of the way.

Musical hosts dominated the variety format for a time. Unlike Sullivan, they participated directly with guests in comedy skits and musical duets. Among the more popular of these shows were those hosted by Perry Como, Dinah Shore, Tennessee Ernie Ford and Andy Williams.

Comedy-based variety accounted for a number of hit shows. Early hosts of successful comedy-variety programs were such colorful personalities as Jackie Gleason, Milton Berle, Red Skelton, Jack Benny and George Gobel.

The 1960s brought the *Smothers Brothers*

Comedy Hour and *Rowan and Martin's Laugh-In.* The Smothers Brothers began with the usual variety show but rapidly became recognized program innovators; Tom and Dick Smothers, Mason Williams, and resident comic Pat Paulsen became heroes to those who felt TV shouldn't shy away from controversy. They had a habit of inviting guests who were politically outspoken.

Often the brothers' material was allowed because their skits were satirical and thus the audience was "not taking them seriously," but when folk singer Joan Baez made some remarks against the war in Vietnam, CBS censors snipped them out. The problem was that TV is a *mass* medium. The network and some sponsors thought a part of the mass audience might become alienated. The Baez incident accelerated the conflict between the

Smothers Brothers and the network, and after extensive discussions and lots of publicity, the show was canceled.

Rowan and Martin's Laugh-In got away with things the Smothers Brothers had only dreamed of. The secret of success was the special form of the show, composed of hundreds of pieces of videotape. There were skits, one-liners, recurring situations, and jokes. *Laugh-In* was the first program to use electronic editing devices extensively to piece together a collection of "out-takes." Dick and Dan would march out on stage at the beginning and say hello. An hour later, they'd come back to say good-bye. In between, anything could happen. There were cameos by John Wayne and Richard Nixon, cream pies and cold showers for the series regulars. Many, including Goldie Hawn and Lily Tomlin, went on to success of their own.

Laugh-In first pointed out that TV audiences could handle a lot more entertainment "information" than other shows were offering. Because it relied so heavily on editing and visual devices, *Laugh-In* was uniquely TV. The mass audience gave thundering approval, and the show (originally scheduled as a 13-week summer replacement) became the most popular on TV. In addition, the critics loved it, and *Laugh-In* won every top award, including a flock of Emmys.

Variety shows of the 1970s borrowed heavily from the *Laugh-In* format. Everything had to be sped up; the more elements the better. These shows depended heavily on technicians and those behind the camera to "create" the visual splendor TV had been lacking. Costuming and set decoration became key factors, as the audience expected to be visually entertained while listening to a song or laughing at a comedy sketch. *Carol Burnett, Sonny and Cher, Donny and Marie,* and others were successful because their producers realized that visual appeal, rapid pacing, and diverse guest lists were a necessity.

The British import *Monty Python* took the *Laugh-In* formula one step further (see 9.4). This show was a nonstop barrage of satirical sketches interspersed with animation in the tradition of the Beatles' animated film *Yellow Submarine.* BBC censorship standards were considerably more relaxed than American counterparts'; nudity and irreverence abounded. The same lack of censorship applied when the show was aired over public TV in America, as there were no irate sponsors to object. Besides, as in *Laugh-In,* everything happened so fast that it was hard to know exactly what was being said.

Monty Python became an underground hit. But when one of the networks bought the rights to the shows and aired them in competition with late-night rock shows, regular *Python* viewers set up a howl. Whole sketches and scenes were missing. The performers themselves finally sued to stop commercial airing unless shows were aired uncut. *Monty Python* quickly disappeared from commercial TV but remained a success on the public network.

Meanwhile in America, NBC's *Saturday Night Live* was breaking ground of its own. There was no regular emcee but a weekly guest host whose role was often overshadowed by the antics of the Not Ready for Prime Time Players. The comic skits offered satire with a bite, and the late-night hour kept network censorship to a minimum. Where else could TV viewers watch a sketch about a brand of soup called Painful Rectal Itch or see a live fish chopped to bits in a blender?

The extraordinary success of the show led to stardom for a number of its talented actors, including Dan Aykroyd, Gilda Radner, and Chevy Chase. But as these stars left the show one by one, they seemed to take a lot of the original energy with them. When NBC reintroduced the program in the fall of 1980, there

9.4

The creators and stars of Monty Python's Flying Circus. Front row (left to right): Eric Idle, Michael Palin, Terry Jones. Back row: Graham Chapman, John Cleese, cartoonist Terry Gilliam.

Often provocative and daring, the humor on Monty Python's Flying Circus was a type rarely seen on American television.

was an entirely new cast of characters. Slow to win followers, the new *Saturday Night Live* nevertheless gradually built its own audience. By 1984 the ratings indicated that the show's regulars were once again becoming stars. Predominant was Eddie Murphy, who also enjoyed success with several comedy albums.

The 1970s also brought a flood of variety-type shows that appealed to a youthful late-night audience. *The Midnight Special, Don Kirshner's Rock Concert*, and *In Concert* all featured rock music. Many were built around major rock personalities, but occasionally a little humor would be thrown in for diversity. Though rock generally was still not popular enough for TV's prime-time audience, the Friday and Saturday late-night spots seemed ripe, and ratings were good.

In general, the variety format had all but disappeared by the early 1980s. Perhaps the idea of "something for everyone" worked more effectively in TV's early years. As programmers became more sophisticated in constructing TV's mediated reality, they were able to focus more directly on the various subaudiences that make up the mass audience. Thus the genre that took the shotgun approach to attracting viewers became less successful.

Westerns

Another genre that enjoyed its biggest success during television's early years was the western. Westerns are uniquely American and make up a large share of the programs that America exports to other countries. As a result, the myths about pioneering and gun-toting Americans get plenty of reinforcement. (Perhaps they should—Americans own more handguns per capita than residents of any other country.) At its best, the western, like all TV genres, can be entertaining, informative, amusing and enlightening. At its worst, it can be trite, boring, and downright offensive.

Gunsmoke (1955–75), the longest-running TV western ever, was a slow-moving, comfortable show with a cast of characters from every age group and social background. Matt (James Arness) was tall, quiet, and rugged. His sidekick, Festus, offered comic relief. Kindly old Doc played the grouch, while attractive Miss Kitty supplied an off-beat romantic angle. Kitty was the stereotype belle of the old West. She was a bit naughty (after all, she did run a saloon) but had a heart of gold and was very virtuous. When *Gunsmoke* finally bit the dust after 20 years, there wasn't a dry eye in the house.

Have Gun, Will Travel (1957–63) and my favorite, *Maverick* (1957–62), merit special consideration because their scripts were often literate. Both took the genre beyond the good guys–bad guys clichés and allowed characters to develop real personalities.

The biggest western of the 1960s was *Bonanza* (1959–73). Interestingly, the NBC show was originally conceived as a showcase for the new color TV sets conveniently being manufactured by parent company RCA. It was one of the first all-color shows to air on network TV and probably was responsible more than any other show for the rapid increase in the sale of color sets during this period. Ben Cartwright and his boys dominated the ratings for years (they were finally knocked out of the number one spot by *Laugh-In*), and the show was a true believer's potpourri of traditional western values with an emphasis on home and family. Cartwright's three sons provided identification enough for everyone. There was Adam, the quiet, articulate man in black; Hoss, the comic relief, with a heart as big as all outdoors and a stomach to match; and Little Joe, the darling of the kids, who saw him as one of their own. Joe often refused to do Pa's bidding and struck out on his own. I doubt if there was any "baby" of the family who didn't readily identify. Landon parlayed his success in *Bonanza* into another long-running NBC hit series, *Little House on the Prairie* (1974–1983).

Ben himself provided a hero image for older viewers, and more than one plot revolved around his straight shooting. He also provided a firm but gentle, understanding father figure. The Cartwrights were the royalty of their land. The Ponderosa was their kingdom. Owning property, of course, is a vital part of the American dream. Plots often involved others' attempts to infringe on the Cartwright domain.

Despite its stereotype trappings, the western format is so flexible that it can meet

9.5

Raymond Burr was the leading character in two long-running TV series, Perry Mason *and* Ironside. *Both have also been successful in syndication.*

virtually all of the 31 needs listed in 9.2. Perhaps this explains the enormous success of the western format during television's early years.

However, with the 1970s came increasing viewer sophistication. As a result, the popularity of the western diminished. New attempts at reviving the western in the early 1980s met with little success.

Doctors and Lawyers

Doctor and lawyer formats enjoyed great popularity during the first two decades of TV. *Dr. Kildare, Ben Casey,* and *Marcus Welby, M.D.* (1969–76) satisfied viewers who had "the

need to share in the suffering of others" and "the desire to believe in the miraculous." The success of these shows probably owes something to the high status we have given the medical profession; the genre has repaid its debt by giving the profession something extra: romantic glamor. Though these men and women were only human, we saw them perform heroically week after week under tremendous pressure, and their patients always seemed to recover.

Television doctors are larger than life size. Many real-life patients have been disappointed because their doctors could not provide the instant cure or hours of personal attention of a Marcus Welby. This "Marcus Welby syndrome" carries over to many facets of real life. We develop expectations about the roles of others from watching TV and are disappointed when they prove erroneous. We expect police officers to solve cases within the hour and lawyers to see justice done whether the client can afford it or not.

The best-known lawyer of television was Perry Mason, played by Raymond Burr (see 9.5). Though it was shot in black and white, *Perry Mason* (1957–66) enjoyed success in syndication during the 1970s and became a television staple. The plot was the same each week: Someone unjustly accused would come to Mason for help. Mason, along with secretary Della Street and detective Paul Drake, would eventually unravel the mystery. Usually Mason would break down the real culprit on the witness stand while his client was being tried.

In the final moments, Mason would meet the client and staff for coffee or a drink and explain how he had figured it out. That portion of the format, known as the *denouement,* was so successful that a number of other shows soon adopted it.

All of these shows cashed in on our desire to experience a happy ending. Of course, the illusion of the happy ending—commonly found in all media—can be a dangerous one. If we expect each episode of our lives to end happily, and if we believe that everything will always turn out for the best, we may often become frustrated and discouraged.

Action-Adventure

The action-adventure program is typically about a police officer or a private eye, but science fiction and other varieties also exist. What they all have in common is *pacing*. The audience is constantly tossed between conversation and car chase, conversation and fistfight, conversation and murder.

Since the beginning, action-adventure shows have come in for a lot of criticism, particularly about their use of violence. There are a couple of schools of thought here: One says that violence on television encourages violence in real life. Another contends that the vicarious experience of violence substitutes for the real thing. If the latter is correct, it would seem the more violence on TV, the better. Generally, network executives have tried to cut down on violence over the years, but the most successful action-adventure series (like *Starsky and Hutch*) were often the most violent as well. Action-adventure series play to the audience's need to share in the suffering of others, to confront the horrible and terrible in a controlled situation, and to see villains in action.

One obvious arena where audiences find gratification is the world of cops and robbers. Some successful action-adventure shows were *Dragnet* (1952–59) and *Highway Patrol* in the 1950s, *The FBI*, *Naked City*, and *Dragnet* (1967–70) in the 1960s, and *Kojak* (see 9.6) and *Hawaii Five-O* in the 1970s. All featured plots in which stars tracked down criminals and brought them to justice with great finesse. Police dramas of the 1970s emphasized the personality of the star. Scripts for *Columbo*, *McCloud*, *Kojak*, and *Baretta* spent

9.6
Telly Savalas played the hard-bitten title character in Kojak, *one of CBS's most successful action-adventure series. His unique personal appearance and mannerisms seemed more important than plot in determining why audiences watched the show.*

as much time developing the hero's character as getting the crooks.

The work of private detectives, too, lends itself to action-adventure gratifications. *77 Sunset Strip* (1958–64) was one of the most successful. In that program the office contained a secretary and a group of "characters" of various ages and social statuses for maximum audience identification. *77 Sunset Strip* starred good-looking, clean-shaven Roger Smith and Efrem Zimbalist, Jr., plus an added attraction: Edd "Kookie" Byrnes. Kookie became somewhat of a cult hero, for he appealed directly to the teenage audience and helped make *77 Sunset Strip* a smash. Later, detective series *Mannix*, *Switch*, *The*

9.7

William Conrad as Frank Cannon, TV's rotund private eye, in his favorite room of the house.

Rockford Files, Charlie's Angels, and *Barnaby Jones* featured heroes, heroines, and villains of various ages and ethnic background. There was something for everybody.

TV critic Horace Newcomb notes that new types of action-adventure characters emerged in the 1970s. They were usually part establishment and part antiestablishment. The kids of the *Mod Squad* were first; then came *Baretta, McCloud,* and others. Though unorthodox, all worked within the system.

Many of the action-adventure series seemed intent on reassuring us that even the fattest *(Cannon)*, clumsiest *(Columbo)*, and most severely handicapped *(Ironside* and *Longstreet)* among us can be heroes. We are *all* potential stars despite our physical and mental shortcomings (see 9.7).

But the most talked-about, most heavily watched action-adventure series was a one-of-a-kind phenomenon. *Star Trek* was on NBC for only three seasons (1966–69), but it still enjoys tremendous ratings as a rerun. Its creator, Gene Roddenberry, described it as a kind of *Wagon Train* of the sky. Each week, the Star Ship *Enterprise* would venture into the universe and right some cosmic wrong. Its five-year mission was to "seek out new life and boldly go where no man has gone before."

Contrary to popular belief, *Star Trek* was not canceled because of some evil Klingon conspiracy. Rather, it was a victim of the ratings system. Ratings measure the *number* of bodies watching TV, but they don't account for the emotional depth of the audience or the loyalty they might have for a given show. *Star Trek*'s viewers were relatively small in number at the time, but they were intensely devoted. When the show was canceled after the second season, they set up an unprecedented howl, enough to keep it on for an extra year.

In the long run, *Star Trek*'s problem was that it was a bit ahead of its time. The integrated crew included blacks, Asians, Russians, and even Vulcans. Women were given roles as geologists and psychiatrists. Plots revolved around war, politics, racism. This would not be unusual for a sitcom of the 1970s, but for an action-adventure show of the 1960s it was unheard of. *Star Trek* got away with it for a while because it was set in the future. Wars were between planets with strange names, and the names of the "races" were equally unfamiliar. In a few years, mass-audience tastes caught up with *Star Trek*, but by then the show was in syndication.

Star Trek was not the only science-fiction program to come to TV (others included *Land of the Giants, Lost in Space,* and *Space 1999*), but it was the only one to offer consistently believable scripts that seemed to center on

THE·WORLD·OF
STAR TREK

Featuring Creator and Producer
GENE RODDENBERRY

See the award winning **"Star Trek"** pilot film, never before shown in its entirety,
and the only authentic showing of the famous blooper reel, both on a full theatre-size screen.
Hear from Gene Roddenberry about the making of the new movie, **"Star Trek"**.
Ask Gene Roddenberry your own questions about **"Star Trek"**.

9.8
Although Star Trek *ended its run in prime time in 1969 producer Gene Roddenberry still draws large crowds when he lectures and shows films of the series. Despite the success of the TV series,* Star Trek *films have not enjoyed the huge box-office grosses of the* Star Wars *films.*

people instead of events. None of *Star Trek's* actors were particularly famous or talented, but the chemistry between them created dialogues that seemed genuine. There was plenty of violence and sex, but the believability of the characters was the key. It created the intense audience involvement that still brings fans out to *Star Trek* conventions and keeps them watching reruns. As a result, *Star Trek* flourishes (see 9.8). KTVU, an independent station in California, has been running the show off and on for years; according to sales manager Jim Diamond, "People just don't ever seem to get tired of the thing."

**Soaps and Scenarios:
Drama in Prime Time**

In the early years of television it was easy to identify prime-time drama, for most theatrical works were simply taken intact from stage to TV. As the form of television programs became more sophisticated and the genres more clearly defined, the distinction between, say, action-adventure and drama became blurred.

Early dramatic efforts were generally anthologies, with stories taken directly from theater or literature. The *Kraft Television*

Theater (1947–58) was one of the most durable, and is remembered fondly by TV's "golden age" enthusiasts. This is also the case with *Playhouse 90* (1956–60), which offered a completely original 90-minute TV drama each week. Most of these shows were done live, which contributed to their theaterlike quality.

The big-budget live shows did not endure as long as a number of other highly regarded dramatic series, many of them of the half-hour variety. *Alfred Hitchcock Presents* (1955–65) was one amusing example, and the program still does quite well in syndication, as does *The Twilight Zone* (1959–64).

The most successful dramatic series of the 1970s was *The Waltons* (1972–81). The Waltons were a Depression family with very little money, but they had a lot of beautiful land and each other. The Depression actually became "the good old days," as John-Boy recalled the hardships and obstacles that led to a weekly renewal of faith in land and family.

The Waltons took place in real time, with children growing up and getting married much as you would expect in real life. Critics had a field day lambasting its "cornball" attitudes toward social problems, but the mass audience loved it. Again, there was a broad range of ages represented. Grandparents were in their 70s, while the youngest children attended elementary school. *The Waltons* seemed to be one of those shows that transcended simplistic scripts and plots to come alive for the mass audience.

Lou Grant first aired in 1977 and immediately found success with the critics who had panned *The Waltons* as too unrealistic. Indeed, the show was advertised as dealing with "stories right out of today's headlines," and plots involved themes like nuclear power, drug use, and freedom of the press.

Realistic drama was also a key element in the success of *Hill Street Blues* (see 9.9) and *St. Elsewhere*. However both shows broke new ground in combining traditional dramatic elements with innovative camera work and scripting. Of particular interest were the developing and ever-changing relationships between regular characters.

In the 1980s, Lorimar Productions, a company that had first found success with *The Waltons*, followed up with two new prime-time dramatic series that were to have far-reaching consequences for the dramatic genre. *Dallas* and its spinoff, *Knots Landing*, became enormously popular. Critics contended that they were mere soap operas in the guise of prime-time drama, and indeed there were "soapy" elements in both shows. It might be said that the *content* of the shows was soap opera, while the *form* was prime time. The Ewings of *Dallas* lived in an expansive ranch outside of town. The action took place outdoors and in expensive-to-shoot locations. Such big-budget luxuries are unknown to most soaps, and they helped distinguish the show from its daytime counterparts. The enormous success of *Dallas* and *Dynasty* seemed to result from their being able to gratify traditional soap-opera-audience needs, such as the need to share in the suffering of others, as well as those more oriented to prime time, such as the desire to live vicariously in a world of significance, intensity, and larger-than-life-size people. In short, prime-time soaps seem to have the best of both worlds, with ratings to match. The emergence of such shows will probably prove to be one of the most significant programming trends of the 1980s.

DAYTIME TV AND THE COMMON COLD

The success of *Dallas* and other prime-time soap operas has sparked an interest in daytime programming among many students.

9.9
Hill Street Blues: A Different Kind of Drama

Several years ago in an episode of *Mork and Mindy,* Mork (Robin Williams) was deeply troubled by a rather perplexing subplot, when he suddenly stopped in the middle of the action, looked into the camera and deadpanned "Oh, wow, this is more confusing than an episode of *Hill Street Blues.*" Confusing or not, *HSB* is the object of attention of millions of television viewers each week.

You may remember that the program did not immediately zoom to the top of the ratings. In fact, when it premiered during the 1980–81 season, it was at the bottom. However, its huge success at Emmy time signaled an upturn, and during the 1981–82 season, *HSB* had more than comfortable ratings.

Trying to understand the program is reminiscent of the story of the six blind men and the elephant. If you'll recall, one blind man held the elephant's tail and described it, another the trunk, a third described the elephant's leg, and so on. All had different perceptions of what an elephant was, and it may be that different viewers have different perceptions of *Hill Street Blues.*

Hill Street does not fit easily into any one of the six genres of prime time. The program actually combines elements of comedy, police-detective, action-adventure, and traditional drama. In addition, its film technique creates a documentary feel. The opening of the show, for example, has a definite documentary look, and credits appearing throughout the first few minutes give it a cinematic quality.

To make matters even more confusing, the show is built on a soap-opera structure similar to that of *Dallas* and the daytime serials. Currently I'm directing a group of students doing in-depth research into why people are so intensely drawn to soap operas. One of our most interesting findings is what we call the "hump factor." The greater number of subplots and characters, the more difficult it is for viewers to "get over the hump" and become regular fans of a particular soap. *HSB,* with its large cast of characters, experienced this problem.

Once the hump has been crossed, we find ourselves getting involved with "real people" and "real emotions" in the same way we did with *Lou Grant. HSB'*s action-adventure elements reminds us of *Magnum, P.I.* and even the ancient *Dragnet.* As with *M*A*S*H,* we see a relatively small amount of bloodshed, but what we do see takes on meaning because we're so involved with the characters who experience it.

The popularity of *HSB* says something significant about the increasing sophistication of television writers and producers *and* the ability of viewers to understand what they're up to. It also provides a measure of satisfaction for those of us who (despite the shrill cries of "boob tube" critics) have contended that the possibilities for the still-developing television art form are both exciting and limitless.

Some are even willing to come forward and confess that they have been daytime-TV fans all along. I was thinking about this during a week when I spent my days (and nights) at home with a temperature of 101° and the usual sinus miseries. During that week I must have seen 100 commercials suggesting remedies for my ailment. I hadn't realized how dependent TV is on the common cold. If it is ever cured, TV is in real trouble!

Colds always seem to come at the wrong time, but this one came at the right time for me. It gave me a chance to make some notes on daytime TV.

1 Game shows are everything you are not when you're sick. Game-show contestants are happy, elated, and competitive. It reminds me of my mother's favorite tongue-in-cheek cliché: "It's not whether you win or lose that counts . . . but the thrill of wiping out a friend." Game-show hosts insist that contestants "know" each other a bit before they do battle.

2 *Hollywood Squares* features form over content. It's not the winning or losing (as with *The Match Game* or *The Price Is Right*); getting there is all the fun. Some of the "stars" are people I've never heard of.

3 Soap operas are by far the most intricate programs offered on television today. The way the writers carefully weave and re-weave characters and situations together is positively incestuous.

4 There is lots more sex on the soaps now than there used to be. Men routinely run around without their shirts on. Women jump in and out of the shower with only a towel wrapped strategically around them.

5 Programs change drastically when the kids get home from school. Lots of cartoons and western reruns are shown after 4:00 P.M.

6 By the time the news comes on, I'm ready for something different, but the news is made up of the same elements as soaps, games, and reruns: suspense, murder, intrigue, money, violence, and uncertainty.

All three major networks derive more advertising revenues from daytime shows than from prime time. Even though each ad costs less in the daytime, there are some 14 hours of TV that are considered non-prime time. These include the daytime hours (7:00 A.M. to 6:00 P.M.) and an increasingly longer late-night period (11:00 P.M. to 2:00 A.M.). Networks supply packaged entertainment to take care of the special audiences that watch during these hours.

In the early years, TV networks supplied no daytime programs. The first major network morning effort was aimed at an audience hungry for information. The *Today* show and later *Good Morning America* featured extensive interviews, film footage of various public figures, and other diversions. The content was often more oriented to entertainment and soft news than the evening newscasts'. These early-morning formats have been very successful. ABC's lively *Good Morning America* finally topped *Today* in the morning ratings in 1979.

Daytime Soap Operas

Though dozens of different daytime formats have been tried, daytime TV is still pretty much soap operas and game shows. The soaps were introduced when daytime TV first began, deriving their name from the soap products that were often sponsors. The soap-opera format was brought intact from radio, and its basic premises have changed little over the years. Protagonists get into conflicts usually involving close friends or relatives, and must make decisions to resolve those conflicts. Some soaps, like *The Guiding Light* and *The Edge of Night*, boast 20 or more years on daytime TV and a loyal audience.

Unlike prime-time shows, soaps are often shot only a day or two before they are aired. This five-show-a-week schedule takes its toll on cast and crew. There is usually little budget for retakes, and sometimes missed cues and blown lines must be aired. It really keeps the cast on its toes. One advantage to the schedule is that the soap script may incorporate recent news events, while prime-time shows, shot as much as six months in advance, cannot.

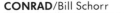

Reprinted by permission: Tribune Company Syndicate, Inc.

The soap opera depends so much on human interaction that we may use the term to describe our own conflicts. ("Gee, my father isn't speaking to my mother, my sister's getting divorced, and I'm flunking out of school. My life is really a soap opera!") In reality, few lives are as troubled and confused as those on the soaps. As with much of TV, our real lives are dull but safe by comparison.

Soap-opera characters are carefully created for the mass audience. They are usually young (25 to 35), well dressed, and financially comfortable. Leading men are doctors and lawyers. Leading women are attractive and well manicured. Indoor sets are unusually large and boast wall-to-wall carpeting, plush drapes, and built-in wet bars. Soap-opera characters tend to do a lot of eating, drinking, and arguing.

Critics contend that all soaps are nauseatingly similar, but actually each is aimed at a special segment of the audience. Although 70 percent of that audience are women, there is an increasing tendency for men and younger viewers to get involved with the soaps.

Soap operas seem to have become increasingly popular with college students in the last few years. On almost any campus you can find students gathered around TV sets during the lunch hour. The marriage of Luke and Laura on ABC's *General Hospital* in 1981 was a major campus event. If you don't schedule your classes around your favorite soaps, you probably know some students who do. In 1983, Agnes Nixon, the creator of *All My Children*, introduced a new half-hour soap, *Loving*. Beginning as a made-for-TV movie, *Loving* was unique in at least one respect: It was the first daytime drama set primarily on a college campus.

Regular viewers can name all the characters in a given soap and describe their history in detail. The casual observer gets lost in the plot, which has more twists and turns than a mountain highway.

Soap operas are a fascinating study of audience-character relationships. There is no other media audience so involved with its programs and so devoted to its characters. When soap characters have an on-camera birthday, they can expect lots of cards from fans. If they are sick, thousands of viewers send get-well greetings. If a popular character dies, viewers protest. And, unlike the prime-time audience, soap watchers tend to have a good handle on what they receive from their programs. The desire to believe in romantic love, the desire to see evil punished and virtue rewarded, and the desire to see others make mistakes are most often cited by viewers themselves. Soap characters are usually good or evil, positive or negative, with well-defined personalities. However, it is not unusual for a character to gradually change from good to evil, then back to good again.

During *Mary Hartman, Mary Hartman*'s run in the mid-1970s, many viewers found themselves hooked on the genre for the first time. Norman Lear's soap was, in his words, "slightly bent." Mary's grandfather (the "Fernwood Flasher") was arrested for exhibitionism, sister Kathy went to work in a massage parlor, and Mary was about to have an affair with a local cop. For all of that, Mary retained her innocence; she was always a victim of circumstance.

While *Mary Hartman, Mary Hartman* represented a departure from traditional soaps (for one thing, it was often aired in the late evening rather than in the daytime), its real significance may be in *how* it got on the air. Despite all of his successes, Lear could not convince any of the three networks to give *Mary* a chance. So he brought the managers of 50 independent TV stations from all over the country to Los Angeles for a quiet dinner on his lawn. Afterward he screened an episode of his new soap and asked them to carry it, sweetening the pot by offering it at budget rates.

Those who accepted were probably grateful. Within weeks the show had doubled existing ratings in its time period for most stations. It was the first time the major networks had been successfully bypassed. Now producers could take more controversial shows directly to the stations, diminishing the power of the networks to dictate what was popular. Dozens of books and hundreds of articles have been written about this problem, but it took Lear's success to prove that the network stranglehold could be broken. In the midst of it all was a show from the most widely criticized genre on television.

Game Shows

Originally introduced to compete with the soaps, game shows now outnumber them. They are actually cheaper to produce, despite the cash they give away. Paying actors, actresses, scriptwriters, and set designers for a soap opera is expensive, but the game show requires only a couple of contestants, a limited production crew, a cheap set with a lot of sequins, and a moderator with a lot of teeth. The audience does the rest.

One game-show producer, interviewed by a network TV crew, was very explicit when asked what he thought was at the bottom of his success: "Greed . . . it's American as apple pie." There is no doubt that the desire to experience financial reward, however vicariously, is at the root of the game format. Often we can't help playing along and trying to outguess the contestants.

Each semester I bring a TV set into the classroom and treat my students to a game show. In the beginning things are rather quiet, but as the show progresses, more begin to participate. At the end everyone is yelling directly at the contestants and criticizing the moderator. The mood is infectious. Even in the college classroom, students who insist they "hate" TV *have* to get involved.

It is precisely this ability to involve the audience that spells game show success. By playing along, we can engage in "risk taking" in a safe and controlled way:

Do you want to keep or trade away your jogging outfit, a year's supply of frozen TV dinners, 200 pet hamsters (with cages), and four thousand eight hundred and twenty-six dollars in cash????? or ????? Do you want what's behind door number two!!!!!?????

The first game shows were a comparatively tranquil lot. *Who Do You Trust?*, *What's*

My Line?, and *You Bet Your Life* were all good-natured get-togethers in which contestants were given time to get acquainted with the emcee. Playing the game was only incidental. This changed in 1955 with the introduction of *The $64,000 Question*. It was the first show to offer really big prize money, and the emphasis shifted to the game itself and the huge financial rewards that went to winners. Contestants were put in an "isolation booth" where they were unable to hear audience hints. Emcee Hal March added to the suspense by constantly reminding the audience: "This question could mean sixty-four thoooouuusand dollars!" Contestants seemed to ponder, look perplexed, sway from side to side, and then suddenly pull the answers out of nowhere. The suspense was unbearable—almost unbelievable.

Before long, we knew it really *was* unbelievable! Participants had been coached ahead of time. In those days, sponsors produced programs, then "rented" space from the networks for airing. As it turned out, executives of Revlon (which had sponsored the show and several offshoots), had decided which contestants could "win" and which were to "lose." A congressional investigation followed, and most quiz shows went off the air. In 1960, networks took control of program production.

By 1960, the last big-money show was off the air, and those that remained, like *The Price Is Right* and *Concentration*, gave away very little cash. Instead, prizes were furnished by sponsors in return for an on-air plug. In 1966, *The Hollywood Squares* premiered, and nine Hollywood personalities began trying to bluff contestants with right or wrong answers to questions based on material from sources like "Dear Abby" and the *National Enquirer*. Again, prizes were furnished by sponsors, but the real show was the stars, who ad-libbed and joked until there wasn't really much time left to play the game.

During the late 1970s, some big-money game shows began to reappear, including *Treasure Hunt* and *Name That Tune*. Ironically, an updated version of the old Revlon favorite, *The $128,000 Question*, was among them. But the new big-money contests were compulsively honest, with answers stored in a computer miles away and sealed envelopes certified by private agencies. Network officials sat in on every taping, and if anything looked remotely fishy, they pulled the plug.

A game-show-junkie friend of mine who lives in Los Angeles attends several tapings daily. One time he got his big chance to become a contestant on *The Hollywood Squares*. After being interviewed several times, he was finally brought to the studio on taping day. The show treats all contestants to lunch at the NBC commissary. There he stood in line with Vincent Price (a *Squares* regular). He asked Price what time it was, and before the star noticed my friend's yellow warning badge, he answered the question. That was all it took; a network supervisor told my friend he could not compete on the show: He and Price might have discussed a possible answer! Disappointed, he pleaded with producers to give him another chance. They told him they'd call the next time Price was off the panel. That was in 1975, and he's still waiting.

Increasingly in the 1970s, game shows seemed bent on milking every last drop of anxiety out of their frantic contestants. *Treasure Hunt* and the durable *Let's Make a Deal* would play the poor contestants' emotions until they were exhausted. One minute they would win, the next they would lose. The emcee would tell them to sit down, then call them up on stage to "give them another chance." Audiences loved it.

The key to success is emotion—the capacity for audiences to identify with contestants and their ups and downs. Little or no skill is required to win big money—just luck.

9.10
Johnny Carson, perennial NBC late-night favorite and reportedly the highest-paid entertainer in television.

TALK SHOWS

Talk shows usually appear late in the afternoon or late in the evening, but seldom in prime time. Many, including those that star Phil Donahue, Mike Douglas and Merv Griffin, are syndicated or produced independently and sold to stations on an individual basis.

The granddaddy of them all is NBC's *Tonight Show*. With its hosts Steve Allen, Jack Paar, and Johnny Carson (along with countless guest hosts), *The Tonight Show* has ruled late-night TV ratings. By the 1980s, Carson had hosted the show for so long that most people simply referred to it as "Carson"—"Did you see Carson last night?" Johnny Carson had become NBC's number one money-

maker (see 9.10). As the late-night audience grew over the years, so did the price sponsors paid to push their dog food or aspirin. *The Tonight Show*'s overhead is comparatively low; the sets are inexpensive and the one production crew is not large. Bob Hope, Jimmy Stewart, and a kazooist from Southeast Asia are all paid the same union minimum (about $600).

Carson's rise to success on *The Tonight Show* was probably due to his own affable personality. Raised in the Midwest, he seems folksy yet smooth. He seldom dominates the show but keeps things going if the guests let down. Most are Hollywood actors and actresses who need little prompting. Again, success is often a matter of chemistry: Carson's on-stage rapport with announcer Ed McMahon and overdressed bandleader Doc Severinsen is legendary.

What do audiences want from a talk show? *The Tonight Show* may offer four or five guests on a given night, some well-known, some lesser known, and some not known at all. Usually there is a vocalist, a comedian, a well-known personality, and a pop "intellectual" guest—perhaps a sociologist explaining some current social or sexual trend. Audiences like this mixed bag because there is something for everybody. The pace is not nearly so frantic as in the prime-time variety shows. Viewers can nod off if they like. For years in most markets, *The Tonight Show* was aired from 11:30 P.M. to 1:00 A.M. and lost half its viewers by sign-off time. However, when NBC signed Carson to a new contract in 1980, part of the agreement was that the show would be reduced to 60 minutes.

Over the years, both ABC and CBS have tried to imitate *The Tonight Show*'s success by offering similar fare. *Joey Bishop* and *Merv Griffin* each lasted less than a year opposite Carson, although Griffin has continued with a successful syndicated show, aired in most markets during the afternoon (see 9.11). Dick

Cavett gave Carson his biggest challenge. Critics loved Cavett, calling him the "thinking man's Johnny Carson." He tried to upgrade the genre by offering the audience in-depth interviews with well-known show people like Marlon Brando and Katharine Hepburn. Cavett also used something called the "theme" show. He'd bring on, say, five singers from the 1930s, or six psychologists to discuss human sexuality. For all his innovations, Cavett's show didn't last. Apparently the mass audience prefers something a little more casual that late at night.

The real key to the talk format may be "talk." We all like to know something about the personal lives of those larger-than-life show-business people. Are they just plain folks in real life, or is there some success secret that may be discovered when they come on stage to be themselves? How close are they to their mediated images?

A 1970s entry in the late-night sweepstakes was NBC's *Tomorrow* show. Shown in most markets from 1:00 A.M. to 2:00 A.M., it began a trend toward late-late programming. Though some affiliated stations did not carry it, those that did found there was indeed life after 1:00 A.M. *Tomorrow* really imitated Dick Cavett; each evening there were one or two guests contributing to a central theme. The success of *Tomorrow* prompted other networks to offer late-late programs (often a movie), and most affiliates stayed on the air.

CHILDREN'S SHOWS

Of all television genres, children's programs are of most concern to researchers. The reason is that children are thought to be the most vulnerable to concepts they find on TV. If TV is as powerful as some say, what kinds of ideas are we putting into the heads of tomorrow's citizens?

9.11
Merv Griffin, one of the most durable talk-show hosts in television, has had a successful syndicated show since the 1960s.

In the beginning, there were *Captain Video*, *Kukla, Fran, and Ollie*, and *Howdy Doody*. These were evening shows (*Howdy Doody* was usually aired at around 5:30 P.M.). When the networks introduced daytime programs, they included *Captain Kangaroo* and other low-key, gentle entertainment designed to amuse the toddlers and keep them occupied. The commercial success of such programs in the 1950s prompted a barrage of children's shows on Saturday mornings.

Most of these slots were filled with cartoons. Though cartoons have changed over the years (there are now fewer animals and more people), the basic formula remains the same. A central character or set of characters is placed in conflict with another character or

set of characters. Action results from the conflict. In the end all is resolved when *our* character wins.

The classic example is the "Roadrunner" series, which still appears on TV and in movie theaters. Roadrunner does nothing but make a pleasant little "beep beep" and run up and down desert paths at 100 miles per hour. He is simple, good, and innocent. Villain Wile E. Coyote plots and schemes to catch Roadrunner, but his elaborate traps always seem to backfire, leaving him the worse for wear. Yet there remains something endearing about both characters. Interestingly, one 1980 study identified *Bugs Bunny-Roadrunner* as the most violent program in all of television.

Occasionally the cartoon format appears in prime time, and audience researchers find that Mom and Dad are looking over their kids' shoulders. *The Flintstones*, *The Jetsons*, and *Top Cat* all made it in the 1960s. The 1970s saw a dozen *Peanuts* specials in prime time and even one featuring the characters from *Doonesbury*.

The only prime-time children's show that spanned all three decades was Walt Disney's (1954–81). (The program had three different names, but they were all essentially the same show.) The Disney show offered cartoons, action-adventure, and other programs appropriate for children. Parents trusted Disney to deliver what was good for their kids; in a sea of sex and violence, it was an island of wholesomeness.

Critics have also been wary of commercials aired during children's shows, asserting that children may be more susceptible to the advertiser's message and should be protected from the gimmicks used to sell products to adults. The products themselves were often criticized. Some claimed that war toys encouraged kids to poke one another's eyes out, and "sugar-coated" cereals turned out to be more sugar than cereal.

Parents are equally uneasy about commercials and children's programs in general. That uneasiness stems from their instinctive knowledge of the power of television. They watch their children gaze hypnotically at the colorful images dashing across the screen and wonder what will come of it all. This was particularly true with parents who experienced the medium for the first time while adults. Today's younger parents grew up with TV and may not fear it as much. "After all," they say, "we watched TV all the time, and we turned out all right." What they may not realize is how much of what they are now is a product of that small screen.

SPORTS

In competition with kids for rights to the family set on weekend mornings is the sports fan. Much has been written about the impact of sports on TV and vice versa. When sports coverage began, it seemed like a natural. After all, TV could "put you there" in a way radio never could. Live sports coverage was a big part of the 1950s. Dominating all was the broadcast of major heavyweight boxing matches and baseball's World Series. The technical capabilities of TV improved to make diversified sports coverage a reality in the 1960s. An experimental broadcast of the 1940 World Series had involved one camera located on the sidelines. By the 1960s there were a dozen cameras, and by the 1980s a roving "mini-cam" had been added along with cameras in helicopters, hot-air balloons, and locker rooms.

But the real story of TV sports is football. The game was a second-class professional sport in the 1950s; more attention was focused on college games. The average National Football League (NFL) player was earning about $6,000 a year. TV changed all that. It was impractical to televise baseball every day; no *one* game ever meant anything, and besides, baseball was so long and drawn out. Football was different; there was plenty of action with balls thrown in the air and guys running into each other all over the place. Football was so, well . . . so *visual!* What's more, when the clock ran out, that was it. No overtime (prior to the 1983 NFL season) meant no unscheduled pre-emptions of other network programs. When TV networks approached the NFL owners, they found them eager to talk. This was in sharp contrast to baseball teams, which enjoyed record attendance and didn't want to rock the boat. The television-football marriage was born.

When the United States Football League (USFL) played its first season in 1983, it was the lucrative TV contracts that made the league financially possible. Despite warnings by some that Americans would tire of football that dragged on into July, early indications were that the league was a success and that the ratings were justifying the millions of dollars spent by commercial, cable, and satellite TV services for rights to the games.

The people of North America watch a lot of football on TV. The Super Bowl seems to break its own rating records year after year. By the 1980s, more than half the men and women in America were tuning in for the annual spectacle. Football provided just the right amount of action (violence, if you like) to make it the perfect TV vehicle. The status of professional football rose accordingly, and by the time the first few Super Bowls were aired, baseball was no longer "the national pastime."

Football provides many of the same gratifications as other TV genres. There is certainly the desire to believe in the "miraculous" ("That catch was a miracle, Howard"). There is the desire to imagine oneself a hero ("Mildred, did you see that? That was just like the touchdown I scored at Tech back in '57—remember?"). There is the need to experience the ugly and the desire to share in the suffering of others ("Look at that field— it must be frozen solid. Why, it's 17 below zero out there").

According to communications researcher Michael Real, football represents a microcosm of American social values. For example, it is a game of territory; the winner is the one who gains the most. Football is competitive, played by the clock, and full of "deadlines" and penalties, much like real life. Of course, football also supplies the heroes with whom we can identify. The Super Bowl in particular is a communal festival. Many Super Bowl watchers interviewed admitted that they seldom watch other football games on TV or in real life but felt that they *had* to watch this one because "everyone is doing it, and everybody will be talking about it tomorrow."

This tremendous sense of participation, of being involved with everyone else in experiencing a spectacle, explains a lot about the popularity of football and other sports on TV. ABC figured this out in the late 1960s and began quietly buying up rights to air the Olympics. By the 1970s, ABC had pulled off a ratings coup, putting the games on night after night in prime time and outrating the competition.

Though the Olympics had been aired before, ABC showed them with a clearer understanding of TV form. The TV audience never had to wait for any event. Olympic schedules were altered so that one event would take place here, another one five minutes later somewhere else. Cameras were set up at every location, and viewers were treated to colorful nonstop action supplemented with "personality profiles." Interviews with Olympic stars were taped in advance but aired just before the crucial moment of "the thrill of victory" or "the agony of defeat."

Sports purists decry such manipulative actions, saying TV has forever altered the true spirit of sport. They point to football referees working directly with TV crews, calling "time out" whenever there is need for a commercial. But these critics miss the point:

Football is not a game played on the gridiron for a few thousand fans, it is a game played on television for millions of fans. Football *is* television, in the truest sense of the word, for many, many viewers. And so are tennis, golf, bowling, basketball, and even baseball.

I was struck by this at a recent baseball game. It was San Francisco at Cincinnati, and we had choice seats just over home plate. I noticed that the guy next to me had a portable television set and a radio. Both were tuned to the game we were watching. After a few beers I got up the courage to ask him, "Why all the paraphernalia?" He looked up from the TV, turned up the radio, and gazed at the field through his binoculars. "Whaddya mean?" he said impatiently. "Why, without this stuff I wouldn't have any idea what was going on."

We need to have real life filtered through mass-media channels before we really feel that we have experienced "the total event." Particularly in sports, the media actually determine the nature of the experience. Media coverage has become more important than the event itself.

The genres of TV combine to give us everything we always wanted in real life and could never have, everything we always wanted in real life but were afraid to have, everything we used to have in real life but lost. In doing this, they have actually become real life, influencing every action we take and every word we say.

REAL LIFE AS MEDIATED REALITY

One notable programming trend in the 1980s is the increase in the "real-life" programs making up part of TV's mediated reality. Of course we have always had talk shows and

9.12
Real People *was the first in a series of "real-life" programs to garner high ratings in the early 1980s.*

news programs. The success of news magazines like *60 Minutes* proved long ago that people can be entertained by fact as well as fiction. Then NBC added a twist. Its *Real People* (see 9.12) was the surprise hit of 1980, and it spawned a number of other shows, including *Those Amazing Animals*, *That's Incredible*, and *Speak Up, America*.

These shows are part of a movement I call "the new populism" in TV programming. The idea is to point out to the viewer that real people are just as fascinating as those fic-

tional characters they have been watching on TV for 30 years. However, the same basic gratifications are involved. Hence, we get lots of sex (the stripper who has "done her thing" non-stop for 13 days), violence (daredevil stunt people driving motorcycles over recreational vehicles and breaking their necks), and all the other ingredients that make up the appeal of fictional programs. TV critics scoffed at most of these shows; whether the real-life phenomenon is a brief fad or will become a new TV genre remains to be seen.

9.13

A scene in the making from An American Family: Filmmakers Alan and Susan Raymond (right) at home with Pat Loud and her son, Grant, in their Santa Barbara, California, living room. For seven months, the Raymonds shared, and captured on film, the day-to-day lives of the seven-member William C. Loud family. The show was so successful PBS produced and aired a follow-up documentary in 1983.

Not all real-life shows have been panned by the critics as extensively as those just mentioned. In fact, some experiments have been met with a certain degree of public acceptance and critical praise. One such show, *An American Family,* was a documentary series aired on PBS in 1973. The crew lived with a real family, the Louds, in their huge house in Santa Barbara, California, for seven months. The result was a 12-hour television production. The Loud family may not have been "typical"—it was certainly not typical of television sitcom families—but it represented what most middle-class Americans were striving for, a chance to succeed and to live out "the good life" in a pleasant environment (see 9.13).

The weekly glimpse into the Loud family also revealed some situations that were definitely not sitcom: Son Lance was a homosexual, and other kids were involved with drugs. In final episodes, Mom and Dad had a series of scathing arguments which ended with separation and divorce. Real-life divorce! Meanwhile, the cameras whirred away, and America tuned in.

Never was the disintegration of a family portrayed with such accuracy and authenticity. Several years later, all were interviewed and asked whether they would do it again. All except wife Pat Loud agreed that they would. By that time, the family was completely scattered: The parents had obtained their final divorce decree, Pat had moved to New York, father Bill had a bachelor pad in Santa Barbara was dating frequently, and son Lance had moved into a shabby New York apartment and was trying to start a rock group.

Many of the episodes had a "home movie" quality about them, but the unique form was apparently part of the tremendous appeal of the series. It became one of the biggest audience draws ever for PBS.

If nothing else can be said for real-life TV, at least it affords us an opportunity to examine the differences between our own everyday experiences and those that form the basis for TV's mediated reality. Exploring and being more aware of those differences should be an important part of your education, one that will help you become a more sophisticated and informed consumer of mass communication in the years to come.

ISSUES AND ANSWERS:
ROOTS, MASS AUDIENCE,
AND SOCIAL AWARENESS

During the winter of 1977, some 130 million Americans took part in a massive sociological experiment. For eight consecutive nights, a TV version of *Roots*, the best-selling family history by Alex Haley, invaded America's living rooms. The story of seven generations of black Americans struggling under suppression and slavery struck a responsive chord in the mass audience. It educated blacks and nonblacks about black history and the struggle for freedom and sparked an interest in genealogy for everyone. While *Roots* was based on facts, parts of it were clearly fiction. But it is fiction in the tradition of *Uncle Tom's Cabin* that often brings about massive social change.

About 750,000 copies of Haley's book had been sold when *Roots* was aired, but for more than 99 percent of TV viewers it was a new story. Clearly it made a distinct impression on them. Many observers felt it would improve race relations, and even the most skeptical admitted it left nonblacks with a more sympathetic view of black history.

Yet *Roots* was not merely popular, it was the most popular prime-time presentation up to that time, nudging aside the prior champ, *Gone with the Wind*. Just as the 1939 film displayed a startling knowledge of movie form, so *Roots* was a brilliant TV production, conceived and designed for the newer medium.

Interestingly, both stories used slavery and the Civil War as a backdrop for a glimpse into the lives of one family. Though both productions were based on a book, the visual presentation seemed to move the mass audience in a way no book could. *Gone with the Wind* told one side of the story, *Roots* another. Both had a profound effect on the mass audience.

Roots, like all prime-time television programs, was not simply a passive body of entertainment but a complex mix of narrative and visual appeal that tells us about audience needs. But at the same time television mirrors society, it also reconstructs it. Though *Roots* may not have set out to accomplish specific goals, it was a social experiment nonetheless. The audience was changed. Black Congressman John Conyers said of the show, "It doesn't cure unemployment or take people out of the ghetto. But it's a democratic statement eloquent as any that's ever been devised, and we've been talking about what can be done with it."

The real lesson in *Roots* may have more to do with television than with black history. For those eight nights, it was obvious that prime-time TV brought an important message to 130 million Americans. How long will it be before we realize that there are many other messages brought to us every night in exactly the same way? *Roots* was not a public-television or government-structured "educational" program, it was *commercial* prime-time viewing. It made the *ongoing*, if invisible, prime-time TV education visible for a short time. It was new and dealt with controversial material; yet the very success of every prime-time genre is based on conflict and controversy.

Perhaps nightly television program content is not always as powerful as *Roots* or *Holocaust*, yet is it so different? It is easy to poke fun at the "idiot box" but far more difficult to unravel its mysteries. Everyone agrees that *Roots* helped us realize the tremendous potential of commercial TV, but in some ways, that potential is *already* being fulfilled.

QUERIES AND CONCEPTS

1 What is your favorite television show? Can you think of ways that it may have affected the person that you are? If you could trade places with any television character for a day, who would it be and why?

2 Name three programs currently on the air that you feel aim for the lowest common denominator and three that do not. Which are the most popular? Why?

3 Check this week's TV schedule and make a list of all prime-time TV series. Then break them down in terms of genre, using the criteria found in this chapter. Does any one particular genre seem to dominate?

4 Using the 31 gratifications listed in 9.2, pick a television show and watch it carefully, keeping the list in front of you at all times. Can you find specific plot instances that match some gratifications? Have a friend do the same and compare notes.

5 Make a list of current heroes and heroines in prime-time TV. What serious character flaws or personality quirks may have contributed to their success?

6 Turn on the TV set at 9:00 A.M. and leave it on all day no matter what. Make notes about what you find. Discuss.

7 Enter the world of children's programming; pick a Saturday morning, turn on the set, and tough it out. Can you spot the shows that appeal to specific age groups? Ask your little brothers, sisters, or neighborhood kids about their favorite programs. Their answers may startle you.

8 What is the total amount of weekend TV time devoted to sports programs? Would you rather watch a favorite sport on TV, view it in person, or directly participate in it?

9 You are a local television reviewer. Sit down and watch a network series that you have never seen before. Write a review based on your knowledge of prime-time programming patterns.

10 Reread the final paragraph of this chapter. Do you agree or disagree? Why?

READINGS AND REFERENCES

Now Back to *Maverick*

John Fiske
John Hartley
Reading Television. London: Methuen, 1978.
 This book is now widely available in the United States and is unique in that it lays the groundwork for new ways of understanding how we perceive television and incorporate it into our lives. Chapters on the functions, modes, codes, and signs of television. Very stimulating. Lots to think about here.

Martin Williams
TV, The Casual Art. New York: Oxford University Press, 1982.

Williams is a regular contributor to New York's *Village Voice*, and his wit and wisdom about the medium provide entertainment as well as vital information. Despite the 1982 publication date, most of the series written about here are those that were popular during the 1950s and 1960s.

From Sitcom to *Star Trek:* The Genres of Prime Time

Tim Brooks
Earle Marsh
The Complete Directory to Prime Time Network TV Shows: 1946–Present. New York: Ballantine Books, 1981.

This is the ultimate book for any TV genre fan. It includes a listing for every network prime-time show that has ever been on the air. Some entries are brief, but the more important shows like *Maverick, I Love Lucy,* and *The Fugitive* receive more extensive treatments. Good for research or just to put on top of the TV set at home. A must for all serious students of the medium. Long awaited and well done. Highly recommended.

Harlan Ellison
The Glass Teat. Moonachie, N.J.: Pyramid Publications, 1975.
The Other Glass Teat. Moonachie, N.J.: Pyramid Publications, 1975.

These are collections of Ellison's columns that originally appeared in the *Los Angeles Free Press.* For many of you, Ellison needs no introduction. He is a prolific writer of science fiction who has also written dozens of television scripts. He won a Hugo award for his *Star Trek* script "The City on the Edge of Forever." Ellison has a tendency to dwell on the sexual implications of TV,

but that makes it all the more fun. You'll read criticism on everything from *The Beverly Hillbillies* to *Star Trek.*

Horace Newcomb
TV: The Most Popular Art. Garden City, N.Y.: Doubleday, 1974.

Includes sections on sitcom, action-adventure, western, and other genres. Newcomb is a TV pioneer, the first to write about the genres of TV with anything less than abhorrence. Instead, he offers insight into *why* these programs are popular. In doing so, he provides a catalog of American myths and values. This may be the most important book ever written on the content of commercial television.

Horace Newcomb, ed.
Television: The Critical View, 3d ed. New York: Oxford University Press, 1982.

A follow-up on *TV: The Most Popular Art,* this time a collection of essays on the genres of TV, plus a section on the meanings behind the myths. Six excellent pieces on the movement toward defining television in terms of mass culture.

Action-Adventure

Stephen E. Whitfield
Gene Roddenberry
The Making of Star Trek. New York: Ballantine Books, 1973.

This is the definitive book on the production of a television show, not only for those who want to produce but also for those interested in what happens from the time the idea is born until the final product appears. Written with reverence by one of *Star Trek*'s fans in collaboration with producer Roddenberry.

Daytime TV and the Common Cold

Charles Sopkin
Seven Glorious Days, Seven Fun-Filled Nights. New York: Simon & Schuster, 1968.
> This bible of commercial TV complaints was created in seven days and nights, but the author never rested. Entertaining and informative.

Daytime Soap Operas

Muriel G. Cantor
Suzanne Pingree
The Soap Opera. Beverly Hills, Calif.: Sage Publications, 1983.
> An academic look at the soap opera genre. Perhaps the most sophisticated approach yet. Includes chapters on radio soaps, content, and the soap audience. An overview into research in the field. Very useful.

Madeleine Edmondson
David Rounds
From Mary Noble *to* Mary Hartman: *The Complete Soap Opera Book*. New York: Stein & Day, 1976.
> This is a thorough history of the soap opera for the more serious student. It contains findings from a number of research studies done on the genre over the years and is comparatively up to date. By the time you read this chapter, there should be a new edition out. Highly recommended.

Robert LaGuardia
The Wonderful World of TV Soap Operas. New York: Ballantine Books, 1977.
> This paperback is strictly for the fans, but it does contain some background information on how soaps are made and why they hold such a tremendous appeal for the mass audience.

Soap Opera Digest, available at the newsstand, delivers capsule plots of all daytime and prime-time shows.

Game Shows; Talk Shows

TV Guide is a good source for current trends in these areas. You'll find it included in the *Popular Periodical Index*. Some back copies are available from Triangle Publications, Radnor, PA 19088.

Children's Shows

Ray Brown
Children and Television. Beverly Hills, Calif.: Sage Publications, 1976.
> A thoughtful empirical analysis of the impact of children's TV programs. Full of insight, this anthology covers all the bases—violence, advertising, and social trends.

Robert M. Liebert
Joyce N. Sprafkin
Emily S. Davidson
The Early Widow: Effects of Television on Children and Youth, 2d ed. New York: Pergamon Press, 1982.
> One of the most up-to-date texts in the field, this covers the thorny issues surrounding children and television as well as any single book can. Like most of the research they report, the authors are generally critical of TV's role in influencing children. Of great value to those interested in the area is Appendix B, which offers a synopsis of each of the important studies done over the years. The references section is also very useful. Highly recommended.

Sports

Michael Real
"Super Bowl: Mythic Spectacle." *Journal of Communication*, Winter 1975, pp. 31–43.

Real Life as Mediated Reality

Michael R. Real
Mass Mediated Culture. Englewood Cliffs, N.J.: Prentice-Hall, 1977.

The author discusses a number of mediated experiences, including Disneyland, Marcus Welby, Billy Graham, and others. Fine introductory chapter on the significance of mass-mediated culture. Highly recommended.

Issues and Answers: *Roots*, Mass Audience, and Social Awareness

"Why 'Roots' Hit Home."
Time, February 14, 1977, pp. 68–71.

10

Sunsets and Scenarios: Film as Popular Art

AMONG MY MOST PRIZED POSSESSIONS IS A BLACK AND WHITE photo of Mary Pickford (10.1). Mary was "America's sweetheart" during the 1920s. She was the picture of innocence. Her blonde hair fell over her shoulders and flowed down her back in long curls. She planted an image in my mind of what innocence was.

Mary Pickford's now dead and buried. Still, the young star lives on because I rush to see her movies, which were made decades before I was born. On the silver screen her innocence was captured forever.

THE AUDIOVISUAL RECORD

Perhaps the most important thing to remember about film is that it started keeping a complete audiovisual history of the world. We see evidence of that today. There are many TV shows set in the 1930s, the 1940s, the 1950s, and so on, but few set in the 1920s. Why? Because we have formed few ideas about what the 1920s were like. We can go back to films from the 1930s to look at the suits and listen to the voices. Film first provided a *multisensory* record of western civilization. That record began in 1927 with the release of *The Jazz Singer*, the first "talkie"—film containing a vocal track (see 10.2). (Actually only a portion of it was in sound.)

Two years later the stock market crashed and the Great Depression began. *The Jazz Singer* is a valuable document of the carefree life and entertainment that existed before the Depression.

People tell me that the movies should be more like real life. I disagree. It is real life that should be more like the movies.

WALTER WINCHELL

10.1

Mary Pickford (1893–1979) reigned supreme as "America's sweetheart" for an entire generation. Her active career spanned 23 years, 125 short features (as the one- and two-reel early silent pictures were called) as well as 52 full-length motion pictures. Cecil B. DeMille, one of her many directors, once wrote about the "America's sweetheart" label that "thousands of such phrases are born daily in Hollywood. . . . About once in a generation such a phrase lives, because it is more than a phrase: it is a fact."

LIFE IS LIKE A MOVIE

Film provides us with a giant mirror—a reflection of the values, the half-truths, and the ideals of society.

It does this because writers, directors, and producers know how to rifle our personal emotional treasure chests and translate their contents to a film. We then buy them back at the box office. The more closely a film approximates our own myths and values, the more likely we are to see it and recommend it to others.

For example, fear is a universal emotion. We have all been afraid at one time or another, afraid we were going to die some horrible, lingering, and unjust death. The master of suspense, Alfred Hitchcock, successfully played to these fears, becoming one of the largest legends in filmdom.

Likewise, *Gone with the Wind* played on our romantic emotions. Rhett Butler was a rogue who had a way with women. Scarlett O'Hara was a beautiful, spoiled belle of the old South whose love affair with Ashley Wilkes was never to be. We wanted to jump into the screen and plead: "Oh Scarlett, can't you see it is Rhett who really loves you?" But she didn't, and her life was ruined.

These are universal emotions—fear, love, disappointment—but few of us have experienced such total ruin, complete love, paralyzing fear, and savage violence. The film blows up universal emotions until they are larger than life. When we come upon something in real life that is profound, we say, "This is just like a movie." Our very way of perceiving intense experience is shaped by what we have seen on film (see 10.3).

In F. Scott Fitzgerald's final novel, *The Last Tycoon*, an admirer marvels at the power a movie producer, Stahr, has had over her life: "Some of my more romantic ideas actually stemmed from pictures. . . . It's more than possible that some of the pictures which Stahr himself conceived had shaped me into what I was."

Indeed, the power of the filmmaker to shape our notions about intense experience, to provide a series of fictional experiences through which we filter real life, is unrivaled in all of

10.2

Time Line: The History of Film in America

1820s In England Peter Mark Roget and John Paris conduct experiments and publish findings involving persistence of vision.

1839 Louis Daguerre in France develops a workable system of still photography

1882 Dr. E. J. Marey, a French physiologist, develops a photographic "gun" that takes 12 pictures per second.

1888 Thomas Edison and assistant William Dickson develop the first workable motion picture camera.

1895 Auguste and Louis Lumière perfect a projection system and exhibit films to a paying public. The movie theater is born.

1900 Edison, Biograph, and Vitagraph are competing companies in the new film industry.

1903 Edwin S. Porter releases *The Great Train Robbery.*

1905–10 Era of the nickelodeons.

1906 British inventors Edward R. Turner and G. Albert Smith devise

Kinemacolor, the first practical natural color film process.

1909 The Motion Picture Patents Company is formed.

1915 D. W. Griffith's *Birth of a Nation* becomes the most successful film yet.

1922 Technicolor is introduced.

1927 *The Jazz Singer* is the first "talkie."

1929 *On with the Show* is the first all-talking color film.

1930 After just three years, almost all new films are talkies.

1933 Fred Astaire and Ginger Rogers team up for *Flying Down to Rio* and become film's most successful couple.

1939 *Gone with the Wind* is the film of the year, sweeping the Oscar awards.

1941 *Citizen Kane,* perhaps the greatest American film of the sound era, is released.

1946 Film's biggest box-office year; 90 million Americans are going to the movies every week.

1950s The film audience is younger than ever. Many adults give up films to watch television.

1960 Alfred Hitchcock's *Psycho* is released.

1969 *Easy Rider* typifies youth-oriented films with a message.

1970s Disaster films *Towering Inferno, Earthquake,* and others are successful.

1972 X-rated *Deep Throat* pioneers pornography for the mass audience.

1975 *Jaws* becomes the most financially successful film to date.

1975 Robert Altman's *Nashville* breaks new ground in entertainment films with the vignette approach.

1977 *Star Wars* breaks theater attendance records, surpasses *Jaws.*

1977 An American Film Institute survey picks *Gone with the Wind* as the top film of all time.

1978 A rash of movies involving popular music appears: *American Hot Wax, FM, Sgt. Pepper's Lonely Hearts Club Band,* and *The Buddy Holly Story* follow on the heels of *Saturday Night Fever.*

1980 *Star Trek: The Motion Picture* costs $40 million but fails at the box office. Meanwhile, *The Empire Strikes Back* draws huge audiences.

1981 The average major feature theatrical film costs $10 million to make and must gross over $16 million to show a profit, according to *Variety.*

1983 The third segment of George Lucas's *Star Wars* trilogy, *Return of the Jedi,* breaks box-office records.

10.3

Scarlett (Vivien Leigh) visits Rhett (Clark Gable) in his prison cell shortly after the end of the war. These love scenes represent our very definition of romance in America.

mass communication. Somehow, the mediated reality we see "up there" takes on an inexplicable significance.

At first glance it's easy to make a distinction between real life and "reel life." If I asked you what the difference was, you would probably respond rather huffily that you could "certainly tell the difference between fact and fiction." However, it's really not that simple.

We have seen how all mass media play a large part in formulating our attitudes, beliefs, and ideals, because we all incorporate perceived mediated reality back into our real lives. For example, most of us have never experienced a major crime firsthand, so we formulate our ideas about it from what we see in films or on television. If we actually do witness a crime, we can't help comparing it with what we have seen on mass media. We might even react to a given situation by imitating behaviors of those we have seen in a film or on TV!

Our notions about romantic love are almost completely derived from mass media, formed by what we have read and seen. All of us are waiting for that great scene when we will take that special person in our arms for the first kiss. It will be a long, smooth, beautiful kiss. Everything will be perfect. The skyrockets will explode, and we will go off and live "happily ever after" just like in the movies.

The problem with this is that real life can't always measure up to the expectations we have formed as the result of watching movies. More

often when you take a special someone in your arms, you find that person is in the middle of a peanut butter candy, or your braces get stuck together.

THE MAGIC LANTERN

Like all mass media, film has two component parts, *form* and *content*. The form of film involves cast, costume, and location, as well as the mechanical phenomena that make it go. The content is the story, plot line, and cast of characters that deliver the "message" to us. When we experience moving pictures, we seldom think of the form but (as with all mass media) concentrate on content to derive the message.

Moving pictures do not actually move, but they seem to because of a physiological process called "persistence of vision." When a series of still pictures is flashed before your eyes faster than you can perceive each one individually, your mind runs them together, creating the illusion of motion—like those cartoon books that instruct you to thumb through rapidly and "watch the characters come to life." The characters appeared to move because of persistence of vision.

This was discovered almost 2,000 years ago by the astronomer Ptolemy, but it was Thomas Edison who put it to work. His incandescent bulb was so strong it could project pictures on a wall, making them visible to a large audience (see 10.4). This is how "moving" pictures differed from other media forms using persistence of vision, which were already popular in the late 19th century. Kinetoscopes and vitascopes were one-person peep shows usually found in a penny arcade. You put in a penny and turned a crank. When turned at the proper speed, the pictures appeared to move.

In the late 1880s, one of Edison's assistants, William Dickson, developed a camera and a projecting device using the new bulb. His first effort at filmmaking was not exactly an aesthetic masterpiece; it lasted 15 seconds and recorded a man sneezing. Yet there were many films with equally dull content—random scenes at a downtown location; the sun rising in a cornfield—that played to large audiences around the turn of the century. (The admission price was usually a nickel, and the theaters were called "nickelodeons.") Such is often the case with a new medium. The new form carries it for a while; refinement of content comes later. (Ask your parents about the early years of television. They'll tell you there was only one station, and when they saw their first television they just stared and stared. It didn't matter what was on the screen—they'd watch *Howdy Doody*, a test pattern, anything.)

10.4
Thomas Edison with an early version of the motion picture projector.

Many who have written of this era have romanticized it or found it "cute," overlooking the seamier side of things. In *Two Reels and a Crank*, Albert E. Smith (who helped found Vitagraph, one of the early motion picture companies), recalls things a little more realistically. There was tremendous competition among early filmmakers to cash in on this new revenue source. Smith admits to "pirating" pictures of major boxing matches by sneaking in a huge camera under his overcoat. He "faked" pictures of major battles of the Spanish-American War and passed them off to an unsuspecting public as the real thing. At the same time, Smith tells fascinating stories of legitimate photographic missions. He claims to have filmed the charge up San Juan Hill with Teddy Roosevelt, who became the first American President introduced to the people via a nonprint mass medium, the film newsreel. Smith was filming a speech by President McKinley when suddenly a shot rang out. The President had been mortally wounded, and it was all on film.

Often the most vicious film battles were fought in the courtroom by competing companies vying for patent rights to cameras and projector components. They "borrowed" one another's inventions shamelessly. For years Edison felt he should receive *all* the revenues from motion pictures, claiming his inventions and patents had made them possible. By the time he organized a court fight, the situation was out of hand. Too many new improvements had come along. In the end a collective was formed, and agreements were reached among the major patent holders. They formed the Motion Picture Patents Company (MPPC) and pooled the use of all patents, giving any additional benefits to the inventors. All movie companies were required to pay a flat fee each time they shot a film. Edison held the largest number of patents, and eventually his share of pool funds reflected it.

Some filmmakers were unhappy with this agreement, particularly smaller companies that operated on very small budgets and preferred to pay no fees at all. Their solution was to leave the East and go so far away that the MPPC would have a hard time tracking them down. Since all films had to be shot outdoors (indoor lighting for film had not been perfected), they decided to locate where there was sun all year round. Most ended up in a remote farm area just north of Los Angeles, called Hollywood. Here was the ideal location for filmmaking, a quiet, sunny area close to a major West Coast town. But it wasn't quiet for long.

Hollywood became a fairy tale land. Even today, for all its tackiness and vulgarity, Hollywood inspires adjectives like beautiful, thrilling, amazing, and spectacular. You can still walk down Hollywood Boulevard and read the names of the stars on the sidewalks or buy a "map to the homes of the stars." Films, movie companies, and stars may come and go, but the myth of Hollywood remains.

THE QUIET YEARS

The birthdate of significant content in film is generally regarded as 1903. An American, Edwin S. Porter, had experimented with moving pictures that told a story in his *Life of an American Fireman* the year before,

but it was quite by accident. Now he set out specifically to construct a "story" film—one that would convey a complete plot, not simply capture an existing event. Porter felt that by using stage actors, a script, and joining disparate pieces of film together he could convey a story to the audience.

It hardly seems revolutionary now, but it was the first time it had been done. Many were skeptical about such a venture, but Porter went ahead anyway, and *The Great Train Robbery* was filmed and released. It was a western, and the plot was pretty flimsy. In the final scene a robber shoots a gun directly toward the audience for no apparent reason. Yet the film was a tremendous commercial success, paving the way for more complex subject matter.

Twelve years later, film took its greatest leap forward. A former Porter actor, D. W. Griffith, had shot a number of short films that were enormously popular. Many were based on American history—pioneering, the West, Indians, and the like. When Griffith decided to make a large-scale film, one subject came to mind. The Civil War was the perfect historical backdrop because it was the most turbulent time in American history, a time when conflicting ideologies were at a peak and unprecedented violence swept the land. But Griffith could not capture such a monumental event while confined to the existing form of film. He expanded it to fit, using a large screen to reproduce marvelously photographed outdoor battle scenes. There were moving shots, extreme close-ups, and a host of other film innovations (see 10.5). *Birth of a Nation* was issued complete with a score to be performed by a full orchestra. No one had ever experienced anything like it. It became a huge box-office success and was the most popular film ever until 1939, when another Civil War epic *(Gone with the Wind)* took its place.

So advanced was *Birth of a Nation* that almost all film critics agree it was the most

10.5
Director D. W. Griffith at work.

influential silent film ever made. It is difficult for a number of reasons for students viewing the film today to assess its impact properly. The film's heroes are members of the Ku Klux Klan. (This reflects Griffith's own racial prejudices and his rural southern background.) Though the content is socially archaic, the achievement of form remains as brilliant today as it was more than half a century ago.

Griffith continued making epic films. His next effort, *Intolerance*, one of the most expensive silent films every made, was on an even grander scale. It contained four interwoven stories, and the film skipped from one to the next. That is a common technique in today's cinema but one that confused the 1916 audience. Griffith was ahead of his time, and he couldn't take the audience with him. In 1948, he died alone and almost forgotten. It was only after his death that his genius was truly recognized.

While moviegoers of the quiet years flocked to see short comedy films with stars like Charlie Chaplin and the Keystone Kops, epic films flourished, too. Audiences now were used to full-length feature films like *Cleopatra*, *Ben-Hur*, and *The Ten Commandments*. These names may be familiar to you, since remakes were done for the sound era.

This tendency to redo existing material did not start when sound came to film. Most films in the quiet years were based on books and stories popular at the time. Griffith's *Birth of a Nation* was taken from the novel *The Clansman*. As the practice became commonplace, many discovered that stories lifted directly from print were simply not the same on the screen. We know now that they couldn't be. Whenever we transfer content from one medium to another, it must change to accommodate the new form. But in the quiet years there was little radio and no television, and audiences were not used to the process of adaptation. According to novelist Elinor Glyn, the transferral process was often painful:

All authors, living or dead, famous or obscure, shared the same fate. Their stories were re-writ-

Miss Lillian Gish
Triangle.

10.6
Lillian Gish (1896–   ) was one of famed director D. W. Griffith's "discoveries" shortly after he joined two other noted directors Thomas W. Ince and Mack Sennet to form Triangle Film Corporation. In The Stars, *film critic Richard Schickel noted that Griffith kept moving his cameras closer and closer to the faces of the actors and actresses, thus his need for "unlined youthful faces for his closeups . . . and unwrinkled minds which he could command absolutely." Apparently Gish filled the bill; she was one of his most successful actresses and starred in a number of his films including* Broken Blossoms *(1919),* Way Down East *(1920), and* Orphans of the Storm *(1921). In 1984, still a working actress, she was presented with the American Film Institute's Lifetime Achievement Award.*

ten and completely altered either by the stenographers and continuity girls of the scenario department, or by the Assistant Director and his lady-love, or by the leading lady, or by anyone else who happened to pass through the studio; and even when at last after infinite struggle a scene was shot which bore some resemblance to the original story it was certain to be left out in the cutting-room or pared away to such an extent that all meaning which it might once have had was lost.

THE STAR IS BORN

But critics and authors had yet to learn what the public knew instinctively: Story content was only part of the film phenomenon. The film audience was becoming less concerned with *what* and more concerned with *who*. The star system was born.

Early silent-film stars came from all walks of life. Some, like Charlie Chaplin, had enormous talent; others had only tremendous visual appeal. Most popular of all were those who projected a romantic, sexual image. Actors Douglas Fairbanks and Rudolph Valentino were cast as romantic rogues, while actresses Lillian Gish (see 10.6) and Mary Pickford projected virginal innocence and breathtaking beauty. Soon, titles of films appeared at the bottom of the marquee—at the top was the name of the film's best-known actor or actress. People began to ask each other: "Have you seen the new Valentino film?" *Story* had been replaced by *star*.

Cults grew around the great stars, and the public became hungry for details of their lives. Fan clubs abounded. The studios were more than happy to cooperate, sensing that a bevy of stars under contract meant financial success. What they did not foresee were the days when stars would make exorbitant salary demands and become "free agents," moving from one studio to the next. Every major film studio in America was built on the star system, yet it was that same system that eventually led to a decline in big-studio control of the industry.

THE MOVIES LEARN TO TALK

In the late 1920s my father played the organ for the silent pictures in one of Los Angeles's major movie houses. He made $60 a week, which was more money than he had ever seen in his life. He drove a brand-new Jowett and, needless to say, this put him at the top of the social heap at Manual Arts High School.

But suddenly tragedy struck. A theater down the street began showing *The Jazz Singer*, and overnight, as he recalls it, the lines in front of his theater dwindled while people waited for hours to see (and hear) the talkies. The theater owner assured him it was "just a fad." The quality of silent pictures produced during the late 1920s was fantastic, whereas the talkies were crude and simplistic by comparison. Surely the audience would soon come to its senses! When it didn't, my father found himself out of a job and playing in bars for two dollars a night. He was understandably bitter; he had to sell the Jowett, and for years refused to go into a theater to see a talkie.

Technological alterations in mass communication can often move so fast that even those closest to media are unable to fathom them. The same producers who had been successful with silent pictures were bewildered with talkies. Studios that got into sound early flourished; others perished. Stars who had commanded five-figure salaries were suddenly unwanted because their voices did not match the voices audiences had created from their visual image. As we have seen, 20 years later radio and television reversed the process. Stars who had been only a "voice" in radio could not make it in a medium where their visual image did not match audience expectations.

Critics of the 1920s were quick to condemn the talkies. Paul Rotha, in *The Film till Now* (1930), wrote:

It may be concluded that a film in which the speech and sound effects are perfectly synchronised and coincide with their visual images on the screen is absolutely contrary to the aim of the cinema. It is a degenerate and misguided attempt to destroy the real use of the film and cannot be accepted as coming within the true boundaries of the cinema. Not only are dialogue films wasting the time of intelligent directors, but they are harmful and detrimental to the culture of the public. The sole aim of their producers is financial gain, and for this reason they are to be resented.

But the public wasn't listening to the critics; it was listening to the sound tracks of the new movies. By 1930 virtually all films appearing for general public release were talkies. The change was sudden, complete, and final.

Talkie producers found that material suitable for silent films did not always work with sound. So they looked to the stage for new stories and fresh faces whose voices were a proven success. This led to a crop of stars with Broadway and other theatrical experience, including Fredric March, James Cagney, Spencer Tracy, and Fred Astaire. A precious few, like Greta Garbo and Marie Dressler, survived the transition from silent to talkie because they had stage experience and their voices were much as silent film fans had imagined.

1930s: THE SOUND AND THE CINEMA

The emphasis on sound led to the birth of the movie musical. After all, now that pictures could talk, why couldn't they sing? Sing they did; most major studios produced a series of musical extravaganzas. MGM's *That's Entertainment* (Parts 1 and 2), released in the early 1970s, is the most complete film record of that wonderful genre.

No single couple dominated entertainment films of the 1930s more than Fred Astaire and Ginger Rogers. They first appeared together in 1933 in *Flying Down to Rio*. Then came a string of box-office smashes, including *The Gay Divorcée, Follow the Fleet*, and the most famous, *Top Hat*. Plots were secondary in the Astaire-Rogers films; emphasis was on the dance numbers sprinkled throughout. Though the formula was redundant, audiences of the 1930s never seemed to tire of it. Most critics argue that the last "great" Astaire-Rogers film was *Carefree* in 1938. There, for the first time, Fred kissed Ginger on screen; for some reason, that seemed to break the spell. Their later films seemed to have lost the magic.

The 1930s films of the Marx Brothers draw large audiences even today. The zany brothers were never concerned with plot. In fact, Groucho would often leave the story altogether while he communicated directly with the audience: "I told you this story would never get beyond the second reel," he'd say impishly and dive back into the action. There were a number of obligatory musical production numbers in Marx films, but the brothers seemed to enjoy doing them. Sound suited the Marxes perfectly, for they delivered an avalanche of dialogue filled with double and triple entendres.

Visually, of course, the Marx films were unrivaled. There were sinks hidden beneath coats, horns and harps under the table, smashed hats and cream pies. The secret of the Marxes' success was their ability to poke fun at authority figures. Kings and queens, dime-store employers, underworld bosses, society matrons, and military commanders were all treated with the same irreverence (see 10.7).

The 1930s also saw a curious public preoccupation with crime. Actors like James Cagney and Edward G. Robinson were filmed fighting and killing one another in an endless parade of St. Valentine's Day Massacres. Perhaps this is one time when mass communication simply reflected a public longing for justice. While hundreds of successful pictures like *Little Caesar* and *Public Enemy* ended with gangsters getting their just deserts, real public enemies Al Capone and Machine Gun Kelly seemed to be, literally, getting away with murder. Nevertheless, these films were often criticized for showing criminals in a sympathetic light and encouraging the hero worship of gangsters among young people.

GONE WITH THE WIND

The one element that seemed to thread through all the successful films of the era was escape from reality. There were few films about real life, because life during the Depression wasn't very entertaining. Films offered an escape from a world of poverty and worry to a world where there was singing, dancing, laughter, justice, and fair play.

10.7

A scene from A Night at the Opera, *one of the Marx Brothers' zaniest films. Their form-over-content approach to films is one reason that their popularity has not diminished in 50 years.*

From the MGM release *A Night at the Opera* © 1935 Metro-Goldwyn-Mayer Corporation. Copyright renewed 1962 by Metro-Goldwyn-Mayer Inc.

The most successful film of the 1930s, *Gone with the Wind*, has entertained generation after generation. *Gone with the Wind* is durable because it had everything: the swaggering Rhett, the ruthless Scarlett, the goody-goody Melanie Wilkes, and the lovable, stereotyped black mammy. Then there was the Civil War: the Yankees, the burning of Atlanta, the carpetbaggers.

The film, adapted from the best-selling book of the time, was produced by David O. Selznick, who spared no expense on lavish sets and period costumes. It was directed by Victor Fleming, whose *Wizard of Oz*, produced the same year, was also a classic.

Gone with the Wind milked every cinematic cliché and success formula that had emerged in the first 40 years of the medium. It stands as a classic, for in it we can see pieces of every one of its successful predecessors. In 1977 an American Film Institute membership survey named it as the greatest film of all time.

1940s: *CITIZEN KANE* AND THE AMERICAN DREAM

The 1940s were a period of abrupt and rapid change for many Americans. Along with increasing prosperity came a devastating war. Likewise, the era was a period of abrupt change in American film and in film all over the world.

Citizen Kane, released in 1941, is considered by many to be the most important American film ever made in the sound era. Like *Birth of a Nation*, it advanced the state of the art by developing entirely new ways of delivering a message on film.

In many ways the story of *Citizen Kane* is the story of one man, Orson Welles. He directed, supervised casting, coauthored the script, and starred. All this is particularly impressive when you consider the film was completed just in time to celebrate his 26th birthday.

Welles had become a national celebrity in

1938 with his *War of the Worlds* broadcast (see Chapter 6). He received several offers to do films, but, according to film critic Pauline Kael, he held out until he could get *complete* artistic freedom and an ample budget. RKO finally gave him that opportunity in 1940, and he moved to Hollywood, bringing his *Mercury Theater on the Air* cast with him. The young sensation looked over the facilities at RKO and exclaimed: "This is the biggest choo-choo train a kid ever had."

It took Welles less than six months to film *Citizen Kane*, and he did it for less than $1 million. The plot was a fictionalized version of the life of Randolph Hearst, the newspaper tycoon, whose reputation for sensationalism and subterfuge was well known to the public at the time. It's not a flattering portrait, and Hearst threatened to sue RKO if it was released. The studio released the film anyway, hoping it would become a money-maker. It didn't, at least not right away. Reviews of the innovative film were mixed, and public response was lukewarm. It took many years for RKO to recoup its initial investment.

For all of its artistic virtues, *Citizen Kane* was not exclusively a "personal statement" in the later tradition of Fellini and Bergman. Rather it was designed to entertain the mass audience. It tells a relatively simple story. In the best tradition of the entertainment film, the tycoon rises to the top and is transformed from a brash, idealistic playboy to a bitter, defeated old man. Sounds like grist for any one of hundreds of films. What made *Citizen Kane* so different?

Plot

The film does not tell the complete story but gives us glimpses into the life of Charles Foster Kane. It begins with Kane's death and works backward. A reporter from a news weekly interviews those closest to Kane and pieces the story together. The opening few minutes of *Citizen Kane* are done as a newsreel: "News on the March" (an imitation of the "March of Time" movie newsreels of the 1940s). This gave the audience the necessary background, and it was so like an actual newsreel that many thought it was real (shades of *War of the Worlds!*).

Sound

Since Welles's background was in radio, he knew the potential of sound to influence the mass audience. Remember, talkies were only beginning their second decade, and the use of sound was still considered an aesthetic handicap to true film art. Welles turned this around by making sound work for him. He used all of the tricks of radio production, including echo, recorded sound effects, and music, to help tell the story.

Approach

Because Welles had never directed a film or even appeared in one, every decision about the storytelling function of film was rethought. Cameramen would scream, "It's never been done," but that didn't stop Welles. For example, in one scene Kane's ex-wife is sitting alone in a large, dark restaurant. Outside the rain is falling; the exterior of the building is bleak and foreboding. The scene begins with a full shot of the neon sign on the roof, which says, "Susan Alexander Kane appearing twice nightly." Then the camera goes *through the skylight* on the roof and zooms in to where Mrs. Kane is talking with the reporter. Welles combined animation and live footage to give the audience the zoom impression, and the scene became the model for many films that followed. This is but one example of the dozens of completely new techniques that *Citizen Kane* contributed to the art of film. There

10.8

Citizen Kane star and director Orson Welles in a scene depicting a festive staff meeting. Note how the ice sculptures in the foreground frame this shot. Innovative visual effects like this helped make *Kane* one of the most important American films ever made.

were new lighting effects and innovative use of mirrors, shadows, and extreme close-ups (see 10.8).

In one scene Kane and his wife are at Xanadu, their mansion in Florida. (Hearst's mansion was at San Simeon in California.) They are having a dispute. The emotional distance between them is symbolically represented by the physical dimensions of the huge room; they are so far apart they practically have to shout to be understood. The camera lens distorts the distance, emphasizing it even more. An echo effect makes their voices seem to rebound against the castle walls.

No discussion of *Citizen Kane*, no matter how brief, would be complete without mentioning "Rosebud." "Rosebud" was the thread that wove the Kane tapestry together. The reporter sets out to find why Kane murmured "Rosebud" just before his death. At the end of the film, the reporter concludes that he'll never find out what Rosebud was. The audience does find out, however, in the last shot of the film. The use of such a hook was not entirely new, but never had it been so skillfully employed, and never had the screen told such a powerful story with such believable irony.

Citizen Kane was successful in bridging the gap between "popular" entertainment designed for the mass audience and a personal "artistic" statement. It remains the most discussed American film of the sound era.

HUMPHREY BOGART AND THE DETECTIVE MOVIE

The most popular single genre of the 1940s was the detective story. Detective films are designed to entertain and intrigue the mass audience, to offer an escape from everyday life into a world of danger and suspense. One of the first great detective films appeared the same year as *Citizen Kane*. John Huston directed *The Maltese Falcon* and cast in the lead an experienced but little-known actor who had mainly played supporting roles in second-rate pictures. His name was Humphrey Bogart.

Bogart became *the* leading man of the 1940s (see 10.9). His successes, *The Maltese Falcon*, *Casablanca*, *Key Largo*, *The Big Sleep*, and *The Treasure of Sierra Madre*, to name just a few, are as well known today as they were when they first thrilled the audiences of their day. Bogart performed equally well as a laconic detective in *The Big Sleep* and as an exuberant mercenary in *The African Queen*. The key to his success seemed to be his image as a loner.

An unlikely hero and an unlikely leading man, Bogart was always tough, streetwise, and looking out for number one. Yet inevitably, plots would lead him to a confrontation that pitted those self-serving values against the public good, law and order, justice. His decision was usually to opt for good in spite of himself.

Bogart wasn't handsome in the Clark Gable or Rudolph Valentino mold. He became the screen's leading man because he projected a visual image that was unique; there was only one Humphrey Bogart. He was tough and tender, selfish and giving, irreverent and sympathetic. As with all successful stars, any picture became *his* picture. Plot was secondary.

Perhaps the ultimate detective film was Howard Hawks's *The Big Sleep*. Bogart starred opposite Lauren Bacall. The great novelist William Faulkner wrote the screenplay from the Raymond Chandler novel. The result was a film that defied understanding. There were so many bodies scattered about and so many evil characters that the audience never did understand "whodunit," but it didn't matter! The real story was Bogart, rescuing damsels in distress and trading sizzling one-liners with Bacall. Dozens of newer films and television programs in the detective genre can be traced directly back to Bogart and his rendering of detectives Sam Spade and Philip Marlowe.

The 1940s saw the full flowering of films in America as far as financial success was concerned. In 1946, over 90 million Americans went to the movies every week. The industry would never have that large an audience again. By the 1970s the figure had dropped to about 20 million each week.

The decline of the movie business in the late 1940s had much to do with new tax regulations, which made films less desirable as investments. There were some anti-monopoly rulings during this period that resulted in the studios' giving up their holdings in the exhibition end of the business. This meant

10.9
Play It, Sam

It started out to be just another spy story and ended up being one of the best-loved movies of all time. *Casablanca,* made in 1942, featured Humphrey Bogart as the proprietor of Rick's Café Americain in occupied Casablanca. He claims he cares not for politics and disdainfully informs the Germans that "the problems of the world are not my department. I'm a saloon keeper." In the end, however, he does "the right thing" and is welcomed back to the fight against the Germans by the man who is married to the only woman Rick ever loved.

Numerous lines from the screenplay (by Julius J. and Philip G. Epstein and Howard Koch) have become famous, including "I'm no good at being noble, but it doesn't take much to see that the problems of three little people don't amount to a hill of beans in this crazy world," and Rick's warning to his beloved Ilsa (played by Ingrid Bergman) to get on a departing plane with her husband or she would hate herself "maybe not today, maybe not tomorrow, but soon, and for the rest of your life."

Most famous of all however, are the moments in the film when Sam, the bar's pianist (played by Dooley Wilson), is asked to "Play it, Sam. Play 'As Time Goes By.' " Woody Allen's film notwithstanding, no one in *Casablanca* ever actually said "Play it *again,* Sam."

Bogart was a star before *Casablanca,* but the success of the film made him one of Hollywood's most famous leading men for the rest of his life. Since his death, his legend—and the audience's fascination with *Casablanca*—seem to increase with each passing year. It would appear that the sentimentalists are right: There will never be another Bogart, or another *Casablanca.*

they no longer controlled the industry as completely as before. Also, the House Un-American Activities Committee was looking into films, and the blacklisting of some top film stars and writers did not help the industry's image. But what really hurt was, of course, television. Within a few years, television would replace movies as America's favorite entertainment pastime. Like radio, film would undergo tremendous change to adjust to its new role as a secondary source of entertainment.

10.10
Moviegoing: The Young Like It Best

These figures represent current estimates of the age of movie-goers as calculated by the Opinion Research Corporation of Princeton, N.J. They clearly show that the younger movie audience dominates. Note that 76 percent of all those attending films are under 30, even though they make up only 41 percent of the total population.

Age	Percent of Total Yearly Admissions	Percent of Resident Civilian Population
12–15	14	10
16–20	31	12
21–24	15	9
25–29	16	10
30–39	13	15
40–49	5	13
50–59	3	18
60 and over	3	18

From Cobbett Steinberg, *Reel Facts: The Movie Book of Records.* Used by permission of Random House, Inc., New York, New York 10022.

1950s: A NEW FILM AUDIENCE

The 1950s film audience demanded that a movie deliver an evening's entertainment different from TV. Perhaps the most significant trend was not in the films but in the audience. Increasingly the movie theater became the habitat of young people. Adults stayed home and watched TV while kids went to the movies to get away from Mom and Dad, engage in a little heavy petting, and nibble a box of popcorn. The youth audience put pressure on filmmakers to produce movies young people could identify with. It remains so today (see 10.10).

The Wild One featured Marlon Brando as a mumbling motorcycle leader whose gang terrorizes a small town, pillages the local shops, and leaves folks devastated in a senseless rampage of violence. Yet Brando emerges as an anti-establishment hero of sorts, a carefree idol on a motorcycle, sought after by the local "good girl." The plot was borrowed from grade-B westerns, with horses replaced by motorcycles. The picture was a huge commercial success.

Another hero in the anti-authority mold was James Dean. His most noted film, *Rebel without a Cause*, told the story of a new kid in school who is roughed up by some juvenile-delinquent types. Dean must take his stand, of course, and this involves a "chickie-run," a contest where he and a rival head their cars for the edge of a cliff and jump out at the last moment. The first one to jump is a "chicken," perhaps the most scathing epithet among youth of that day. More telling than any other scene in the film is the confrontation between Dean and his father (played by Jim Backus). When his son asks if he should go ahead with the chickie-run, Dad says simply: "In 10 or 15 years, none of this will be important to you."

Like rock music, *Rebel without a Cause* seemed to strike a responsive chord with a bored teen audience. James Dean was some-one they could look up to, a younger Humphrey Bogart whose main concern was his most cherished possession, his automobile. So strong was audience identification with Dean that he became something of a cult hero after his early death in a car accident. Though he starred in only three pictures (*East of Eden* and *Giant* were the other two), he was probably the era's greatest youth hero besides Elvis.

There was also a market in the 1950s for a new kind of horror movie—the science-fiction film. True SF buffs will recoil when I use the term to describe movies like *The Fly*, *The Thing*, and *The Blob*, yet these films were a product of the time, representing millions of dollars in box-office revenues. Usually there was some technological disaster that transformed men and women into robots, automatons, insects, or the like. Often the culprit was a visitor from outer space, bent on conquering and destroying the earth. Usually there was a scientist in charge of the good guys, and his teenaged son/daughter/student would play a role in the victory, allowing the young audience to identify. These films were often made by small, independent studios like American International Pictures. But their success caused the major studios to rethink some policies. Many ventured into the B-film business while continuing to issue their "major" releases.

Many of the greatest westerns were made during the 1950s. *High Noon* and *Shane* both drew attention to the genre from film critics. The western remains one of the most popular movie types, though its TV heyday has come and gone. More than any other entertainment form, the western is *totally* American. The story of the American cowboy is a vital component of the American dream. Like the detective story, the western also offers the vicarious violence of which Americans seem so fond.

The need for vicarious physical experience of a different kind may also explain the success of those forgettable films starring sex queens of the 1950s, most notably Marilyn Monroe and Jayne Mansfield. Plot served as vehicle for the sex goddess to parade her charms before the camera. Like violence, sex became a vital ingredient to the success of many movies. There had been sex in the cinema long before the 1950s, but it was usually an appetizer, not the main course.

1960s: THE YOUNG AND THE RESTLESS

Movies in the 1960s continued the accent on youth and reflected the anxieties of a generation born into the atomic age. The period was one of tremendous social upheaval, and some of it ended up on film.

Psycho (1960) was perhaps Alfred Hitchcock's greatest horror film. There have been hundreds of horror films, some good and most bad, but film critics and the moviegoing public agreed *Psycho* was a masterpiece.

Janet Leigh plays a character who steals money from her greedy, insensitive boss and absconds to a motel. But by the time a half hour has passed, she decides to turn the money back in and face the music. She steps into the shower and lets the water run down her body as if to cleanse it of this terrible sin she has committed. Then an unknown person pulls the shower curtain back and stabs her repeatedly. The audience has no idea why; it all seems so senseless. Suddenly we are transferred from one story to another far more brutal and terrifying.

The stabbing itself is a miracle of cinema. We never actually *see* the knife enter her body, but through hundreds of short, quick shots we watch the knife gleam, see the flesh gyrate, and gasp as blood mixes with the swirling water. It is probably the most violent and chilling piece of film ever shot, yet the murder happens entirely in the viewer's imagination. (I remember seeing the film shortly after it came out—I couldn't take a shower for a month afterward.)

Hitchcock was called the "master of suspense" because he was most successful in creating that suspense in the minds of his audience. The famous director was an artist but said he was "merely an entertainer." Perhaps exact definitions of the two will always be blurred, but Hitchcock paid special attention to his audience, and the result was a string of commercial successes.

Another successful 1960s film was Stanley Kubrick's *Dr. Strangelove.* Made not long after the frightening Cuban missile crisis of 1962, it brought the possibility of nuclear holocaust home to the nervous public. Fear of the bomb had been an American preoccupation since 1945, and during the late 1950s and early 1960s many Americans had spent a lot of time and money building bomb shelters in their basements. *Dr. Strangelove* played on this phobia for laughs, but the humor was very black indeed. The military elite were portrayed as mindless puppets reveling in the ultimate destruction. Kubrick uses the film to mock the military-industrial complex, and we laugh until we cry. *Dr. Strangelove* still attracts large audiences whenever it plays, despite frequent appearances on television. Perhaps its popularity during the latter part of the 1960s was bolstered by the opposition to the Vietnam War. Young moviegoers, suspicious of the military and its motives, approved of Kubrick's message.

In a less serious vein, three films starring the Beatles rang up box-office profits during the 1960s. *A Hard Day's Night, Help!,* and *Yellow Submarine* were all resounding commercial successes. Though the popularity of the group as rock musicians was a vital component of the films' success, film critics are beginning to realize that the genius of the Beatles infected their other media efforts. On film the group performed very much like the Marx Brothers. There was little plot; rather, the screen was a vehicle for music and madness.

As with the Marxes, so *much* happens in a Beatles movie that you find something new each time you watch it. There are puns galore, along with message and music. All three films went much further than simply setting film to music. They explored how each medium could reinforce and expand the other. The significance of that contribution becomes more apparent as filmmakers discover that devotion to rock can spell box-office success.

In 1969, the commercial success of *Easy Rider* set off a wave of youth-oriented "protest" pictures. Dennis Hopper, who directed and starred in the film, may have been the first American director since Orson Welles to have so much freedom with his product. *Easy Rider* was privately financed (costing a comparatively low $370,000) and wasn't under the direction of any major studio. Those who had the chance turned it down, feeling the plot was an open endorsement of drugs and would scare away the mass audience.

What it actually did was bring them in. *Easy Rider* connected with the youth audience because it articulated, in the most graphic and basic way, the concerns of the 1960s. Two long-haired trippers, Captain America and Billy, set off on their motorcycles to chase down the American Dream. Along the way they visit a commune, a couple of prostitutes, and a southern lawyer (Jack Nicholson), who gets them out of the local jail. Nicholson is the first to die a violent death at the hands of the rednecks. Both Captain America and Billy die at the end of the film. In between there is talk of politics and the use of drugs. *Easy Rider* vindicated a large subculture of people who had been using marijuana for years.

Audiences left the theater stunned by the

violent ending. The film provided a warning to society and a plea for understanding. It also provided music, lots of it. The use of songs like "Born to Be Wild" solidified youth identification and made *Easy Rider* one of the most significant social films of the decade.

1970s: SNATCHING VICTORY FROM THE JAWS OF DISASTER

The key to big box office in the 1970s was disaster. A string of hits beginning with *The Poseidon Adventure* (about the shipwreck of a luxury liner) proved that the mass audience was hungry for giant films, giant stars, and giant catastrophes. *The Towering Inferno* was the story of a huge office-building fire. *Earthquake* told of the inevitable destruction that finally came to Los Angeles. It also featured sound so loud it practically shook the audience out of the seats.

But a bigger box-office success than all these was a disaster film of a different color. *Jaws*, about a shark that devours tourists at an East Cost beach resort, played to millions of people and became one of the most talked-about movies ever. It broke all box-office records and became the biggest money maker until surpassed in 1977 by *Star Wars*.

Jaws pitted humanity against beast in the *King Kong* tradition and involved the audience in the struggle. Millions screamed in anguish as the skilled camera crew convinced them the giant shark was about to come out of the screen and eat them alive.

Jaws, *The Exorcist*, *King Kong*, and the other disaster films shared one common trait: They were able to take the audience along for the nightmare. Critics argue that moviegoers are becoming jaded, that they demand increasing doses of titillation. Perhaps this is so; as soon as we thought we had reached the ultimate in vicarious thrills, along comes *Jaws* to show us we had just begun.

All of this raises a more significant issue. Are there moral implications to this symbiotic relationship between audience and filmmaker? Can the audience that gasps when a shark gobbles up a victim's leg be somehow damaged in real life? When does manufactured anxiety become destructive? Those questions have yet to be answered, and they become enormously important as audience manipulation becomes easier for filmmakers.

NASHVILLE AND *NETWORK*

Many have argued that the movies of the 1970s were devoid of aesthetic merit, that films were notable only for their commercial success. Two films about mass media defy this analysis: Robert Altman's *Nashville* and Paddy Chayefsky's *Network* (directed by Sidney Lumet). Altman has directed a number of first-rate films, including *M*A*S*H*, *McCabe and Mrs. Miller*, and *California Split*, but *Nashville* is his masterpiece.

Nashville defied film convention. It is almost a documentary, tracing the paths of dozens of characters as they attempt to crawl to the top of the country and western music scene in Nashville. There is the established C&W star, the teenybopper just in from California, the bevy of C&W starlets eager to make their way in the music business, the politician who sends advance men to convince a country group that this is a good time to support his candidacy, the promotion man's wife who sleeps with the young lead singer, and the singer himself, who lives and loves one day at a time and sings his one "special" song to every woman in the room.

There's also the music—more than a dozen country and western tunes sung by superstars and would-be superstars. All the songs in the film were written by the performers, few of whom had any real professional musical experience. This didn't keep Keith Carradine from winning the Academy Award for best song, "I'm Easy."

Oddly enough, that's the only Oscar the film won, though it was lauded by reviewers. Although it was not a complete commercial failure, it failed to live up to the predictions of the critics.

The form of *Nashville* is both its strongest virtue and its greatest handicap. The dozens of subplots are interwoven in a series of vignettes so the audience never has a chance to get to know the characters as well as it does in other films. Yet Altman turns this into a strength, because *Nashville* is not the story of one star but the story of the star system. It doesn't matter what kind of stardom you're after (film, C&W, rock and roll), *Nashville* tells a universal story of media power and prestige and its glorious, but arbitrary, rewards.

The film points out that arbitrary success works for singers and politicians alike. The political figure of the film, Hal Philip Walker, is out to "use" the glitter of the stars to his own advantage. His advance men hint that a C&W superstar (played by Henry Gibson) might eventually become governor if he'll "only go along." In the chilling final moments of the film we see a gunman stalk his famous prey and, when the shooting comes, it reminds us all too clearly of those we have seen in real life. Though this film was released four years before the John Lennon shooting, there are similarities to be explored.

We still cannot understand *Nashville* completely; perhaps we never will, but its significance will become increasingly apparent. Already critics keep mentioning it in conjunction with a new technique here, a new approach there, a whole new kind of film

somewhere else. In the decade when the film industry seemed interested only in box-office numbers, *Nashville* stood out like a beacon.

More commercially successful was Paddy Chayefsky's *Network*. The 1976 film captured several Oscars, including those for best actor and best actress. The story involves the behind-the-scenes activities at UBC, a mythical fourth TV network. When a wild-eyed anchorman goes off the deep end on camera, ratings skyrocket. He's left on the air despite his strange ravings because it is UBC's first hit show.

The story is told in a very traditional manner, but it is an important story. Chayefsky's animosity toward the influence of television struck a very responsive chord in the film-going audience. Both the real audience and the depicted TV audience seem to respond unanimously when the anchorman urges them to begin shouting (for no special reason), "I'm mad as hell and I'm not going to take it anymore!" *Network* proved that, though the protests of the 1960s had subsided, there remained a bubbling undercurrent of frustration. Ironically, the film was sold for airing on television in 1978.

THE 1980s: SIMPLE STORIES AND GALACTIC ALLEGORIES?

Recent successful films have been hard to stereotype. George Lucas's successful trilogy *Star Wars*, *The Empire Strikes Back*, and *Return of the Jedi* told straightforward stories involving danger and heroism (see 10.11). Audiences' need for these simple story lines, plus the spectacular form of the space epics with their colossal special effects, spelled success.

Meanwhile, *Breaking Away* represented another kind of vision and one with which a

Guest Essay by Patrick Smith Understanding the Movies: Another View

While the critics tend to focus on movies as holistic works, there are a number of possible ways to look at a feature film. In this essay the author suggests that one way to enjoy a film is by getting acquainted with some of the myriad roles played by individuals who collaborate to produce the final product. Patrick Smith chairs the English Department at the University of San Francisco. He is an author, poet, and sculptor and teaches a number of courses involving film and film technique.

Feature films, *the movies* we have all seen from our earliest days, are among the most complicated aesthetic objects that criticism has to analyze. These "stories" that sweep us along and make a hundred minutes seem like a single moment are really made by the craftsmanship of hundreds of people, the authoritative artistic contributions of at least ten, and the mingling of drama, music, fiction, graphic art, history—and virtually every other form of communication and expression.

Reviewers, critics, and scholars try to reduce a film's complexity by assuming that it has the unity of an aesthetic object. That is, they talk about it as if its parts all were made to fit together by some single intellect, some controlling intention. The person most usually credited with this power is the director. By assuming that a film is a single object with a single "meaning," we are able to demand that it "make sense" or

lot of people, and a lot of film critics, could identify. It's set in a small college town in Indiana and pits the local high school graduates against the out-of-town college kids. It also tells the story of one young man in his struggle for maturity. At first he tries to be something he's not; then he learns to live with himself and, finally, to be proud of what he is.

Two other popular films dealt with similar problems. *Ordinary People*, directed by Robert Reford and starring Mary Tyler Moore, is a taut psychological drama set in suburban America where again a young man tries to come to grips with himself, often with disturbing consequences. The same could be said of *Chariots of Fire*, a film about men who compete and their search for excellence.

The 1980s have also been a time when films explored the social, political, and personal issues that had roots in the women's move-

be like life. We can quarrel with the judgments the film passes on our life and our society.

Yet films are made of bits and pieces. The elementary aspect of a movie is its editing—it is made up of thousands of pieces of film, spliced together to make us think or feel that the actions on the screen took place in some unified "time" of our imagination. You can look "backstage" at this illusion if you compare the face of an actor as it appears in a medium shot and the same face—registering the same emotion—in the close shot that follows. In one you will see a softer expression, a more general emotion; in the other you will see intensity, detail, emotional complexity. Is this a "mistake"? Is this careless direction or editing? Only if you want to keep your illusions that movies are just the story. But if you want to know about the real existence of one of the most secretly democratic, anarchic art objects the world has ever

sponsored, you will want to learn about the seams of the movies, those lines through which you can see the work of the entire production company going on—or at least the evidence of that work as it appears through these secret openings. Your map to these openings is shown in its broadest lines in the part of the movie you may not pay much attention to: the credits. Listed here are talents that contributed to the final product. If you know the contribution each skill makes and you understand that a movie is the record of the struggles between all these talents, then you will know how to measure individual contributions.

The actress's move toward a window may begin with one sort of expression and end up with another in the close-up. Between the two expressions lies the sum of the idea she has had about this scene. But who sent her to the window? Is that motion a motif in the film and thus a sign of the director's con-

trol? And who put the window behind her? Did the cinematographer suggest that the camera placements used would give a certain graphic shape to the motions on the flattened image that reaches the screen? And, to go back even further, who made the window in the first place? The art designer, it has been said, is the first director, because it is he or she who makes the floor plan on which all the actions must be "blocked." Music, costume, makeup, the quality of the sets, and the production value of the location can all be seen as the active contributions of some filmmaking role. And once they are, you will be able to read autobiographies of all those persons to help you understand what they can add or subtract. Then when you read production accounts in the professional quarterlies, or even in the gossip columns, you will be enlarging the eye with which you enjoy yourself at the movies.

ment of the 1970s. *Lianna* explored with sensitivity the problems encountered in a lesbian relationship. *Terms of Endearment* spotlighted the evolution of a mother–daughter relationship. *Silkwood* was based on the real-life story of a female nuclear plant worker who exposed unsafe working conditions.

E.T., the biggest film success of 1982, centered on the impact of a visitor from outer space on an average American family. Compared to Lucas's space epics, this Steven

Spielberg film featured more heartwarming drama and fewer special effects. Other 1982 success stories were *Tootsie*, featuring Dustin Hoffman as a soap opera actress, and *Gandhi*, a powerful epic-length movie. Also popular in the '80s were *Raiders of the Lost Ark* and its sequel, *Indiana Jones and the Temple of Doom*. Like so many other recent films, these movies' combination of special effects and escapism lured many young people to the theaters.

10.11
George Lucas: "Walt Disney of the '80s"

As a child, George Lucas seemed less like a budding film executive and more like an impossible dreamer. The producer and creator of the *Star Wars* trilogy spent most of his childhood lost in comic books or in front of the television set. Perhaps that is why he is so much in touch with today's generation of children.

Lucas graduated from high school in Modesto, California (later the setting for his *American Graffiti*), attended a community college for two years, and eventually wound up in film school at the University of Southern California. It was there that he met Francis Coppola. The rest is history. Coppola went on to direct *The Godfather* and helped Lucas

One exception to the escapist rule was *The Big Chill*, a 1983 film that won both popular acceptance and critical praise. The plot centered on the reunion of seven college friends from the 1960s. Each had found different ways of coping with the "real world," but each in one way or another felt that their college years in that turbulent time represented the finest part of their lives. Another critically acclaimed film from this same period was *The Right Stuff*. Loosely based on Tom Wolfe's book, it told the story of the first U.S. astronauts and centered on their relations with the media.

Critics have not been happy with the general escapist nature of many of most successful films of the '80s, yet generally escapism seems to have been the key to big box-office grosses during this period. Perhaps with so much serious drama available on television and cable, the movie theater seems more suited to epic adventures in 70 millimeter and Dolby stereo. There can be no question that

find financial backing for *THX 1138,* a film about a futuristic world that served as a kind of prototype for *Star Wars.*

The two collaborated on *American Graffiti,* a film reflecting Lucas's own boyhood in Modesto. *Graffiti,* made for a scant $780,000, has returned some $145 million in box-office revenues worldwide. That success led to the making of *Star Wars.* Its $10 million budget seemed high at the time, but it already has in excess of $500 million in box-office revenues, making it far and away the most financially successful film in history.

As you may already know, the third *Star Wars* film, *Return of the Jedi,* is but one more chapter in what Lucas hopes will eventually be a nine-film series. In fact, at the beginning of *Jedi,* it is identified as episode VI. The three existing films form a middle trilogy for the most ambitious mythical undertaking in the history of entertainment. Indeed, Walt Disney himself could not have created a fairy tale on any grander scale.

How much of Lucas can be found in the *Star Wars* sagas? In an interview with *Time* magazine, Lucas says: "A lot of the stuff in there is very personal. There's more of me in *Star Wars* than I care to admit." After all, Luke Skywalker didn't get to be called Luke by accident. Lucas admits that the character played by Mark Hamill is, in many ways, his alter ego.

Lucas currently presides over a 3,000-acre filmmaker's paradise in Northern California called "Skywalker Ranch." The ranch is a magnet for filmmakers from all over the world. His Lucasfilm company, located near the ranch, oversees the millions of details associated with a project the size of the *Star Wars* trilogy. Once *Jedi* was launched in mid-1983,

Lucas announced he was taking a two-year sabbatical, and rumors have circulated about a possible retirement. Money is certainly no problem at this point.

Yet Lucas proudly shows interviewers the large binder that contains notes on the entire nine-part *Star Wars* saga. One gets the feeling that it won't be too long before he's back into production with another segment. At least that's what the millions of *Star Wars* fans throughout the world are hoping for.

Lucas's talent for tapping into the collective imagination of so many people of all ages and all walks of life is truly unique. In many ways he has become, as *Time* put it, the Walt Disney of the 1980s. Everything Lucas has accomplished thus far was completed before his 40th birthday. Everyone feels there is much more to come.

films of the *Star Wars* genre lose something when transferred to the small screen.

THE CRITICS, PROMOTION, AND SUCCESS

Throughout this chapter I have continually referred to "the critics" as if they were a consolidated body of snobs who perceive film on an altogether different plane from the mass audience. Although this portrayal is somewhat simplistic, there may be some truth in it. Film critics do not generally reflect the mass audience's taste, and therefore they don't have the power to "make or break" a film the way a record reviewer for *Rolling Stone* can make or break an album.

For example, there are hundreds of successful films that have received nothing but poor reviews from all major film critics. Among

10.12
The Top Money-Making Films

Each year *Variety* magazine publishes an updated list of the films that have compiled the highest rental fee receipts. These 1984 figures represent the amount of money the theater has paid to the distributor—not box-office grosses, as is widely believed.

These figures are for North American rentals only; worldwide revenues generally run about double.

The list is top-heavy with recent films, partly because of inflation. A recent study by the accounting firm of Laventhol and Horwath used these figures as a base but allowed for inflation. The results? *Gone With the Wind* was the clear winner with $321 million in "constant" rentals. (The constant rental figures are hypothetical dollar amounts allowing for inflation.) Under these conditions older films such as *The Ten Commandments* and *Dr. Zhivago* would move into the top 20 while more recent successes would drop off the list.

Title	Date Released	Dollars Paid to Distributor
E.T. The Extra-Terrestrial	1982	$209,567,000
Star Wars	1977	193,500,000
Return of the Jedi	1983	165,500,000
The Empire Strikes Back	1980	141,600,000
Jaws	1975	133,435,000
Raiders of the Lost Ark	1981	115,598,000
Grease	1978	96,300,000
Tootsie	1982	94,571,613
The Exorcist	1973	89,000,000
The Godfather	1972	86,275,000
Close Encounters of the Third Kind	1977/1980	83,452,000
Superman	1978	82,800,000
The Sound of Music	1965	79,748,000
The Sting	1973	79,419,900
Gone with the Wind	1939	76,700,000
Saturday Night Fever	1977	74,100,000
Nat'l Lampoon's Animal House	1978	74,000,000
Nine to Five	1980	66,200,000
Rocky III	1982	65,763,177
Superman II	1981	65,100,000
On Golden Pond	1981	63,000,000
Kramer vs. Kramer	1979	61,734,000
Smokey and the Bandit	1977	61,055,000
One Flew Over the Cuckoo's Nest	1975	59,205,793
Stir Crazy	1980	58,408,000

Figures through December 1983

Source: *Variety,* vol. 313 no. 11 (78th annual anniversary issue). Wednesday, January 11, 1984, p. 16. (Variety, Inc., 154 W. 46th St., New York, NY 10036) Used by permission.

the top money makers of all time (see 10.12), not one has really had the critical acclaim of *Nashville* or *Citizen Kane*. Yet those listed are indeed the most popular films ever made.

Film has been around a lot longer than radio or television, and it has developed a certain artistic integrity in the minds of the cultural elite. Like the novel, film has a swarm of reviewers who make a living judging each new effort and pronouncing its place among all other works. Radio and television have few such critics. Broadcast-media programs are noted only for their ability to get and hold a large audience. The TV and radio shows that attract the most attention from critics are those known to the mass audience: *I Love Lucy*, *The Mary Tyler Moore Show*, and *Happy Days*, for example. But the films that most critics like to talk about, "artistic" films like *Rules of the Game*, *Jules and Jim*, and *8½*, may be virtually unknown to the mass audience. There is a clear difference between the elite interpretation of film as art and the mass-audience perception of film as entertainment. Film critics like to think of themselves as celluloid gourmets, telling the public what tastes good and what's in good taste. The public seems to develop its own tastes, however, and the critics are largely ignored.

For this reason, movie studios do not go overboard trying to woo the critics. Instead, they try to appeal directly to the buying public through publicity and promotion. But even these tools do not always do the job. For example, *The Great Gatsby* was released in 1974 amid one of the greatest ballyhoos of the decade. Everyone was rereading the Fitzgerald novel. The studio spared no expense hiring Robert Redford to play Gatsby and Mia Farrow for Daisy. *Time* magazine put it on the cover, and everyone was set for a box-office bonanza. Within a few weeks most theaters showing the film were empty. The word was out: *Gatsby* was a bomb, and no amount of publicity could save it. Six months later it was on television.

Most movie producers agree that film, more than any other medium, has one elusive requirement for commercial success: word of mouth. The audience sees a film and tells their friends. They in turn see the film and pass the word along. Pretty soon there are long lines waiting to see film A, while film B, which cost the same to produce, opened at the theater next door, and enjoyed an equal amount of advance promotion and critical acclaim, goes begging.

At the heart of the problem is the intricate relationship between studio, critic, and audience. Critics want movies that advance the state of the art or make strong social statements or both. The public seems content with simple stories. The studio would like to produce winners that are loved by mass audience and critic alike, but its primary concern is the mass audience. No amount of critical acclaim or advance promotion can guarantee money in the bank.

ISSUES AND ANSWERS: THE REGULATION OF SELF

Looking back over the successful movies of the last 30 years, we can identify some patterns. For example, the trend toward explicit sexuality in films in the 1950s culminated with a series of movies that seemed to capitalize on an increasingly permissive society in the 1960s. A Swedish import, *I Am Curious (Yellow)* (1967) showed sexual intercourse on the screen. Parents seemed reluctant to send their children to see anything but Walt Disney films for fear the kids would be exposed to language and behavior they considered unsuitable.

Seeing a threat to their pocketbooks, the members of the Motion Picture Association of America (MPAA), a trade organization, instituted a rating system designed to give audiences an idea of what kind of picture they were going to see. After some modifications, the four now-familiar categories of films emerged.

G: For all ages; no nudity or sex and only a minimal amount of violence.

PG: Parental guidance suggested. Some portions may not be suitable for young children. Some mild profanity may be present, and violence is permitted as long as it is not "excessive." A glimpse of a nude body is permitted, but anything more makes it R.

R: Restricted; those under 17 must be accompanied by a parent. This is an adult film in every sense of the word and may contain very rough violence, explicit nudity, or love making.

X: No one under 17 is admitted, with or without a parent. This rating is generally reserved for films that are openly pornographic, though some serious films by noted filmmakers have been rated X.

The ratings do not represent censorship per se, since filmmakers usually have the final say. But studios know, in most cases, that the more acceptable the rating, the larger the potential audience. With the emphasis on youth, major studios hesitate to make films that will exclude everyone under 17. Though the absurdity of rating or evaluating a film according to the number of seconds a bare buttock appears on the screen is self-evident, the ratings seem to have accomplished what they set out to do.

The ratings have the same problem as all attempts to identify what makes a media presentation "objectionable." Guidelines must be flexible enough to incorporate shifting community standards, but which community? Frontal nudity on the screen may be commonplace in Manhattan but unheard of in Milpitas.

Millions of words have been written attempting to define obscenity. But it's an elusive term; today's obscenity is tomorrow's art. No attempt will be made to define obscenity here, but it's worth taking a moment to think about the code itself and what it may hold in store for other mass media.

The most obvious flaw in the code is its approach to violence. Though hundreds of sexually explicit films received the X rating, it wasn't until 1974 that a martial-arts film, *The Street Fighter*, received it for showing objectionable violence. The implication seems to be that our society will tolerate arbitrary violence but objects to arbitrary sex.

During the 1970s, television networks began to show more explicit material (usually films) but preceded it with a "warning" that parental discretion was advised. Some cable TV companies showed uncut X-rated movies during late hours. The time slot of a network show sent a message to the audience. The "family hour" experiment that began in the mid-1970s was designed to reassure parents that their children would be safe watching shows during the early evening.

The "success" of the MPAA rating scheme may eventually lead to a similar code for radio and television programs. The large audiences watching controversial TV shows like *Saturday Night Live* and listening to deejays like New York's Don Imus (see Chapter 6) mean there is a segment of the public that is ready for "adult" broadcast programs. But their desires often conflict with those determined to protect kids by keeping sex and violence off the air. A self-imposed rating system could go a long way toward resolving this conflict.

QUERIES AND CONCEPTS

1 Choose three top films now showing in your local theaters. Can you make a list of myths and values that may be associated with each?

2 Make arrangements to see a silent film. (There is probably one available through your library, and public television stations show them often.) Keep a journal of observations regarding the differences between silents and talkies. Which seem to move faster? Which use the visual aspect of film more effectively?

3 Are there any young film stars of today that enjoy the idol worship of James Dean? If so, who are they and *why* are they? If not, why not?

4 Prediction time: When the 1980s are over, we will look back and write about the film trends of that decade just as the 1940s through the 1970s are assessed here. What will those trends be?

5 Devise a set of guidelines for self-regulation of TV programming. What type of material should not be shown under any circumstance?

6 In one concise page describe the standards that you feel are prevalent in your community with respect to obscenity. Can you think of any films or publications that seem to violate these standards?

READINGS AND REFERENCES

America's Sweetheart

Raymond Lee
The Films of Mary Pickford. Cranbury, N.J.: A.S. Barnes, 1970.
    I bought this book on sale for one dollar . . . here's hoping you have that kind of luck. There is a very short introduction and then hundreds of incredible stills from Pickford's most famous films.

The Audiovisual Record; Life Is Like a Movie

These areas often go unexplored in books on film. The best single source on the lingering emotional impact of film is F. Scott Fitzgerald's *The Last Tycoon* (New York: Scribner's, 1941). Some social approaches to film may be found in *The Movies As Medium* (New York: Farrar, Straus and Giroux, 1970), an anthology edited by Lewis Jacobs, and in Arthur Knight's *The Liveliest Art* (New York: New American Library, 1971).

The Magic Lantern

Albert Smith
Two Reels and a Crank. Garden City, N.Y.: Doubleday, 1952.
    This is a particularly rewarding first-person account of the early years of film from nickelodeon to the silent screen. Told with relish and conviction.

The Quiet Years

Edward Wagenknecht
The Movies in the Age of Innocence. Norman: University of Oklahoma Press, 1962.
Silent screen star Lillian Gish calls this "the best book on films I've ever read." It turns out she is a personal friend of the author, but her enthusiasm is warranted. The book concentrates on the silent film, particularly its heroines.

The Star Is Born

Richard Schickel
Allen Hurlbut
The Stars. New York: Dial Press, 1962.
Schickel has been a film critic for *Life* and *Time*, so this is more than a fan's-eye view of the stars. Their lives and influences are examined in the context of their audiences. Good reading, plenty of lavish pictures.

The Movies Learn to Talk

Thomas W. Bohn
Richard Stromgren
Light and Shadows: A History of Motion Pictures. Sherman Oaks, Calif.: Alfred, 1975.
One of the newer historical accounts of the rise of cinema. See particularly Chapters 3–6 on the rise and influence of the silent film. Chapter 7 deals exclusively with the impact of sound.

Richard Griffith
Arthur Mayer
The Movies. New York: Simon & Schuster, 1970.
A decade-by-decade fan's-eye view that covers film into the 1960s. The largest (9″x12″) and most enthusiastic history around.

Paul Rotha
Richard Griffith
The Film till Now. New York: Springs Books, 1967.
This book was originally written in 1930 and is obviously dated. Yet it was the first monumental history of film ever written, compiled before the intellectual establishment was taking film seriously. Rotha notes in an updated introduction that he would like to take back some of his earlier opinions, particularly those on sound films. (He thought it was a passing fad.)

1930s through 1970s

William Bayer
The Great Movies. New York: Grosset & Dunlap, 1973.
This is the best single source for great films of the sound era. Easy and fun to read. Bayer is a sharp film critic with a gift for getting to the point. It is filled with more than 300 photographs and a text that provides convincing rationale for his choice of the 60 greatest films ever made.

Two general historical accounts of the movies provide excellent background material for those seeking specific information on specific films. Gerald Mast's *A Short History of the Movies*, 3d ed. (Indianapolis, Ind.: Bobbs-Merrill, 1981) is just that, but it covers virtually every important film ever made from an international perspective and includes sections on the rise of the film industry. John L. Fell's *A History of Films* (New York: Holt, Rinehart & Winston, 1979) covers similar turf in somewhat less detail but emphasizes the medium's more daring and avant-garde directors such as Fellini, Antonioni, Godard, and Bergman.

1940s: *Citizen Kane* and the American Dream

Pauline Kael
The Citizen Kane Book. New York: Bantam Books, 1973.

    This includes the original review by Kael as well as the full shooting script and over 100 hard-to-find stills from the film. Once you have seen *Citizen Kane* you will probably want to pick it up. Now available in paperback.

The Critics, Promotion, and Success

Pauline Kael
Kiss Kiss Bang Bang. Boston: Little, Brown, 1968.

    The New Yorker's witty and often cynical film reviewer issues a book every few years containing her best reviews and longer pieces about film. This is one of her most entertaining.

Cobbett Steinberg, ed.
Reel Facts: The Movie Book of Records. New York: Vintage Books, 1982.

    Everything you always wanted to know about movie facts and figures. A massive "book of lists" for the movie buff. Included are sections covering the Academy Awards and all other major awards, the marketplace (most popular films on TV, annual box-office receipts), the studios, stars, and festivals. Plus a section on the codes and regulatory functions of the industry. Lots of information. No index.

David Thomson
America in the Dark: Hollywood and the Gift of Unreality. New York: William Morrow, 1977.

    Thomson feels that most of us really are "in the dark" where the movies are concerned. His analysis of the *process* of making and distributing films is a paradox. On the one hand, he is drawn to films and obviously loves them. On the other hand, he seems to despise the movies and those who make them for their cynicism and "lowest common denominator" approach. Interesting criticism. You figure it out.

    Note: See David Shaw, "The Film Critics—Power of Pen Has Sharp Limits" from the *Los Angeles Times*, July 6, 1976 (p. 1), for a discussion of popular versus critically acclaimed films.

Issues and Answers: The Regulation of Self

Bohn and Stromgren's *Light and Shadows: A History of Motion Pictures* (Sherman Oaks, Calif.: Alfred, 1975) gives equal time to sex, violence, and race and their roles in the MPAA ratings. There's a brief discussion of movie ratings in Agee, Ault, and Emery's *Introduction to Mass Communications*, 7th ed. (New York: Harper & Row, 1982); check the index under "film."

PART THREE
Beyond the Media: The Phenomena of Mass Communication

SO FAR WE HAVE CONCENTRATED ON THE MEDIA THEM-selves—what they are, what they have been, and what they have done. This final section explores a few media-related areas chosen after some thought about what might be of most importance to you as well as to the study of mass communication.

News has always been with us, and many people still think of mass media primarily as conveyors of news. As you will see, that concept is becoming outmoded.

Advertising and public relations play unique and controversial roles in our mass-communication system. Without them, the system as we know it would not exist.

Popular culture is a new academic discipline that is attracting a lot of students and teachers alike. I hope the chapter devoted to it will lead you to further thought about the meaning of it in your everyday lives. Like the media themselves, the implications of popular culture are worldwide.

Media research of the empirical kind is being conducted daily to answer many of the questions that have been posed in this book. But there are many ways to conduct research, and lay people can be easily influenced by articles that attempt to simplify findings. Let Chapter 14 be an introduction for you and a kind of "consumer's guide" to reading about empirical research and the effects of mass media.

The final chapter deals with some of the ways our mass-communication systems are changing as a result of the application of new technologies. In the past, we have tended to think of technological breakthroughs as isolated scientific curiosities. But things are changing so rapidly in mass communication that the form and content of the information we receive may be radically different a few years from now than it is today.

11

And Now the News . . .

WHEN DAN RATHER TOOK OVER FOR WALTER CRONKITE ON *The CBS Evening News* in 1981, I panicked. What would I do now? After all, for years I had rushed home each evening from work in time to tune in "Uncle Wally" (see 11.1). Walter Cronkite and I had been friends for a long time. We'd weathered floods, storms, airline crashes, Watergate, the hostages, and the election of Ronald Reagan. Through it all, Wally had remained as faithful, sober, and credible as any human being could. I could *count* on him to give me all the news—fairly, concisely, objectively.

Yet he was not without emotion. The day that President Richard Nixon resigned, I thought I saw a faint look of relief in Wally's face for just a moment. During the Bicentennial, he beamed as the gaily decorated schooners glided across the color screen.

Cronkite was the last word. If there were doubts or anxieties about the world situation, he could put them to rest with the shuffle of a paper. At the end of his newscast, I knew that I was truly informed, for Wally always assured me solemnly, "That's the way it is . . . ".

WHAT'S NEWS?

Our tremendous dependence on broadcasters like Walter Cronkite—and journalists in general—raises the question of why news has come to be regarded as so important in our mediated America. At the heart of this question is the issue of how those who present "the news" to us make their decisions about what it is. Experienced news editors know that a story

"It is our assumption there may be those in this country who would be disrespectful to the President but that no one would be disrespectful to Walter Cronkite," White House Press Secretary Jody Powell said.

ASSOCIATED PRESS, MARCH 5, 1977

11.1

"Uncle Wally" as he appeared while still anchoring The CBS Evening News. *From 1962– 1981 his familiar face could be seen each weekday evening. Douglas Edwards had anchored before him for 14 years. Thus, Dan Rather became only the third CBS anchorman since the show's inception in 1948.*

must have certain attributes to qualify as news. They decide what goes in the paper and on the air using time-honored criteria. These criteria are not always what you might imagine. There is more to be asked than "Is it important to the audience?" (Actually, that might be one of the last considerations of some newspapers and newscasts.) We have already discussed hard news versus soft news and the role that each plays in the content of newspapers (see Chapter 3). Comparatively little hard news may be included in newscasts as well, because editors have learned that hard news doesn't always sell.

Newsmakers

Some people make news no matter what they do. The President of the United States, a wealthy Arab leader, Jackie Onassis, Queen Elizabeth are always worthy of a story.

Regional or Local Interest

The editor must decide if the audience will want to know about an event because *it happened here.* If a bridge falls and two are killed in Paris, it doesn't "play in Peoria." If the Peoria bridge goes out, it's on the front page of the Peoria newspaper, the lead story on the Peoria evening news.

Rewards

Wilbur Schramm, perhaps the best known of all communication researchers, says that news stories have either *immediate* or *delayed* rewards that satisfy a need. We all need to feel informed, and immediate-reward news stories provide instant satisfaction. We can laugh, cry, sympathize, or become angry about them right away. Stories concerning disaster, crime, sports, and social events all give us immediate rewards. Delayed-reward news stories may be about public affairs, business, finance, or other complex matters. These stories don't carry any immediate relevance to our lives, and increasingly, editors are finding less room for them.

Human Interest

These stories are becoming more common on the nation's news pages and newscasts. They're heart tuggers: the "miracle baby" who grew outside the womb, the handicapped man who rises to an important government position. Editors are finding that an increasing number of readers want the "human side" of the

day's events. Perhaps this reflects a general feeling of disaffiliation with government and world affairs.

These criteria are not universal or all-inclusive, but they are some of the most common. The unusual, the unique, the sensational—this is the stuff of the day's news.

It is also important to remember that reporters find news *where the editors tell them to look.* In this sense, the news is institutional, predictable, and likely to come from the same sources day in and day out.

GOOD NEWS IS NO NEWS

One of the most frequent complaints an editor hears is, "How come you guys never run any *good* news?" It's true that reporters seek out stories about murders that did happen, not about murders that didn't.

Perhaps this is human nature. We don't usually go out of our way to tell people how *good* we feel, but if something is bothering us, we let them know.

Chet Huntley, the late teammate of David Brinkley on the NBC news, once said flatly, "Journalists were never intended to be the cheerleaders of society." For print journalists this is particularly true. Reporters often see themselves as the thin buffer between people and their government. The relationship can be a difficult one. When the U.S. invaded the small nation of Grenada in 1983, the press was virtually barred from being on the scene. Reaction was negative, for reporters felt that they were being kept from doing their job. Most feel that their duty is to report what goes wrong. Implicit is the feeling that if these wrongs are reported, others may learn a lesson.

Clearly this was the motivation for the investigative reporting so much in vogue during the 1970s (see 11.2). When Don Bolles, an Arizona newspaper reporter, was killed in 1975 while investigating white-collar crime, a blue-ribbon panel of three dozen journalists descended on the area. After six months of exhaustive research, they published a series of articles implicating prominent Arizonans in a web of crime.

In 1977, several Hanafi Muslim leaders held 134 Washington residents captive for several days. Afterward, the news media were resoundingly criticized for "overcovering" the event. Many said such coverage encourages

11.2
The New Muckrakers

The most widely read and best-known reporters of the 1970s were those who specialized in investigative reporting, a group journalism writer Leonard Downie, Jr., calls "the modern muckrakers."

Bob Woodward and Carl Bernstein are probably the most famous newspaper reporters in America. They broke the Watergate story, and their pursuit of the Nixon connection was made into the popular film *All the President's Men.* Woodward admits, "It's almost a perverse pleasure. I like going out and finding something that is going wrong . . . and then putting it into the newspaper."

Seymour Hersh, a Washington correspondent for the *New York Times* during the Watergate era, is often disturbed by the ground rules of investigative journalism. "One of the bad things about the newspaper business is that the stories have to be so dry and stick to proven facts." Hersh has been given credit for breaking the My Lai massacre story, and he played a key role in the investigation of the CIA's illegal activities in Chile.

Donald Barlett and James Steele are specialists at digging into public records and focusing attention on corruption in government. One particular triumph was a 1973 series of articles for the *Philadelphia Inquirer* revealing corruption in the judiciary, routine court payoffs, and unequal dispensation of justice. The following year, they won a Pulitzer Prize for stories uncovering preferential IRS treatment of wealthy taxpayers.

Jack Anderson worked for two decades as an understudy to the famous muckraker Drew Pearson. When Pearson died, Anderson took over his "Washington Merry-Go-Round" and

Jack Anderson: "It's a really sexy way to make a living!"

has kept the noted column in motion. He has been threatened, beaten, and drugged by his enemies, but it doesn't seem to deter him. When asked why he continues, Anderson replies casually, "It's a really sexy way to make a living!"

others to commit crimes. Journalists responded by defending their actions on the basis of truth. "If we neglect to report some news because we think suppression is in the public interest," they said, "we'll lose our credibility as impartial news reporters." That impartiality may already be suspect, given the criteria for news selection, but the point is well taken. There is a difference between *selection* of news and *suppression* of news.

A similar dilemma came to the public's attention in 1983. An intoxicated man with a

history of instability called a small TV station in Alabama and urged a camera crew to meet him in the town square in ten minutes "if you want to see someone set himself on fire . . ."

The station notified the police, then went to the square to "cover the story." Through a series of miscommunications, the police left before the camera crew arrived. When the crew got there and set up their lights, the man who had called appeared. While the cameras rolled, he spent 37 seconds and several matches trying to set himself on fire. He was finally successful, just as a member of the crew tried to approach him and force him to stop.

Footage of the immolation appeared on all three major networks, prompting debate about what is ethically appropriate in these situations. Reacting to criticism, one crew member said: "My job is to record events as they happen." Critics contended that the decision to send the crew at all was wrong. Others felt that even though the station had the footage of the incident, they were wrong to air it.

The nation's dependence on TV news and the nature of competition between various stations for high news ratings has created new moral and ethical quandaries for those who make coverage decisions.

NEWSPAPERS

Most of us get all our late-breaking news from three media: newspapers, radio, and television. From newspapers—at least traditional newspapers—come detailed, factual, dispassionate accounts of the day's events. Television supplies a visual depth, while radio keeps us up to the minute with the latest headlines as we drive, work, or play.

The average daily newspaper runs almost 60 pages. More than half that space is for advertising, but some 25 pages are devoted to editorial content—the stuff we call the news.

The circulation of weekly newspapers is close to 35 million. Weeklies are most often found in rural areas that cannot support a daily. Weekly readers are loyal to their product, since it may be their only source of community information. Readers of other types of weeklies may share ethnic or social interests. Many religious groups publish their own newspapers, giving members a particular perspective on world events.

Staff sizes vary tremendously from one newspaper to the next. The typical large daily newspaper employs a full-time editorial staff of 75 to 100 people. Major dailies like the *Washington Post* may have several hundred editorial staffers. Small rural weeklies are often "mom and pop" operations run entirely by one family or (in some cases) one person.

THE NEWSPAPER YOU NEVER SEE

We all have a picture of the investigative reporter in our mind. We know about the crusading editor or publisher. But, as with all media, these people represent only the tip of the iceberg. There are dozens of lesser-known jobs; many are those in which a recent graduate can break into the business. All are vital to getting the paper out on time. In an average metropolitan daily the major departments break down this way:

Owner-Publisher

This can be one person or many. The *Kansas City Star* was even owned by its own employees. For a number of years it was the only totally employee-owned metro in the country, though this ended when the employees sold the paper in 1977. The owner-publisher hires the editors and fills key editorial positions.

Editors

The editor-in-chief is in charge of all editorial functions but delegates the power of review to individual specialized editors in all but the most extraordinary cases. These specialized editors include the managing editor, city editor, news editor, wire editor, and editors of various sections, including sports, editorial, financial, education, science, religion, and life-style. These specialists make decisions about which reporters will cover a story and where it will be placed.

Business Manager

This person ranks equally with the editor-in-chief. The business manager is in charge of advertising, promotion, circulation, and accounting. A good business manager makes sure the paper is earning a profit. He or she reports directly to the owner-publisher.

Production Manager

This person is in charge of the workers and equipment needed to print the paper. The production manager reports directly to the owner-publisher.

Reporters and Photographers

These people work under the city editor or are assigned to an editor in a special department. There are about 15 reporters on a crew of 75, so they actually represent about 20 percent of the total editorial staff. However, like the radio disc jockeys, they are the staff members best known to the average reader. There are general reporters (taking a number of diverse assignments) and those assigned as columnists or who have special beats like city hall or the courts. Photographers usually work with reporters and are often assigned to a story with a good "picture possibility."

Copy Editors

These are the unsung champions of the newsroom. Without them all articles would read strangely. I've never known a reporter who could hand in a story with every word spelled correctly and every punctuation mark in place. Copy editors "clean up" copy before it goes to the composing room. This job is absolutely vital, since readership studies indicate that spelling mistakes and grammatical errors detract from a story's credibility. The content may be correct, but if form is poor the reader is skeptical. Copy editors usually write all headlines.

Stringers

Most newspapers employ a shadow staff of occasional contributors. Often these are young journalists still in school or those working full time in other jobs, many of whom hope to break in as full-time reporters. "Stringers" are usually paid by the column inch. A newspaper with a full-time editorial staff of 75 people may use 15 or 20 stringers.

Naturally, no two newspaper staffs are exactly alike; all functions vary according to individual editorial needs and staff abilities. Most major dailies have a separate art department with editorial cartoonists and illustrators. Often there are special correspondents at the state and federal levels to give the "local angle" to regional and national news. In large labor towns like Detroit and San Francisco, there are often a labor editor and a staff of reporters to cover the union beat.

NEWSPAPER LAYOUT: THE EYES HAVE IT

In 1919 Joseph Patterson decided New York City was ripe for a new kind of newspaper. For a number of years, staid papers like the *New York Times* had been tops in circulation, and Patterson thought the city was ready for a no-holds-barred journal more in the tradition of the yellow papers of the 1890s. His *Illustrated Daily News* (later simply the *New York Daily News*) sported a tabloid format and coupled it with a strong emphasis on photography. On some days the entire front page consisted of masthead, photograph, and caption.

This caught the eye of New Yorkers who had not been daily newspaper readers. While the circulation of most city papers remained the same, the *Daily News* became the largest-selling daily in the country, and is currently second largest, after the *Wall Street Journal*. Sensational weeklies like the *National Enquirer* later copied the layout formula and prospered. Patterson's was a new kind of journalism that seemed to typify the "jazz age" of the 1920s. It became known as "jazz journalism."

Of course, jazz journalism was much more than visual appeal, but layout was an undeniably important reason for the phenomenal success of the *Daily News*. Since that time, all newspapers have become more aware of how necessary visual appeal and graphics are to hold the attention of the reader. Newspapers now have to compete with TV, a visual medium. Graphics research is done to determine reader preferences for various typefaces. Editors have found that most readers prefer bigger pictures, larger headlines, and more eye-catching material.

There is an increased awareness that newspaper *form* as well as *content* is crucial in getting and holding a large readership. The average 60-page newspaper is read in just less than half an hour. That's about two pages a minute. Readers make critical decisions about what they will read by glancing at a headline or photograph.

An awareness of this process has led to increasing specialization in most daily newspapers. In the future, *your* newspaper may be quite different from the one delivered next door, though both come off the same press. If your neighbors are executives, they may get a larger business section. The technology is not quite here yet, but newspaper people know they must help readers find the news they want.

There are now special magazines, inserts, and advertising supplements for individual areas of interest. In addition, there are more advice columns, soft news, and how-to and where-to news in the daily paper than ever before.

STRAIGHT FROM THE WIRES

As local newspapers have increased their emphasis on features, inserts, supplements, and other local-interest stories, they have relegated their regional, national, and international news-gathering functions to the *wire services*, so called because they send their stories to subscribers via wire or phone lines. In recent years wire services have also utilized satellite technology to distribute news to their clients.

Average news consumers have no idea how reliant on the wires their local paper as well as radio stations and TV stations are. If you look through the newspaper in your own town you'll probably find that the majority of its stories are "wire copy." Even big-budget dailies like the *Washington Post* and the *Los Angeles Times* with their own foreign and national correspondents rely heavily on wire copy.

It all began back in 1848 at the *New York Sun*, where a number of New York newspaper publishers met to form a cooperative news-gathering association called the Associated

Press. The idea was simple: Each newspaper would receive stories from its member newspapers, and some of the wasteful duplication made necessary by intense competition to "scoop" their rivals would be eliminated. The telegraph, which came into common use shortly after the forming of the AP, meant that newspapers all over the country could receive instantaneous news. Thus there was a rapid dissemination of the day's important stories. The public now had access to information that had once taken weeks or even months to reach them.

The AP's rival, the United Press, was formed in 1907 as a combination of several smaller news services that had tried to compete with the AP. In 1958 the UP merged with the International News Service and became United Press International. While the AP was the leading service for many years, UPI was first to recognize that service to broadcasters would become big business, and it got a head start in that area. UPI was also first to provide radio stations with wire "actualities," or tapes recorded on-the-scene at important news events. The AP lagged behind in this area until finally launching its own AP audio wire in 1974.

The two wire services are by far the nation's largest news-gathering agencies, with offices in each major city and reporters on every important beat around the world. So dependent have local newspapers become on the wires that they often wait for wire copy on major events in their own cities just to be sure they have all of the background material and other information necessary for in-depth coverage.

In addition to the two major wires, there are hundreds of foreign and special wire services supplying an endless array of copy. The largest of these is Reuters, a British news service that also specializes in financial infor-

mation. The Lumber Instant News (LIN) carries prices and other information of special interest to lumber companies as well as newspapers in areas where lumber is news. Grain Information News (GIN) and Poultry and Egg News (PEN) are examples of other special-interest wire services.

In addition, large newspapers like the *Los Angeles Times*, *Washington Post*, and *New York Times* operate their own news services, as do newspaper chains like Gannett and Knight-Ridder.

The AP and UPI were originally conceived to serve newspapers and other print media. Yet broadcast stations have also become increasingly dependent on the wires. This trend began with a battle between newspapers and radio stations over radio's access to the wire information.

RADIO: THE NEW KID IN TOWN

During the early 1920s, radio broadcasters were not very interested in news. There were no radio reporters, and most news came directly from newspapers and sounded rather dull on the air. Advertisers expressed little enthusiasm for sponsoring news broadcasts, preferring to back more popular entertainment and music shows. Yet there were some news events that seemed designed for radio coverage.

The Hoover-Smith presidential election of 1928 was fully covered by the new medium. The three wire services (AP, UP, and INS) supplied radio with details of the campaign and official election results. Listeners found that they could get the returns via radio without having to wait until the next morning for printed results. The candidates themselves spent almost $1 million on radio advertising. The age of radio news and public affairs had arrived. By the time the Depression began in 1929, some stations had as many as ten reporters whose sole job was to cover the news.

Newspapers were among the first to feel the economic pinch of the Depression, and they were not about to sit by and lose advertisers to radio. They reasoned that radio was supposed to provide entertainment, but real news coverage should remain exclusively the job of print. In 1933, a majority of Associated Press members fired the first volley of the press-radio war by refusing to provide wire-service information to radio networks. This forced newscasters to go to the early editions of newspapers for their news, but the AP soon went to court to stop even that practice. NBC and CBS then set up their own news-gathering bureaus.

A compromise was tried: In exchange for the networks' dropping their plans to expand radio news coverage, a newly created "Press-Radio Bureau" would supply two five-minute newscasts daily, culled from wire service stories. But that wasn't enough. Radio stations and listeners demanded more. In no time there were half a dozen competing radio news services.

Radio bypassed traditional news channels to bring listeners the events leading to World War II. Edward R. Murrow (see 11.3) organized a series of broadcasts for CBS from the capitals of Europe. As Hitler's demands became more preposterous, listeners heard reporters describe the tense situation. All this culminated in Murrow's 1940 broadcasts from London. While bombs burst all around him, Murrow told the sad tale of England's struggle to survive the war. This sense of immediacy and involvement would not soon be forgotten by the millions of Americans glued to their radios. Radio had won the press-radio struggle and achieved its rightful place in news reporting.

RIP AND READ

Despite this exciting beginning, radio news has made few major advances since World War II. No sooner had radio established personalities like Murrow and Eric Sevareid than television came along and offered them a more exciting challenge.

Most radio networks were forced to cut back on expensive news operations when radio began losing lucrative entertainment advertising dollars to TV. Many continued to provide affiliates with five minutes of national news each hour, most of it ripped and read from the "radio wire," which provided news copy, and a limited number of actualities or taped broadcasts from reporters in the field.

In 1975, NBC merged existing news facilities with a new radio news service dubbed the "News and Information Service" (NIS). NIS provided affiliates (both NBC and non-NBC stations) with 50 minutes of radio news an hour, allowing them to become "all-news" stations overnight simply by plugging in. NIS featured imaginative interpretative reporting and a barrage of feature material. Despite the popularity of the all-news format in many markets, NIS folded in 1977.

Prompted by the increase in popularity of the all-news and news-talk formats (see 11.4), the Cable News Network (CNN) began a 24-hour all-news and news-talk service and made it available to radio stations nationwide in 1982. CNN radio, like CNN TV, was the brainchild of Atlanta's TV "superstation" owner Ted Turner. CNN offers potential affiliates the possibility of becoming all-news at the push of a button. Whether CNN will go the way of NIS or become successful remains to be seen.

11.3
Edward R. Murrow: Patron Saint of Broadcast Journalism

The voice that so many Americans came to trust during World War II was that of Edward R. Murrow. Christened Egbert Murrow in 1908, he was the youngest of three sons born to Scottish immigrant parents. Though they began American life in Kentucky, the Murrows soon moved to a small town in Washington State.

Egbert's education began at home; with his mother's patient tutoring he had a head start on his classmates. Young Egbert always liked school. Mrs. Murrow also instilled in her son the firm belief in a solid day's work. Later, he was to admit that he would feel "miserable" if he didn't work and that he was not "equipped for fun."

After high school, Murrow briefly attended the University of Virginia before returning to enroll at Washington State. There he came under the influence of Ida Lou Anderson, an instructor in speech. She taught him speech, diction, and presence. Always a debate enthusiast, Murrow worked hard and was regarded by Anderson as her most promising pupil. It was she who suggested later that Murrow pause after the first word of his introduction to his London broadcasts. Thus, "This is London" became "This . . . is London," the phrase that was to become a Murrow trademark.

After working briefly in several radio-related jobs, Murrow joined the CBS radio network in 1935 as "director of talks" through the recommendation of an old friend, Fred Willis, who was then special assistant to CBS president William Paley; Murrow soon proved his worth.

The talks director set a prec-

edent for CBS by hiring reporters, rather than announcers, to broadcast the news in Europe. Some of these, like Walter Cronkite and Robert Trout, would go on to become famous television journalists. Murrow expected superhuman effort from his staffers, but he was no less dedicated himself. During one crisis, he made 35 broad-

THE COMMENTATORS

Radio commentators have a unique voice or delivery—the most recognizable "byline" ever. The brief listing below highlights a few newscasters who pioneered a new brand of "audio journalism."

Paul Harvey was still going strong in the mid-1980s. His delivery includes long pauses that drive the point home. Seldom does Harvey have to let his audience know how he feels about a subject. His tone tells all. Harvey has said: "The cold hard facts have to be salted and peppered to make them palatable. Since objectivity is impossible, I make no pretense of it—I just let it all hang out."

His daily newscasts seem to strike a particularly responsive chord in small-town and rural America. Stories include the big news of the day as well as the story of the couple who has been married "68 years today . . . and still holding." His trademark sign-off is punctuated by five seconds of silence. "This is Paul Harvey . . . . . Good day."

Gabriel Heatter had a flair for the emotion-packed human-interest story while with

casts in less than three weeks and arranged for 116 others from 18 points in Europe.

After returning from Europe in 1946, his name now a household word, the still young (38) Murrow was named CBS vice president in charge of news, education, and discussion programs. He was joined a year later by his lifetime friend and mentor, Fred Friendly, and together they produced the popular news show *Hear It Now*. The program was unusual in that it blended straight, or hard, news stories with the interpretative reports Murrow dubbed "think pieces."

In 1951 *Hear It Now* became *See It Now*. The face that went with the famous voice was introduced to American television viewers. Critic Gilbert Seldes called *See It Now* the most important show on the air—"not only for the solutions it found to some problems but also for the problems it tackled without finding the right answers."

Murrow was to narrate many famous broadcasts, including a blistering attack on Senator Joseph McCarthy in 1954 and a famous CBS documentary, "Harvest of Shame," which explored the tragic conditions of American migrant farm workers. All of this was not without its consequences.

Though originally a Murrow admirer, Paley eventually grew disenchanted with Murrow and *See It Now*. The controversy, he said, upset his stomach. This precipitated a falling-out of sorts between Murrow and CBS. There was an extended sabbatical, and finally Murrow left the network to head the United States Information Agency under the John F. Kennedy administration. According to one biographer, the last straw involved Murrow's being denied his usual "instant access" to Paley.

Ironically, *See It Now* was the first television program to openly discuss the possibility that cigarette smoking might lead to lung cancer. For years, Murrow's trademark had been his endless chain of cigarettes and the smoke curling across the screen. In 1965, after a long battle with lung cancer, he assembled his family for a last air appearance, a public-service announcement urging Americans to quit smoking. He died in April of that year.

Perhaps his accomplishments were best summed up by Friendly: "He laid down a standard of responsibility for radio and television broadcast journalists, a standard lacking before his time and seldom measured up to since."

From Edward Jay Whetmore, *The Magic Medium: An Introduction to Radio in America.* © 1981 by Wadsworth, Inc.

---

the Mutual network during the 1920s and 1930s. Heatter's name became a household word. He was one of the first to be strongly identified by voice and broadcast style. Along with Fulton Lewis, Jr., and Elmer Davis, he pioneered the 15-minute "news commentary" format.

H. V. Kaltenborn started broadcasting in 1922 and joined CBS eight years later. He was probably the best-known radio commentator of his day. The height of his fame came during a 20-day crisis in 1938 when Hitler made a number of demands on Czechoslovakia. Europe appeared on the brink of war, and Kaltenborn set up a cot in his famous "Studio Nine" to give listeners all the latest. During those three weeks, he did more than 80 broadcasts, including a number of long commentaries. Never had Americans heard so much news and comment.

Lowell Thomas began at Pittsburgh's KDKA in 1925 and worked until his death in 1981. Thomas had a unique, brash, but sincere delivery that caught on with the public. His era of reporting stretched from the Spanish Civil War to the war in Vietnam. Thomas's

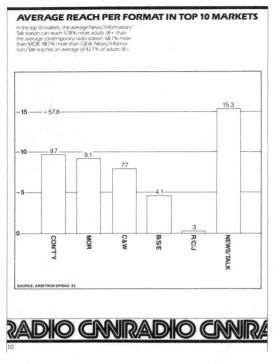

AVERAGE REACH PER FORMAT IN TOP 10 MARKETS

In the top 10 markets, the average News/Information/Talk station can reach 578% more adults 18+ than the average contemporary radio station; 68.1% more than MOR; 98.7% more than C&W. News/Information/Talk reaches an average of 42.7% of adults 18+.

SOURCE: ARBITRON SPRING '82

11.4

This chart reflects the widespread audience interest in the Information/Talk format in most major markets. It was used by Turner Broadcasting to help market their CNN format to would-be subscribers.

Turner Broadcasting Systems, Inc., 1982. Used by permission.

trademark was his introduction: "From Moscow to the Suez Canal [the day's top datelines] comes today's news. Good evening everybody, this is Lowell Thomas for CBS news . . ."

Walter Winchell may be remembered by some of you as the machine-gun staccato voice that introduced the old *Untouchables* series. Winchell was a New York newspaper columnist who got into radio as a sideline. Unlike his other radio colleagues, Winchell was strictly in the entertainment business, supplying

humorous tidbits and personal "secrets" (see 11.5). His popularity among peers faded somewhat in the 1950s. He once accused Lucille Ball of being a communist and sided with Senator McCarthy against Murrow in the famous 1954 TV battle.

TELEVISION NEWS: THE TOSSED SALAD

Television news began as a simple rip-and-read operation. TV newscasters delivered the script taken directly from the AP and UPI radio wires. A considerable amount of TV news still reaches us this way. Local newscasts are often a "tossed salad" culled from radio wire copy, newspapers, and other sources. Still slides are used along with 16-mm film. None of these media are television in the strictest sense of the word.

Walter Cronkite has observed that the concept of an anchorperson unifying these separate parts may become a thing of the past:

If we can illustrate all stories there is no further need of a news broadcaster to read half the items to the public. Disembodied voices can narrate the film, reporters on the scene will be seen when the situation demands, and there will be no need for a news master of ceremonies in the studio.

Indeed, the whole idea of an anchorperson may be left over from commentators of the radio era. Yet today's anchorpeople seem far less opinionated and pioneering than their radio counterparts. Of more importance is their visual appeal to the audience. According to author Irving Fang, the five most important qualities for the TV anchorperson are:

1. Speaking clearly.
2. Imparting the sense of the news.
3. Convincing viewers you know what you are talking about.

11.5

Walter Winchell in 1944 on the NBC Blue network, tapping out his famous "Morse code" signature.

4. Keeping the newscast running smoothly.
5. Maintaining contact with the audience.

Nowhere on the list do we find skills involving more traditional journalistic practices or ethics.

Perhaps the ultimate extension of this trend came when ERA, a San Francisco research firm, was hired by Los Angeles's KNXT-TV to find out why their news ratings were slipping. Viewers were chosen at random, and their galvanic skin response (GSR) was measured while they were shown film clips of the station's anchorpeople. GSR works like a lie detector test; when viewers get excited, they begin to sweat slightly, and GSR picks up the subtle difference. Newscasters that produced sufficient GSR responses were kept; those who didn't were fired.

George Putnam, a rival newscaster and long-time Los Angeles TV personality noted for his own ability to elicit emotional audience response, objected to the practice. "This ERA thing is frightening. I'm sure if they showed Adolf Hitler up there on the screen the needle would jump right out of the glass. But that's no reason to let Adolf anchor the five o'clock news!"

Nevertheless, those who anchor newscasts realize that their jobs are as much cosmetic as substantive (see 11.6). When ABC paid Barbara Walters $5 million to co-anchor its evening newscast, it was not because it seriously felt she could add substance. What she would add (it hoped) were style and flair—that indescribable something that seemed to be working for many local male-female co-anchors. Alas, the match between Walters and co-anchor Harry Reasoner was far from perfect. Before long she had returned to doing prime-time interview specials, and Reasoner had gone back to CBS.

FRIENDLY TEAMNESS . . . TEEMING FRIENDLINESS

ABC-owned stations in San Francisco and New York pioneered the "Eyewitness news" format in the early 1970s. These shows have also been called "friendly teamness" and "happy news." They differ from other local newscasts in a number of ways, but most notably in the way members of the news team relate to one another. Gone is the old stiff-collared, serious approach. Friendly team members are relaxed and at ease with their news.

In between stories there is light chitchat about the day's events and whatever else comes to mind. News stories emphasize human interest. There's a group of Boy Scouts going on a hike in Tarzana, a new flower seller on Fourth Street.

Journalists debate the ethics of "friendly news," but no one debates its success. ABC hit the ratings jackpot in both San Francisco and New York. The network promptly supplied the format outline to local affiliates, and soon eyewitness news teams began to spring up in most of the country's major markets. Other newscasts were forced to copy them in hopes of winning back viewers.

In part, this is a product of the new competitiveness among local newscasts. In recent years local newscasts in large markets have begun to show a profit, despite high costs.

In addition, for many stations the local news is directly followed by prime-time offerings. If a large audience is tuned in for the local news, more will stay tuned when it's over. So "teeming friendliness" is desirable because it means a larger audience than the more traditional approach. Why?

ABC called in Marshall McLuhan to explain the phenomenon. McLuhan contended that friendly newscasters *share* the news with the audience rather than reporting it in a more objective way. The happy chat between newscasters lets the audience in on what's happening. "The press," he says, "is concerned with what *has* happened. TV news is more successful when it concerns itself with what *is* happening."

Eyewitness news is really "I" witness news. It's a warmer, friendlier, more relaxed coverage of events that allows the viewer to participate. The news team has direct dialogue with the audience. The old newscaster says, "That's the way it is"; the friendly news team says, "This is the way *we are*." In this way, the reporting of the event *becomes* the event, overshadowing the original story.

The same can be true of news at the national level. Famous anchorpeople are stars or celebrities in their own right. When Barbara Walters goes to interview an official in Kuwait, she is actually the story, since she's far better known than her interviewee.

11.6

Not Just Another Pretty Face: The Christine Craft Case

Christine Craft was relatively happy in her job as anchor of the evening newscast on KEYT-TV in Santa Barbara, California. A media consulting firm liked what it saw and, without her knowledge, sent a tape of one of her newscasts to Kansas City's KMBC-TV, a station in search of a new female anchor. KMBC contacted Craft and in January 1981 hired her away at almost double her KEYT salary.

While Craft was being interviewed for the Kansas City job, she told them she resented the treatment she had gotten while working for CBS Sports. In 1978 they had insisted she bleach her hair blonde and change her makeup technique. Despite the changes she was eventually fired, and she didn't want a repeat performance. Ironically, that is exactly what she got.

From the day she arrived at KMBC, she was told what to wear, when to wear it, and what kind of makeup to apply. Craft didn't like it but went along. Despite a rise in the program's ratings she was fired seven months after she began. The station manager told her that a consulting firm had found that she was "too old, too unattractive, and not deferential enough to men." Craft sued Metromedia

Inc., owner of the station, charging sex discrimination. "No one cares what John Chancellor and Roger Mudd look like," she told *People* magazine. "If we can have uncles on television, why can't we have aunts?"

During the trial it became clear that it was the consultant's findings regarding her looks that had cost her the job. A member of the firm had been taped in a conversation with viewers where he declared, "Let's spend 30 seconds destroying Chris Craft. Is she a mutt?" In addition, the consultants reported that she did not appeal to men and "the women viewers dislike you the most. They resent the fact that you don't hide your intelligence."

With that kind of evidence, it didn't take the jury long to decide. On August 8, 1983, they awarded her $500,000 in damages and urged the judge to find the station guilty of sex discrimination. The jury foreman said "We hope we have helped women in broadcasting."

The decision sent shock waves through the industry and raised some questions about TV news practices. Should anchors be hired for their journalistic skills and experience or is the way they look of prime importance? TV executives say they must be free to hire and fire anchors and other news "personalities" at will as they struggle to compete for ratings. ABC News Vice President David

Burke was quoted as saying "Women in this business face pressures that men do not, but those pressures often stem from the public." Indeed, one research firm conducted a survey of 1,200 anchors and found that almost half of the men but only 3 percent of the women anchors were over 40.

The 38-year-old Craft returned briefly to her Santa Barbara job but quit shortly after the 1983 judgment was awarded to write and speak on the lecture circuit. Currently Craft carries on the battle for changes in TV news practices but sees it as uphill. Shortly after the verdict she admitted, "This is a victory for civil rights, but I have no illusions that it will make a huge difference in TV news."

The August 8 verdict, however, was thrown out by U.S. District Judge Joseph F. Stevens in October 1983. A retrial was scheduled, and on January 13, 1984, the new jury awarded Craft $325,000—$225,000 for actual damages and $100,000 in punitive damages. Craft's lawyer argued that punitive damages should be awarded for their "deterrent effect," to discourage other stations from similar practices. At this writing Metromedia Inc. plans further appeal. The debate over the appropriate weighting of form and content, of viewer appeal and solid journalistic practice continues.

11.7

Anchorpeople Lois Hart and David Walker in the Atlanta newsroom-set of the Cable News Network.

TV NEWS IN THE 1980s

TV's emphasis on friendly news reveals the changing nature of local TV news. Once upon a time, it was thought that local news was something you had to put on to keep the FCC off your back. Most stations tried to keep it to a minimum, and budgets were meager. But in the last decade or so, the audience for local TV news seems to have multiplied exponentially. Now local TV newscasts vie for ratings points just like game shows and prime-time movies.

The cost of producing a top-quality local newscast is tremendous. There are salaries, sets, and expensive electronic equipment. Yet local newscasts in most metropolitan markets make a good profit.

This turn of events came about as a result of an increasing public hunger for news and information of every kind. The truth is that we are consuming more information via mass media than ever before. This was the theory behind the founding of all-news radio in the 1960s. The success of that format led the way

to increasing TV news coverage. As early as 1970 one Los Angeles TV station was presenting two and a half hours of local news each evening.

A major breakthrough came in 1980 when Ted Turner, the controversial cable TV tycoon, inaugurated his Cable News Network (CNN) (see 11.7). Fed to approximately 3.7 million cable news subscribers all over the country, CNN was the first 24-hour-a-day, seven-day-a-week TV news service.

In its first two years of operation, CNN increased its potential audience immensely and can now be received in over 15 million homes. In addition, Turner inaugurated a second service, CNN 2, which provides "news headlines" and rapid updates on a 24-hour basis.

Though still in the red financially, CNN and CNN 2 are supported by Turner's "superstation," WTBS Atlanta, which now enjoys annual profits in the $40 million range. It's clear that Turner has become, in the words of *Business Week* magazine, "the man to beat in news-for-cable-TV audiences."

In mid-1982, Satellite News Channel, a joint

NOW WE HAVE TIME TO GIVE YOU THE NEWS AS WELL AS TAKE IT APART.

Great news for newswatchers. After seven years of bringing you news analysis, Robert MacNeil and Jim Lehrer now report the day's news, too. On the new MacNeil/Lehrer NewsHour.

Now they have a full hour. That's enough time to give you news summaries for the day, and to go on to examine stories in depth with expert guests and special reports from around the world.

So start getting the news where you've been getting the analysis.

Major funding is provided by AT&T, the national corporate underwriter.

 AT&T

A production of WNET/THIRTEEN, New York, WETA, Washington, D.C., and MacNeil-Lehrer-Gannett Productions. Funded by AT&T, Public Television Stations, and the Corporation for Public Broadcasting.

The MacNeil/Lehrer NEWSHOUR
Weeknights on PBS

11.8

Amid the intense ratings race of the commercial networks, PBS announced its own entry in 1983. The half-hour Mac-Neil/Lehrer Report, *a news analysis program, was being expanded to an hour and would now include a full-range report on the day's events. Long among the most respected of all TV journalists, Robert MacNeil and Jim Lehrer seemed at home with the new format almost immediately. The long-term effect on the commercial network newscasts? Too soon to tell, perhaps, but the appeal of a full hour of news anchored by such prestigious journalists and including no commercials must have raised a few eyebrows at the offices of the big three.*

venture of ABC Video Enterprises and Group W Satellite Communications, went on the air to compete with CNN. Turner contends that the new news channel is intended to compete only with CNN 2 and terms the intrusion "a pathetic way to counterattack." Within a year Turner announced plans to buy the new network and add its subscribers and facilities to CNN. It appears that there is an unexpectedly large audience out there ready for continuous TV news.

The networks have responded to this in a number of ways. In 1983 ABC expanded its successful *Nightline* from a half hour to an hour each weekday evening. Meanwhile, CBS inaugurated an overnight (early-early morning, if you like) news service seen in many markets. NBC now airs a complete newscast before the *Today* show, and of course *Today* has always had a large news component. Even the noncommercial network has been affected by the national thirst for news (see 11.8).

BROADCAST EDITORIALS

The concept of the broadcast editorial, now a regular part of most TV newscasts, was borrowed from print. Editorial expression has, of course, been around since the beginning of mass media, but the earliest separate editorial pages appeared in Horace Greeley's *New York Tribune* in the 1840s. Though Greeley was a great moralist, he felt the place for opinion was on a separate page, not mixed up with the news. The editorial page was a permanent fixture by the end of the century.

When radio appeared in the 1920s, there was no thought to giving a point of view. But as radio news went into high gear, some stations offered programs of news and comment, calling them "newspapers of the air." By 1940, WAAB in Boston was offering regular opinions on the qualifications of political candidates and other controversial public issues.

Some complaints to the FCC surfaced in 1941 when WAAB applied for a license renewal. Hearings were held. In what became known as the "Mayflower Decision," the FCC concluded:

A radio station cannot be used to advocate the causes of the licensee. It cannot be used to support the candidacy of his friends. It cannot be devoted to the support of principles he happens to regard most favorably. In brief, the broadcaster cannot be an advocate.

WAAB saw the writing on the wall and stopped editorializing. Without ever being tested by the courts, the right to editorialize was relinquished by broadcasters. Debate ensued during the next eight years about what the rights and responsibilities of a "truly free radio station" should be. Many broadcasters were alarmed, contending that the FCC had overstepped its authority. In 1949, the commission reversed the Mayflower Decision and said that in the interest of the public's right to hear all points of view (and of broadcasters' right of free speech), editorials would be allowed. It established guidelines for those who would editorialize, reminding them that the right to editorialize carried with it an obligation to make sure those with opposing points of view were heard.

The commission said, "In such presentation of news and comment the public interest requires that the licensee must operate on a basis of overall fairness." This came to be known as the "fairness doctrine." The policy became more important in 1959, as Congress (through an amendment of section 315 of the Communication Act) began to *encourage* broadcasters to editorialize, and in the 1960s, with encouragement from FCC Chairman Newton Minow. In essense Congress said that it was not only broadcasters' *right* to editorialize (and offer equal time), it was also their *responsibility*. In this way, the public could hear all sides of controversial issues.

In the 1969 Red Lion Decision, the U.S. Supreme Court went even further, saying the rights of viewers and listeners come before those of broadcasters. The Red Lion Broadcasting Company ran a small Pennsylvania radio station that advocated right wing politics and conservative religious practices. When they refused to allow opposing forces equal time to respond to one particular program, the case went to the FCC. The Commission held that broadcasters may not systematically exclude a program or a reply because they feared that it would be too controversial or that some listeners may find it objectionable. They have a duty to present provocative programs and diverse points of view.

By the mid-1970s, two of every three commercial TV stations in the country were carrying some sort of editorials. But only one station in seven carried a *daily* editorial or reply. What's more, the subject matter for those editorials was often innocuous or relatively trivial. Some stations still stayed away from more substantive issues for fear of offending viewers or sponsors. Two out of three commercial AM radio stations and half of the FM stations editorialized. Congress has forbidden public radio and TV stations from editorializing, fearing that public broadcasting funds might be used to support a particular candidate. The constitutionality of forbidding public stations to editorialize while demanding it from commercial stations remains to be tested.

ISSUES AND ANSWERS: WHO OWNS THE MEDIA?

We are surrounded by thousands of media outlets supplying countless billions of words, sounds, and pictures. Our right to get news and opinion from these diversified media has been affirmed by the Supreme Court. We have a tradition of a free press and a free marketplace of ideas where all can speak their mind as they see fit.

But the marketplace of ideas is also a marketplace of free enterprise. Media ownership trends in recent years have some critics worried. We know that the power of media is the greatest single power in our society. Control of media means control of the information channels we use to decide political and social issues. We may try to counteract this control by getting our news from a variety of media. But if the newspaper we read, the radio station we hear, and the television channels we watch are all owned by one person or corporation, where does that leave us? Are we being denied our chance to get more diversified information?

The proliferation of vast corporations—some owning 50 or more newspapers, some even owning two in a single market—is cause for concern. The latest available figures indicate that the 12 largest newspaper corporations own a total of 245 newspapers with a combined circulation of 23.4 million, or 38 percent of the 61 million individual newspapers distributed in America each day. To make matters worse, many of these same chains maintain broadcast interests.

During the 1970s, a series of FCC decisions made it clear that owning broadcast and newspaper outlets in the same market was not desirable. But to break up existing combinations would mean the sale or trade of stations in 43 states and most major markets. So, while the FCC decided to approve no more cross-ownership deals, it let those that existed remain. A 1977 U.S. Circuit Court of Appeals decision took the FCC ruling one step further, saying that broadcasters must either prove that such arrangements are "in the public interest" or divest themselves of multiple outlets.

Former FCC Commissioner Nicholas Johnson hailed the decision as a landmark victory for freedom of speech and First Amendment rights. Long a critic of those he calls "the media barons," Johnson says the FCC is our only hope of continuing diversified information. Once, he says, the FCC took this responsibility seriously.

In 1941, they ordered NBC to divest itself of one of its radio networks and in that same year, they set limits on the total number of broadcast licenses any individual can hold. . . . but since the New Deal generation left the command posts of the FCC, this agency has lost much of its zeal for combatting concentration. . . . atrophy has reached an advanced state.

Johnson notes that the question is basic. Can the government or its agency really *control* an industry that in turn controls the access of government officials to the electorate? Perhaps this is why the FCC has been timid in recent years and why it took the court of appeals to prod it into doing its job.

Media owners were outraged at these events, pointing out that profitable broadcast stations often support money-losing newspapers. Without the broadcast income, they claim, many newspapers would cease publication. Yet the power of owning several media outlets in one community is awesome. It may be better to have no newspaper than to have one controlled by owners who already run AM, FM, and TV stations. If the FCC can't or won't force the issue, the problem will have to be left to the judiciary.

The Department of Justice has authority under the antitrust laws to break up combinations that "restrain trade" or "tend to lessen competition." These laws apply to media as they do to any other industry. Johnson argues convincingly that if it is in the public interest to have different brands of steel and different kinds of automobiles, it is certainly in our interest to have diverse sources of information.

QUERIES AND CONCEPTS

1 Compare a local daily paper and a weekly paper. What are the differences in size? Amount of advertising? Editorial content?

2 Make up your own list of criteria defining "what's news." How does it differ from the editor's list included here? How would newspapers be better if they followed your list?

3 Dig through your library or newspaper's files to find a newspaper printed 30 years ago. Does the visual style differ from that of today? How about the use of pictures? Headlines?

4 Do a comparative analysis of newspaper, radio, and TV news. Simply list all stories in the news sections of the paper, all stories covered by a five-minute radio newscast, and all stories covered by a half-hour TV newscast on the same day. Which does the best job of covering the day's news? Why?

5 Check your local TV newscast for any possible influence of the "friendly team" approach. You might want to look at all TV newscasts in your market and decide which has the friendliest team.

6 Do some research on the ownership of media outlets in your market. Does any one single person or corporation own more than one? How might this affect the news you receive?

7 Reread 11.6 regarding the Christine Craft case. Make up a list of all the qualities that should be considered when stations are looking for a new anchor. What priorities should each of these qualities be awarded?

READINGS AND REFERENCES

What's News?

For a number of articles groping with definitions for news, see the special section, "What Is News," *Journal of Communication*, Autumn 1976, p. 4.

The Newspaper You Never See

One excellent staff chart of a typical newspaper appears in Chapter 14 of *Mass Media* by Hiebert, Ungurait, and Bohn (New York: David McKay, 1974).

Newspaper Layout: The Eyes Have It

Arthur T. Turnbull
Russell N. Baird
The Graphics of Communication: Practical Exercises in Typography, Layout and Design, 4th ed. New York: Holt, Rinehart & Winston, 1980.

> This is the complete book of newspaper design, covering graphics, typography, and layout. Though it is dated, its historical perspective and basic premises remain applicable to today's visual trends.

Radio: The New Kid in Town; Rip and Read

Edward Jay Whetmore
The Magic Medium: An Introduction to Radio in America. Belmont, Calif.: Wadsworth, 1981.

> The history and evolution of radio is covered in Chapter 2. Chapter 5 deals exclusively with news and sports, including an analysis of the all-news format.

The Commentators

You'll find an interesting discussion of Paul Harvey and his influence in William L. Rivers's *The Mass Media*, 2d ed. (New York: Harper & Row, 1975). Edward R. Murrow's biography, *Prime Time: The Life of Edward R. Murrow*, by Alexander Kendrick (New York: Avon Books, 1970) is the most complete account of the highly revered newsman. See also *CBS: Reflections in a Bloodshot Eye* by Robert Metz (New York: New American Library, 1976) for the "inside story" of early CBS radio and TV commentators and stars.

Television News: The Tossed Salad

Irving E. Fang
Television News, Radio News, 3rd rev. ed. Champlin, Minn.: Rada Press, 1980. (Original title: *Television News*.)

> Originally devoted to television news, this expanded and updated edition covers both radio and TV. Chapters cover writing for the ear, news copy, reporting for radio and TV, weather, sports, and every aspect of field work. A popular text in radio and TV news courses.

Alfred W. Friendly
Due to Circumstances Beyond Our Control. New York: Random House, 1967.

> The man who co-produced *See It Now* with Ed Murrow reminisces about his broadcasting career and his final years as president of CBS News. He quit in 1966 when the network chose to air a rerun of *I Love Lucy* instead of important public hearings on Vietnam.

12

Advertising and Public Relations: The Pretty Package

STANDARD OIL. CALVIN KLEIN JEANS. GOODYEAR TIRE AND Rubber Company. Adidas. Ronald Reagan. Edward Kennedy. Social Security. In our information environment, countless thousands of such entities compete for our attention on a daily basis. Each employs a full-time staff of advertising and public-relations professionals whose job it is to influence *you*, the information consumer.

THE INFORMATION ENVIRONMENT

Our image of Standard Oil can be a public-minded company attempting to serve the public interest, or a greedy conglomerate out to rip off all consumers. We can believe that Adidas makes athletic equipment to help us all become healthier, or we can believe they are in business only to make money. It is the job of advertising and public relations professionals to *influence* our attitudes in very specific ways.

To accomplish this they use two general strategies we might label *covert* and *overt*. Overt strategies are direct. Buy this! Send in the coupon! You must own this! Overt strategies comprise what we call *advertising*. Covert strategies are far more subtle. Goodyear sends a press release to the media announcing their support of National Motherhood Week. They wait. They hope the media responds by passing along to the public, the consumers, word of their corporate good deeds. If and when that happens perhaps the consumer will buy more Goodyear tires. These covert efforts are known as *public relations* (PR).

Media visionary McLuhan reminded us that the world has

> **News, by its very definition, is bad; if one hears good news— it must be advertising or PR. . . .**
> MARSHALL MCLUHAN

259

changed rapidly in the last several decades. We have, in a sense, gone from an industrial society to an information society. We have witnessed "the creation of a worldwide information environment. Information itself has become by far our largest business and commodity."

In some ways, advertising and PR differ little from mass media themselves. As in print, radio, and television, a message is created from real life, and a mediated reality is constructed and designed to reach a mass audience (see 12.1). But the advertising message must do more than keep the audience's attention. It must influence attitudes, beliefs, and behaviors. No matter how clever a message campaign may be, if it fails to influence, it fails. What's more, you may have only 30 seconds of air time or a few column inches of space to make it happen.

Let's look at another example. A large oil company's drilling operations have accidentally spilled 2 million gallons of oil on Miami Beach. That is a hell of a PR problem. The PR staff advises how to rectify the damage to the company's image. There will be a press release to explain company efforts to clean up the beach, advertising to counteract public outrage, and publicity concerning a new company-instituted safety regulation.

At the same time, the advertising department of the same oil company will continue as if the oil spill had never happened. Its job is simply (as we'll see, it's not really all that simple) to urge people to buy the company's brand of oil.

Advertising and PR are *message businesses*. But these messages are often aimed at only small segments of the mass audience. For example, a PR campaign may be aimed at only those who have negative feelings about a particular company. An advertising campaign may be aimed at only those affluent enough to buy a Mercedes Benz. PR and advertising practitioners are *information specialists*.

THE ADVERTISING BUSINESS DEVELOPS

Mass advertising developed along with mass media. Early ad forms were handbills and printed signs. Actually, newspapers first developed as vehicles for advertising. By the early 1800s there were thousands of such publications. Most transactions were made at the local level, but as marketing techniques became more sophisticated and long-distance travel more common, many businesses wanted to expand to new markets.

Into this dilemma came the advertising *agency*. Volney Palmer organized the first one in the United States in 1841. Early agencies represented publishers, not products, going to potential advertisers to offer space for sale. They were given a small fee by the publishers, usually based on the total amount of revenues they brought in.

Soon the advertising business was becoming unwieldy. Companies that advertised their products were constantly in doubt as to which publications to place their ads in and what their ads should say. Circulation figures were suspect, and advertisers had no way of knowing the real "cost per thousand" of readers reached. Into this vacuum stepped the N. W. Ayer & Son Agency. In 1875, it began offering ad counseling directly to the people with the products, advising them how to get more for their advertising dollar. The idea was a great success, and the basic structure of advertising remains the same today.

Advertising agencies represent clients, dream up copy for their ads, recommend media outlets, and are paid a percentage of the total advertising dollars spent (usually 15 percent). One additional twist makes the relationship between agency and client interesting. Though agencies are paid a percentage of their client's advertising dollars, the client doesn't always actually pay. Most media outlets offer a 15 percent *agency discount* on all ad rates. Clients are getting the services of their agencies free—or at least it appears that way in theory.

EARLY EXCESSES

Advertising practices during the first half of the 20th century were often more expedient than ethical. Print media and radio stations received consumer complaints by the thousands, accusing advertisers of making exaggerated claims for their products.

In 1911, a crusade was started by advertisers to clean up the industry. This was in large part a reaction against the shady campaigns of purveyors of patent medicines. A number of organizations tried to adopt codes of ethics to encourage truth in advertising and discourage questionable practices. They reasoned that the public might come to distrust all advertising.

The 1929 code of ethics of the National Association of Broadcasters laid down guidelines for the regulation of commercials, placing the responsibility for commercial content on the broadcast licensee. Broadcasters were urged to prohibit advertising making "false, deceptive, or grossly exaggerated claims." Obscene material was to be banned. The client's business product should be mentioned "succinctly to ensure an adequate return on his investment, but never to the extent that it loses listeners to the station." That's a magic formula most stations would still like to have today!

The problem comes in defining the terms used in the 1929 code or in any of the dozens of advertising codes that followed. At what point do we reach "excessive" advertising claims? When does zealous representation of the product end and exaggeration begin? Advertising remains "advocacy" for a product. Most consumers know by now that advertising agencies exist to portray the sponsor's product in the most favorable light. A product's weaknesses are going to be ignored and the competition's exploited.

TRUTH IN ADVERTISING

In an effort to keep advertisers and advertising honest, dozens of government and private agencies have become involved. At one time or another the Federal Trade Commission, the FCC, the U.S. Postal Service, the Food and Drug Administration, the Securities and Exchange Commission, and the Public Health Service have all acted as consumer watchdogs. Consumer advocate Ralph Nader and his Center for the Study of Responsive Law is one of the best known of the independent, nongovernmental forces in the consumer arena. The last decade or so has brought about a tremendous increase in the consumer-advocacy movement. With it has come an increasingly critical focus on advertising practices.

In addition, the courts have generally become more favorable toward the consumer in cases where consumer interest and advertising practices conflict. Severe judgments have been made against companies by judges and juries sympathetic to the consumer perspective. In short, more than ever advertisers are *liable* for what they advertise.

In *The Advertising Answerbook*, Hal Betancourt lists five general rules of thumb for the advertiser and the agency that wish to stay out of hot water:

1. Refrain from advertising a product that is unsafe or potentially hazardous.

12.1

This two-page layout for Creamer, Incorporated, stresses the versatility of the agency by displaying some successful ads for clients.

2. Refrain from false claims that lead a customer to expect a better product than he or she will actually get.
3. Refrain from creating false impressions—by the use of the word "free," or testimonials, or reduced special prices that are phony—in order to motivate sales.
4. Refrain from unfairly hurting competition through comparative advertising that disparages a competitor's products.
5. Refrain from making claims for a product without substantiation or some reasonable basis for making such claims.

He concludes with a simple statement: "Fooling the customer these days is a risky

and expensive proposition." He is only one of a growing number of advertising professionals who believe that we have gone from a society that once said "caveat emptor" (let the buyer beware) to one that now says "caveat venditor" (let the seller beware).

The Printer's Ink Model Statute, a strongly worded model for legislation against false and deceptive advertising practices, has been passed in one version or another in 44 states. The statute spells out specific guidelines for advertisers and identifies practices which are "deceptive or misleading." It covers radio and television as well as print practices and is responsible, in part, for a growing movement toward truth in advertising.

RADIO ADVERTISING

There has always been a difference between public perceptions of print and of broadcast advertising. From the beginning, people seemed to take print advertising for granted. No one seemed to object in the 1800s when most newspapers developed a heavy dependence on advertising. For example, it's easy to see the benefits of newspaper classified advertising to everyone involved. But broadcasting was different. The public seemed to feel that broadcast ads were an intrusion into their own private space. Many still do.

From the time the first radio ad ran in 1922, it took only five years before radio advertising was commonplace. Advertiser claims and counterclaims were chaotic. Into all this stepped the federal government, and in 1927 the first major radio act was passed. The provisions of the act made it obvious that the American system of broadcasting was to be "commercial." What might have happened had the government taken a different tack? In Britain and many other European nations, all broadcasting was put under control of the national government. No advertising was allowed, and listeners paid for their entertainment via a special tax on home receivers.

The commercial nature of American radio continued to be challenged. As late as 1929, the National Association of Broadcasters, an industry organization, was trying to discourage advertising during what we now call "prime time." Its code of ethics stated that there was a "decided difference between what may be broadcast before 6:00 P.M. and what may be broadcast after 6:00 P.M." They reasoned that before 6:00 P.M., radio is part of the listener's business day. But after that time,

radio should be used for "recreation and relaxation." The 1929 code limited advertising between 6:00 P.M. and 11:00 P.M. to a dignified identification of sponsors.

Such idealism soon gave way to a more pragmatic approach. It was precisely during prime time that most people were listening, and broadcasters quickly learned that they could charge more for advertising time when the audience was large.

By 1930, the CBS and dual NBC radio networks were going strong. Between them, they boasted more than 100 affiliates. Programs supplied through the networks were not their own creations, but those of sponsors and their advertising agencies. Thus during the 1920s and 1930s many successful programs bore the names of products: *Lux Radio Theatre*, *The Eveready Hour*, and *The Purina Chow Checkerboard Boys*. Often the name of the product was woven into the theme song of the show. Radio stars unabashedly endorsed everything from soap to cigarettes.

Today advertisers pay over $3 billion each year to tout their products on local radio stations (see 12.2). Unlike the early sponsored shows, virtually all radio advertising is now done on a "spot" basis, with advertisers running their brief commercials during various times of the day. In radio the most sought-after periods are the crucial drive-time slots: 6 to 9 in the morning and 3 to 6 in the afternoon. During these periods the radio audience swells as commuters tune in.

TELEVISION: THE ULTIMATE ADVERTISING MEDIUM

Though radio remains a vital force in advertising, it is generally acknowledged that after World War II television became the dominant American entertainment medium. It was only

How do you spell "relief" from the pain of high TV costs?

The jump in cost of television is giving a lot of local and national advertisers acid indigestion.

This season, for example, a thirty-second commercial on one of those humorous situation comedies could cost you a not-very-funny $120,000.

It's no wonder so many national and local advertisers are turning to R-A-D-I-O for fast, fast relief.

But, despite its high costs, some advertisers continue to buy TV because they want "impact."

Radio does much more, however, than control costs. It produces proven sales results the way some advertisers used to believe only television could.

Revlon's Oxy 5 used radio as its primary medium and became the number one acne product in America.

Maxwell House Coffee did a searching study of alternatives to remaining virtually an all-TV advertiser. They moved big dollars into radio.

Western Union summed up what so many well-operated companies have discovered when they said, "Radio gives us the impact of television, at a fraction of the cost." (Mailgram used radio as their primary medium to triple sales.)

Maybe it's time your business took a big dose of radio for relief. For more facts, write to Radio Advertising Bureau, 485 Lexington Avenue, New York, N.Y. 10017. Or call us at (212) 599-6666 and ask for the Radio Facts Book.

12.2

The high cost of advertising on television is the theme from this ad, designed to reach advertisers and agencies. Radio has had an uphill battle to hold on to its share of revenues since TV, the "ultimate advertising medium," was introduced in the late 1940s.

natural that it should become the dominant advertising medium as well. Network radio no longer attracted the mass audience. Advertisers were among the first to perceive this change, and TV was quickly flooded with commercials. Since the new medium reached a heterogeneous audience, products most likely to benefit from TV exposure were those almost everyone could use: toothpaste, aspirin, soap, and cigarettes.

Television was a new challenge for advertisers, since they could now picture the product as well as describe it. A lesson first learned in radio was doubly applicable to television: In a marketplace flooded with similar products, the form of the ad was at least as important as the content. Cigarette commercials in the mid-1950s, for example, showed scene after scene of lush springtime countryside. A playful couple cavorted flirtatiously while smoking. Clearly the message was that smoking (for whatever unknown reason) is like a springtime experience, embodying all the joys of youth, love, and an ant-free picnic.

In 1952 the sale of radio time still accounted for more than 60 percent of every broadcast advertising dollar, but two years later television surpassed radio with sales that exceeded $500 million. By 1956, the total spent buying network radio time had dropped to $44 million, about a third of what it had been at the beginning of the decade.

As in radio, most network television programs were *sponsored*—conceived, created, and paid for by sponsors and their agencies. In 1959, the public was outraged at having been deceived by those rigged quiz shows and blamed the networks. With some justification all three maintained that they were only conduits, selling time to others who created the shows, but it didn't seem to matter.

Networks quickly realized that they would have to control more carefully the content of programs they aired. Increasingly, new shows were conceived and produced by the networks themselves. This led to a decline of the sponsorships of shows and the rise of spot advertising. The spot advertiser does not buy any one show but hundreds of 30- or 60-second spots to be run at specified times.

SAVE ME A SPOT

Spot advertising is the backbone of broadcast advertising. Here's how it works:

1 The ad agency meets with the client and determines media strategies most appropriate for the product.

2 A time buyer employed by the agency meets with a station representative, who may handle dozens of radio and TV stations. Together they try to determine which "buys" will be most effective for the client.

3 The station rep designs a package of buys, specifying stations and air times.

Sometimes a client will intervene by putting other constraints on the time buyer. Often the station rep will try to stick time buyers with the less than desirable times they are under pressure to sell. Eventually the client's spot, conceived and produced by the agency, appears on the station at the time and date specified.

What I've just described is a simplified version of what happens at the national or regional level. At the local level, sponsors may deal directly with the station sales people. In very small markets, those sales people may also be on-the-air personalities or perform some other function for the station.

ADVERTISING: MAKING A LIVING

There are more than half a million people employed in advertising in America today. Some of these are station reps and time buyers. Some deal exclusively in print: layout, design, illustrations, and graphics. Others work for newspapers, magazines, or other media outlets. Some are involved with broadcast copywriting and production.

A typical advertising agency is run by a board of directors that chooses a president. The president then deals with department heads, each of whom has a specialized staff.

Market Research

This is the agency's statistical arm, which informs clients of the most lucrative geographic and demographic targets for their products. Often market research involves field interviews with potential buyers.

Media Selection

This is done by the print space buyers and the broadcast time buyers, who do their best to place the client's message where it is likely to get maximum response.

Creative Activity

Creativity is what most of us think of when we imagine an advertising agency. It involves the people who write the copy and create the visuals of the ads we see and hear each day. Photographers, graphics experts, copywriters, and others are often employed by the agency on a full-time basis. However, much of this work is also farmed out to production companies or freelancers.

Account Management

These are the account executives, who deal directly with the client and who are constantly on the lookout for new clients to bring into the agency fold. Account executives, like radio and TV sales people and media buyers, are generally among the highest-paid staffers. Without them, there would be no need for other staff members, since there would be no clients.

Most graduates lucky enough to land an entry-level advertising position start as sales people at local media outlets. If you go to an agency, you could start as a copywriter, particularly if you are a man. Most of the ad agencies I know still hire women college graduates only as clerk typists, though they adamantly insist that they practice equal opportunity employment.

However, women will find that initiative is rewarded more rapidly in advertising than anywhere else in media—not because ad agencies are feminist, but because they are pro-achievement. Advertising is a very upwardly mobile business. Once you get over the demeaning lower hurdles, you'll be able to rise as far as your brains and talent will take you. You'll have a much better chance if you're competitive, aggressive, hardworking, and mix well with all kinds of people, regardless of political persuasion. The world of advertising is one of *compromise*. Ad people are hard-headed realists: Their business is to help clients sell. *What* they're selling makes little difference.

Advertising can be used effectively in "selling" many things that are not products in the traditional sense (see 12.3). It was the TV antismoking campaigns that helped lead to a ban of cigarette commercials on the medium. Many of the top advertising agencies regularly contribute their time and energies to worthwhile causes and charities.

One tangible reward awaits those who do break into advertising: money. Even at the lowest levels, advertising positions tend to pay substantially more than comparable media jobs. A beginning copywriter at an agency can expect to earn 20 percent more than someone doing the same thing at radio or TV stations. This holds true for employees in production, art, and other areas as well.

CASE IN POINT: THE GREAT PET-FOOD WAR

> *I want tuna,*
> *I want liver,*
> *I want chicken,*
> *Please deliver.*

The cat that sang this refrain for Meow Mix was supposed to persuade us that our cats would never be happy until we delivered the product to them. This is one of the dozens of pet-food commercials in recent years that have "humanized" pets. But when you stop

12.3

Advertisers remind readers that they sell education, health, and peace as well as products—and themselves.

ADVERTISING SELLS A LOT MORE THAN CARS, COOKIES AND COMPUTERS.

Just name the good cause and chances are awfully good that advertising has given it a helping hand.

Corporations, advertising agencies, and communications media—through the Advertising Council—have been donating their time, talent and money for 30 years.

Because advertising works for cars and cookies and computers. And it works just as hard for education and health and peace.

and think about it, pets aren't human at all. Or are they?

Behind these commercials are thousands of hours of research designed to exploit our feelings about pets and to sell us one particular brand of pet food over another. Most veterinarians agree that pets are color blind and that even the taste of a particular food matters very little. Yet most of us are con-vinced about the virtues of the pet food we buy. Why?

Pet-food commercials afford the perfect example of the victory of form over content in advertising. In Europe, most animals get along on table scraps, but the American pet must have pet food.

This phenomenon is a fairly recent one. According to an article in *The New Yorker*, until about 1960 there were only a few pet foods on the market. But by 1965, Americans were spending $700 million on their pets, and a scant 15 years later that figure had jumped to over $3.2 *billion*. Virtually all of this can be attributed to advertising. Our pets may be no healthier or happier, yet we believe they *must* have these products.

The advertising agencies have us neatly divided into three camps. There's the "premium" buyer, who buys only the best—brands advertised as "100 percent meat and meat by-products." Then there's the "practical" or "functional" consumer, who buys whatever is cheapest—the cereal products. In the middle is the buyer of the "moist meal" pet foods, packaged in convenient foil pouches but supposedly tasting like they "just came out of the can."

The most celebrated coup in the industry was the triumph of the Alpo campaign of the middle 1960s, which insisted "Your dog *needs* meat." The goal was simple: to convince owners that their dogs *had* to have the premium-priced Alpo brand. In 1970, the Federal Trade Commission intervened. Their tests indicated that pets really didn't *need* meat at all. In fact, all pet foods—canned, moist, and cereal—had long been meeting government regulations requiring certain minimum nutritional content.

The new Alpo cry was: "Your dog *loves* meat!" Alpo, of course, was not the only pet food manufacturer to use slogans. Ralston Purina asserted that its Chuck Wagon was "meaty, juicy, chunky." However, Chuck Wagon did not contain one speck of meat.

What motivates us to spend all this money on our pets? The first response is obvious—we love them. We want them to have a "balanced diet," one that's good for them. We have feelings about our pets that have been successfully exploited by sponsors and their agencies. Besides, who can resist a close-up of a kitten or puppy (see 12.4), or the antics

of Morris the "finicky" cat? Pets are so . . . well . . . visual! That's why pet-food commercials work so well on television. Despite healthy budgets for radio and print, TV remains first in the pet-food ad business.

Television advertising has been the biggest single contributor to the rapid economic growth of many key industries like pet foods, which sell their products to a large number of consumers. Through heavy use of TV, today's unfamiliar brand name becomes tomorrow's institution.

Of course, the pet-food war is but one example of thousands of wars being waged for our consumer dollars every day by advertisers. Vance Packard pointed out in *The Hidden Persuaders* that advertisers exploit our fears, hopes, dreams, and anxieties. We must become more aware of this process if we are to make sensible choices about how we spend our money.

Packard feels that advertisers with their "depth manipulation" often make us do things that are irrational and illogical.

At times it is pleasanter or easier to be nonlogical. But I prefer being nonlogical by my own free will and impulse rather than to find myself manipulated into such acts.

The most serious offense many of the depth manipulators commit, it seems to me, is that they try to invade the privacy of our minds. It is this right to privacy in our minds—privacy to be either rational or irrational—that I believe we must strive to protect.

More recent controversy along these lines has centered on the debate about so-called *subliminal* advertising, or the use of hidden images in magazine and TV ads (see Guest Essay). A 1973 book exposing this practice, *Subliminal Seduction* by Wilson Bryan Key, stirred quite a response from the industry and the public as well.

12.4

Form or content? Purina contends that it puts more "wow" in its cat food. What is wow?

FORM AND CONTENT: HOW ADVERTISING WORKS

The effectiveness of advertising is due to the considerable media skills of people in the industry. The cleverest copywriters, best artists, and most talented graphic designers labor over the national advertising campaigns that bombard us. This led Marshall McLuhan to observe: "The ad is the meeting place for all the arts, skills, and all the media of the American environment."

The television-commercial scriptwriter has only 30 seconds to tell the story. Television advertising dispenses with plot line and brings us action and visuals (see 12.5). The scene may shift several dozen times in that 30 seconds. First a close-up of a hand holding a drink—suddenly a plane flies overhead—a

12.5

The Best Thing on TV: Commercials

In his 1978 book *Commercials: The Best Thing on TV* author Jonathan Price extols the virtues of the TV commercial. While we are conditioned to think of these 10-, 30-, and 60-second messages as mere interruptions, Price maintains that they involve the audience far more than the programs themselves.

More fun than a gorilla with a suitcase, more explosive than a camera that blows up, more entertaining than the programs they interrupt, more informative than most network news, commercials are often the best thing on TV. And the best commercials outpace the television programs they sponsor in at least a dozen ways.

- Commercials are dangerous to make: The admen who go out on location often risk their lives for even less than an Oscar; they do death-defying stunts for the sake of five seconds of film to advertise a car—or peanut butter.
- They're violent to products: Unlike regular programs, commercials don't hurt people; they torture products.
- They're almost obscene: Also unlike regular programs, commercials hint and flash but never deliver; the suggestions are enough to arouse, but these clean scenes never come to climax.
- They're emotional: In thirty seconds, not thirty minutes, a commercial can make your eyes moisten, your adrenaline accelerate, and your heart thump.
- They're coldly calculated: Since a commercial is designed as part of a marketing strategy, its objectives are studiously worked out beforehand; compared to program writers, the creators of commercials are far more con-scious of the impact they are making.
- They're carefully written: Since every second costs more than two thousand dollars, crack writers sand every idea and plan every camera angle for maximum effect, making the authors of *60 Minutes* look like tourists casually writing home.
- They're overdirected: Shooting one hundred feet of film for every one they use, commercial directors caress every detail until it glows; particularly on food, hair, and cars, the results are bravura.
- They're star-studded: There are more Oscar winners playing the breaks than the shows, and commercials sometimes turn unknowns into superstars in a few months.
- They're extravagantly produced: Since more money goes into the production of some thirty-second spots than into half-hour shows, commercials often have flashier locations, bigger casts, stranger sets, snappier graphics, and funnier ideas.
- They're highly edited: Our culture is learning faster perception per second thanks to editing techniques that show us a hundred bottles of beer on a wall in twenty-seven seconds or sixty-five pictures of McDonald's breakfasts in sixty seconds; we follow them, and when we return to the slower editing of regular programming—not to mention the scenes of real life—we may find the pace unaccountably dull.
- They're regulated and censored: Commercials have to submit to many more censors and many more taboos than regular programming; since freedom of expression does not apply to advertisers, the commercials must do a fine tap dance down the line of conventions, a discipline that keeps commercials politically agile and diplomatically astute.
- They're even rated PG: When parents cannot ban products, they band together to prevent advertisers from mentioning the rotten stuff to kids; as a result, ads to children are now much more honest than the programs—and kids still like candy.

Culturally, commercials have trained our eye to accept fast cuts, dense and highly paced imagery, very brief scenes, connections that are implied but not spelled out—in brief, a new style of visual entertainment.

Historically, we see commercials more often than the shows (the same spot may be run six to sixty times a season), and we recall them in more detail, often with more fondness. People feel great nostalgia for the White Knight, the Green Giant, Speedy Alka-Seltzer, Tony the Tiger, Snap, Crackle, and Pop—these are the elves of our country's imagination.

Financially, commercials represent the pinnacle of our popular culture's artistic expression. More money per second goes into their making, more cash flows from their impact, more business thinking goes into each word than in any movie, opera, stage play, painting, or videotape. If commercials are artful, then the art is objective, not subjective; capitalist, not rebellious; part of a social activity rather than a personal search for expression; more like a Roman road than a lyric poem. Their beauty is economic.

Yes, some are dumb. Some guy leaning out of the screen to yell at us because we supposedly tried to make him change beers just makes us hate Schlitz. People going gaga when they walk into a bank, just because the bank accepts savings accounts, make me gag. But then I don't love Lucy much. And I'm glad Gilligan has to stay on his island.

Commercials are not all superb. But the best are lively, very American mini-dramas, tiny films, high-speed epics. Taken as a whole, commercials offer a rough catalogue of our consumer economy and a wild tour of our unconscious fantasies.

Guest Essay by Luigi Manca and Allesandra Maclean Manca

The Siren's Song: A Theory of Subliminal Seduction

Luigi Manca and Allesandra McLean Manca were teaching and studying mass media and sociology, respectively, in New Orleans, where they were involved in research related to subliminal images. Here they suggest some reasons why such images are used and why we "need" the amazing things advertisers promise us.

In the mid-1950s Vance Packard exposed the extensive use of hidden, or subliminal, messages by advertisers selling products. In the 1970s Wilson Bryan Key began to find all kinds of sex and death images embedded in magazine ads and radio and TV commercials. Inspired by their books, an alert student in a Loyola University mass-persuasion course discovered the words "you love" delicately, but unmistakably, traced in the shadow by Ted Kennedy's nose on the cover of the November 5, 1979, issue of *Time*.

Apparently we are being bombarded with a variety of subliminal stimuli. But, with the possible exception of Professor Key and his students, those of us who are supposed to study and teach mass-media practices really do not know very much about what is going on. What's more, we do not know what sort of social impact or significance the use of subliminal communication may have.

Among all the media enterprises, the advertising industry is the most directly involved in systematically using subliminal stimuli to manipulate consumer behavior. As Packard pointed out, at first advertisers were concerned primarily with informing the public about the quality and the availability of their products. Eventually, however, marketing research demonstrated that most consumers were not persuaded to buy by cool, logical arguments but rather by hidden, seemingly irrational motivations. Advertising, therefore, could no longer be based on a cool mode of communication but had to rely on emotional and aesthetic appeals. The manipulation of consumers through subliminal stimuli was a logical consequence.

Since subliminal communication has become a part of our daily lives and, therefore, our culture, the role it plays in our society should certainly be examined. It may be that subliminal communication is part of what we may call the emotional-aesthetic dimension of our mass culture and that it is being used in certain media in the creation of a feeling of mass intimacy and spirituality.

Since it is no longer a matter of cool, logical transmission of information in order to persuade reasonable people, the concept of truth in advertising has acquired a novel dimension. Are the popular images used to appeal to emotional and aesthetic values true or false?

When Catherine Deneuve greets TV viewers with a throaty meow from atop a luxury sedan, is the meow true or false? In a sense, the ad is certainly false, since at a subconscious level it is promising the male consumer a sexy European blonde and the female consumer her glamour and sex appeal as part of the package. And we know that Catherine Deneuve definitely does not come with the car. Or does she?

As Ernest Dichter pointed out, consumers tend to act toward a product as if it had a soul or a personality of its own. The function of advertising is therefore to suggest or even create this soul in the minds of the consumers. In the case of the luxury sedan, the soul is the sexy European blonde. It follows that in a consumer society, commodities are no longer marketed for what they really are but for the fantasies and ideals they represent to the buyer.

For example, Marlboro and Virginia Slims are both manufactured by Philip Morris and probably contain essentially the same tobacco. But the soul of the Marlboro is the rugged cowboy roughing it in the untamed West, while that of Virginia Slims is a sleek, svelte woman with a chic touch of liberation.

On the surface, most of us simply dismiss such ads as so

Of all the sports cars available to you, this is the one—the ultimate cat.

Because it offers what the others can't offer: the Jaguar V-12 engine.

And that changes the discussion from *what* a sports car can do to *how well* it can do it.

That's what the Jaguar E-type V-12 is all about. How well it glides from zero to fifty. How well it accelerates out of a pack and into the clear. Even how well it behaves in downtown traffic at quitting time before a holiday weekend.

In a word, the Jaguar V-12 is smooth. It's smooth going up the scale from zero and it's smooth going from cruising speed to passing speed. It's even smooth waiting for the light to change.

Because, from an engineering viewpoint, the Jaguar V-12 is in perfect balance. Since its 5.3 litres of capacity are divided by twelve—not eight or six—the forces are spread more evenly over the crankshaft by delivering smaller but more frequent pulses of power.

What is the effect like? Well, it's something like a turbine. And it's something like an express elevator. But it's not *exactly* like anything else. That's why you have to drive a Jaguar E-type V-12 before you decide on anybody else's sports car.

Since it is a Jaguar, it has independent front and rear suspension with "anti-dive" control. Power-assisted rack

and pinion steering. Power-assisted disc brakes on all four wheels—ventilated in the front. A four-speed manual is standard, an automatic is optional.

So see the Jaguar E-type V-12. It's the only production V-12 sports car in town. And that makes it second to none.

For your dealer's name and for information about overseas delivery, call (800) 447-4700. In Illinois, call (800) 322-4400. Calls are toll free.

BRITISH LEYLAND MOTORS INC., LEONIA, N. J. 07605

Does the woman come with the car?

much Madison Avenue fluff. However, their impact on our behavior is very real. The same people who laugh at the ads when they see them in a magazine would not even consider buying the cigarette whose soul was of the opposite gender.

At a subconscious level, the preoccupation with the soul of

the products we consume seems to have given an almost spiritual dimension to what used to be (and in reality still is) a basically materialistic society. We are promised the experience of a nearly transcendental joy as we caress the upholstery of our shiny new cars or take the Nestea plunge. We should feel a

Guest Essay by Luigi Manca and Allesandra Maclean Manca (continued)

deep, forbidden thrill when we finally get to squeeze the Charmin or rub our armpits with Tickle. We'll see the light with 7-Up . . . and we know, of course, that Coke adds life.

This is obviously a pseudo-spirituality. Viewing the crime, fear, organized violence, poverty, racism, and genocide that are also part of our daily lives, it seems likely that we actually have a great spiritual void. Perhaps our ability to perceive the suffering of other human beings as something touching us has been numbed by the siren's song.

What particular market might this ad be aimed at?

flight attendant pours a cup of coffee—a child laughs in glee while being served a hot dog as the clouds roll by outside the window.

Form is the important thing; content is secondary. The ad for a shirt company shows a field of daisies; there's no shirt and no people. The voice-over tells us: "This shirt makes you *feel* like a daisy." It's like Picasso's painting

Man in Chair. There is no man, no chair, only a collection of skewed lines that represent what it *feels like* to sit in a chair.

Print media, particularly magazines, are replete with examples. A full-page ad for silverware pictures a tree (see 12.6). A Marlboro ad pictures a man herding horses down a hillside (see 12.7). The cigarette packages

In Subliminal Seduction, *Wilson Key suggests that liquor ads often use distorted and grotesque faces hidden among glass and ice cubes to play on the death wish of alcoholics. The face circled in this Crown Royal ad seems to verify this. Can you find any other hidden images here?*

Have you ever seen a grown man cry?

are almost hidden in the lower right-hand corner, and the rest of the page is devoted to trees and a mountain stream. In another ad, a tiny GM logo is in a lower left-hand corner, and the Chevrolet is unrecognizably dwarfed by a huge canyon (see 12.8). In each case, visual space is given over to a scene that has a minimal "logical" connection with the prod-uct. The theory is that by surrounding the product with a pleasant environment, the medium can entice the consumer to try it.

But the consumer is also busy learning other things. Ads tell us a great deal about our society, and they help to influence and change that society. Although the first business of ads is to sell products, their influence

12.6
The ad seems to imply that a spoon is like a tree. Is it?

True beauty is timeless.

ONEIDA

For a 22" x 28" poster of this page, send 50¢ to: Evergreen Poster, P.O. Box 1, Oneida, N. Y. 13421. Offer expires 9/30/76. © Oneida Ltd., 1976

doesn't stop there. In fact, that's where it begins. As McLuhan points out, "Advertising itself is an information commodity far greater than anything it advertises." In their rush to sell a product, advertisers sometimes don't even recognize the more important effects of their collective art—selling life-styles and social values to an entire generation of Americans.

Advertising is the first to reflect and encourage social trends. According to McLuhan, advertising "responds instantly to any social change, making ads in themselves invaluable means of knowing where it's at." For example, America's interest in ecology during the 1970s showed up often in advertising: ads featuring the "natural" environment to sell, as noted, everything from cig-

12.7

The Western image has long been associated with Marlboro cigarettes. Ironically Marlboros were originally designed to appeal to women.

arettes to silverware. The women's movement had barely gotten started when television ads began picturing women as mechanics and bank presidents. Ads are first to reflect social trends because they *have* to be one step ahead. Competition in advertising is far fiercer than in programming or editorial content, so advertising is often more interesting than the program or article itself.

Advertising also teaches us how to behave through little socialization lessons. As we've noted, ads teach us that if we love our pets, we must feed them a special kind of food. And they teach us how and when to love each other. A wife makes her husband happy by straining his coffee through a special filter. Ads also provide a context and a meaning for all sorts of everyday experiences. A smelly house

12.8

The sweeping view certainly commands the reader's attention. But can you find the car?

Chevrolet returns to Castle Rock.

means social disapproval from important guests.

PUBLIC RELATIONS: MASTERING THE SUBTLE SEMANTICS

Once upon a time there was a PR practitioner who approached a large corporation for a job and was interviewed by a hiring committee.

"What have you done?" they asked.

"Why, I'm responsible for the best PR campaign of all time. I was called in as a consultant by a young lady who was having terrible problems. She was living with seven strange men and people were beginning to talk." "Oh, really? Did you do her any good?"

"Oh, c'mon," he said impatiently. "Haven't you heard of Snow White and the Seven Dwarfs?"

Embodied in this story is the central function of public relations: to present the "image" of the client in the best possible light.

Many institutions and organizations, from university administrators to tavern owners, employ someone in a public-relations capacity. The PR agent acts as a liaison between client and public. Whereas advertising agencies generally try to reach the public directly through paid messages in the mass media, PR practitioners usually deal with editors and reporters, who then disseminate information to the public via the media. Sometimes the job is only a matter of answering the phone and giving information. More often it requires skills in journalism, broadcasting, advertising, and more. Like advertising, PR jobs are financially rewarding. Again, the job can be more demanding, more frustrating, and more rewarding than other media employment.

PRESS-AGENTRY PIONEERS: P. T. BARNUM & CO.

PR is as old as media. As long as there have been public-information channels, there have been people who would use them to influence public opinion. The acknowledged king of PR pioneers was Phineas Taylor Barnum. He was responsible for the success of midget Tom Thumb and of Jenny Lind, the "Swedish Nightingale." Barnum made these people and many others into legends. Then of course there was the circus that bore his name. Barnum's favorite phrase, "There's a sucker born every minute," is still heard often. So effective was Barnum's PR that it remains a part of Americana almost 100 years after his death!

The term *public relations* did not come into being until the 20th century. Before that, PR was known as press agentry. The press agents were masters at planting stories in newspapers. This kind of publicity was much more

valuable than paid-for advertising, and it was free. There were many such campaigns during the late 19th century, but most notable, according to historian Marshall Fishwick, was the rise of Buffalo Bill.

Fishwick notes that a half dozen writers helped shape Buffalo Bill into the greatest American folk hero of all. "No one should underestimate their endeavors. More spectacular men had to be outdistanced. Mountains had to be made out of molehills." Almost all of the folk heroes from this era were virtually created through press agentry, among them Wyatt Earp, Calamity Jane, and Wild Bill Hickok. Some stories began with fact but all were eventually mostly fiction.

PR also moved into politics. The 1896 McKinley-Bryan presidential race was the beginning of modern political campaigning methods. There were posters, pamphlets, and publicity, much of it concocted by party press agents. The information tools have changed a bit and candidates have moved to the electronic stage, but tactics remain essentially the same today.

Patent-medicine scandals and questionable business practices that came to light just before the turn of the century helped give rise to the PR industry. Business leaders became convinced that they could no longer ignore public opinion.

Public pressure on government and governmental agencies became so great that a number of business reform bills were passed, making things more difficult for large corporations.

By the 1920s, the use of PR and its necessity in an increasingly complex business environment had become a generally accepted practice.

Most PR pioneers were ex–newspaper reporters who became famous for successful publicity campaigns for railroads, steel corporations, and others.

PUBLIC RELATIONS IN
THE GLOBAL VILLAGE

Even this relatively brief introduction to the practice of public relations would be incomplete without mentioning the size of the PR industry. Today in America there are probably 2,000 different PR agencies, and over 100,000 people are actively employed in the field. Many work in creative capacities as writers, media producers, and directors. Virtually every media position open to the entry-level employee has a counterpart in PR. PR is by far the fastest-growing arm of mass communication and, as such, supplies an increasingly large number of beginning jobs for those desiring a career in the media. Administration, finance, research, and even legal departments flourish at most medium and large agencies. Small agencies offer the beginner the opportunity to gain experience in many facets of media, experience that might take years to acquire in other fields.

One reason for the PR boom is the increasing value—and the increasing cost—of access to media channels themselves. Sponsors may pay $400,000 for one commercial during the Super Bowl. The average 30-second spot on network prime-time TV costs about $200,000. As media have become more powerful, obtaining advertising space has become more desirable and more difficult. Many turn to the PR specialist, whose prime function is snaring that space free of charge. (An extreme example of free media coverage happens when fringe political groups kidnap or assassinate well-known people just to focus attention on their concerns.)

Each of the 200 largest corporations in America employs a public-relations staff of at least 75. Large PR firms may have as many as 500 employees. Reporters who leave journalism for PR can expect an immediate salary increase of 25 percent or so. The chances are very good that when they return to the newsroom to see old friends ten years later, these "defectors" will be earning double the salary of colleagues who stayed. Though writing is the skill most often mentioned as necessary for entry to PR, those who specialize in public speaking, group communication skills, and electronic media production are finding PR positions, too.

In large corporations, the PR staff has monumental responsibilities. Stockholders want maximum return for their investment, employees want higher wages, and the public is convinced that all corporations are run by criminals. The PR department is expected to make everyone happy. It attempts to do so by using the one tool of the trade: information. Stockholders' meetings are held, and quarterly reports are issued that speak in glowing terms of profits. Employee newsletters help create a sense of community and harmony. News releases tell of acts of benevolence performed by corporation executives.

There are lots of PR people who work exclusively for nonprofit foundations and charities. The Camp Fire Girls, for example, maintains a full-time public-relations staff who help plan national campaigns and the inevitable candy sales. PR staffs can also be found working for labor unions, government agencies, and churches. In each case, the job involves getting specific information to the public via the news media.

ETHICS, JOURNALISTS,
AND PR

It is ironic that the industry in charge of maintaining a good public image for its clients seems unable to do the same for itself. The public at large may not even distinguish between advertising and PR, but when it does, PR is often perceived as a shady practice.

Part of this public mistrust is probably due to a lack of information about what PR people actually do. Part of it also centers on the relationship between PR practitioners and journalists. Journalists call PR practitioners "flacks" (the term originally meant the publicity itself, and was probably derived from the word *flak* because of its scattershot nature). The Associated Press managing editor's guidelines define a "flack" as:

. . . a person who makes all or part of his income by obtaining space in newspapers without cost to himself or his clients. Usually a professional . . . they are known formally as public relations men. A flack is a flack. His job is to say kind things about his client. He will not lie very often, but much of the time he tells less than the whole story. You do not owe the PR man anything. The owner of the newspaper, not the flack, pays your salary. Your immediate job is to serve the readers, not the man who would raid your columns.

The most common complaint against flacks concerns their attempts to "color" the news or grab free advertising for their clients. Reporters also resent the fact that many of their own give up reporting for higher-paying PR positions.

PR practitioners have their own complaints against journalists. They often claim that their clients are victims of sensational reporting of news. Quotes and other information from releases are taken out of context.

The Public Relations Society of America has been active in promoting PR as a positive and integral part of the mass-communication system. In 1954 they adopted a Code of Professional Standards and at times they have acted to penalize and expel members for violating that code.

ISSUES AND ANSWERS: THE SELLING OF THE PRESIDENT

Back in 1960, when the role of advertising and PR in politics first became apparent, *Life* magazine quoted one campaign strategist as saying, "I can elect any person to office if he has $60,000, an IQ of at least 120, and can keep his mouth shut."

Since the 1896 campaign, the election of a President has been determined largely by the ability of information specialists to generate favorable publicity. In recent years that publicity has been supplanted by heavy spot buying on electronic media.

The most talked-about medium in American politics is television. Highly publicized debates between candidates in 1960, 1976, and 1980 appear to have affected the outcomes. Richard Nixon (the early favorite) would probably not have lost to John Kennedy were it not for his poor showing on TV (see 12.9). Similarly, the 1976 debates probably clinched Jimmy Carter's narrow victory over Gerald Ford, and Ronald Reagan outshone Carter in the 1980 debates.

Yet there were other elections where, according to political analyst Edward Chester, no amount of TV exposure could have changed the outcome: Barry Goldwater versus Lyndon Johnson in 1964 and Nixon versus George McGovern in 1972. Television commercials seem to work best in close elections or in those where there is a large undecided vote. According to the Associated Press, Ford's TV spots during the 1976 campaign probably swung over 100,000

12.9

The first televised presidential debates stirred controversy about TV's role in politics and helped establish the charismatic Kennedy image in the minds of the electorate.

undecided voters a day during the last few months of the campaign. Nevertheless, he lost the election.

What effect does television have on the candidates themselves? It dictates priorities that are different from those of an earlier day. The physical appearance of the candidate is increasingly important. Does he or she look fit, well-rested, secure? Losing candidates like Adlai Stevenson, Hubert Humphrey, and Richard Nixon all seemed to look "bad" on TV. Nixon overcame this

problem in 1972 with ads that featured longer shots of him being "presidential"—flying off to China, for example. Close-ups were avoided.

Both Kennedy and Carter seemed more at home with the medium, perhaps because both were youthful, informal, and physically active outdoor types. Dwight Eisenhower and Lyndon Johnson seemed to have a paternal, fatherly image on the small screen. All of the recent Presidents have learned how to use the medium to their advantage, to "stage" events so as to receive maximum favorable coverage. This has added to the already awesome power of the incumbency.

Television has diminished the significance of issues. It can be argued that since the 1960 presidential debates, we have elected people, not platforms. This is a major departure from earlier years. Franklin Roosevelt's radio charisma cannot be denied, but he was swept to power by one issue— the Great Depression.

All the print information we now receive is simpler and more condensed than ever before. Issues and print go together. Television is *images*, not issues. We develop a more personal, emotional feeling about the candidates. Jimmy Carter's spectacular rise to power was a testament to this new image orientation. No one really knew *what* he was going to do when he took office, since his entire campaign had been geared toward developing a relationship of trust with the electorate. "Trust me," he said. "I'll never lie to you."

A more recent example was the election of Reagan in 1980. For some, this represented the ultimate television victory. After all, what other country can claim that it has elected an actor President? It can be argued that Americans were tired of Carter and that Reagan simply offered an alternative. Yet throughout the campaign he offered us a media "vision" of a "shining city on a hill." And what about his constant references to John Wayne, one of the "last great Americans"?

My father, a long-time politician in southern California, used to say, "The worst thing a candidate can do is get bogged down in the issues." This trend has alarmed countless media critics. Politicians, newscasters, and others have stood in line to denounce it. They assert that the important thing is *what the candidates stand for*, not the candidates themselves. Almost everyone seems to agree that television has been detrimental to American politics; it has clouded the issues and confused the electorate.

Media researchers Thomas E. Patterson and Robert D. McClure say the power of TV has been overrated and that (1) "Viewers of the nightly network newscasts learn almost nothing of importance about a presidential election," and (2) "People are not taken in by advertising hyperbole and imagery. . . . exposure to televised ads has *no effect on voters' images of the candidates*." [italics mine] I disagree on both counts.

If the Watergate mess proved anything, it was that we need a President we feel we *know* and can *trust*. Print afforded us no opportunity to get a "feel" for the person. We could study the issues, read the speeches, yes—but how would we "know" the candidate as we might a neighbor or casual acquaintance? Television (and television advertising) provides an audiovisual record of the candidate under all sorts of circumstances. It is with that knowledge that we can choose someone of integrity, at least someone with honorable intentions.

Of course, TV cannot guarantee honest candidates, but we rejected Richard Nixon in 1960 and we might have again had he not so successfully *avoided* any informal coverage. (He wouldn't let TV newscasters near him unless he had a suit on. For all we knew he wore a suit while walking on the beach.) Once he was President, it was the intimate nature of the medium that helped bring him down. Even his well-rehearsed Watergate denials wouldn't work. He would sit there surrounded by flags and piles of transcripts and swear he was innocent. Yet the sweat on his brow and the look in his eyes seemed to confirm his guilt.

Issues come and go, but we elect *people* to the presidency. In this fast-moving information environment, today's burning issue is tomorrow's historical footnote. It's far more important to develop a sense of what kind of person we are electing to the nation's highest office. Television affords us that opportunity in a way no other medium can.

QUERIES AND CONCEPTS

1 Design a print ad for your favorite product. Then follow up by writing copy for a 60-second television or radio ad. Which most effectively sells the product? Why?

2 Find three examples of magazine advertisements you feel are in bad taste. How could they be changed so they still sell the product without using the tactics you consider offensive?

3 Think of the television commercial that you hate more than any other. Write three paragraphs on what you find so objectionable about it. No fair using general words like *stupid* or *dumb*—be *specific*. Have you ever used the product?

4 Who feeds the pet in your house? Interview some pet owners about their pets' eating habits. What brand do they usually buy and why?

5 You are a public-relations agent for a baseball player who has held out for a $15 million contract and has been booted off the team. In a fit of rage, he has beaten up the owner and his manager. The press is calling for a statement, and you can't find your client anywhere. What do you do?

6 Using a cassette recorder, tape five TV commercials. Is there anything in any of them that might violate the truth-in-advertising guidelines given in this chapter?

READINGS AND REFERENCES

The Information Environment

Steven M. L. Aronson
Hype. New York: William Morrow, 1983.
How are superstars born? Reborn? How does one get into exclusive New York restaurants without a reservation? These intriguing questions are answered in this flip and devastating treatise on information manipulation. Fun to read.

Philip Ward Burton
William Ryan
Advertising Fundamentals, 3rd ed.
Columbus, Ohio: Grid, 1980.
A management-oriented text that discusses the business of advertising. Designed for the student who wants to become involved in the business. Sec-

tions include "Structure of Advertising," "Promotional Aids," and "Creative Advertising." A thorough job of assessing typical tasks in the field.

Scott M. Cutlip
Allen H. Center
Effective Public Relations, 5th rev. ed. Englewood Cliffs, N.J.: Prentice-Hall, 1982.

First written in 1952, this text has become a standard in the field. It is written by two authors heavily committed to the "positive" aspects of PR, and it reflects that perspective. It is comprehensive and includes historical information on the pioneers of PR.

David Ogilvy
Confessions of an Advertising Man. New York: Atheneum, 1980.

A how-to book laced with humor. The author immodestly opens Chapter 2 with: "Fifteen years ago I was an obscure tobacco farmer in Pennsylvania. Today I preside over one of the best advertising agencies in the United States with billings of $55 million a year, a payroll of $5 million and offices in New York, Chicago, Los Angeles, San Francisco and Toronto." Includes chapters on how to get clients, how to build a great campaign, and TV commercials. Fun.

The Advertising Business Develops

Maurice Mandell
Advertising, 3d ed. Englewood Cliffs, N.J.: Prentice-Hall, 1980.

This is probably the most comprehensive and thorough textbook on advertising available today. It covers history, control, marketing, radio, TV, outdoor advertising, and much more.

A nice five-page mini-history of advertising is found in Agee, Ault, and Emery's *Introduction to Mass Communications*, 7th ed. (New York: Dodd, Mead, 1982).

Radio Advertising; Television: The Ultimate Advertising Medium; Save Me a Spot

Arlen, Michael J.
Thirty Seconds. New York: Farrar, Straus & Giroux, 1980.

A rather hilarious step-by-step account of the making of one thirty-second commercial. The subject is one of AT&T's "reach out and touch someone" spots; Arlen's sense of humor about the extraordinary lengths involved in manufacturing such a spot is obvious when, for example, he interviews the man whose job it is to "soften" the colors to give them just the right luster. Nevertheless, this is not a technical book by any means.

Huntley Baldwin
Creating Effective TV Commercials. Chicago: Crain Books, 1982.

Chapters on strategy, how to come up with ideas, visual storytelling, storyboards, preproduction and production, and much more. An excellent how-to text on the production of TV commercials by someone who knows the business inside out.

Elizabeth Heighton
Don R. Cunningham
Advertising in the Broadcast and Cable Media, 2d ed. Belmont, Calif.: Wadsworth, 1984.

A solid treatment of real-world advertising practices in the broadcast media. Well illustrated and very easy for the beginning student to read. There are chapters on audience research and spot sales, and an entire section is devoted to social responsibility. Highly recommended.

Advertising: Making a Living

Hal Betancourt
The Advertising Answerbook: A Guide for Business and Professional People. Englewood Cliffs, N.J.: Prentice-Hall, 1982.
   Agencies, budgets, copywriting, artwork . . . you name it, it's here. A professional hands-on approach to the advertising business. Highly recommended.

A. Jerome Jeweler
Creative Strategy in Advertising. Belmont, Calif.: Wadsworth, 1981.
   The first text I know of to deal exclusively with the problems of the advertising copywriter. Offers a practical, step-by-step approach to solving various advertising writing and layout problems.

Case in Point: The Great Pet-Food War

Thomas Whiteside
"Onward and Upward with the Arts (Pet Food)." *The New Yorker,* November 1, 1976, pp. 51–98.

Form and Content: How Advertising Works

Marshall McLuhan
Culture Is Our Business. New York: Ballantine Books, 1972.

This is McLuhan on advertising and its social and cultural consequences. He juxtaposes full-page ads from magazines with a series of "probes," exploring the way advertising creates cultural norms and predicts social trends. Fascinating stuff, but take it in small doses. The book is now out of print but is available in most libraries.

Subliminal Seduction

Wilson Bryan Key
Subliminal Seduction. Englewood Cliffs, N.J.: Prentice-Hall, 1973.

Media Sexploitation. Englewood Cliffs, N.J.: Prentice-Hall, 1976. (Available in paperback from New American Library, 1977.)
   These two books present Key's controversial and thought-provoking theories. Both are easy to read and include ample illustrations. Highly recommended.

Public Relations: Mastering the Subtle Semantics; Press-Agentry Pioneers: P. T. Barnum & Co.; Public Relations in the Global Village

For an up-to-date discussion of current trends, see the *Readers' Guide to Periodical Literature. U.S. News & World Report* is often a good source.

Doug Newsom
Alan Scott
This is PR: The Realities of Public Relations, 3d ed. Belmont, Calif.: Wadsworth, 1985.
   This up-to-date text is one of the standards in the field. Includes chapters on

PR activities, research, and the PR audience.

Doug Newsom
Tom Siegfried
Writing in Public Relations Practice: Form and Style. Belmont, Calif.: Wadsworth, 1981.

A practical how-to text. Includes chapters on writing principles and writing for the general and special-interest audiences. There is a special "project" chapter at the end. Good background for any student seriously thinking about PR as a career.

**Issues and Answers:
The Selling of the
President**

Edward W. Chester
Radio, Television and American Politics. New York: Sheed & Ward, 1969.

A good basic introduction to the field; covers developments through the 1960s.

Dan D. Nimmo
James E. Combs
Mediated Political Realities. New York: Longman, 1983.

A thoughtful analysis of the relationship between politics and the media. Chapters on the mediated world of election campaigns, TV news as fantasyland, political celebrity in popular magazines, and more. Solid material with touches of humor. Must reading for those interested in the subject.

Thomas E. Patterson
The Mass Media Election: How Americans Choose Their President. New York: Praeger, 1980.

One of the more outspoken and rigorous critics of the American political system presents a series of important studies on the involvement of mass media in the electoral process. Difficult reading in places for the beginning student, but definitely worth the effort.

Thomas E. Patterson
Robert D. McClure
The Unseeing Eye: The Myth of Television Power in National Politics. New York: G. P. Putnam's, 1976.

The authors argue that the influence of TV has been far overrated by media analysts. The book is, in part, the result of a grant from the National Science Foundation. One problem: Much data for the empirical conclusions is taken from the 1972 Nixon-McGovern race, an atypical election in a number of ways. Fascinating reading.

For fascinating reading on the relationship between press and presidential candidates, read Timothy Crouse's *The Boys on the Bus* (Westminster, Md.: Random House, 1973; paperback from Ballantine, 1976).

The Global Village: Popular Culture and International Mass Communication

13

IN THE SUMMER OF 1980 I FINALLY TOOK MY FIRST TRIP TO Europe. After the long trip to London I arrived at Heathrow Airport complete with baggage and a fresh copy of *Europe on $15 a Day*. I tried to call a few of the bed-and-breakfast hotels listed in the book but had a hard time figuring out how the pay phones worked. You had to put the money in *after* dialing the number and receiving an answer. Finally I made a connection and took the Underground, or subway, to Kensington.

Once there I spent several hours lugging my bags up and down the street trying to find the hotel. Seems as if the streets changed names at will, and the numbers would climb up and down without any real rhyme or reason. "Everything is so *different* here," I thought. When I stopped and asked directions, I could barely understand what I was being told. Those thick British accents I'd heard on PBS were great for drama but not so good for understanding directions.

Finally I arrived at the small hotel and paid for my first night's lodging. When the man asked for 8 pounds 60, I could barely figure out which coins I was supposed to hand him. After unpacking I wandered up to the lobby area and settled into the TV room. I was ready for some of that amazing British television I'd heard so much about. Instead, there were some very familiar figures parading across the screen. You guessed it— it was J.R., Bobby, and the gang. *Dallas* reruns were being aired by the BBC.

This was my initiation into European culture. There were two distinct lessons to be learned. First, things are very different all over the world. Sometimes we get so wrapped up in our own country that we forget it is but one small part of the planet. But at the same time, our world is growing smaller, and mass communication plays a large part in that process.

> The new electronic interdependence re-creates the world in the image of a global village. . . .
>
> MARSHALL McLUHAN

> Pop is an unflinching look at the real world today; a fascination with and acceptance of our mechanized, trivialized, urbanized environment; a mirror held up to life, full of motion and madness.
>
> MARSHALL FISHWICK

While each country has its own unique characteristics and mass-media systems, all of us increasingly share a common culture, one that is facilitated by the mass-communication process. That common experience is largely in the realm of popular culture.

DEFINING POPULAR CULTURE

What is *popular culture*? It consists primarily of the "stuff of everyday life." That means that there was popular culture in ancient Greece, during the Renaissance, and so on. However, most of it was local and regional by nature. With the coming of mass-communication technology, more and more of our popular culture is national and global. The term *mass culture* is used to identify those everyday things that we all share through mass media and industrial technology. By definition, that which is mass produced (and successful) is "popular," thus becoming part of our popular culture.

Some examples of popular culture at work involve the icons and artifacts of our society: McDonald's golden arches, the Kodak camera, the Coke bottle, and the T-shirt. These things are produced for and consumed by ordinary people all over the world.

Popular culture is so pervasive that it is almost invisible. Marshall McLuhan (see 13.1) contended that all environments are invisible, and he used the fairy tale of the emperor's new clothes to illustrate that we see only what we are conditioned to see. All the well-conditioned subjects saw the emperor's new clothes; it took the unconditioned child to exclaim, "But he has nothing on at all!" One instructor likes to begin his mass-media course each semester by writing on the blackboard, "The fish will be the last creature on earth to discover water." Mass communication and popular culture are so much a part of our everyday life that we have to step back from participating in order to see them.

Another way to define popular culture is by what it *isn't*. It isn't *elite* culture. Our elite culture, which comes primarily from the European tradition, is anything deemed worthy of study and included in the traditional curricula of colleges and universities: art, history, medicine, law, philosophy, and science. In contrast, popular culture is not what we study, but what we live with. Popular culture represents a common denominator, something that cuts across most economic, social, and educational barriers.

In America, Rembrandt represents elite culture, but Norman Rockwell is popular culture. Chamber music is elite, but punk rock is popular. (The Balinese have no word for *art;* they say they simply do everything as well as they can. For the Balinese there is little difference between popular and elite culture.)

Some advocates of elite culture argue that the masses would be better off if they became "cultured." But the masses are already steeped in culture—mass culture. And much of the mass culture of today will be the elite culture of the future. Shakespeare, whose plays are now considered the epitome of elite culture, supplied sex and violence to the masses of his day. Someday *Star Trek* may become elite culture; it can be argued that *Star Trek* provides much the same sort of material to the masses today that Shakespeare did in the 17th century.

Mass culture is largely uncharted as far as academic study is concerned. We have been studying the elite for so long that we have ignored the culture we all have in common. But this is changing, and popular culture is becoming at last an object of serious study at some universities. Bowling Green State University in Ohio, which boasts the nation's leading department of popular culture, has close to 1,000 students discovering the social significance of things like Volkswagens, comic books, science fiction, sports, film theory, women in literature, and more. According to department head Ray Browne: "Popular culture is a very important segment of our society. The contemporary scene is holding us up to ourselves to see; it can tell us who we are, what we are, and why."

Of course, popular culture is an even newer academic discipline than communication. As a result, there is a great deal of debate about exactly what it is and whether it's an academic discipline at all. In this respect, it's developing like such disciplines as psychology, sociology, journalism, and business administration, all of which had to "earn their way" into acceptance during the first half of the 20th century.

In academe, the study of popular culture draws on many disciplines, including American studies, sociology, psychology, anthropology, and communication. But it is with communication that it seems most at home, for mass culture has become the consequence of mass communication; print, radio, film, and television are today's channels of popular culture.

POPULAR CULTURE AND MASS COMMUNICATION

Before Gutenberg, the artist survived through subsidies from the wealthy classes. This is how we derived the term *patron of the arts*. Novelists, poets, and painters would dedicate and/or deliver their work to those who could afford to support them.

With the rise of mass literacy came a new kind of patron and a change in the relationship between patron and artist. Artists were at the beck and call of not one patron, but thousands. The newly literate consumer had tastes that were noticeably different from those of the wealthy elite. If the artist were

to profit, these tastes had to be satisfied— hence the arrival of the "commercial," or popular, artist and the popular arts.

Print was the first medium to offer a new palette for the commercial artist, and eventually came radio and television. These newer mass media have been almost exclusively given over to the popular arts. Electronic media are in the business of attracting the largest possible audience; this means catering to public tastes. The popular artist, now as always, calculates the wants and needs of the mass audience, creates a work in response to those needs, and delivers it to millions of patrons through mass-media channels. What's more, it is done very quickly. The 15th-century writer may have taken years to complete a book. The modern mystery novelist may take only a few weeks. Some television scripts are written in even less time. Popular art is art in a hurry.

Researchers have long debated whether the mass media create popular culture or simply act as a mirror reflecting popular tastes and values. Actually, TV and all mass media probably *refract* reality. The mediated reality we see on the TV screen, for example, is similar to real life yet distorted. It is America as seen through the eyes and minds of producers, directors, and scriptwriters. It "imitates" life while creating a separate reality for the mass audience. Those who disdain popular culture feel that this distortion may be harmful.

Yet it can be argued that the often simplistic world of mass media may offer consumers a buffer between themselves and modern life with all its complexity and technology. Further study could reveal that one function of mass media in our time has been to ease the transition from the relatively simple life-styles of a few decades ago to the accelerated and stress-filled life-styles of today and tomorrow. If TV is partly responsible for what author Alvin Toffler calls "future shock,"

13.1
Who Was Marshall McLuhan?

Herbert Marshall McLuhan was the director of the University of Toronto's Center for Culture and Technology. Although he received his Ph.D. in English, he concentrated on developing a group of theories about the impact of electronic media.

McLuhan was the most controversial figure in mass communication and popular culture. Shunning traditional research methods, he liked to tell his critics: "I don't pretend to understand all my stuff—after all, I'm very difficult!"

Empirical researchers seem most upset by his complete lack of "proof" to back countless assertions. McLuhan offered a theory, gave one or two brief examples, and then went on to the next theory. He seldom cited serious academic research or offered footnotes. To those who criticized this technique, McLuhan responded, "I don't explain, I explore."

His argument that it is how, not what, a medium communicates that matters seems to defy common sense. He maintained that watching television actually requires more involvement than reading a book and that it is the amateur, not the professional, who can best solve complex technical problems in everything from physics to marketing.

In person, he delivered lec-

Photo © by Harry Benson, 1976.

tures in an offhand and matter-of-fact way, as if everyone should see the obvious logic of his argument. (If you saw Woody Allen's film *Annie Hall*, then you caught a glimpse of McLuhan in action.) His books are hard to read, since he jumps from one thought to another with very little connection. When criticized for his writing style, he simply maintained that it used what he called "interface," or the placing side by side of two things

that seem unrelated until you look more closely.

Though he was accused of favoring electronic media over print, McLuhan spent most of his time reading and said he watched very little television. He was called everything from the "electronic guru" to "that nutty professor from Canada." When he died in 1980, we lost one of the most original media observers in recent memory. A synopsis of "The Gospel According to McLuhan":

History: 600 Years of Linear Thought

Since Gutenberg, humans have been trained to believe that all "real" truth and knowledge are in books and printed material. This has perpetrated the fallacy of linear thought. We live our lives the way we read, knowing this is the "correct way." We discuss one topic at a time, take things and teach things in "logical" sequence. YOU HAVE TO WALK BEFORE YOU RUN, YOU HAVE TO CRAWL BEFORE YOU WALK! McLuhan says walking may come first, or running may come first. "There is absolutely no inevitability as long as there is a willingness to contemplate what is happening."

What: The Medium Is the Message/Massage

The medium is the *message* because our technological and social progress has always been affected more by the nature of what we communicate *with* than by individual messages contained in the communication.

The medium is the *massage* because it "massages" us thousands of times each day. We are virtual prisoners in an infinite collection of unrelenting media form and content. These media have a profound effect on the way we think and behave toward one another.

The Media and Technologies: Human Extensions

The media, like other technological innovations, have been designed by us to extend the functions of the body and brain. The radio is an extension of the ear, just as the wheel is an extension of the foot, and the computer an extension of the central nervous system. Radio and television have catapulted music to a mass emotional experience unprecedented in the history of art.

Where: The Global Village

Early people clustered in small villages for convenience and self-protection. Enter industrial progress and the population explosion. Tribes grew bigger and bigger, jobs became more specialized, and a change in identity developed. Rivalries became more acute. People were now grouped in cities, towns, and nations. Print encouraged factions to develop, because it failed to perceive the whole. Now air travel and the electronic media are "shrinking" the world back to tribal size, and tribalization is encouraged by the demise of print. Hence we are becoming once again a "village," but this time a "global village." Such upheavals do not always come easily. According to Alfred North Whitehead, "The major advances in civilization are processes that all but wreck the societies in which they occur."

How: Collide-o-Scope/ Breaking Down the Walls

The electronic media tend to break down the social and ethnic barriers between people by familiarizing everyone with everyone. Information is instantaneous. The poor see the rich, blacks see whites, and with an increased awareness comes increasing unrest. The electronic media are both the enemy of ignorance and factors in social havoc. Then they *amplify* that same havoc through instant news coverage. They bring together divergent ideas, views, and ethics in a collide-o-scope of change.

When: Speed/ Instantaneous Communication and Information

The electronic media make possible instant communication worldwide with radio, TV, telephone, and other devices. Technology provides instant access to all but a few forms of private communication. Their privacy violated and their most cherished patterns threatened, generations raised without these electronic media are bombarded with them in later stages of life when they are less able to accept rapid change. This fact (plus the H-bomb, a technological extension of the club) has created a unique fissure between the postwar generation and its elders.

Who: We Are Them!

It becomes increasingly absurd to talk about protecting "us" from "them." The global village is running out of elbow room. Pollution, radiation, and other related problems are of concern to all of us. We are "them." We are the children of the global village. We are the tribal members of humanity.

it may also provide a temporary cure. To know for sure, we must put popular culture under the microscope of serious academic investigation.

Some research has been done, and much remains to be done. But everyone agrees there is an important link between mass media and popular culture. If the mass media do not actually create popular art and popular culture, they certainly help make it conspicuous and available. People who favor elite art feel (with some justification) that they are drowning in a sea of popular culture, promoted and perpetrated by the mass media. In any event, popular culture is so much a part of our mass communication system that distinctions between mass media and popular culture have become increasingly blurred.

ICONS AND ARTIFACTS

Though there are a number of ways to examine the impact of popular culture, one of the most useful and interesting is to look at icons and artifacts. Icons are special symbols that tend to be idolized in a particular culture. Artifacts are objects that receive less attention.

To really understand the importance of icons, we need to try to imagine a world without words. For the cave-dwelling family, communication was a system of grunts and gestures. Cave dwellers drew pictures of animals and of themselves, leaving them for future generations. Early tribal civilizations lived in a world of symbols, just as we do today. But their symbols were *visual*, more direct than the written word.

In a sense, words take us away from all that is direct and create a complex and confusing system of communication. Inside all of us, there is a cave dweller yearning to be free.

So we develop a devotion to *things*, visual two- or three-dimensional objects.

Religion and politics have always made use of icons: the crucifix, the St. Christopher medal, the Union Jack, the swastika. Icons have become an especially visible part of our lives since our "retribalization" by television. TV has reintroduced us to thinking in pictures. So, like the cave dwellers, we are beginning to rely more on visual and three-dimensional objects for communication and as symbols of worth.

Among the more treasured icons is the automobile. Our cars have always been more than just a way to get from one place to another. They reflect and communicate our values, hopes, and dreams. Are you the practical, no-nonsense driver of an economy model? Or perhaps the proud owner of a luxurious, comfortable gas guzzler? Whatever the case, you have developed a personal and emotional commitment to your choice of automobile.

"Diamonds are a girl's best friend," while "clothes make the man." Even a book can be an icon, appreciated more for form than for content. Have you ever been to a house full of tastefully bound leather books that had never been opened? The television set is an icon of paramount importance. Likewise, the stereo can be a status symbol.

But one does not need to be wealthy to have a hoard of personal icons. Marshall Fishwick points out:

Even the poorest among us has his private icon bank. We make deposits there regularly, and withdraw more than we know. Just as we tuck away special treasures (notes, emblems, photos, medals) in the corners of drawers, so do we tuck away iconic images in the corners of our mind. We draw interest from our deposits. Icons have a way of funding us, sustaining whatever sense and form our lives assume. When we can no longer draw from an icon bank, we quickly go bankrupt.

So it would seem that our icons are essential to our emotional well-being. They are with us now more than ever, encouraged by mass advertising.

A thousand years from now, archaeologists will measure the worth of our culture from the objects we have left behind. As with the cultures of old, the objects most likely to remain are icons. Cultural artifacts disappear because they are thrown away. We may keep the wine bottle and throw away the cork. We keep our books but throw away our magazines. An icon is forever.

But what about our artifacts? Andy Warhol's painting of a Campbell's tomato soup can and Claes Oldenburg's pop depiction of the hamburger serve to remind us that it is the everyday things in our consumer society that make up our lives. It is as if the artists are saying, "For better or worse, this is *your* art; these are the objects you have chosen." So in a sense, even our artifacts can be icons if they have a special symbolic meaning for us. The Coke bottle, for example, is perhaps the best-known American icon; its shape—and its meaning (things go better with Coke!)—are recognized in every corner of the globe.

THE EVENTS OF POPULAR CULTURE

Each year during the third week of January, 70 million Americans sit down in front of their television sets and spend a few hours watching a small army of uniformed men carry a pigskin ball up and down a hundred yards of real or artificial grass. The event is the Super Bowl, and the teams are the winners of the National and American Conferences of the National Football League. To decide which team is "the best," there is a one-game playoff.

The Super Bowl, the World Series, and other mass-communicated sports events are a vital part of our culture, reflecting its priorities and values. As with all popular culture, careful study yields clues about the sociological and psychological games we play in everyday life (see Guest Essay).

THE CULT IN POPULAR CULTURE

Webster's New World Dictionary defines *cult* as "devoted attachment to, or extravagant admiration for, a person, principle, etc., especially when regarded as a fad." In most cases, mass media play an important role in bringing about popular cults.

Cults may form around political candidates or other opinion leaders who strike a responsive chord among a segment of the population.

When thousands of long-haired, brightly clad hippies invaded San Francisco in the summer of 1967, they had a number of political and social beliefs in common, many dealing with questions of religion. That movement, fanned by mass-media coverage, can be justifiably labeled a cult.

It is not surprising that cults, like most aspects of popular culture, often involve mass media in some way. Certainly the tribal ritualistic gatherings at rock concerts to hear Bob Dylan, the Beatles, Elvis Presley, and others were cult-like. In the eyes of the devoted, these figures could do no wrong. In their presence, followers found a symbolic or mythic truth.

A tremendous cult sprang up around *Star Wars, The Empire Strikes Back*, and *Return of the Jedi*. Some devotees claimed that they had seen the movies hundreds of times. Box-office figures indicated that a large number of people saw them more than once. Similar responses have been mentioned in connection

Guest Essay by Marshall Fishwick God and the Super Bowl

Dr. Fishwick is one of the best known of all scholars in the field of popular culture. He is a past president of the Popular Culture Association and has written more than a dozen books on American history and popular culture. He is professor of humanities at Virginia Polytechnic Institute in Blacksburg.

An Episcopal bishop recently commented that he was tiring of the NFL—it was too High Church. He gave this version of the Lord's Prayer:

*Our football, which art on
     television
Hallowed be thy game.
Thy fullback run, thy pass be
     flung*

*In Miami as it is in Dallas.
Give us this day our four
     quarters
And forgive us our trips to the
     bathroom
As we forgive our fumblers.
And lead us not into
     conversation,
But deliver us from off-sides;
For this is the power and the
     popular culture
Forever and ever. Amen.*

The Super Bowl provides the basis not only for recreation but for religion as well. This application of the word *religion* offends because our way of regarding religion as an institution prevents us from seeing the "sacred" or sacrosanct in everyday life. We *want* religion locked into a pietistic Sunday morning service, and we mold our language accordingly. Look at the faces of people listening to Easter sermons on the church's Super Sunday (Easter), and compare them with faces watching football's Super Sun-

day. Where is there more involvement?

Several years ago in Colorado (where the Denver Broncos roam), a fan attempted suicide by shooting himself in the head on the day after the Bron-

with a wide range of films, including *Woodstock, The Wall, Harold and Maude,* and especially *The Rocky Horror Picture Show.* Likewise some television programs, such as *Leave it to Beaver* and *The Twilight Zone,* can best be described as "cult classics."

One of the most widespread cults to center on a television program is that of the Trekkies, fanatic devotees of the *Star Trek* series. Trekkies come in all ages, though most are 15–35 years old. Each year thousands of

them gather at conventions ("cons") held in various major cities. Here they view *Start Trek* episodes they have seen countless times before. There are exhibitors selling everything from plastic Spock ears to metal phaser guns.

The Trekkies do not sit passively and observe. Many dress up in the costumes of their favorite heroes and heroines: Captain Kirk, Mr. Spock, Klingons, robots, even "Tribbles," the round, faceless, furry creatures featured in an early episode.

cos fumbled seven times against the Chicago Bears.

"I have been a Broncos fan since they got organized," he wrote in his suicide note. "I can't stand their fumbling anymore."

He fumbled, too—the bullet did not reach a vital spot. Otherwise it would have been a classic example of blood sacrifice demanded by a merciless God.

Traditional rituals were attuned to the seasons; throughout central North America, say anthropologists, they took the form of war games between tribes. How has this come down to our times? As battles between rival teams, with incantations, cheerleaders, and fans (short for *fanatic*) to urge armed (at least padded) warriors forward.

This "friendly game" is a minutely observed and monitored battle between aggressive male teams, who use cunning, deceit, and violence to attain their ends. Does this sound like a corporation or bureaucracy? Is the Bowl merely a mirror image of life out there?

And what about up there? Teams both play and pray to win. George Allen of the Washington Redskins insists on locker room prayers. The Miami Dolphins have a public pregame prayer. "How touching a scene," reports Colman McCarthy of the *Washington Post*. "Giant men, bruised and asweat, kneeling to acknowledge that however almighty their win may have been, there is still another Almighty, the Divine Coach. . . ." In such a scene the true meaning of popular culture can be found—if only we know how to find it.

Super Sunday dawns. Ten times ten thousand go to the Bowl itself. Millions more witness the events on television screens, "against the beautiful skyline." The destiny-laden pre-game coin flip (the coin, incidentally, is worth $4,000) sets the scene. Players come onto the field, amidst acclamations louder than any heard outside ancient Jerusalem's walls. They run, collide, bruise, bash. Now for the halftime festivities. Ten lines of young people march forth, precise as pistons in a well-tuned engine . . . females in yellow or orange, males in blue, white teeth shining as they sing, "It's a Good Time to Know Your Neighbor." Four priest warriors dance on the drumhead/godhead. Now the hundred thousand worshippers are on their feet, tears in their eyes, singing:

America, America,
God shed his grace on thee. . . .

Amen.

Participants swap stories about their favorite episodes and trade trivia questions. Several years ago I participated in an academic panel at a Los Angeles con. There were half a dozen of us who had taught seminars on *Star Trek* or used it as a jumping-off point for analyses of TV's influence in society.

I thought I was quite an expert, having read every available book and even talked with Gene Roddenberry (the creator and producer of the series). I quickly discovered I was among the most poorly informed at the con. These people had spent hours every day for years learning every detail. At a moment's notice they could tell you who starred in a given episode, what it was about, and even describe the scene before the first commercial! More recently, the life of the Star Trek phenomenon has been prolonged by the success of a series of films documenting the continuing adventures of the crew of the Enterprise. To the delight of Trekkies, the widescreen versions sport obscure references to their favorite TV episodes.

ISSUES AND ANSWERS: THE DILEMMA OF POPULAR CULTURE

One of the reasons for including popular culture in a book about mass media is to interest you in the global consequences of mass communication at the earliest possible moment. I have found that my own students are willing to spend more time investigating history and current issues if they can link them up to the real world around them.

For too long we have ignored popular culture in favor of a more traditional historical approach. Mass media and popular culture are important because you *live* them every day. You wake up to popular culture in the morning and fall asleep to it each night.

You should also wake up to things around you. What you find in textbooks (including this one) may not be much help. You need to examine your own life-style, icons, artifacts, television viewing habits, favorite singers, and favorite foods in order to understand yourself and your relationships with others.

Because you *live* popular culture, you may not think it is important. Nothing could be further from the truth. Yet you will probably get little encouragement or support from your professors. This may indeed be something you need to do on your own, but it is critical. When Socrates said, "The unexamined life is not worth living," he could hardly have envisioned our vast electronic environment full of instant gratification and information. If he were here today, he might add, "The unexamined environment is not worth living *in*."

INTERNATIONAL MEDIA SYSTEMS

In this book I have been concerned primarily with the development of mass-communication systems within the United States. But every country has developed its own methods for using mass-media technology. Perhaps soon there will be enough information to add a section in this chapter on the People's Republic of China. Certainly this rapidly emerging portion of the global village will be an interesting media use case study. In any event, with each new system comes a unique set of problems. Most countries have not opted for a commercial system to the extent that the United States has. In fact, some countries severely restrict the kinds of advertising allowed. Some allow no advertising on TV or radio at all. To give you an idea of how a few other nations control their mass media, we'll take a closer look at the United Kingdom, Canada, Mexico, the Netherlands, the Soviet Union, and Japan.

THE UNITED KINGDOM: MEDIA IN THE MOTHERLAND

My trip to Great Britain was, in part, a chance to experience a media system that has been praised by many in America as far superior to ours. Our impression of England is largely formed by the popular culture that is exported here. We think of Fleet Street, the Beatles, *Upstairs, Downstairs,* and doubledecker buses. At the same time, they think of *Dallas,* Elvis Presley, the Wild West, and Ronald Reagan. Obviously both impressions are incomplete.

Regular mass-produced newspapers were available in England as early as 1622. The British were interested enough in radio to support Italian inventor Guglielmo Marconi's efforts to make the "wireless" a practical communication system. When radio grew to become a consumer-oriented medium in the early 1920s, the British were ready. The British Broadcasting Company (BBC) was formed in 1922 and became a corporation in 1927. The BBC is independent, being financed by a license fee collected from each citizen who owns a radio or television set. It uses these revenues to build and maintain its various radio and television stations and to pay for the programming that is broadcast from them.

Today there are four BBC radio channels, which can be heard throughout the country. BBC 1 and BBC 2 carry popular music. The first is a rough equivalent of our Top-40 format and plays the songs that are selling in the record stores. BBC 2 is more like our album-oriented rock stations, playing selected album cuts as well as the hits. These two channels are by far the most popular, and together they account for about four of every five radio listeners. Like their counterparts in America, they also offer news, weather, and traffic reports.

BBC 3 programs classical music, drama, and other more elite cultural fare, including discussion programs about philosophical and sociological questions. BBC 4 offers many programs similar to our news and news-talk formats. Especially popular are the "news magazine" shows such as *The World in Focus* and *PM Reports.*

Experimental television in England began in 1936. Just as in America, the development of TV took a back seat to World War II. However, there was regular BBC-TV programming available before the war, and it resumed in 1946. Most of the programs are produced by the BBC, but some came from independent producers both at home and abroad. BBC-TV programming is world famous, and its productions air in over 100 nations.

In 1954 the government established the Independent Broadcasting Authority (IBA). The IBA operates the Independent Television (ITV) and Independent Local Radio (ILR) stations throughout the country.

Unlike the BBC, these stations are commercial; each is allowed to carry a specified number of commercials each hour. Each IBA radio and television station is responsible for its own success or failure, and each must answer to the IBA for the quality of its programming. IBA stations have been quite successful in competition with the BBC, though they do not dominate the airwaves the way the commercial stations in this country overpower PBS. In fact, it wasn't until 1982 that viewers all over the United Kingdom could receive a second commercial television channel. A total of four channels is now available to British viewers: two run by the BBC and two independent commercial outlets.

Perhaps our admiration for the British media system comes from the feeling that people there enjoy "the best of both worlds" by having access to commercial and noncommercial outlets in more or less equal measure. In addition, the British are voracious readers and support dozens of daily newspapers, ranging from sensationalistic tabloids that print pictures of nude women every day to the detailed coverage of the day's events found in the London *Times.* In any event, most everyone agrees that American media outlets have much to learn from those in the Motherland.

THE CANADIAN COMPROMISE

Like Great Britain, Canada has long had a tradition of quality mass communication. The first Canadian newspapers were printed in 1751. Many of the newspapers have taken their lead from developments in England. At the same time, many magazines and some newspapers have patterned their approach after successful counterparts in the United States.

Since Newfoundland was chosen as the reception point for Marconi's first transatlantic wireless experiments, Canada has been a leader in establishing radio communication. Broadcasting is regulated by the Canadian Radio-Television Commission (CRTC), an agency of the government somewhat analogous to the FCC. The CRTC consists of five full-time members and ten part-time members, whose votes are always taken on crucial issues such as license revocation.

The Broadcasting Act of 1968 states clearly that the airwaves belong to the public and that licensees "have a reponsibility for programs they broadcast, but the right to freedom of expression and the right of persons to receive programs . . . is unquestioned."

Like Britain, Canada has a strong government-owned broadcasting service. The Canadian Broadcasting Corporation (CBC) offers many news, public affairs, and documentary shows as well as entertainment fare. Unlike its British counterpart, however, the CBC does accept commercials. There is also a CTV television network, the counterpart of Britain's ITV. These stations are privately owned and are operated for a profit.

Of special concern over the years has been competition from nearby media outlets in the United States. Some major U.S. magazines produce a Canadian edition. In addition, since most of Canada's population lives near the American border, there has always been a lively competition between U.S. and Canadian broadcast stations. The Canadian government moved to restrict Canadian advertising on U.S. stations some time ago by limiting the tax deductions Canadian businesses can take on such expenditures. For some time many Canadian radio stations were prohibited from playing too many songs by American artists.

The unique characteristics of the Canadian population create another problem. In order to serve all the people, much of what appears in the print and broadcast media must be duplicated for the French-speaking segment of the population. Most feel that there is adequate service for both segments, but the issue has heated up as a result of a separatist movement among French-speaking Canadians.

Another concern involves cross-media ownership and monopoly. One report indicated that over half of all daily newspaper circulation is controlled by two large corporations. Just as in the U.S., this calls up the question of news manipulation and control and could mean that Canadians are not getting as much diversity in their news as some think they should.

In many ways, the Canadian media system is a compromise between England's and America's. Canadian broadcast media, especially, seem to be able to maintain the fine tradition of the BBC while bending to some of the economic realities that seem to govern broadcasting in the United States.

THE MEXICAN CHALLENGE: SERVING ALL THE PEOPLE

Since the first newspaper was founded in 1722, there has been a rich tradition of print media in Mexico. Despite this, the country's literacy rate has consistently lagged behind that of its northern neighbor. Today, however, more Mexican citizens can read than ever before.

The Mexican broadcast system is dominated by the government. Three agencies are involved with radio and television at various levels: the Ministry of Transport and Communications, the Ministry of Internal Affairs, and the Ministry of Education. These agencies oversee the government-operated stations. In addition, all privately owned stations must give up 12.5 percent of their air time to the government.

Four television channels are loosely affiliated in a federation known as *Televisa*. Each channel is programmed to reach different segments of the population during various time periods. Here viewers can find most anything they would find in the United States, including a Mexican version of *Sesame Street*, game shows, soap operas, and talk shows. In addition, some American, Japanese, and British programs are shown regularly. However, there has been some concern in recent years that certain programs from the United States and elsewhere may be too violent or otherwise unacceptable by Mexican standards. Another concern has been radio stations situated on the U.S. border. These stations are licensed by the Mexican government but aim virtually all of their programming and advertising at the more affluent audience to the north.

THE NETHERLANDS: PRINT LEADS THE WAY

It has been said that nowhere in the world are people more dependent on print than in the Netherlands. Indeed, over 98 percent of the population is literate, and the Dutch have a huge appetite for print, especially books and newspapers. They take their politics seriously; hence the newspapers generally take a stand on most issues of the day. Despite their political orientation, however, the Dutch have achieved worldwide recognition for their objectivity.

This interest in politics carries over to the broadcast system, which is a unique experiment in democracy. Major social, political, and religious groups can band together to form a broadcast association and petition the government for air time. About 70 percent of all broadcast programming is created by these groups, with the rest used for educational and entertainment purposes. To form a group, you must get 40,000 members, and that number must increase to 100,000 within two years if you are to remain on the air. The broadcast group then becomes a part of the Dutch Broadcast Foundation, which oversees operations.

While broadcasting is under the jurisdiction of the Ministry of Cultural Recreation and Social Work, no government agency has the right to edit or censor programs aired by participating groups, despite their occasional inflammatory nature. There are restrictions on the use of obscenities and other obviously objectionable programming, however. This open system of broadcasting typifies the rather enlightened perspective of the country.

Until the late 1960s no advertising was allowed on Dutch broadcast stations. Today, however, the broadcast media are supported by advertising as well as a license-fee structure similar to that of the United Kingdom. Unlike other programming forms, radio and TV news is produced by an independent group without political or religious affiliations. News shows carry out the print tradition of in-depth reporting and objectivity. Many feel that the media system of the Netherlands is the best in Europe, if not the world. At the very least it presents a unique example of experimentation that the rest of the world can watch with interest.

BACK IN THE USSR: THE SOVIET MODEL

Unlike the other media systems you have learned about thus far, the Soviet system exists for one central purpose only: to perpetuate the Communist Party and help fulfill its goals. There are no privately owned newspapers or broadcast outlets in the country, and there is no advertising per se, though some information about available goods may be passed along to consumers.

The most popular and most widely distributed newspaper is *Pravda (Truth)*, which is printed in over two dozen cities throughout the country. Though most of its editorial staff is in Moscow, over half of all *Pravda's* readers live outside the capital.

It is estimated that over 4,000 magazines are printed regularly, some of them exclusively for the audience outside the country. All Soviet media are regarded as potential propaganda tools to further the aims of the state. In a country where over 60 languages are spoken, it is a difficult task to ensure that media are available for all the people, but generally there is something for everyone.

Tass is the central news agency from which most news emanates. It serves a function similar to that of wire services in other countries, since its dispatches form a basis for much of what is printed in the U.S.S.R.

The government operates four radio networks and four television networks. Each of these has distinct programming. The usual fare includes classical music (over half of all music broadcast in the country is classical), drama, and news. Unlike their U.S. counterparts, Soviet news outlets do not try to "scoop" one another on stories. The general approach is to stay away from fast-breaking news events until the official perspective is passed along from party leaders.

No mention of the Soviet media system would be complete without a passing reference to the film industry. While there are only about 60 million radio sets and 60 million TV sets to serve over 250 million people, attendance at the 100,000 movie theaters exceeds 5 billion each year. Soviet films have long been famous for their artistic quality, and many are used as models for films produced in other European countries.

MADE IN JAPAN: TECHNOLOGY AND MORE

There can be little doubt that Japan's mass-communication system is technologically the most highly developed in the world. This is surprising in that it got off to a relatively late start. The first Japanese newspaper did not appear on a regular basis until 1864, and as late as World War II the Japanese media were considered quaint and rather sluggish by western standards. Since the war, however, the Japanese have developed technology to the fullest, especially in broadcasting.

One need only think of the quality of the electronic products of Japanese firms such as Sony, Panasonic, and Mitsubishi to get some idea of just how far the country has come in a short time. The vast majority of all video recorders for sale in the United States are made in Japan, and virtually all of the various models were designed there.

Currently the Japanese are the world leader in fiber-optics application (see Chapter 15) and have developed some cable and closed-circuit TV systems that would put any in the West to shame.

Nippon Hōsō Kyōkai (NHK) is the government broadcast service, and it has been compared favorably with the BBC. The system is financed by license fees similar to those in Britain and the Netherlands. The service offers both traditional Japanese theater and cultural programs as well as numerous reruns of popular programs from other countries, notably the United States. The NHK also operates a radio network with stations tailored to local and regional interests.

Since 1950, the NHK has had to compete with numerous commercial broadcasters as well. The result of this has been an abundance of programs for Japanese citizens. The small country is served by over 6,000 radio and television stations. Japan's success in developing broadcasting has amazed the world.

THE GLOBAL VILLAGE

We have seen that each country has developed its own media system in response to its own political, cultural, and sociological needs. At the same time, we can readily see numerous similarities in the approaches most have taken. The new information technologies will probably lead us to a great common understanding and appreciation for the unique aspects that make up the global village. That means a common set of experiences for all of the world's population and, eventually, a common popular culture. It is to be hoped that these new developments will lead us to a better understanding of one another in the years ahead.

QUERIES AND CONCEPTS

1 Make a list of your five favorite books. Which would be considered popular culture and which elite? Why?

2 Investigate your wallet and dresser drawers to find your own icons. Why are you saving them? Write a paragraph about each, justifying your actions. (If you can't justify them, throw them away!)

3 The Super Bowl is not the only event of popular culture that takes on overtly spiritual overtones. Can you think of others? Are there any television shows that involve religious values?

4 Can you think of several popular cults not mentioned in the text? Are you a member of any organization, formal or informal, that could be considered a popular cult?

5 Who are in the best position to investigate and evaluate popular culture: (1) those in elite culture who have risen above it, (2) those who experience it firsthand all the time, or (3) Martians coming to Earth for the first time? Choose one and explain why.

READINGS AND REFERENCES

Defining Popular Culture

Marshall Fishwick
Parameters of Popular Culture. Bowling Green, Ohio: Bowling Green University, Popular Press, 1974.

This is a collection of Fishwick's original essays, which probe into definitions of popular culture and include pieces on "Fakelore," "Theology," "Mythology," and "Art."

The emperor's new clothes analogy is from Quentin Fiore and Marshall McLuhan's *The Medium is the Massage* (Westminster, Md.: Random House, 1967).

Popular Culture and Mass Communication

Ray B. Browne
David Madden
The Popular Culture Explosion: Experiencing Mass Media. Dubuque, Iowa: Wm. C. Brown, 1972.

Here is a magazine-style book that defines popular culture and answers the question "Why study popular culture?" Hundreds of examples from newspapers and magazines are included.

Stuart and Elizabeth Ewen
Channels of Desire: Mass Images and the Shaping of American Consciousness.
New York: McGraw-Hill, 1982.

This upbeat and thoroughly readable book deals with the relationship between mass communication (the channels) and popular culture (the desire). A good hard look at our consumer culture; a must for students interested in popular culture and mass communication.

Icons and Artifacts

Marshall Fishwick
Ray B. Browne
Icons of America. Bowling Green, Ohio: Bowling Green University, Popular Press, 1978.

Now in its third edition, this standard includes articles on the most talked-about modern icons. A highly recommended anthology.

The Events of Popular Culture

For Michael Real's analysis of the Super Bowl as mythic spectacle, see Readings and References in Chapter 9.

The Cult in Popular Culture

The best coverage of the various movements in popular culture is in Russel Nye's *The Unembarrassed Muse: The Popular Arts in America* (New York: Dial Press, 1970).

Susan Sackett's *Letters to Star Trek* (New York: Ballantine Books, 1977) traces the Trekkie saga.

Issues and Answers: The Dilemma of Popular Culture

These issues are thoroughly covered in Herbert J. Gans's *Popular Culture and High Culture: An Analysis and Evaluation of Taste* (New York: Basic Books, 1977).

John M. Phelan's *Mediaworld: Programming the Public* (New York: Seabury Press, 1977) explores the ways mass media are taking over the interpersonal functions of popular culture.

The *Journal of Popular Culture, Journal of International Popular Culture*, and *Journal of American Culture* are available in many university libraries, and some come free with a membership in the Popular Culture Association. There are reduced rates for students. Those interested can write to the association at 101 University Hall, Bowling Green State University, Bowling Green, Ohio 43403.

International Media Systems

Heinz-Dietrich Fischer and Stefan Reinhard Melnik, eds. *Entertainment: A Cross-Cultural Examination.* New York: Hastings House, 1979.
  A compendium of articles from all over the world covering such topics as the "middle age" of British television and the "Misunderstood Best Seller" in West Germany. A little something for everyone, from everywhere.

Wilbur Schramm *Mass Media and National Development.* Palo Alto, Calif.: Stanford University Press, 1964.
  A look at how mass media systems and political realities interface in emerging Third World nations. Considered a classic in the field.

14

Mass-Communication Research: A Beginner's Guide

THE STUDY OF MASS MEDIA IS RELATIVELY NEW. WHEN COM-pared with medicine, which is thousands of years old, or even with modern psychology, which is a product of this century, the formal study of communication is a babe. We have only begun to research the effects of mass media, a dynamic force that is reshaping our lives.

PATTERNS IN MASS-COMMUNICATION RESEARCH

The direction of research in mass media is largely determined by the people who hold the purse strings. Much of the funding for large-scale studies comes from some level of government. These studies are often about violence or involve the interests of minority or unfairly treated groups like blacks or women. They are prompted by the concern of the people (as expressed through their government) that certain media programs or practices may be harmful to society.

A second group of studies is done by students who write theses and dissertations in graduate schools. Usually these are directed by senior-level faculty members, who either steer students to favorite research topics or let them make their own decisions. Studies are also funded by universities or private sources.

All these efforts contribute *something* to the accumulated knowledge that we have about issues in mass communication. But because research in mass media is so new, we have very few hard and fast conclusions. Not enough studies have been done in most areas to give us conclusive results.

Another problem involves the *situational perspective* that we have on our media consumption. In brief, not all media consumption affects everyone in the same way. Violence on TV may stimulate certain types of young people to behave

Social scientists insist that any important conclusions about the effects of media be supported by solid evidence . . . most are quite wary of any simple answers or unverified conclusions concerning causal relations between media content and undesirable conduct. . . .

MELVIN DeFLEUR

It is surely no wonder that a bewildered public should regard with cynicism a research tradition which supplies, instead of answers, a plethora of relevant, but inconclusive, and, at times, seemingly contradictory findings

JOSEPH KLAPPER

violently in real life; for others it may have the opposite effect. All studies that involve large numbers of subjects inherently assume that those subjects are somehow similar. But in the real world we are all very different.

We need more research in mass media because the media themselves are constantly changing. They are not stable, like a chemical formula; instead, they are flexible and changing in both form and content. I spent three years working on a dissertation involving sex-role socialization on four popular TV shows. All of them are now off the air. This can be very frustrating. But it shows that we need more research in the field to help us keep current and cope with change.

The study of mass media is so new that there is still some debate about whether it should be housed with arts, humanities, or the social sciences. The creation of effective mass communication via print, radio, television, or film is an art. It involves the efforts of one or more artists. Each medium can point to its best and proudly proclaim it a unique art form. But mass communication is also a branch of human learning and belongs with the rest of the humanities, like English and foreign languages. Each medium has a "literature" all its own: In radio, it's sound; in television, pictures.

As far as research is concerned, mass communication is a social science. To understand its effects we borrow procedures from psychology and sociology. In fact, many of the most important communication researchers are psychologists and sociologists. They have developed methods for examining attitudes, beliefs, and behaviors. They admit that the methods of the social scientist are not as exact or as pure as those of the physical scientist, since human behavior is simply not as predictable as a chemical solution or a physics experiment. But it *is* predictable to some degree. Social scientists adopt many of the statistical procedures used in the physical sciences in order to make more definite predictions about human behavior.

PROCEDURES AND PROBLEMS OF COMMUNICATION RESEARCH

We all have opinions about the influence of mass media, just as we have opinions about everything. These opinions are often based on information we have gathered and things we have been taught by our parents, teachers, and television sets. Occasionally we engage in debate with others. We match our opinions against theirs and offer "facts" to back them. But if that's all we do, then what we end up with is what we started with: *opinions*.

Of course, it is possible to gather opinions in a systematic way. We might go to everyone in the country and ask what he or she thinks about TV and violence. We might find that 76.2 percent feel there is a relationship between TV viewing and violence. But this does not mean there *is* a relationship, only that more than three-quarters of the people *think there is*.

In recent years all social sciences have placed more and more emphasis on empirical research, which relies not on gathering opinions but on observing behaviors. The researcher gathers data systematically and makes conclusions based on the data. There are several steps involved in designing an empirical study, and each has its own pitfalls.

The first step is to identify an idea that is to be tested. The field is wide open, with an unlimited number of hypotheses—some far too general to be tested and some so small or obvious that they are not worth testing. The beginning research student often makes the mistake of asking too large a question. It might be impractical, for instance, to test whether TV violence causes violence in real life, but we could design a nice study documenting the TV viewing habits among inmates of a juvenile detention school versus those of students in a public school. By obtaining this information we might contribute a small bit of data to help resolve the larger question.

A common way to test a hypothesis is to go at it backwards: to gather data in an attempt to disprove a *null hypothesis*. The null hypothesis claims that there is no relationship between the elements in question. In this case our null hypothesis would be: There is no difference between the viewing habits and program preferences of the two groups being studied.

Then we must make a decision about research design. How can we gather data to test our null hypothesis? Are we going to ask these kids to report how many hours they watch TV per day? That's one simple way, but does it tell us what we want to know? And how do we know their answers will be accurate? Some subjects may report fewer hours than they actually watch, since there is a social stigma attached to spending too much time with the "boob tube." And since TV watching is something we do on an irregular basis (some days we watch five hours, other days none), the chances are great that some error will be made. It would help if we could just station someone by the TV set both in private homes and in a detention home and see how many hours each kid watches it, but that's going to be difficult and time-consuming. Moreover, if we do manage to observe the subjects, are they going to watch what they normally would? These are just some of the problems of research design.

Once we have data, we have the job of analyzing and interpreting it. The first question is: Did we get enough data? Perhaps our N (number in the sample) was only 20. Does this really represent the institution and the school?

The community? Children in the United States? Children of the world? We must be careful when inferring that others behave like our test group.

The greatest pitfall in empirical research involves the problem of establishing causal inferences. It is all too easy to leap to conclusions. We may *infer*, for example, that since Lee Harvey Oswald was an ex-Marine, and since he allegedly shot John F. Kennedy, all ex-Marines are somewhat prone to violence, and therefore military training tends to make trainees more violent. But someone else might respond by saying that an acquaintance was in the Marines and now heads a committee for strict gun-control legislation, and therefore experience in the Marines makes someone realize how destructive guns can be. Who is right?

Most of what we hear and read about mass communication is the opinion of others. It is generally assumed that the more education or experience someone has in the field, the more valuable the opinion is. Still, even the most educated and experienced people can and do disagree.

That is why the social-science methodology, which tries to go beyond gathering opinions, has become increasingly accepted among those who teach mass communication. Without it, there is really no way for us to go beyond the opinion stage. There are so many urgent social problems relating to mass media that we cannot ignore methods that provide us with new and more conclusive information. A theory that remains untested remains just a theory.

And so, should you go on to graduate school in mass communication, you will most likely need a passing knowledge of social-science methods to conduct your own research.

To test a theory the researcher attempts to establish *causality*, that is, the relationship of one phenomenon to another. Richard J. Hill, editor of *Sociometry* and a leading authority on statistical research, used to tell a story that illustrates the problem of establishing causality. He said that many years ago researchers discovered that the water level of the Potomac River dropped in direct proportion to the number of peanuts consumed in Washington, D.C. The more peanuts consumed, the less water there was in the river. The obvious conclusion? People eating all those salted peanuts got thirsty and drank up the water!

This makes sense, of a sort, but it doesn't have anything to do with reality. In the spring, ice melts and the river rises. In the summer, water evaporates and the level goes down. Meanwhile, baseball season goes into full swing (Washington had a team in those days), and the number of peanuts consumed rises, thanks to peanut-hungry fans. Baseball and melting ice were *intervening variables* that accounted for the peanut and water levels.

We must be careful not to establish causality simply because the statistics (data) seem to support a certain theory. It is one thing to say that real-life crime rates and the number of crimes committed on TV have both risen in the last ten years. It is quite another to establish a *causal relationship*, to say that one "causes" the other.

Causal ordering is another problem. It seemed to make sense that the peanut consumption caused the lower water levels, but the statistics offered equal support for the theory that lower water levels caused a higher consumption of peanuts. Of course, both hypotheses are nonsense, but causal ordering can be critical. If more real-life crimes encourage TV writers to think more about crime and put it into their scripts, that's one thing. If the true causal ordering is the reverse, we have an entirely different problem.

Finally, there is always a great temptation to yield to our own opinions and biases in such cases or to design studies so that results will verify gut-level feelings. Yet it is the difference between gut-level feelings and empirical research that gives credibility to a point of view.

To avoid all these pitfalls we must choose the right statistical method to test our theories. A battery of tests is available to help us decide if any significant difference exists between groups. There will always be differences between any two groups; we want to know if there are any *statistically significant* differences that relate to our hypothesis. Choosing the appropriate statistical test helps us make that decision. All such tests have limitations. Some can be used only for certain kinds of data, others only when N is large.

A SAMPLER OF RESEARCH STUDIES

The balance of this chapter contains three research articles that were published in two communication journals. These journals are designed primarily for graduate students, researchers, and college professors. Yet some of their articles can be useful to the undergraduate student.

Each article deals with an important area of mass-communication research. Obviously it would not be possible to present or summarize all of the relevant articles in each area or to try to represent all of the areas that are being investigated. However, you may want to use these articles as a jumping-off point to learn more about research and about the questions being studied by mass-communication researchers across the country.

To help guide you through each article, there is a list of "Tips and Touts" for each study as well as annotated material. These should be useful in helping you understand the unique aspects of each of the three research examples.

Television Network News Reporting by Female Correspondents: An Update

by Loy A. Singleton and Stephanie L. Cook

One of the principal tools of communications researchers is a technique known as content analysis, *using a careful, objective collection of data that can be counted in some way. This research involves a content analysis of 1,247 network news reports and contends that there is still a significant difference between male- and female-reported story topics on network news reports.*

Tips and Touts

1 Note that the authors have counted over 1,200 stories reported on network news, then analyzed them to see if there are *systematic* biases with respect to which reporters were chosen to cover the stories. Such a large sample helps give the study credibility.

2 When discussing the .05 level, the authors mean that they are looking for any story assignment biases that occur as a result of some systematic problem, not merely the results of chance occurrences.

3 The authors state that more women were assigned to domestic government stories than were assigned to cover foreign affairs. Can you think of what image this might leave in the mind of the viewer?

4 In Table 1 under the p column, the authors mean that any area with a p score of .05 or less (all of the .001 scores, for example) may indicate a systematic editorial bias of some kind.

5 The authors conclude that sexual stereotyping may still exist in TV newsrooms. After reading the study do you agree or disagree?

Loy A. Singleton is an assistant professor in the Department of Radio, Television and Motion Pictures, University of North Carolina at Chapel Hill. He received his Ph.D. degree from the University of Texas at Austin in 1979. His research interests are in telecommunications policy and economics.

Stephanie L. Cook is an English-language instructor in Osaka, Japan. She received her M.A. degree from the University of North Carolina at Chapel Hill in 1980.

This article first appeared in the Winter 1982 issue of the *Journal of Broadcasting*. Used by permission of *Journal of Broadcasting*.

Women have been reporting the news on television since the earliest days of the medium. In 1947 Dorothy Fuldheim became the nation's first television news anchorwoman on WEWS-TV, Cleveland.[1] A year later Pauline Frederick became the first female television network news reporter when she was hired by ABC.[2] However, over the next 20 years relatively few women joined network news staffs.

This began to change in the 1970s when, aided by federal affirmative-action policies and citizen-group agreements, more female reporters began to appear on local and network news programs. From 1971 to 1977 female reporters and newscasters achieved the largest employment gains of any broadcasting industry employee category.[3] By 1977 the number of on-air network newswomen had doubled to 25.[4] By late 1979, 37 of the 180 correspondents who had appeared on the three commercial television networks that year were women.[5]

The increased employment of women as television news reporters and anchors has given rise to studies comparing their effectiveness and credibility with their male colleagues.[6] However, an area of concern to female reporters which has received little empirical investigation is the types of news stories assigned to males and females. In 1974 Bowman concluded that female reporters in print and electronic media consistently were being assigned less newsworthy beats than males.[7] The U.S. Commission on Civil Rights reported that, in a 1974–1975 sample of network television news programs, female reporters tended to cover stories limited to women's interests.[8] In a 1977 follow-up study of television network news programming, the Commission concluded that female correspondents had made some gains in the variety and importance of their assignments but did not report detailed information on differences in male and female coverage responsibilities.[9]

The present study undertook to update these earlier efforts and to assess what differences still may exist in the subjects of network news stories covered by male and female reporters. Specifically, it addressed the research question: Do female correspondents generally report the same kinds of news stories as their male counterparts, or are there significant differences in the topics of the stories they are assigned?

Method

A systematic probability sample of ten weeks in 1979 was drawn, beginning with the seventh week of the year, which was randomly selected, then selecting every fifth week thereafter. Using

Note here that the authors have "set the stage" for their study by expressing a particular point of view about the subject matter.

the *Television News Index and Abstracts*,[10] all 150 early evening newscasts of the three commercial networks which were broadcast during the sample weeks were examined. The unit of analysis was the news report, that is, any report filed by a single correspondent. In the case of a multi-part report each segment reported by a single correspondent was coded separately.

The sample contained 1,247 reports. These were coded as to position in the newscast, correspondent sex and topic.[11] A portion of the reports could not be coded satisfactorily into discrete topic categories. Rather than "force" the topic coding, these reports were analyzed separately. They revealed the same general assignment patterns as the remaining 91 percent and, in the interest of concise presentation of data, have been omitted from the Table discussed below.

A test for the significance of the difference between two proportions was applied to each topic to compare the percentage of all male-reported stories falling under that topic with the percentage of all female-reported stories.[12]

Examining such a large number of reports helps the authors gain credibility for their findings.

Results

Stories dealing with foreign affairs, the federal government and the economy predominated.[13] The Table compares the distribution of report topics for male reporters with the distribution for female reporters. There were several topics for which the proportions of male and female reports were significantly different at the .05 level or below: Women reported proportionately less foreign affairs, economy, disaster and feature stories than male reporters. In contrast, women were significantly over-assigned stories dealing with US government, environment and social problems.

In the transportation and sports categories women were under-represented, but the difference only approached the .05 level. Three other categories yielded significant differences (religion, weather report and other), but the small number of reports in these categories and the presence of zeros as the female proportions reduce their utility. Generally, the results suggest that, compared to male reporters, females are assigned more U.S. government stories and less foreign affairs, more social problems and fewer disasters, more "women's issues" and fewer stereotypically male-associated topics such as business and sports.

The relative importance of stories reported by female correspondents was also examined. The positioning of a report in

Table 1: News Report Distribution by Reporter Sex

Report Topic*	Male-reported (percent of male stories)	Female-reported (percent of female stories)	Z	p
Foreign affairs	298(31.0)	33(19.5)	6.35	<.001
U.S. government	122(12.7)	44(26.0)	8.10	<.001
Economy	123(12.7)	16(9.5)	2.42	.016
Disaster	67(6.9)	7(4.1)	2.92	.004
Energy	53(5.5)	8(4.7)	.86	.389
Feature	51(5.3)	6(3.6)	1.96	.050
Environment	38(3.9)	15(7.7)	3.88	<.001
Crime	40(4.2)	6(3.6)	.74	.459
Social problems	28(2.9)	14(8.3)	5.62	<.001
Transportation	29(3.0)	3(1.8)	1.87	.061
Courts	27(2.8)	4(2.4)	.60	.549
Science	27(2.7)	4(2.4)	.45	.653
Entertainment	21(2.2)	3(1.8)	.68	.497
Sports	13(1.4)	1(0.6)	1.91	.056
Religion	8(0.8)	— 0 —	3.02	.003
Women's	3(0.3)	5(3.0)	5.07	<.001
Weather report	5(0.5)	— 0 —	2.38	.017
Consumer	4(0.4)	1(0.6)	.67	.503
Institutions	4(0.4)	1(0.6)	.67	.503
Other	1(0.1)	— 0 —	3.38	<.001
Total	961	169		

* See footnote 11 for full titles of report categories.

Gazing down the list above, do any conclusions spring to mind?

a network television newscast is a useful indicator of that story's perceived importance or news value. Overall, female reporters were well represented in coverage of lead stories in the newscast sample. Of the network reporters whose stories fell into the sample, 83 percent were male and 17 percent female. Females filed 16.2 percent of the lead-off or number one stories, 15.5 percent of the number two stories and 18.2 percent of the third-place reports. In all, females reported 16.1 percent of stories appearing either first, second, or third. This compares favorably with their numerical representation in the sample and is a marked improvement over the 2 percent coverage of such stories reported in a 1974–1975 study.[14]

Discussion

These results are noteworthy in light of Pauline Frederick's comment in 1975 that, although opportunities for women in television news had increased over the years, "there is still a considerable distance to go until women have completely equal treatment in hiring, assignments and promotions."[15] Although trends in particular topic assignments are not yet clear due to a lack of detailed previous research, the data suggest that generally the scope and importance of women's reporting assignments have improved in recent years. But they also indicate that a measurable differential still exists in the overall coverage responsibilities of male and female reporters.

The causes of this differential should be more clearly defined by future research. Variables such as professional background or seniority no doubt affect the types of assignments made available to female correspondents. These and numerous other factors pertinent to the assignment process can be examined using more comprehensive multivariate approaches.

Here the authors discuss other variables—reasons that could help explain their findings. Social scientists realize that more than one factor is potentially involved.

Meanwhile, recalling the complaints of female reporters in the early 1970s that their coverage opportunities were being limited, news producers should consider whether they to any extent underestimate or misapply the capabilities of their female correspondents. Although rudimentary, the data in this study do imply that remnants of sexual stereotyping may still exist in the assignment of television network news stories.

References

1.   Nancy K. Gray, "Before Barbara Walters There was Dorothy Fuldheim," *Ms.* (December 1976), p. 40.

2.   "Prime Time for TV Newswomen," *Time* (21 March 1977), p. 85.

3.   Marvin Barrett, *Rich News, Poor News* (New York: Thomas Y. Crowell Co., 1978), p. 151.

4.   "Prime Time," p. 85.

5.   Judith Adler Hennessee, "What It Takes to Anchor the News." *Ms.* (August 1979), p. 93.

6.   Generally, studies have found no significant difference in the perceived credibility of males versus females; see Vernon A. Stone, "Attitudes Toward Television Newswomen," *Journal of Broadcasting* 18 (Winter 1974), p. 54; Susan Whittaker and Ron Whittaker, "Relative Effectiveness of Male and Female Newscasters," *Journal of Broadcasting* 20 (Spring 1976), p. 177; Suzanne Savary, "An Experimental Investigation of the Effect of the Medium of Communication, Sex of Source and Sex of Perceiver on Perceived Credibility of the Source" (Ph.D. dissertation, New York University, 1978).

7.   William W. Bowan, "Distaff Journalists: Women as a Minority Group in the News Media" (Ph.D. dissertation, University of Illinois at Chicago Circle, 1974).

8.   *Window Dressing on the Set: Women and Minorities in Television* (Washington, D.C.: U.S. Commission on Civil Rights, 1977), p. 51.

9. *Window Dressing on the Set: An Update* (Washington, D.C.: U.S. Commission on Civil Rights, 1979), p. 31.

10. *Television News Index and Abstracts* (Nashville, Tennessee: Vanderbilt Television News Archive, 1979).

11. The following categories were used: U.S. Government, Science, Disaster/Accident, Standard Weather Report, Crime, Labor/Economy/Business, Sports, Human Interest/People/Feature, Foreign Affairs, Consumer Protection, Social Problems, Entertainment/Culture/Arts, Institutions, Environment, Transportation, Energy, Religion, Courts, Women's Issues, Other. A single coder was used and reliability was checked by a panel of six graduate students who each coded 77 reports randomly selected from the same sample. Average agreement between the coder and panel members was 79 percent across the 20 topic categories.

12. See J. L. Bruning and B. L. Kintz, *Computational Handbook of Statistics* (Glenview, Ill.: Scott, Foresman, 1968), p. 199.

13. A similar pattern was also noted in an earlier study of network news. See *Window Dressing* (1977), p. 50.

14. Marion Marzolf, *Up From the Footnote* (New York: Hastings House, 1977), p. 197.

15. See, for example, Connie Chung's remarks in "The New Breed," *Newsweek* (30 August 1971), p. 62; Judith S. Gelfman, *Women in Television News* (New York: Columbia University Press, 1976), p. 41 and Marzolf, *op. cit.*

The Treatment and Resolution of Moral Violations on Soap Operas

by John C. Sutherland and Shelley J. Siniawsky

Soap operas have been increasingly analyzed in research journals. It is important to note that this research used content-analysis technique, but that the source is a secondary one. Rather than analyze a year's worth of episodes of All My Children *and* General Hospital, *the authors have chosen to accept the condensation in* Soap Opera Digest *as their source. Nevertheless, the findings refute one of the most often voiced objections to daytime drama: that soap operas condone or encourage immoral behavior.*

Tips and Touts

1 Note how the authors present several points of view about the moral point of view of soap operas before discussing their own findings. This is often done in research studies to help present a "balanced" perspective.

2 Note the list of 14 moral "stands" which the authors chose to represent "established" moral codes. Do you agree with all of these? How about your community at large?

3 Note in Table 4 that over 60 percent of all of the moral issues were not resolved or resolved in an unclear manner. This means that the study's conclusions are actually based on the minority of issues that were resolved.

4 In the final paragraph of the study, the authors make an excellent point that relates to all content analysis. Simply "counting" how often things occur in the media (x number of murders, for example) does not tell us nearly as much as when further analysis can be applied in some way, as has been attempted here.

John C. Sutherland is assistant professor and Shelley J. Siniawsky is a graduate student, both in the College of Journalism and Communications, University of Florida.

This article originally appeared in the Spring 1982 issue of the *Journal of Communication.* Reprinted by permission of the *Journal of Communication.*

5 The numbers at the end of the sentences in this study refer to other related studies which are listed by number at the end. Those interested in a particular point may track down the original study for more information.

As with most studies, different points of view about the question are discussed and summarized. Those interested in the studies mentioned may read them in full using information from these citations.

A frequent criticism of soap operas is that they present and condone immorality. According to Herzog (12), soap operas function as a "school of life," where moral truths are taught by example and advice. Similarly, soap operas fit into Chesebro's (4) mimetic form of communication, as a reflection of ordinary life. Over repeated exposures, some critics maintain, viewers come to believe that the behavior and moral stands to which they are exposed are socially accepted. According to Katzman (13), soap operas "suggest how people should act in certain situations. . . . They can legitimize behavior and remove taboos. . . ." As morals are treated more liberally and violators of moral standards are unpunished, so this argument goes, viewers learn more liberal and perhaps new moral standards.

Other critics take a middle ground. Modleski (14, p. 15) maintains that soap operas only introduce those issues that can be forgiven in the long run, but that soap operas may ultimately have a liberalizing effect. Comstock (5) suggests that while television program content cannot transgress established morals and beliefs, programming does flirt with nonconformity.

Finally, some critics believe that soap operas are only "propaganda for the status quo" (1, p. 43), and that soap opera content has not changed since the days of radio (8). If soap operas have such a strong effect on moral standards, these critics might ask, why have these standards changed so little over time?

The opinion of the public on the effects of soap operas on morality is mixed as well. Over half the respondents in a 1970 Canadian survey (3) believed television contributed to a breakdown of morals. In a 1971 Harris poll only 26 percent of those interviewed believed soap operas are "meant for me" (6, p. 40). Polls conducted for NBC by the Roper Organization and for ABC by the National Survey Research Group found that few viewers scorn television violence and sex (9). The Roper poll concluded, "There is little dissatisfaction with the treatment of sex, less dissatisfaction with violence, and even less sentiment for taking these programs off the air because of sex, profanity or violence." Sixty-four percent of the respondents to the ABC poll believed that "primary responsibility to determine what is acceptable belongs to the individual viewer."

Research of soap opera and other programming content has attempted to clarify the issues. Goldsen (10) and Katzman (13) analyzed soap operas to determine their moral content. These studies found plots revolving around murder, child abuse, poisonings, infidelity, illegitimacy, and incest. Durdeen-Smith's analysis of CBS and ABC soap operas found emphasis placed on moral and emotional crises rather than on characters (7, p. 19). Ryan's (16) analysis of one episode of "Kung Fu" found the major character to have a highly developed moral system; villains had less developed moral systems. Examining violent content in films, Martin (cited in 17, p. 153) argued that the effect of violence is mediated by the reason for it; violence for the sake of decency should be less "harmful" to viewers. A similar conclusion was reached in a 1976 Canadian Senate content analysis of programming (19), which maintained that strong conclusions could not be reached about television content without studying how the the audience perceived that content.

Previous research on soap operas has focused on the moral content of the programs and the number of instances in which moral dilemmas arise. However, merely tabulating the instances in which moral questions arise does not reveal how these questions were resolved. It may be that moral dilemmas are treated and resolved in a manner that is consistent with a moral code.

We selected two popular soap operas for analysis—*All My Children* and *General Hospital*, both highly rated, one-hour shows on ABC. While the results of this study clearly cannot be generalized to all soap operas, our objectives here were best met by examining popular, trend-setting soap operas which are frequently criticized. Each report of these two soap operas in issues of *Soap Opera Digest* from January 8–December 23, 1980, was analyzed. Since each issue of *Soap Opera Digest* covers about two weeks of programming or ten episodes, this study analyzed roughly 440 episodes (220 episodes per series).

While there are limitations inherent in the use of such a secondary source, only two present serious difficulties (11). First, because *Soap Opera Digest* runs several weeks behind regularly scheduled broadcasts, and the number of episodes reported in each *Digest* varies, it was impossible to determine accurately exactly when events occurred. However, this was not considered relevant to our study. The second limitation is more serious. Written capsule descriptions cannot provide all the information presented in a television broadcast. Hence subtle messages conveyed by music, facial expressions, and voice inflections could not be taken into account. Given soap operas' use of repetition and their heavy reliance on dialogue, however, this limitation was not considered a debilitating one. The benefit in using *Soap Opera Digest* was that it permitted analysis

The question of "moral points of view" is raised often in media research. Perhaps you have one particular favorite program. Can you see any implications here for the characters on that show?

Here the authors must deal with the fact that using Soap Opera Digest is not exactly the same as watching the shows themselves. However they feel that the differences are not significant enough when compared with the benefit of being able to "monitor" the shows for such a lengthy period. This is a methodological "short cut"; such practices are common in research. Can you think of any problems such a short cut might pose?

of a full year of programming, which we considered necessary to allow story lines to reach resolutions. The time and costs of analyzing one year of broadcasts would have been prohibitive.

Moral standards are difficult to define because they differ among individuals and they are continuously evolving. We reviewed soap opera criticism and discovered 14 moral standards frequently claimed by critics to be violated on soap operas.

1. Premarital/extramarital sex is wrong (8, 10, 13, 14, 15).
2. Bigamy is extramarital sex and wrong (10, 13).
3. Children should be born in wedlock (8, 10, 13, 15).
4. Abortion is wrong (8, 14, 15).
5. Incest is wrong (18).
6. Rape is wrong (15).
7. Divorce must be carefully considered and not rushed into (10, 14, 15).
8. Parents should not neglect their children (10).
9. Children should obey their parents (15).
10. Alcohol abuse/addiction is wrong (8, 14).
11. Drug abuse/addiction is wrong (13, 15).
12. Deception of others is wrong (5).
13. Blackmail is wrong (13, 14).
14. Murder is wrong (13).

Each instance of a moral violation was coded according to the action taken. Instances in which the character intended to violate a moral but took no action were coded as "intended"— for example, if a character purchased a gun to commit murder but did not attempt the murder. Instances in which a character attempted an action that violated a moral standard but was unsuccessful were coded as "attempted"—for example, if a character fired a weapon at a victim with the intent to kill, but missed; or if a male attacked a female with the intent to rape, but was stopped by another character's intervention. Instances were coded as "actual" if a character carried out an action that violated a moral standard.

Treatment, or what happens to the character who violates a moral, was coded into three categories. Treatment was considered "condoned" if a character's immoral action was supported either socially or economically in the story line. For example, if one who violated a moral standard was agreed with or offered aid, this was considered a "condoned" treatment. When Palmer and Myra allowed Daisy to remain in Pine Valley without revealing her true identity to Nina on *All My Children*, they "condoned" her deceit. Treatment was "not condoned" when immoral action was opposed, as, for example, when the transgressing character was "warned" by another, was "suspected," or suffered social or economic penalties. This category was also indicated by emotional reactions, such as guilt, shock, or worry. Complications, such as a "close call" or an argument, also indicated treatment that was "not condoned." Finally, "not indicated" covered a situation in which the violation was mentioned but no reaction was described. For example, a reporter told Anne the details of Paul's affair with Ellen on *All My Children*, but according to the description Anne did not exhibit emotion or use the information in any way.

Every story involving a moral dilemma was examined for the moral lesson in its conclusion. This concluding lesson was the resolution. If the resolution was punishment, the resolution was coded as "consistent"; if the resolution was reward, it was coded as "inconsistent." For example, on *All My Children*, Claudette Montgomery killed Eddie Dorrance. Although she was not accused of murder for six months, others began to suspect her. When Claudette was chased by the police, she drove her car into a river. She died in the hospital after confessing. Since Claudette was punished for her actions, this resolution was coded as being "consistent" with the moral injunction "do not kill." If a character violated a moral injunction but was rewarded, the resolution was coded as "inconsistent" with the moral code. In some instances the resolution was coded as "not clear." On *General Hospital*, for instance, Mitch and Susan had an affair. There was no clear reward or punishment; the affair ended because of extraneous circumstances. Finally, story lines not resolved by the end of the *Soap Opera Digest* year were coded as "not resolved."

There were 68 instances of moral issues coded, 36 on *All My Children* and 32 on *General Hospital*. As shown in Table 1, deceit was the most frequently raised moral issue, followed by murder and premarital and extramarital sex. No other moral issue arose more than five times. Neither incest, illegitimacy, nor bigamy was addressed. As a result, all moral issues except deceit, murder, and sex were collapsed into an "all other" category for analysis.

Table 2 shows that the majority (72.1 percent) of the moral issues involved actual violations: someone told a lie; someone murdered someone; or someone had premarital or extramarital sex. The remaining instances involved intent to violate a moral injunction (19.1 percent) or attempted violations (8.8 percent). The majority of situations involving murder led to intended or

It is common practice to give examples of situations and how they affected the collection of the data. Obviously some subjectivity on the part of the researchers is called for here, in terms of how they categorized what they saw. Such subjectivity may influence a study's findings.

In other words, when examining the "moral issues" they had identified, the plot resolutions usually involved some rejection of the notion that it was "O.K." to lie or cheat in some way.

attempted violations; most of the instances involving other moral issues resulted in actual violations.

There were 489 treatments of moral issues, 298 on *All My Children* and 191 on *General Hospital*, an average of 7.19 treatments per moral. As shown in Table 3, the majority of moral violations (64 percent) were not condoned, more than the combined number of treatments condoning the violation and treatments where the stand taken was not indicated. The percentage of treatments condoned on *General Hospital* was greater than on *All My Children*, as was the percentage of situations in which the stand was not indicated. However, for both soap operas, more than half the treatments did not condone the moral violation.

Of the 68 instances of moral issues raised, 44.1 percent were not resolved during the time frame of this study (see Table 4).

Table 1: Moral Issues Addressed by *All My Children* and *General Hospital*

Moral issues	n	%	Moral issues	n	%
Deceit	20	29.4	Drinking	1	1.5
Murder	16	23.5	Child obedience	1	1.5
Premarital/extramarital sex	11	16.2	Parents must not neglect		
Blackmail	5	7.4	their children	1	1.5
Drugs	4	5.9	Incest	0	0.0
Other	4	5.9	Illegitimacy	0	0.0
Divorce	2	2.9	Bigamy	0	0.0
Rape	2	2.9			
Abortion	1	1.5	Total	68	100.1

Table 2: Moral Issues by Type of Violation on *All My Children* and *General Hospital*

	Intended		Type of Violation Attempted		Actual	
Moral issue	n	% of total	n	% of total	n	% of total
Deceit	1	5.0	0	0.0	19	95.0
Murder	9	56.3	2	12.5	5	31.2
Sex	2	18.2	0	0.0	9	81.8
All others	1	4.8	4	19.0	16	76.2
All moral issues	13	19.1	6	8.8	49	72.1

$\chi^2 = 19.691$, df = 6, p < .05. Blalock's (2) correction for continuity was used for small expected values.

Of the remaining 38, 56.1 percent were resolved in a manner consistent with moral standards, 18.4 percent were resolved inconsistently with moral standards, and 29 percent were resolved in an ambiguous way. The majority of the latter violations involved deceit and the "all other" category, which included the more controversial issues. No difference in resolution was found between soap operas. Nor were there differences in the type of resolutions among the different moral violations. Regardless of type, moral violations tended to be resolved consistently with moral standards.

While there was no significant difference between male and female characters in terms of the percentage of violations committed, there was such a difference for the types of morals they violated. As shown in Table 5, male characters were more often involved with murder, while female characters were more often involved with deceit.

While it is true that moral issues are frequently discussed on these soap operas, the most frequently raised moral issues—murder, deceit, and sex—have always been the mainstay of dramatic conflict. More controversial moral topics, such as incest, illegitimacy, bigamy, abortion, and drugs, were rarely raised.

This is interesting in light of the fact that we usually assume these issues are soap opera staples.

Table 3: Treatment of Moral Issues on *All My Children* and *General Hospital*

	All My Children		General Hospital		Total	
	n	%	n	%	n	%
Condoned	41	13.7	31	16.2	72	14.7
Not condoned	203	68.1	110	57.6	313	64.0
Not indicated	54	18.1	50	26.1	104	21.3
Total	298	99.9	191	99.9	489	100.0

Table 4: Resolution of Moral Issues on *All My Children* and *General Hospital*

	n	% of total	% of total resolved
Resolved consistent with moral standards	20	29.4	52.6
Resolved inconsistent with moral standards	7	10.3	18.4
Resolution not clear	11	16.2	29.0
Not resolved	30	44.1	—
Total	68	100.0	100.0

**Table 5: Sex of Characters
(Perpetrators) Involved in Moral Issues
on *All My Children* and *General Hospital***

Moral issue	Male n	Female n	Total n
Deceit	7	14	21
Murder	14	2	16
Sex	6	8	14
All others	14	7	21
Total	41	31	72

$\chi^2 = 12.81$, df = 3, p < .05.

The soap operas analyzed also tend to punish those who violate moral standards, either socially or economically; they support the status quo. Although almost half the violations were not resolved during our one-year time period, those that were resolved tended to be resolved consistently with "traditional" moral standards. Many of the resolutions were left open to viewers' interpretations; traditional attitude theory would suggest that the audience is most likely to perceive such situations in a manner consistent with their existing beliefs and morals, which should further support the status quo. Many of these instances tended to involve the more controversial moral issues.

There are instances, although they constituted a minority, when soap operas do allow a person who violates a moral to "get away with it." Some characters do "get away with" murder, deceit, and/or premarital or extramarital sex.

In sum, the issue of soap operas' presentation of moral issues is not as clear-cut as many would have the public believe. Research that simply counts the number of instances in which moral issues are raised without taking into account the treatment and resolution of these issues adds little to an understanding of the interaction of soap opera content and societal morals.

References

1. Barnouw, E. "Television as a Medium," *Performance*, July/August 1972.

2. Blalock, H. M., Jr. *Social Statistics* (2d ed.). New York: McGraw-Hill, 1972.

3. Canadian Government, Special Senate Committee on Mass Media. *Mass Media*, Volume 3: *Good, Bad or Simply Inevitable*. Ottawa, Ontario: Queen's Printer for Canada, 1970.

4. Chesebro, J. "Communication, Values, and Popular TV Series—A Four-Year Assessment." In G. Gumpert and R. Cathcart (Eds.) *Inter-Media: Interpersonal Communication in a Media World*. New York: Oxford University Press, 1979.

5. Comstock, G. *Television in America*. Beverly Hills, Cal.: Sage, 1980.

6. "Do We Like What We Watch?" *Life* 71(11), September 10, 1971.

7. Durdeen-Smith, J. "Daytime TV—Soft-Soaping the American Woman," *Village Voice*, February 8, 1973.

8. Edmondson, M. and D. Rounds. *From* Mary Noble *to* Mary Hartman: *The Complete Soap Opera Book*. New York: Stein and Day, 1976.

9. "Few Scorn TV Sex, Violence," *Tampa Tribune*, June 20, 1981.

10. Goldsen, R. K. *The Show and Tell Machine: How Television Works and Works You Over*. New York: Dial Press, 1977.

11. Gordon, Ruth. *Soap Opera Digest*. Telephone interview, April 17, 1980.

12. Herzog, H. "Daytime Serials." In P. Lazarsfeld and F. Stanton (Eds.) *Radio Research 1942–1943*. New York: Essential Books, 1944.

13. Katzman, N. "Television Soap Operas: What's Been Going on Anyway?" *Public Opinion Quarterly* 36(2), 1972, pp. 200–212.

14. Modleski, T. "The Search for Tomorrow in Today's Soap Operas." *Film Quarterly* 33, Fall 1979.

15. Ramsdell, M. L. "The Trauma of TV's Troubled Soap Families." *The Family Coordinator*, July 1973.

16. Ryan, K. "TV as a Moral Educator." In D. Cater and R. Adler (Eds.) *Television as a Social Force: New Approaches to TV Criticism*. New York: Praeger, 1976.

17. Skornia, H. J. *Television and Society*. New York: McGraw-Hill, 1965.

18. Soares, M. *The Soap Opera Book*. New York: Harmony Books, 1978.

19. Williams, T. M., M. L. Zabrack, and L. A. Joy. "A Content Analysis of Entertainment TV Programs." *Report of the Royal Commission on Violence in the Communication Industry*, Volume 3. Ottawa, Ontario: J. C. Thatcher, Queen's Printer for Canada, 1976.

Popular Music: Resistance to New Wave

by James Lull

There are a number of things that make this article unique. New-wave music specifically and popular music in general are rarely the subjects of empirical research. The technique involved in gathering the research data involves the formation of a questionnaire designed to measure the attitudes and preferences of a group. The author has attempted to solve one of the most vexing problems of mass communication, and of popular culture, namely: What attitudes impede the acceptance of a new popular art form?

James Lull is assistant professor in the Department of Speech, University of California at Santa Barbara, and program director, KTYD-FM, Santa Barbara.

This article originally appeared in the Winter 1982 issue of the *Journal of Communication*. Reprinted by permission of the *Journal of Communication*.

Tips and Touts

1 As with the previous study, the numbers at the end of the sentences refer to other related studies which are listed by number at the end. That way those interested in a particular point may track down the original study for additional scrutiny.

2 In the first few paragraphs, the authors comment on the relationship between British bands and their culture, and note that their impact here may be different because of the differences between Britain and the United States.

3 This article was written in 1981. If it were updated, do you think the authors would find more or less acceptance of new wave? Why?

4 Note how the author's findings that the "beat" was the most important aspect of these songs is consistent with the material you read in Chapter 7.

5 Table 3 lists the responses to "open-ended" questions about the differences between new wave and traditional popular music. Open-ended questions allow the audience to respond in any way they choose, hence researchers gather more in-depth information that is harder to classify and categorize. Closed-ended questions simply give research subjects the

chance to respond yes or no, agree or disagree, or choose one of several options: A, B, C . . . This information is easier to categorize and classify but it does not tell us as much as open-ended responses, since the response range has been dictated by the researchers rather than the subjects themselves.

As rock and roll music has shifted from subcultural status into the mainstream of popular culture, it has distributed messages of social deviance, class consciousness, and even revolution to a wide audience. In the process, exotic subcultural values may have been legitimized (30) and social class relations identified and interpreted (9). The very origins of rock and roll music in the United States and England are class-related, grounded in the day-to-day experiences of working-class white and black youth (29). Advanced sound-recording techniques and the emergence of specialized radio formats in the United States have extended the range of rock music's influence by transporting the sounds to young middle- and upper-class listeners. However, the proliferation of a new form of subcultural music, known as new wave, is meeting with resistance from two principal sources—culture industries that are inclined to produce only "safe" marketplace commodities and audience members who have yet to accept the unfamiliar sounds.

In England, the relationship between working-class youth and music has been a colorful one. Unconventional British youth of the 1950s (teddy boys), the 1960s (rockers, mods, skinheads), and the 1970s and 1980s (punks) have used forms of rock and roll, including its nonmusical cultural features, as objects of communal symbolic resistance to a class-based social system that provokes feelings of economic despair (16, 32). Many of England's first punk-rock bands such as the Sex Pistols and the Clash wrote and recorded fierce anthems that denounced perceived government-enforced practices of socioeconomic injustice. The punk movement in England has been noted for its oppositional "extremism" (loud, short, up-tempo songs created by men and women who wear short, spiky haircuts, tattered clothing, and safety pins piercing the skin). Political and social consciousness continues to be reflected in the lyrics of music made by British bands such as the Gang of Four and Au Pairs, during what has been termed a period of "post-punk pop avant-garde" (27).

More generally, punk rock and its up-tempo musical derivatives represent what is now widely labeled new-wave music. Much of this music is based on distinctive, evocative sounds

The relationship between economics and rock and roll has firm roots in England but seems less pronounced here. However, some recent songs and videos (Billy Joel's Uptown Girl) have dealt with these issues in America.

that derive from black-originated reggae and ska bassline-oriented rhythms combined with tempered British punk music (15). The music is still characterized by fastness and clarity of beat, features believed to have special appeal to youthful working-class audiences (34).

There is empirical evidence to support the conclusion that U.S. audiences are not united behind the emerging musical form as a medium for the expression of unified, class-based social protest (6, 10). While various identifiable themes appear in the lyrics of popular songs at different historical periods (3, 14), and although these themes sometimes reflect social protest (5, 13), there is some evidence that today's audiences do not listen carefully to lyrics (7, 8). Indeed, the widespread acceptance of new wave's immediate predecessors—apolitical rhythm and blues music, heavy metal rock, and disco—reflects an apparent preoccupation by audience members with the sound of the music rather than its lyrics.

This point was discussed in this book in Chapter 7.

The recording industry, like other culture industries, typically avoids contractual agreements with "high risk" products such as nontraditional musical forms (22). Consequently, many new-wave artists and groups have been shunned by the major record labels and have been forced to sign with small, independent companies, if they can find support at all (20). These small recording companies may not be able to market their product effectively because of their small budgets for promotion.

Although it is difficult to measure with validity the popularity of music (17), it is generally understood that sales depend on exposure (19). The principal medium for exposure, of course, is radio. There is clear evidence that fragmentation is taking place in radio in terms of the numbers of different formats on the air (*Broadcasting*, Aug. 25, 1980, p. 52; 31), the music and other program content that define the formats (1, 18), the demography of subaudiences (26, 28), and the media consumption patterns of listeners to the various popular formats (25). Ultimately, the subdividing of the overall radio audience may help separate and legitimate subcultures through differential listening patterns characteristic of different age groups (21).

Nevertheless, a major factor in the continued lack of popular acceptance of new-wave music in the United States is that the songs are not regularly played on the radio. The predicament faced by new-wave artists attempting to receive exposure via radio is somewhat remindful of the relationship between progressive rock music and FM radio in the 1960s. At that time, however, owners of FM stations were more willing to experiment with the profit potential of programming the "radical" new music, since many frequency-modulated stations were financially impoverished.

At present, the most likely outlet for airplay of new-wave music is the popular album-oriented rock stations (formerly progressive rock stations), but programmers of these stations have resisted playing the hard-edged new music. New-wave music, like other innovative subcultural materials, may soften over time in order to be absorbed into media systems managed by the culture producers (2). New-wave recording artists, independent record companies, and alternative radio stations and record stores already have an impact on the popular music market from its periphery, but entry to the popular consciousness is still likely to be fundamentally controlled by mainstream recording artists and their corporate recording and distributional networks. Nonetheless, access to the new sounds has not been completely stifled.

I assessed the impact of this new musical form on a major component of the U.S. record-buying public—college students. Media habits, musical preferences, and attitudes toward new-wave music were ascertained by means of a series of fixed-item and open-ended questions that were asked of 375 students at the University of California, Santa Barbara. Respondents were member of a large introductory communications class who completed questionnaires during the first class meeting. They were young (97 percent between 18 and 24), Caucasian (94 percent), and generally from middle- to upper-middle-class homes. There was no reason to suspect that course content or other external factors influenced the results.

Using a Likert-type scale, I asked respondents to evaluate their feelings toward "traditional, mainstream rock-and-roll music" and toward "new-wave music." The findings indicate that students still prefer "traditional" rock-and-roll music to new-wave music (t = 12.55, df = 374, p < .001). No obvious systematic explanatory factors were found. Men and women did not differ in their attitudes toward either traditional or new-wave rock music. Quantitative ratings of new-wave music were uncorrelated with attitudes toward mainstream rock and roll and uncorrelated with the amount of time spent with radio, records, and tapes. Further, one-way analyses of variance revealed no significant effect of political identification on respondents' attitudes toward new-wave music. Political orientation (expressed as conservative, liberal, independent, or don't know/care, rather than party affiliation) was likewise

The Likert scale is one standard way of measuring the degree of subject like or dislike of some phenomenon.

Table 1: Respondent Identification of New-Wave Artists and Groups (n = 375)

Rank	Artist/group	f	% of sample mentioning artist/group
1	B-52s	180	48
2	Devo	148	40
3	Blondie	144	38
4	Pretenders	128	34
5	Elvis Costello	124	33
6	Cars	85	23
7.5	Talking Heads	49	13
7.5	Clash	49	13
9	X	41	11
10.5	Motels	37	10
10.5	Joe Jackson	37	10

unrelated to attitudes toward traditional rock-and-roll music and unrelated to amount of time spent with radio, records, and tapes.

In general, when asked to list their favorite artists, college students mentioned those who made their reputations in music many years ago. The top-rated recording group was the Beatles, a band that had been dissolved for more than 10 years at the time the data were gathered. Other preferred groups, such as the original Genesis and Crosby, Stills and Nash, are no longer recording music. Several of the more popular performers began to achieve their popularity in the 1960s (Rolling Stones, The Who, Led Zeppelin, James Taylor, Neil Young, Fleetwood Mac) or the early 1970s (Jackson Browne, Kenny Loggins, Supertramp, Eagles, Doobie Brothers, Bruce Springsteen).

Only one new-wave artist, Elvis Costello, was ranked among the top 20 favorites. New-wave bands apparently are not yet competitive with established traditional rock acts or the musical vestiges of former groups. When asked on an open-ended question to name new-wave artists or bands (Table 1), 94 percent of the sample could name at least one, and 59 percent could name as many as five; but even the most frequently named of these new-wave artists (B-52s, Devo) were rarely mentioned as overall favorites.

Each student was given an opportunity to establish and express his or her own criteria for defining new-wave music. The typology that appears in Table 2 was constructed by distilling the written open-ended definitions into categories. The

Table 2: Respondents' Descriptions of New-Wave Music

Characteristic	No. of mentions	Characteristic	No. of mentions
Total mentions	728	Cultural phenomenon	
		Unique culture, lifestyle	20
General		Bands look unusual	20
Primitive, crude, simple	39	Faddish	10
Original, different	38	Bands act unusual	6
Bizarre, exotic, strange	30	Subtotal	56
Rebellious, antisocial	24	% of total mentions	8
Meaningless, vacuous,		Music	
stupid	23	Repetitious, constant,	
Cynical, negative,		monotonous beat	66
sarcastic	19	Fast, upbeat, energetic	65
Violent, aggressive	11	Dance, jump, pogo	34
Expressive	7	Technological, synthesized	33
Vulgar	3	Harsh instrumentation	10
Subtotal	194	Different vocals	3
% of total mentions	27	Harsh vocals	2
		Subtotal	229
Genre		% of total mentions	32
New form of rock music	49	Lyrics	
Sounds like '50s and '60s		Social/political comment	31
music	41	Original, different	12
Is punk rock	39	Strange	11
Between rock and		Harsh	4
punk rock	39	Can't understand	4
Of British origin	16	Simple	3
Subtotal	184	Subtotal	65
% of total mentions	25	% of total mentions	9

first three identifiable comments from each respondent's written remarks that defined the genre were coded and placed into one of 32 categories. Using this approach, 92 percent of the sample could render at least one definition of new-wave music.

Many of the comments, which fell into five major areas, were of a general nature, referring to the new music in terms not obviously related to particular attributes of its technical structure or content. These remarks reflected a fundamental belief that the music is unusual, forceful, and undesirable.

Many respondents defined new-wave music in terms of its historical or aesthetic location. Some said that they believed new wave was simply a new form of rock music; that it resembles British hardcore punk music; or that it is a contemporary derivative of the rock and roll of the 1950s and/or 1960s.

The remaining three definitional categories provide more specific information. The largest share of comments defined

The table of open-ended responses above allows us to get a good sense of how the students perceived the music in question. Note how many times certain words and phrases emerged.

new-wave music in terms of its *sound*. The most frequently mentioned definitional feature of new-wave music was the *beat*, described as repetitious, constant, monotonous, fast, or energetic. Further, respondents believed that the definite beat made the music especially danceable, although new-wave dancing is characterized more by the pogo (vertical jumping) or the skank (simple rhythmic motion of the arms and hips) than by sophisticated dance floor maneuvers. Little emphasis was placed on the vocal textures of the music or on its lyrical content. Some respondents said that the lyrics contain social or political commentary. Others considered them to be original, different, or strange.

A very small number of the comments defined new-wave music in a way that distinguished it as a distinctive subculture or lifestyle; few respondents made a connection between the music and its relation to social class. This content analysis of listener responses, therefore, shows that new-wave music is being defined primarily by its sound or general characteristics rather than by its lyrics or subcultural associations.

Note here how the sound and the beat—the form aspects of the music—were mentioned as opposed to the content factors, such as lyrics.

Using procedures similar to those used in Table 2, 86 percent of the sample was able to provide at least one meaningful comment to describe what they perceived as a difference between new wave and traditional rock music (see Table 3). Comments about the sound of new-wave music in contrast to traditional rock music accounted for half of the remarks made. Again, respondents were particularly likely to mention the beat, calling it more repetitive, definite, monotonous, faster, more pronounced, or just different from mainstream rock music. Remarks about lyrical content were about half as numerous and reflected some awareness of the critical or revolutionary nature of some new-wave songs. The genre was recognized as more active, unusual, and violent than mainstream rock and roll. Very few respondents distinguished the two rock forms in terms of cultural or lifestyle attributes.

The final open-ended question asked for respondents' personal feelings about new-wave music. No quantification of these data was made because of the nonspecificity of the question. Nonetheless, the comments made can be interpreted thematically. They reveal perhaps the most interesting dimensions of personal resistance to and acceptance of new-wave music, since they allowed respondents to report freely their own sentiments. The question seems to be a more direct measure of attitude than were the definitional indices.

Mood. A frequent comment was that new-wave music was acceptable only when the respondent was in the "right mood."

Table 3: Respondents' Descriptions of How New-Wave Music Differs from Traditional Rock and Roll

Difference	No. of mentions	Difference	No. of mentions
Total mentions	706	Music	
General		Harder, faster, more	
Less talent required	20	pronounced beat	69
More crude, blatant	17	More repetitious,	
More disturbing,		definite beat	68
irritating	16	Different beat	41
More bizarre, weird	16	More instrumentation,	
More active, wild, intense	16	noisy	41
More violent, hostile,		Simpler, cleaner	34
aggressive	15	More vocal variation	25
More creative,		More danceable	22
imaginative	13	Less melodic	20
More involving	10	No solos, leads	14
More relaxing	8	Less instrumentation	12
More seductive, sensual	5	Variety of beats involved	10
More fun	5	Subtotal	356
More future-oriented	5	% of total mentions	50
Subtotal	146	Lyrics	
% of total mentions	21	More critical, revolutionary	47
Cultural phenomenon		Wider or narrower content	41
Different culture,		Less meaningful	30
lifestyle	22	Less romantic	12
Stranger appearance		Simpler	11
of band	18	Less understandable	10
More trendy, faddish	10	Harsher	3
Subtotal	50	Subtotal	154
% of total mentions	7	% of total mentions	22

Descriptors of the appropriate mood for enjoying new-wave music were: rowdy, crazy, radical, energetic, hyped-up, when you feel like fooling around, when you want to dance, when you're drunk or stoned. So, the music is considered acceptable by some listeners under certain conditions having to do with mood.

History. Many people said that they already had their musical preferences in place and would not permit new-wave music to disturb loyalties to their pre-established favorites. Some listeners believed that new-wave rock and roll is an "attack" on established rock and roll, and some recognized their defensiveness. One male respondent said:

Sometimes I feel like my parents and how they feel towards what I listen to. So, maybe I'm getting old-fashioned in my early twenties,

Hardly an original finding, but an interesting one. Think of how your own mood often dictates the type of music that you prefer.

for I prefer the music I grew up with (soft rock and roll) and I'm set in my ways. I think I now understand why my parents like the classical music they grew up with.

Traditional rock music may represent a kind of security to some young listeners whose preferences were formed during their pre-adolescent and adolescent years.

Confusion. Many respondents said that they did not understand what new-wave music means and therefore they did not like it. Comments such as "it makes no sense," "has no value," "is too complex," "can't identify with it," "is too abstract," or "sounds stupid" were common.

Lifestyle. New-wave music is considered by some young people to be more than just a preference for a particular kind of music. The subcultural features of the genre extend toward what is described as an intense, alienated lifestyle. The subculture was described as "sick," "kinky," or "not fun." The dancing was said to be violent and the clothes worn by "new wavers" were described as "like a costume. They think it's Halloween all the time." Several respondents indicated that to appreciate new-wave music a set of preconditions for entrance into the alternative lifestyle must be met. These include at least clothing, dance style, and peculiar social attitudes.

Social function. Certain personal or social objectives typically facilitated by music cannot be met with new-wave music, according to several respondents. Those who believe that music is an agent for relaxing or romanticizing were generally convinced that new-wave music is not attractive. These reasons were sufficient for many of them to consider new wave inappropriate for some of the roles music plays in their lives.

Emotional discomfort. The experience of listening to new-wave music creates intense and uncomfortable emotional (and sometimes physiological) feelings for some people. The music was often described by these persons as angry, negative, weird, critical, or even warlike. These people claimed to feel tense, unsettled, annoyed, unpleasant, or haunted after listening to new-wave music; many said it gave them a headache. One woman reported that she invariably has nightmares after listening to new-wave music.

Frivolity. A final major classification indicates that many listeners do not take new-wave music seriously. They consider it "funny," "a joke," or "an opportunity for normal people to go crazy for a little while." New-wave music is regarded by some of these listeners as a temporary escape from their regular experiences with music, but not as a competitor for their loy-

Popular music, like all media form and content, offers the audience a chance to escape from their own everyday lives and enter the world of mediated reality.

alties to particular artists, groups, or types of music.

Although many more objected to new-wave music than liked it, many students did indicate curiosity, interest, or excitement about its newness and uniqueness. These people often said they liked it simply because it was different. Many of them were intrigued by some of the same attributes of the music that negatively affected other respondents. Some expressed a belief that new wave is "this generation's music." Since most new-wave artists are young and the sound differs noticeably from traditional rock and roll music, these respondents may be identifying with new wave as a cultural phenomenon that they can help create rather than simply inherit. The perceived complexity or sophistication of the music, including its lyrics, fascinated some listeners. Many said they appreciated its energy and excitement, referring to the music as "vital," "stimulating," "refreshing," "fun," or music that "sets me free." Some listeners claimed to find beauty in the vulgarity of the more hardcore elements of new-wave music. Others remarked that new wave helps create a social awareness that they find necessary.

Many respondents said that they had become less opposed to new-wave music after listening to it several times. This exposure was typically facilitated by friends who were often devotees of the new music. These friendship networks and their opinion leaders eventually may help popularize new-wave music.

Although ideological themes persist in the lyrics of some contemporary new-wave music, this audience did not respond primarily to the lyrics and themes of class domination that some of the songs contain. Similarly, the agitated beat of new-wave music was widely noticed but not ideologically interpreted. The fundamental characteristic for young listeners appears to be the overall sound, especially the beat, rather than the lyrical content (see also 29). If there is differentiation in response to new-wave music, it may lead listeners to react as politically benign taste cultures (4, 11, 23) rather than as class cultures (24) or social strata.

The data presented here indicate that the new music may not meet a primary functional expectation of audiences for popular music, at least for college-aged listeners—to make them feel relaxed or happy (12). Younger listeners in junior high and high school, another active component of the record-buying public, may find new wave more satisfying or serving different needs if their tastes are less well-formed than college-age listeners. The functional roles too could change (see also 33), as many recent new-wave albums are softer in texture and presumably more attractive and accessible to the record-buying

As with all media content, there are a number of factors that determine the acceptance or rejection of a particular artistic force or practice. Obviously those factors center around the cultural and social backgrounds of the audience.

public than were the early songs. The buzzsaw sound of the pioneer element of new wave, punk rock, generally has been supplanted by more melodic arrangements. Some new-wave bands such as the highly recognized B-52s rely completely on festive melodies and apolitical lyrics.

New-wave music has achieved a notable degree of familiarity among the listeners sampled here, but many objections to it, grounded in the personal, social, and cultural predispositions of audience members, apparently have curtailed its widespread acceptance. Although new-wave music has some unique characteristics, obstacles that impede its popular acceptance may not differ much from those that confront other cultural phenomena. The resistance observed among audience members and in the day-to-day practices of culture producers and distributors must be overcome if the genre is to transcend its subcultural status and extend its range of influence.

References

1. Anderson, Bruce, Peter Hesbacher, K. Peter Etzkorn, and R. Serge Denisoff. "Hit Record Trends, 1940–1977." *Journal of Communication* 30(2), Spring 1980, pp. 31–43.

2. Cantor, Muriel G. *Prime-Time Television: Content and Control.* Beverly Hills, Cal.: Sage, 1980.

3. Carey, James. "The Ideology of Autonomy in Popular Lyrics: A Content Analysis." *Psychiatry* 32(2), May 1969, pp. 150–164.

4. Carey, James and Albert Kreiling. "Popular Culture and Uses and Gratifications: Notes Toward an Accommodation." In Jay G. Blumler and Elihu Katz (Eds.) *The Uses of Mass Communication.* Beverly Hills, Cal.: Sage, 1974, pp. 225–246.

5. Cole, Richard. "Top Songs in the Sixties: A Content Analysis of Popular Lyrics." *American Behavioral Scientist* 14(3), January–February 1971, pp. 389–400.

6. Dancis, Bruce. "Safety Pins and Class Struggle: Punk Rock and the American Left." *Socialist Review* 8(2), May–June 1978, pp. 156–181.

7. Denisoff, R. Serge and Mark H. Levine. "Generations and Counterculture: A Study in the Ideology of Music." *Youth and Society* 2(1), September 1970, pp. 33–58.

8. Denisoff, R. Serge and Mark H. Levine. "The Popular Protest Songs: The Case of 'Eve of Destruction.' " *Public Opinion Quarterly* 35(1), Spring 1971, pp. 117–122.

9. Denisoff, R. Serge and Richard A. Peterson. *The Sounds of Social Change.* Chicago: Rand-McNally, 1972.

10. Dixon, Richard D., Fred R. Ingram, Richard M. Levinson, and Catherine L. Putnam. "The Cultural Diffusion of Punk Rock in the United States." *Popular Music and Society* 6(3), 1979, pp. 21–28.

11. Gans, Herbert. *Popular Culture and High Culture: An Analysis and Evaluation of Taste.* New York: Basic Books, 1974.

12. Gantz, Walter, Howard M. Gartenberg, Martin L. Pearson, and Seth O. Schiller. "Gratifications and Expectations Associated with Pop Music Among Adolescents." *Popular Music and Society* 6(1), 1978, pp. 81–89.

13. Gray, J. Patrick. "Rock as a Chaos Model Ritual." *Popular Music and Society* 7(2), 1980, pp. 75–83.

14. Harmon, James. "The New Music and Counter Culture Values." *Youth and Society* 4(1), September 1972, pp. 61–83.

15. Hebdige, Dick. "Reggae, Rastas and Rudies." In James Curran, Michael Gurevitch, and Janet Woollacott (Eds.) *Mass Communication and Society.* Beverly Hills, Cal.: Sage, 1979, pp. 426–439.

16. Hebdige, Dick. *Subculture: The Meaning of Style.* London: Methuen, 1979.

17. Hesbacher, Peter. "Sound Exposure in Radio: The Misleading Nature of the Station Playlist." *Popular Music and Society* 3(2), 1974, pp. 189–201.

18. Hesbacher, Peter, Nancy Clasby, Bruce Anderson, and David G. Berger. "Radio Format Strategies," *Journal of Communication* 26(1), Winter 1976, pp. 110–119.

19. Hesbacher, Peter, Robert Downing, and David G. Berger. "Record Roulette: What Makes It Spin?" *Journal of Communication* 25(3), Summer 1975, pp. 74–85.

20. Hilburn, Robert. "X Marks the Heart of L.A.'s Rock Scene." *Los Angeles Times*, June 22, 1980.

21. Hirsch, Paul M. "The Economics of Rock." *The Nation*, March 9, 1970.

22. Hirsch, Paul M. "Processing Fads and Fashions: An Organization Set Analysis of Cultural Industry Systems." *American Journal of Sociology* 77(4), January 1972, pp. 639–659.

23. Kreiling, Albert. "Toward a Cultural Studies Approach for the Sociology of Popular Culture." *Communication Research* 5(3), July 1978, pp. 240–263.

24. Lewis, George H. "Taste Cultures and Culture Classes in Mass Society." *International Review of the Aesthetics and Sociology of Music* 8(1), 1977, pp. 39–48.

25. Lull, James, Lawrence M. Johnson, and Donald Edmond. "Radio Listeners' Electronic Media Habits." *Journal of Broadcasting* 25(1), Winter 1981, pp. 1–12.

26. Lull, James, Lawrence M. Johnson, and Carol Sweeny. "Audiences for Contemporary Radio Formats." *Journal of Broadcasting* 22(4), Fall 1978, pp. 439–453.

27. Marcus, Greil. "Wake Up!" *Rolling Stone*, July 24, 1980.

28. Peterson, Richard A. and Russell B. Davis, Jr. "The Contemporary American Radio Audience." *Popular Music and Society* 3(4), 1974, pp. 299–314.

29. Robinson, John and Paul Hirsch. "It's the Sound That Does It." In Leonard L. Sellers and William L. Rivers (Eds.) *Mass Media Issues.* Englewood Cliffs, N.J.: Prentice-Hall, 1977, pp. 153–158.

30. Robinson, John, Robert Pilskaln, and Paul Hirsch. "Protest Rock and Drugs." *Journal of Communication* 26(4), Fall 1976, pp. 125–136.

31. Routt, Edd, James B. McGrath, and Frederic A. Weiss. *The Radio Format Conundrum.* New York: Hastings House, 1978.

32. Tanner, Julian. "Pop, Punk and Subcultural Solutions." *Popular Music and Society* 6(1), 1978, pp. 68–71.

33. Tillman, Robert. "Punk Rock and the Construction of 'Pseudo-Political' Movements." *Popular Music and Society* 7(3), 1980, pp. 165–175.

34. Willis, Paul. "The Triple X Boys." *New Society* 23(547), 1973, pp. 693–695.

ISSUES AND ANSWERS: MASS-COMMUNICATION RESEARCH AND YOU

You've now had the opportunity to read a few of the hundreds of mass-communication research studies that are published each year. Such research is important because it represents the only way that we can go beyond speculation and our own aesthetic responses and make definitive statements about the effects of mass communication.

A number of complex issues involving mass communication face us today. We need to know more about how TV affects children and how newspapers influence our political decisions. We need to know how women pictured in magazine ads affect our perception of women and our interpersonal relationships in general. We may speculate all we like about these things, but until we have

definitive research along the lines of the examples presented here, we can't be sure what to do about it all. To put it as plainly as possible, we need more legitimate mass-communication research, and we need it to be as concise as possible.

To accomplish this, we'll eventually need a lot of help from students like yourselves. Those of you considering teaching careers should think seriously about the possibility of contributing to efforts such as those presented here. Each completed study adds something to our total knowledge and takes us one step closer to a true, comprehensive understanding of the mass-communication process.

QUERIES AND CONCEPTS

1 Give several examples of communication as art, language, and social science that are not mentioned in the text.

2 In a few paragraphs, describe a study you would like to do and how it would avoid the pitfalls described in the text.

3 Make a list of ten statements that include causal inferences. How many of these could be tested empirically?

4 Other than those mentioned in the text, can you think of at least three important

media-related questions that might be addressed by research projects such as those reported here?

5 Identify at least three areas where you feel media research would be valuable. Based on what you have learned in this chapter, briefly describe how you might go about setting up a study in each of these areas.

READINGS AND REFERENCES

Mass-Communication Research

Hubert M. Blalock, Jr.
Ann B. Blalock
An Introduction to Social Research, 2nd ed. Englewood Cliffs, N.J.: Prentice-Hall, 1982.

This is the easiest-to-understand introduction I know of for students who want to find out what research methodology is all about. Blalock is an acknowledged leader in the field and has written some texts that easily mystify the amateur; this one is brief, simple, and in paperback.

Hubert M. Blalock, Jr.
Causal Inferences in Nonexperimental Research. Chapel Hill: University of North Carolina Press, 1964.

The introductory chapter offers a simple introduction to causal thinking and theory, along with problems in the field and the causal model.

Dennis K. Davis
Stanley J. Baran
Mass Communication and Everyday Life: A Perspective on Theory and Effects. Belmont, Calif.: Wadsworth, 1981.

The dilemma of the application of social-science research to the "real world" of media consumption is the formidable task the authors set up for themselves here. This one-of-a-kind approach to understanding communication research is required reading for all students interested in the area. Highly recommended.

Philip Emmert
William D. Brooks
Methods of Research in Communication. Boston: Houghton Mifflin, 1970.

This is a text designed for the student seeking basic information about communication research. The book's three sections are "Research Design and Setting," "Research Methods," and "Instruments and Research Technologies." Standard fare for most beginning graduate courses in communication research. Straightforward.

R. Gerald Kline and Phillip Tichenor, eds.
Current Perspectives in Mass Communication Research. Beverly Hills: Sage Publications, annual.

Each year Sage publishes an additional volume in this set, covering important issues in communication research. Extremely useful bibliographies and articles from top names in the field.

Roger D. Wimmer
Joseph R. Dominick
Mass Media Research: An Introduction. Belmont, Calif.: Wadsworth, 1983.

A clear introduction to the research process and to various approaches to mass media research. Recommended for students wanting to know more about research methods and their applications to mass media problems.

15

New Technologies and the Future of Mass Communication

FOR DECADES, MASS-COMMUNICATION TEXTS AND THE TEACHers who use them have talked of the "communications revolution." It has been widely projected as a time when new technological devices would change the way we communicate with one another. Those changes in turn were expected to radically alter our daily lives.

While the communications revolution has been decidedly slower to arrive than expected, it now appears that the next decade will transform our communication patterns and our daily lives in ways that even the most radical visionaries failed to anticipate. The communications revolution is here at last. In his book *The Coming Information Age*, Wilson P. Dizard explains how this came to be.

The so-called communications revolution is, in reality, a succession of three overlapping technological stages that have taken place during the past one hundred and fifty years. The first of these was the Wire Age (1844–1900), the second was the Wireless Age (1900–1970), and the third is the one we are now entering—the Integrated Grid Age, in which wire and wireless technology are brought together in powerful combinations which will form the structure of the future global information utility. The technological advances that occurred between the beginning of the Wire Age and the present are awesome. The early Western Union telegraph machines that opened the Wire Age could relay about forty words a minute. Western Union's first domestic communications satellite, the successor to the old telegraph line, was placed in orbit in 1975 with a capability of transmitting eight million words a *second*.

It is the business of the future to be dangerous.
ALFRED NORTH
WHITEHEAD

Throughout this book we have explored some of the ways that the introduction of technological devices, from the printing press to television, have altered the outlook of the population of what the late Buckminster Fuller called the "spaceship earth." What follows is a brief overview of the new technologies and some of the things we might expect to happen as they become increasingly significant in our everyday lives.

One of the reasons the communications revolution has been so late in arriving involves economic reality. No communication device can have much impact until it is used by a significant subgroup of the population. Consumers must be able to afford to buy a new device or hook up to a new service before it can become part of their lives. The innovations made possible by the computer microchip, fiber optics, and satellites are already at work in millions of living rooms across the nation. We are all touched by the new technologies. Our task now is to understand them and ultimately control them. As with all media, the destiny of the new technologies is strictly up to us.

LINKUPS: THE FOUNDATION OF THE COMMUNICATIONS REVOLUTION

To understand all that is happening with the new technologies requires far more information than is possible to include in this brief overview. However, any understanding begins with an awareness of the basic elements at work in the revolution. Some of the elements can also be understood by being aware of how they work together to produce results you're already familiar with.

A case in point is Ted Turner (see Chapter 11) and his Atlanta-based superstation,

WTBS. Turner bought the failing UHF station for $2.5 million in 1970, against the advice of just about everyone he knew in the industry. His idea was relatively simple: Why not "link up" the station's output of old movies, syndicated reruns, and sports programs with some of the thousands of cable systems across the country? Once this was accomplished, his audience would be truly national and the rates he could charge advertisers would be multiplied.

Using Home Box Office (HBO) as his model, Turner rented the facilities of a communication satellite to beam his signal to the local cable companies, who in turn distributed it to their subscribers. Cable operators got another reason to urge potential subscribers to sign up and Turner got his national audience. By 1983 WTBS was earning profits of $40 million annually.

Turner's feat was a stunning accomplishment for a number of reasons. Most "high tech" endeavors take years to turn a profit. Many may never show a profit. MTV, despite all its publicity, has been a money-loser so far for Warner Amex. Sponsors are reluctant to try a new medium, and competition in all areas of the new technologies is intense. Turner overcame these odds. WTBS became a prototype for media to come.

At the heart of this success story is the marriage of two of the new technologies, *cable television* (CATV) and *satellite communication*. These two elements have now been joined by *computers* and dozens of new *home video* products to form the basis for the communications revolution.

CABLE TV

Former FCC member Nicholas Johnson (see Chapter 8) has said that "the difference between ordinary television and cable is the difference between a garden hose and Niagara Falls." This analogy is not as farfetched as it may seem. Whereas the ordinary TV set has a limited channel capacity and may carry only a handful of stations, state-of-the-art cable systems now deliver over 100 channels of programming. Of course, not all of those channels are always used, but the proliferation of services to fill them staggers the imagination.

Currently most cable services offer dozens of special-program channels, including the HBO, Showtime, and Cinemax movie channels. There is also WTBS, Cable News Network (CNN), Entertainment and Sports Programming (ESPN), and the USA Cable Network. *Network* is an appropriate term for all these services, since they structurally duplicate what ABC, CBS, and NBC do, that is, they can be received simultaneously across the country.

They have not yet had the impact of the "big three" only because they are received just by those who subscribe to a cable service. In most cases, these subscribers must also pay an extra service charge to receive the new networks. Yet "networks" like WTBS, CNN, USA, and MTV (see 15.1) are generally available to all who pay the basic rate. In addition, all come via satellite, and would not exist were it not for that element of the new technology. HBO, the first satellite cable network, began in 1975. By 1984 it had 12 million subscribers and had made substantial inroads in many cable markets.

Little by little, these new networks are eating away at the big piece of the pie long enjoyed by the big three. Since 1975, the number of viewers who tune in to the big three during prime time has dropped from over 90 percent to less than 80 percent, and that number is growing smaller each year.

The situation is complex, but the basic reason is simple. CBS can't offer 24 hours of movies without commercials each day. NBC can't run 24 hours of music. ABC can't offer nonstop sports. They must cater to a large general audience. The smaller networks with lower costs zero in on various demographic groups and offer them exactly what they want. This process (sometimes called *narrowcasting*) involves target programming for target audiences and has long been a factor in all mass-media marketing strategies. Narrowcasting is good news for advertisers who wish to reach these types of special audiences.

By 1982, over one-third of all the nation's homes were subscribing to a cable service. By 1983, there were over 5,000 different cable systems serving some 30 million households. We are rapidly becoming a "wired nation" tuned in to what some call the "television of abundance."

Of course, *more* is not necessarily *better*. There is no shortage of ideas for new services and new communication possibilities, but whether these will result in an aesthetically improved product remains to be seen. And there are marketplace constraints. Just how much television do we really want? How much can we afford? Cable operators have found that consumers are willing to pay extra for certain selections. In 1981, over 500,000 homes paid up to $25 each to see a boxing match between Sugar Ray Leonard and Thomas Hearns on a *pay-per-view* basis.

Fiber Optics

An engineering breakthrough pioneered by Western Electric is bound to have great impact on cable. *Fiber optics* has made it possible to carry 100,000 phone calls or transmit the entire broadcast spectrum through a cable the size of a human hair (15.2). While traditional wires use radio signals for transmission, fiber optics employs light waves. It may soon be possible to use one wire to receive

15.1
I Want My MTV!

You turn on the set and suddenly there's Tom Petty on a barren desert, Randy Newman tooling around L.A. in an old Buick convertible, Phil Collins's eerily disembodied head moaning a refrain. You haven't been transported to the Twilight Zone . . . you've just entered the world of MTV!

Initiated in August 1981, MTV now reaches some 10 million households nationwide and is increasing its audience daily—thanks, in part, to an insistent advertising campaign that implores potential viewers to call up their local cable systems and say "I want my MTV!"

The idea was simple. Why not create an album-oriented rock station for television? Warner Amex Satellite Entertainment company did just that, using videos supplied by record companies. In between the videos, viewers are treated to comments by "veejays" who are peers of MTV's target audience of 12- to 23-year-olds. The veejays rattle off the latest concert information, and you never know when Thomas Dolby or Boy George might drop by to talk about his latest video.

Most observers agree that two relatively unexpected consequences have resulted from MTV. Virtually every new band now makes at least one video in addition to their first album with the hope of breaking into MTV's closely monitored playlist. A second consequence is the impact of MTV and other rock video programs on the music industry itself. A Nielsen survey of 2,000 rock enthusiasts indicated that about 70 percent of them felt that MTV was important in determining their record-buying decisions. Since MTV programmers take a special interest in "breaking" new bands, they have turned the usually predictable sales figures for new music upside down. Radio is now not the only outlet for new music; MTV's decision to place a new band in their rotation can be very influential. In 1982 an obscure Australian group, Men at Work, received MTV exposure and went on to become that year's hottest group. In 1983 MTV was among the first to play songs from the Police's *Synchronicity* album and shamelessly promoted the group's summer tour, even going so far as to have veejays host concerts in some major cities. The Police had the best-selling single and the best-selling album that summer.

Generally the videos shown on MTV and other rock video programs fall into two categories: (1) concert footage and (2) stories or series of images that somehow complement or visually amplify the music. The latter videos are more intriguing; certainly they qualify as a new hybrid art form. The recording companies associated with groups like Fleetwood Mac and solo performers like Michael Jackson may spend in excess of $100,000 for the few minutes of videotape that finally reaches MTV's studio. Of course, this is not philanthropy. Rock videos increase album sales.

---

phone, TV, and all other electronic communication.

In fact, fiber optics is already in use in some international phone services. It carries with it exciting possibilities, since it represents almost unlimited channel capacity.

What began as a way for those with poor TV reception to receive a clear picture has blossomed into an entirely new industry, as revolutionary as printing or television itself.

It is only now that we are beginning to realize it.

SATELLITE COMMUNICATION

When Telstar, the first communication satellite, was launched in 1962 a new concept was launched with it. Five years earlier the

Some have credited MTV for single-handedly pulling the sagging popular-music industry out of the financial doldrums. It certainly is safe to say that it has been instrumental in ushering in the new music that has swept the pop scene (see Chapter 7).

Not everyone is overjoyed with MTV or the concept of rock videos in general. Some critics maintain that it is "mindless" entertainment. But these tend to be the same critics who have felt that way about rock and roll all along. A more serious charge was leveled by black entertainers, who felt that some of their music had been excluded from MTV. Bob Cavallo, who represents Earth, Wind and Fire, has called MTV "racist." Successful black artists such as Marvin Gaye, Rick James, and Donna Summer were conspicuously absent from MTV's playlist for its first few years of operation.

According to MTV vice president John Sykes, it was not a question of race but of format. He insisted, "We're not dealing with racism. Right from the start we geared this towards a rock-and-roll format. For the same reason we are not playing country, we're not playing classical, and we're not playing adult contemporary, we're not playing rhythm and blues. There aren't [a lot of blacks on MTV] because it just so happens that in rock and roll there aren't a lot of blacks." Interestingly, his response could very well have been that of any AOR radio programmer.

Whatever its shortcomings, MTV has been incredibly successful. It was only a matter of time before MTV would be imitated. In 1982 the USA Cable Network began offering *Night Flite,* a program devoted to video in the MTV manner. *Radio 1990,* a similar program, is now offered five nights each week. HBO and Showtime now play videos aimed at the younger audience to help fill the gap between movies. Many independent stations and even the "big three" now air an hour or more of videos each week and in 1984 *Hot,* a video top 10 countdown, appeared in many markets. Meanwhile, the Nashville Network programs non-stop country music entertainment.

Nonetheless, MTV remains the only 24-hour-a-day channel devoted exclusively to rock music, at least for the moment. Since it plays 80 percent new music, it has become a potent force in the music business and may be on the way to becoming a great commercial TV success for Warner Amex. Perhaps more important, it has become a fixture in the homes, hearts, and minds of millions of music enthusiasts all over the country. And it may be transforming our very notion of what popular music is. During the '50s, '60s, and '70s, rock fans grew up with the sounds that would forever be etched into their lives. But the rock fans of the '80s have the *sights* as well as the sounds. It will be interesting to see what effects those sights have in the years to come, and how they are remembered by the first rock video generation.

Soviet Union had shaken the world by launching Sputnik I. America soon followed with Explorer I. These early efforts were aimed at increasing our knowledge of space. As it turned out, the real role of satellites would be not in exploring space but in transforming life on earth through the infusion of new communication channels. Telstar was the first satellite designed exclusively for such purposes.

The theory behind satellite communication is fairly simple. The satellites actually act as radio relay stations, receiving electronic messages from the ground that are transmitted through "uplinks" in earth stations. The satellites then retransmit them to "dishes" in other earth stations ("downlinks").

Satellites can relay such information with relative ease because they are placed in a syn-

Can you make the ends of these glass fibers fit together precisely?

WE will. Someday, you may be communicating over beams of light. Thousands of people already are. Their calls are carried through glass fibers using a new technology called lightwave communication.

But before this innovative technology could be put to work, Western Electric had to solve a major problem: how to splice threads of glass.

Western Electric, working from a Bell Labs idea, developed a solution: "honeycombs" of precisely etched crystal that can hold the fibers in perfect alignment. A unique process guarantees that all of the honeycombs will be identical. So no two fibers are ever more than one eight-thousandth of an inch out of line.

Glass fibers can carry hundreds of times more information than copper wire.

This helps the Bell System keep down the cost of your phone service.

Western Electric products have helped to make your communications system the best in the world. And we're working hard to keep it that way.

Western Electric

15.2

Western Electric has been a pioneer in the fiber optics field.

chronous orbit approximately 22,000 miles above the earth: The satellites revolve around the earth at the same speed the earth rotates on its axis, so they are constantly in the same position in relation to the earth stations. This gives them the ability to beam signals all over the planet with equal ease (though rarely with equal signal strength), something that no ground-to-ground device could possibly do at such a comparatively small cost.

Put most simply, satellites like Telstar have made instantaneous global communication possible. By the mid-1980s, there were 20 such satellites owned by America in the air. Meanwhile, the Japanese and European communities have built and launched "birds" of their own.

In 1975 when Home Box Office began using Satcom I to transmit its movies, it became the first satellite network and altered forever the shape of the television landscape. No longer was television earthbound, tied to phone lines or other ground devices used by the big three.

Nevertheless, the average consumer is probably not aware of the technology that makes HBO or any of the other services possible. But that consumer will become more aware of satellite services with the proliferation of personal satellite receiving dishes. Currently about 35,000 homes have an earth station, which enables them to receive most or all of the signals being fed to satellites. A new publication, *Satellite TV Week*, is a *TV*

Guide for earth-station owners, showing them what they can receive from each satellite (15.3). Of course, these TV buffs also receive material designed for viewing at a later time, news feeds, sporting events, and the like, as well as radio signals that use satellite distribution.

Those who are sending their signals via satellite are not particularly pleased with these "signal pirates" (as they refer to them)—dish owners do not pay any fee to receive the signals. The legality of dish ownership and the ownership of the signals themselves is still being debated in the courts. Earth-station owners contend they're simply receiving information that should be free to all, just as radio and TV earthbound signals are free to all. Those paying large fees to utilize satellite distribution feel they're being cheated by not receiving revenues from the "pirates." In 1984, HBO announced it would begin "scrambling" its signals to thwart signal pirates. It may be years before the courts make final decisions regarding these issues. In the meantime, dish sales continue to be brisk, despite the $3,500–$10,000 required to purchase and set up an earth station.

DBS: Direct-Broadcast Satellites

A variation on the home dish is the direct-broadcast satellite (DBS). Unlike HBO or Showtime, DBS signals are intended to go directly to the consumer, without benefit of a cable "middleman" (15.4). These services beam several program channels to consumers who have specially equipped dishes installed on their roofs. The dish combined with a descrambler unit allows the consumer to receive satellite transmissions beamed directly to them, thanks to a technological development providing transmission of a signal up to 40 times greater than those used for other transmissions. As a result, the dish is comparatively small (about the size of an umbrella) and considerably easier and less expensive to operate than a traditional dish. Of course, DBS enthusiasts can receive only what is beamed to them, and they are charged a monthly fee. Nevertheless, the future of DBS is intriguing from an economic point of view. It is the first technology that lets consumers bypass traditional TV stations, networks, and cable systems. The immediate future for DBS may be in areas where cable is not available. By some estimates, up to 30 percent of all U.S. homes are unable to be wired economically; these should be prime markets for satellite programming.

The first experimental DBS transmissions began in 1983. However, there are a number of potential problems, including an FCC decision about how much of the broadcast spectrum will be allotted to DBS. Because DBS signals are so strong, they require a much wider band width than ordinary satellite transmissions. In addition, the FCC is considering setting aside part of the DBS spectrum for experiments with high-definition television (HDTV). This new type of television transmission would use 1,125 lines rather than the 525 presently used. HDTV would require a lot of special equipment, and at present it is only experimental. The potential advantages are great, however, since HDTV picture quality would far surpass whatever is currently available anywhere in the world.

As strange as it may seem, there is already talk about the limitations of satellite technology. The single most important element in satellite technology is the *transponder*. Each transponder is capable of relaying one color television channel or handling over 1,000 phone calls. Most current satellites pack a payload of 24 transponders, but those to be launched during the 1990s could carry 40 or more. Even so, there is considerably more demand for satellite use than there are satellites.

☆ ☆ ☆ 📡 Satellite

Tr. No.	WESTAR 2 79°W [W-2]	SATCOM 4 83°W [F4]	COMSTAR 3 87°W [D3]	WESTAR 3 91°W [W3]	COMSTAR 2 95°W [D2]	TELSTAR 301 96°W [T1]	WESTAR 4 99°W [W4]	ANIK D 104.5°W [A]
1		SIN	NBC Network Programs (east)	o/v		1D		
2		FNN BRAVO	SPN			1X	o/v	
3	o/v	SPN				2D		
4		Home Sports Ent. Warner Amex			o/v	2X	o/v	
5	ABC (feeds)	ABC (feeds)	sports o/v	CNN (feeds)		3D	Bonneville Sat. Corp. CTNA	
6						3X	XEW-TV Mexico City	
7		NCN				4D		
8			Wold/ABC o/v			4X	o/v	CHCH Hamilton (enc.)
9				o/v	o/v	5D	Wold/ o/v	
10			Wold/CBS o/v			5X	o/v	
11	o/v	Netcom/Warner Amex Home Sports Ent Wold/ o/v		o/v	o/v	6D	Wold/ o/v	
12		Playboy			o/v	6X		
13		Cinemax spare	ABC Network Programs (east)	o/v		7D		
14					o/v	7X	o/v	TCTV Montreal (enc.)
15		(Viacom/Group W) American Bus. Net		o/v		8D	PBS-A	
16					o/v	8X	CNN feeds	(CBC) House of Comm French
17		Trinity Broadcasting	CBS Network Programs (east)	o/v		9D	PBS-B	
18						9X		CITV Edmonton (enc.)
19	o/v	American Medical Bldgs.	Telstar Hotel Net	Hughes TV Net sports o/v		10D	Wold o/v	
20						10X	ABC Contract Chan. feeds	
21		o/v		o/v INN News/CBS	o/v	11D	PBS-C	
22		ABC Network Programs (west)			o/v	11X	o/v	BCTV Vancouver B.C. (en)
23	o/v	Galavision o/v		o/v BAMC-HSC		12D	U.S. News Ag. PBS o/v	
24		NBC (feeds)			o/v	12X	o/v	(CBC) House of Comm English

NOTES:
a) Transponder numbers are the dial position on a standard 24-channel receiver.
b) Polarization on 12 transponder satellites is all horizontal.
c) On Satcom and Comstar 24 transponder satellites polarization is ODD-Vertical and EVEN-Horizontal.
d) On Westar 24 transpnder satellites polarization is EVEN-Vertical and ODD-Horizontal.

D = Horizontal polarity
X = Vertical polarity
(enc.) = encripted
o/v = occasional video
s.s. = stereo subcarrier
nd = narrow discreet

AUDIO-ONLY STEREO:
03 [F3] — WFMT (Chicago); fine arts and classical (6.3-6.48 chns.)
Satellite Music Network; popular, country (5.58-5.76 chns. pop — 5.94-6.12 chns. ctry.)

15.3

At what point will viewers feel they have enough programming?

Used by permission of *Satellite TV Week.*

Commercial Uses

In *The Communications Revolution*, Frederick Williams lists a number of commercial applications that will be possible with the construction of "communication platforms"—giant satellites that can be put into

15.4

U.S. Satellite Broadcasting Company is trying a slightly different approach to the satellite game. Rather than have their signals piped in by cable, they offer them to local stations that can set up their own dish and then beam the signals to the viewers via their transmitter. The ad implies that the stations can do this at no cost to themselves since the signal also carries commercials which "pay" for the service.

Pioneer Television's New Frontier!

Most direct-to-home satellite services by-pass local participation. But one group in the satellite space-race believes that free TV delivered with the help of local television stations has a bright future. United States Satellite Broadcasting Company, Inc.

We're adding space-age technology to local service ... making free, advertiser-supported news, sports and first-run entertainment available to every American home via satellite with local station participation!

Pioneer the future! Join us!
Call Bob Fransen at (813) 576-4444 or (612) 642-4467 today.

United States Satellite Broadcasting Company, Inc.
3415 University Avenue St. Paul, Minnesota 55114
Pending F.C.C. approval.

systems for computer-assisted management or design;

- linkage of small hand-held computer terminals, like pocket calculators, with sources of information such as banking records, the stock market, transportation scheduling, a library of games, or useful computer programs;
- movement toward electronic mail systems where electron movement replaces paper movement;
- nationwide educational communications network, one capable of supplying instructional materials from a central library, of supporting computer-assisted instructional systems now too costly for schools, even systems which can link into the home.

Among the most innovative business uses currently available is *videoconferencing*. By using satellite signals, corporations with branches spread out across the nation or all over the world can hold "meetings" without having to pay costly plane fares and hotel bills. Executives simply gather where there is an uplink and downlink and communicate via giant TV screens. The Hilton Communications Network currently offers such services for about $90 a person for 1,000 people in 10 locations and about $80 a person for 2,000 people in 20 locations. Though that may seem like a lot of money, it is comparatively cheap given the cost of travel and accommodations. By the early 1980s, videoconferencing was a $30-million-a-year industry and growing rapidly.

Though business meetings and conferences are the most immediately applicable use of this new technology, some envision college classrooms and universities without walls using satellite transmissions.

In August 1982, 500,000 followers of the controversial TV evangelist Kenneth Copeland were involved in a five-continent revival meeting that cost an estimated $2 million. Some evangelists have been hugely successful at using TV to raise funds and reach their constituents; many of them are looking toward satellite technology to expand their following.

In summary, satellite technology combined with cable is the most immediately applicable and financially practical marriage among the new technologies. Such a marriage combines wireless and wired technologies and forms the basis for what Dizard calls the "integrated grid age."

THE COMPUTER AGE

Already millions of American households contain some kind of personal computer. It won't be long before using a computer will be second nature to a new generation of consumers. As home computer systems become more sophisticated, we will find added uses for them.

If you've walked by a video arcade recently, you don't have to be reminded that the use of video games is growing at what some feel is an alarming rate. In 1981 the movie industry grossed $3 billion while video games took in an estimated $6 billion. That gives you some idea of just how big these "sugar-coated computers" (as they are sometimes called) have become.

Video games employ the same technology as personal computers, and indeed many who have bought personal computers have done so primarily so they can play games at home, thus saving their quarters. But video games are just a small part of the computer boom. The combination of computer technology with satellites and cable promises innovations that would have seemed astonishing just a few years ago.

Two-Way TV

In 1977 Warner Amex pioneered two-way TV with its pilot QUBE system in Columbus, Ohio. A later version was introduced in Pittsburgh in 1982 and utilized 63 of 80 available channels for a variety of programs, some of which use two-way communication. Two-way technology has appeared in a number of other cities as well. Here's how it works. Viewers see a speech by the President, for example, and then are able to respond to a series of questions about the speech by using a small unit resembling a TV remote-control box (see 15.5). A large computer tallies the results, and in seconds they're flashed on the screen.

Many see this as a perfect opportunity to "talk back" to their television sets. Cities now granting franchises to cable operators routinely require that new systems have two-way capability. Not all the uses are as serious as the one described above, however. Pittsburgh's QUBE also offers viewers the chance to vote on which suitor should date an available young lady in a kind of electronic version of *The Dating Game* called *Singles Magazine*.

15.5

This interactive terminal is used by subscribers to Warner's QUBE system to "talk back" to their TV sets.

The present computer technology also allows for a *sweep* every six seconds of viewers who have their sets turned on that supplies precise information as to what they're watching. Even the best ratings services can provide only estimates.

Pittsburgh's QUBE (15.5) is also getting set to offer *teleshopping*, a service where viewers can "shop" for goods pictured on the screen. When they find something they like, they need only push a few buttons to order the product, which is sent directly to them. The bill can be part of their monthly cable charges. Though teleshopping is not operational as of this writing, it will be soon. Needless to say, advertisers are excited about the possibilities.

Electronic Mail

Another direct application of computer technology is electronic mail. Business interests have led the way in developing this application. Letters are typed into a computer, which then feeds the information to a satellite uplink. On the other end, a downlink decodes the message and the letter appears on a video screen. This could pose a real threat to the U.S. Postal Service, which reports that 80 percent of all first-class letters are business-oriented.

Electronic mail is but one service made possible by a system known as *videotex*. Videotex transforms the ordinary TV screen into a display terminal and opens the door for electronic publishing. For years we have heard about the possibility of receiving the morning paper electronically. Videotex has made that a reality in several cities, where viewers can now receive newspaper-type information—stock quotations, weather reports, sports scores, and the like—on their screens.

Though there are some technological and marketing problems still to be solved, we are told that the day when all cable systems are thus equipped may not be far away. A simple link from cable to TV to computer printer can provide printed copy. The cost of such equipment is dropping all the time.

Computer technology coupled with cable systems has also made home banking a reality in several markets. Customers can move funds from one account to another, pay bills, check account balances, and so on without leaving their living rooms. Banks see this as a way to expand their markets without building costly new branches.

A less exotic form of this technology is also employed in *teletext*, a one-way service that can utilize some or all of the 525 TV screen lines to transmit printed information directly to the consumer. Present teletext services include sports scores, television listings, and stock quotations, at a minimal cost. Some of these services are sponsored, so viewers are treated to a built-in commercial along with their weather report. The most popular current use of this technology is for closed-caption messages for the hearing-impaired. "Telecaption," a service run by Sears and the National Captioning Institute, serves over 60,000 subscribers.

HOME VIDEO: THE CONSUMER TAKES CONTROL

Yet another element in the communication revolution is home video. In 1975 Sony introduced Betamax, the first video cassette recording device (VCR) intended for home use (15.6). VCRs are now in about 5 million homes, or about 5 percent of all homes with a television set. What can be accomplished with a state-of-the-art VCR is truly amazing. Shows can be taped and played back at a later, more convenient time. One show can be taped while another is being watched, since a VCR is actually a small "recording" TV set without the picture tube.

Unfortunately, VCRs are sold in two non-compatible formats (15.7), VHS and Beta. Beta fans argue that picture quality is slightly better with this format, while VHS fans note that their systems allow more hours per tape (eight compared with Beta's four and a half). It appears that VHS is winning the battle—about three-fourths of all units sold today are VHS.

The latest VCRs also offer the viewer the options to watch programs in slow motion and to utilize freeze frame. Most important from a consumer point of view is the scan feature, which allows viewers to skip through commercials and record entire programs virtually uninterrupted.

15.6

Sony pioneered home video recording when it offered the Betamax unit in 1975. The "two shows at once" and time shift functions are still major marketing sales features for all of today's VCR manufacturers.

A new system pioneered in Japan uses one-quarter-inch tape rather than the standard half-inch format and entered the U.S. market in 1984. This format could very well replace both Beta and VHS and become the standard for the industry. The new system will offer cassettes barely larger than audio cassettes with no noticeable difference in quality. Consumers will need less space to house their treasured video memories. Marketing research indicates that while consumers erase many programs as soon as they've viewed them, they also keep a fairly large number of all-time favorites in storage.

The popularity of these machines has increased as the price has dropped. Currently VCRs can be found for as little as $300 or as much as $1,600, depending on the options chosen.

Meanwhile the legality of home taping was in question for some time. Originally the courts had held that such taping, even for private

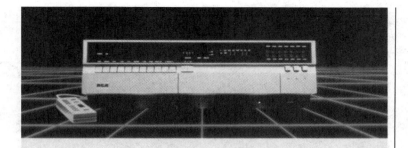

15.7

The RCA Selectavision was one of the first "high-tech" design video recorders to hit the market. The VHS format utilized by this unit was soon to surpass the Beta format pioneered by Sony. Currently about 75 percent of all home video recorders sold are VHS models.

home use, may be in violation of copyright law. The case was finally settled in 1984 when the Supreme Court ruled 5–4 that such taping was legal. Video manufacturers and VCR owners breathed a sigh of relief. Meanwhile those who own the rights to movies and television programs put pressure on Congress to enact a special tax on machines and tapes to make sure they were getting appropriate residuals. The ultimate fate of such legislation may not be known for some time. Currently Congress is considering amending the Act to exclude videotaping. Meanwhile, an extra tax on the machines or on the tapes themselves or both has been offered as a compromise. Whatever happens, it appears that the VCR is here to stay.

Laser Discs

Competing with VCRs for the home video market are *video disc players* (see 15.8).

15.8

Magnavox obviously does not want to be left out of the home video revolution. Here their ad stresses a complete home video system including a television, video game unit, a home video recording system that records off the air (as well as allowing the consumer to make home video movies with the addition of a camera), and "Discovision," a video disc system.

Unlike VCRs, these units cannot record; they use prerecorded programming. Currently there are two noncompatible systems: the RCA video disc, and the technologically superior Laservision format, offered by Phillips and Pioneer. Both feature high-quality sound and picture, surpassing all VCRs in these crucial categories. However, the public has clearly shown a preference for VCRs, with their ability to record, play back, and erase.

Currently, disc programming is primarily movies, but VCRs may have cornered that market. So disc makers are now planning more interactive software: cooking demonstrations, exercise programs, and the like. Such programs utilize disc capabilities much more effectively, but the public will have to be educated in these.

The real significance of discs is only beginning to be discovered by consumers. When linked to a computer, the laser disc becomes a magic carpet ride. Each side of the disc contains 54,000 frames of information, which can be played in any order and at various speeds. One disc could contain all the great paintings from all the great museums of the

world, for example, on call at the pleasure of the consumer. Textual information could appear with them on an adjacent frame.

In 1977 a team from the Massachusetts Institute of Technology created the Movie Map Disc. This revolutionary disc allows the viewer to "drive" down the streets of Aspen, Colorado, making left turns and right turns at will. When the viewer wishes to stop and examine a building, he or she can "enter" simply by touching another button. The day may not be far away when any city can be thus visited. The enormous storage capacity of the laser disc coupled with the use of computers may change forever our perception of video. Of all of the home video technologies, laser discs appear to have the brightest long-term future and the most intriguing possibilities.

Three other home video technologies seem poised for major marketing breakthroughs in the 1980s. These are stereo TV, big-screen TV, and "Watchman" miniature TVs. Stereo TV already exists in Germany and Japan, and some Japanese sets marketed in America today have stereo capability. Music buffs will be among the first to try these expensive new machines; if previous patterns are any indication, it won't be long before the prices begin to drop.

Big-screen or projection TV has been around for at least a decade, but sales have been slow, hampered by $3,000 price tags and pictures that don't approach the clarity of the smaller screens. Some of this may be solved by rear projection units, which offer a clearer and brighter picture. Still, it appears that it will be several years before big-screen TV will have much of an impact in the marketplace. Currently about 200,000 units are sold each year—but that's about the same as the number of television sets sold in a single week. Everyone seems to feel that the large screen

is TV's ultimate destiny, but no one yet seems to know when the bugs will be worked out or when prices may drop. In addition, large-screen picture clarity is lessened somewhat by the use of VCRs, since recorded programs don't have the sharpness of the originals. This is hardly noticeable on smaller screens but becomes a glaring problem when the picture is "blown up."

In 1983 Sony introduced the Watchman to American consumers. Utilizing new miniature circuitry and the ability to place the picture tube under the screen instead of behind it, the Watchman may finally become the Dick Tracy "two-way wrist TV" that we've so long awaited.

ISSUES AND ANSWERS: THE COMMUNICATIONS FUTURE

I hear two major concerns most often about the new technologies from students and others. One involves the fear that machines will "take over" or somehow usurp the human experience and leave us emotionally bankrupt. The second, often mentioned in connection with video games, is familiar because it has been put forth by the opponents of television for years: Are we increasingly "escaping" from reality into a world of fantasy made possible by the new technologies? Both of these concerns are real, and arguments can be made on each side. On balance, it seems to me that both concerns are essentially without substance.

A special issue of *Channels* magazine on the new technologies argued convincingly for the acceptance of "technology without fear." There is no more reason to be put off by communications technology than by jet

planes, automatic dishwashers, or old-fashioned radios.

To utilize the new technologies, we don't need to know everything about what makes them work, any more than we need to know how a TV set works in order to watch it. Devices are becoming increasingly complex, but unless they are (as the computer buffs say) "user-friendly"—comprehensible to the average consumer without too much trouble—they will never be widely used or accepted.

Another thing that seems promising about the new technologies is that they allow the consumer to control more of what he or she sees, hears, and experiences. Cable TV and satellite delivery systems allow us to choose from dozens of entertainment and instructional channels, freeing us from the "tyranny" of the big three. Computers give us instant access to information in a way that is unprecedented in human history. Home video technologies enable us to watch what we want to watch when we want to watch it. In short, the new technologies have delivered a means to put us in control of our own mediated reality as never before.

As to the charge that we are "escaping" reality, mediated reality is another form of reality, not an escape from it. Back in Chapter 1 we discussed the crucial differences between real life and mediated reality. These are especially important in light of the proliferation of the new technologies, each with their own mediated content. To turn on the screen or pick up the videotex version of the day's news is to still enter the world of mediated reality. Through media courses such as the one you're taking right now, we're learning more about the nature of mediated reality as it exists and as it may exist in the future.

While we should not embrace change for its own sake, neither should we reject it out of fear, anxiety, or lack of knowledge. The technological outlines of Mediamerica are changing more rapidly now than ever before. Never has there been a better time for you to develop your skills as a critical consumer of mass-mediated information. To do this, you will need to be open to change, because it is inevitable. It may be "the business of the future to be dangerous," but the danger is within us. Your increased awareness and sensitivity to the changes to come can only help enhance your experiences with mediated reality as well as real life. That awareness can be the key to making the Mediamerica of the future a more positive and meaningful one for all of us.

QUERIES AND CONCEPTS

1 A research project: What is the impact of cable and the other new technologies in your community? See if you can obtain data concerning the availability and the success of these new program sources. Can you speculate as to what impact some of these new programs might be having in your area?

2 If you currently receive MTV or a similar program in your area, do a brief content analysis of the rock videos you find there. How many are straight concert footage and how many involve some kind of storytelling? What percentage of videos currently involve at least one black performer?

3 In one page: Should signals coming from satellites be free to all those who have purchased the equipment to receive them? What are the economic implications of your conclusion?

4 You are about to buy your first computer. How many tasks that you do on a regular basis could possibly be accomplished more efficiently with a computer? You'll need to spend some time at your local computer outlet to learn more about current computer capabilities.

READINGS AND REFERENCES

Thomas F. Baldwin
D. Stevens McVoy
Cable Communication. Englewood Cliffs,
N.J.: Prentice-Hall, 1983.
   A broad overview of the impact of
   cable: past, present, and future. The
   authors deal with cable's pre-eminent
   position in the communications future.
   Special chapters on pay television, two-
   way services, public policy, satellite-
   delivered programming, and cable
   radio. Tough reading and perhaps
   overly technical, in places, for the
   beginning student, the book nevertheless delivers a variety of vital
   information.

Wilson P. Dizard, Jr.
The Coming Information Age. New York:
Longman, 1982.
   A highly regarded work in the field,
   Dizard brings direct insights into the
   new age of communication technology.
   Chapters on the economics of the new
   age, the politics of change, exporting
   the information society, and what he
   calls the "open loop future." His
   thoughts regarding the three technological stages mentioned in this chapter
   can be found on pp. 47–48. Highly
   recommended.

Lynne Schafer Gross
The New Television Technologies.
Dubuque, Iowa: Wm. C. Brown, 1983.
   Things are moving so quickly in the
   new-technologies area that I chose this
   text as a good primer currently available for those interested in the field.
   Chapter 1 is on the scope of the new
   technologies with each of them then
   listed in a separate chapter. Information can be found on videocassettes,
   videotex, video discs, direct-broadcast
   satellites, and more.

Frederick Williams
The Communications Revolution. New
York: New American Library, 1983.
   Of all the popular books available on the
   subject of the new technologies, this is
   perhaps the most accessible to the
   beginning student. Concise, easy to
   understand. Williams covers computers, satellites, microprocessors,
   cable, videotex, and much more.

Frederick Williams
The New Communications. Belmont,
Calif.: Wadsworth, 1984.
   Williams's ability to take complex material and make it comprehensible to students is demonstrated in this "breakthrough text." Designed for beginning
   communications classes, it covers traditional areas such as interpersonal, small
   group, and intrapersonal communication against the backdrop of technological change. Chapters on mass communication and the impact of the new
   technologies.

Note: Students interested in the latest
developments would do well to consult
magazines such as *Cablevision, Broadcasting, Broadcast Engineering,* and
Channels. I am especially indebted to
the *Channels* special field guide issue
(November/December 1982) for many of
the facts included in this chapter.

Index

A Team, The, 98, 159
Abrams, Lee, 112
Account management, 267
Accuracy, in communication, 6
Adorno, Theodor W., 146
Advertising, 259–78; activities in, 266–67; compromise in, 267; early radio, 96; ethical questions, 261; form/content in, 270, 274–78; jobs in, 266–67; in magazines, 77, 80–83; in mass communication, 235; mass media and, 13; mediated reality in, 260; in Netherlands broadcasting, 301; newspaper, 34; pay in, 267; pet-food war, 267–69; in politics, 281–84; prime-time revenue, 186; psychology of, 270–78; radio, 264; rate card, 81; revenues from, 33, 71, 186; socialization via, 277; spot, 266; subliminal, 269, 272–75; truth in, 261–64; TV, 149, 152, 264–66, 271
See also Commercials
Advocacy journalism, 38, 39
African Queen, The, 217
Aldridge, Alan, 145
Alexander, Shana, 79
Alfred Hitchcock Presents, 184
Alger, Horatio, 20–21
All in the Family, 151, 173
All My Children, 187, 319–24
All the President's Men, 43, 240
All Things Considered, 116
Allen, George, 297
Allen, Gracie, 100
Allen, Woody, 218, 292
Altman, Robert, 139, 222–23
American Bandstand, 129–30
American Blade, 86
American Broadcasting Company (ABC): early, 99; radio,

97; TV, 147, 151, 153, 155, 157, 194, 253
American Family, An, 196
American Hot Wax, 205
American Magazine, 70, 72
American Marconi Company, 94
American Newspaper Guild, 37
American Shipper, 80
American Society of Composers, Authors, and Publishers (ASCAP), 128, 129
American Society of Newspaper Editors, 37, 44, 56
American Telephone and Telegraph (AT&T), 94–95, 96
American Top 40, 108, 109
American Women in Radio and Television (AWRT), 162
Amos 'n' Andy, 96, 98, 162
Anderson, Jack, 240
Anderson, Laurie, 134
Animals, 132
Anka, Paul, 130
Annie Hall, 292
Apartment 3G, 61
"April Come She Will," 138
Arbitron book, 114–15, 153
Arbitron, Inc., 152, 153
Arlen, Michael J., 285
Armstrong, Edwin, 96, 117, 118
Arnaz, Desi, 173
Arness, James, 179
Aronson, Steven M. L., 284
"As Time Goes By," 218
Asner, Ed, 174
Associated Press (AP), 36, 37, 40, 45, 237, 243–44, 245
Astaire, Fred, 205, 213
Atlantic Monthly, 55
Audiences, mass vs. special-interest, 33
Au Pairs, 327
Avalon, Frankie, 130
Ayer, N. W., & Son Agency, 260
Aykroyd, Dan, 177

Baby and Child Care, 24
Bacall, Lauren, 217
Backus, Jim, 219
Baez, Joan, 176
Baird, Russell N., 257
Balance, Bill, 120
Baldwin, Huntley, 285
Baldwin, Thomas F., 360
Ball, Lucille, 173, 248
Ball Four, 141
Bank Systems & Equipment, 79–80
Banzhaf, John, 165
Baran, Stanley J., 339
Baretta, 181, 182
Barnaby Jones, 182
Barnouw, Erik, 121, 166
Barnum, P. T., 279
Barron, Jerome A., 54
Bartlett, Donald, 240
Baseball, 193
Batman, 61
Bayer, William, 232
Bayes, Nora, 129
Bayh, Birch, 49
B.C., 61
Beatles, 109, 126; in films, 221; rock music and, 130, 131, 132, 136; on TV, 175, 177
"Behind Closed Doors," 140
Bell, Alexander Graham, 126
Bellow, Saul, 22
Belz, Carl, 144–45
Ben Casey, 180
Ben-Hur, 210
Bennett, James Gordon, 36
Benny, Jack, 99, 173, 176
Benson, 162
Bergen, Edgar, 100
Berger, Arthur Asa, 61, 67
Bergman, Ingrid, 218
Bergreen, Laurence, 166
Berkeley Barb, 37, 46
Berle, Milton, 148, 176
Berlin, 134

Bernstein, Carl, 37, 65, 240
Betamax, 353
Betancourt, Hal, 261–63, 286
Better Homes and Gardens, 70, 74
Beverly Hillbillies, The, 150
B-52s, 330
Bible, 9, 20
Big bands, 112, 128
Big Chill, The, 225–26
Big Sleep, The, 217
Biker/Hiker, 80
Billboard, 108, 140, 142, 143
Biographies in Sound, 103
Birth of a Nation, 205, 209–10
Bishop, Joey, 190
Bittner, Denise A., 123
Bittner, John R., 123
Black, Hugo, 65
"Black and Blue," 137
Blackboard Jungle, 129
Blacks, in broadcast media, 162
Blalock, Ann B., 339
Blalock, Hubert M., Jr., 339
Blob, The, 220
"Blonde in the Bleachers," 139
Blondie, 61
Bloom County, 63, 64
"Blowin' in the Wind," 139
Bogart, Humphrey, 217, 218
Bogart, Leo, 35
Bohn, Thomas W., 232, 233
Bolles, Don, 239
Bombeck, Erma, 59
Bonanza, 151, 179
Book clubs, 22
Books, 17–26; in America, 20–23; best sellers, 22–23; binding of, 18, 20; business of, 23–24; censorship of, 24–26; early forms of, 19–20; electronic media vs., 10; as mass medium, 7; paperback, 22; permanence of, 17–20; publishing eras of, 23–24; sales of, 22
"Born to Be Wild," 222
Boston Globe, 37
Bouton, Jim, 141
Bovies, 23
Bowie, David, 126, 132
Boyer, Paul S., 24, 28
Bradbury, Ray, 24

Bradford, Andrew, 70, 72
Brady, John, 76–77
Brando, Marlon, 191, 219
Breaking Away, 223–24
Brenda Starr, 61
Breslin, Jimmy, 37
Brinkley, David, 239
British Broadcasting Company (BBC), 298–99
Broadcast Music, Incorporated (BMI), 128, 129
Broadcasting: censorship of, 97; in Japan, 302–3; in the Netherlands, 301. *See also* Radio; Television
Broadcasting, 113, 117, 154
Broadcasting Act of 1968 (Canada), 300
Broken Blossoms, 211
Bronze Thrills, 86
Brooks, Tim, 199
Brooks, William D., 339
Broom Hilda, 61
Brown, James, 140
Brown, Jerry, 62
Browne, Jackson, 330
Browne, Ray, 200, 291, 304
Buddy Holly Story, The, 205
Buffalo Bill, 279
Bugs Bunny, 192
Burdon, Eric, 132
Burger, Warren, 26, 47
Burke, David, 251
Burnett, Carol, 58, 177
Burns, George, 99
Burns and Allen, 173
Burr, Raymond, 180
Burton, Philip Ward, 284
Business Week, 30
Buxton, Frank, 122
Bylines: in magazines, 87; voice as, 246
Byrds, 132
Byrnes, Edd "Kookie," 181
Byte, 80

Cable News Network (CNN), 245, 248, 252–53, 343
Cable TV, 12, 342–45; FCC and, 151; fiber optics and, 343–44; in Japan, 302; programming, 173; two-way, 351–52

Cagney, James, 213
Califano, Joseph A., 123
California Chicano News Media Association, 162
California Split, 222
Calling All Cars, 98
Canada, 299–300
Canadian Radio-Television Commission (CRTC), 300
Candy, 26
Cannon, 182
Canons of Journalism, 37
"Can't Buy Me Love," 130
Canterbury Tales, 9, 20
Cantor, Eddie, 129
Cantor, Muriel G., 200
Capitol Cloakroom, 103
Capote, Truman, 85
Captain Kangaroo, 191
Captain Marvel, 61
Captain Video, 191
Carefree, 213
Carey, Matthew, 23
Carlin, George, 120
Carpenters, 110
Carradine, Keith, 223
Carson, Johnny, 190–91
Carter, Jimmy, 281, 282, 283
Cartoons, 43, 61–64, 192
Caruso, Enrico, 127
Casablanca, 217, 218
Cashbox, 142
Cathy, 61, 64
Causality, 309–10
Cavallo, Bob, 345
Cavett, Dick, 191
Censorship: of books, 24–26; of broadcasting, 97; by CBS, 176–77; of newspapers, 38, 46–50; by school boards, 26; of TV, 176, 177; voluntary, 37
Center, Allen H., 285
Chandler, Raymond, 217
Changing Times, 82, 83
Channel capacity, 9
Chaplin, Charlie, 210, 211
Chapman, Graham, 178
Chariots of Fire, 224
Charles, Ray, 140
Charlie's Angels, 154, 157, 182
Chase, Chevy, 177
Chaucer, Geoffrey, 9, 20

Chayefsky, Paddy, 222, 223
Chester, Edward, 281, 287
Children's Digest, 80
Churchill, Winston, 78
Cigarette commercials, 265–66, 273
Cinemax, 343
Citizen Kane, 42–43, 205, 214–17, 227
Citizens' band (CB) radio, 97
Civilisation, 159
Clansman, The, 210
Clark, Bernadine, 89
Clark, Dick, 129
Clark, Ruth, 66
Clash, 134, 139, 327
Classical music: on radio, 112; recording of, 127
Cleese, John, 178
Cleopatra, 210
Close Encounters of the Third Kind, 228
CMR. *See* Constructed mediated reality
"Code of Wartime Practices for the American Press," 37
Codex, 20
Cohen, Bernard, 33
College Quiz Bowl, 103
Colley, John, 140
Collier's, 71, 73
Columbia Broadcasting System (CBS): censorship, 176–77; early, 95, 96, 99–100; TV, 147, 148, 151, 155, 253
Columbia Journalism Review, 47
Columbo, 181, 182
Combat Rock, 108
Combs, James E., 287
"Come Monday," 139
Comets, 97, 129
Comic strips, 43, 61–64
Coming Information Age, The, 341
Commercials: in children's shows, 192; cigarette, 265–66, 273; in daytime TV, 186. *See also* Advertising
Commercials: The Best Thing on TV, 271
Communication: accuracy in, 6; consequences of, 6; content

of, 5, 7–8; defined, 4–6; form of, 5, 6–7; interpersonal, 5, 6, 7; intrapersonal, 5, 6, 7; modes of, 5–6. *See also* Mass communication
Communications Act of 1934, 96, 119, 121
Communications Revolution, The, 348
Communicology, 12
Como, Perry, 128, 176
Compact Electronic Disc (CED), 356
Compaine, Benjamin M., 28
Compressed Air, 86
Compute! 80
Computer typesetting, 20
Computers, 351–53
Comstock, Anthony, 24, 25
Concentration, 189
Conde Naste, 73
Cone effect, 10–12, 170, 171
Conrad, William, 103, 182
Constructed mediated reality (CMR), 10–11, 106–7, 171
Content, of commucation, 5, 7–8
"Convoy," 140
Cook, Stephanie L., 311
Cooper, Alice, 132–33
Copeland, Kenneth, 351
Copywriter, radio, 105–6
Corporation for Public Broadcasting (CPB), 116, 117
Cosby, Bill, 103
Coser, Lewis A., 28
Cosmopolitan, 70, 71, 72, 73, 74
Costello, Elvis, 134, 330
Country and western music, 110, 139–40, 141
Cousins, Norman, 25
Craft, Christine, 251
Creamer, Inc., 262–63
Creative Computing, 80
Cronkite, Walter, 237, 238, 248
Crosby, Bing, 100, 109
Crosby, David, 138
Crosby, Stills, Nash, and Young, 132, 330
Crouse, Timothy, 287
Cruikshank, George, 61

Cults, 295–97
Culture: in book publishing, 25; mass, 8–9; mass-mediated, 13–14; popular, 290–98
Culture Club, 134
Cunningham, Don R., 167, 285
Cure, 134
Curtis, Cyrus, 71, 72
Cutlip, Scott M., 285

Daguerre, Louis, 205
Dagwood, 61, 64
Dallas, 147, 151, 155, 174, 184, 289
Damone, Vic, 128
Dance, Frank E. X., 4–5, 6, 15
"Dangling Conversation," 138
Danny and the Juniors, 130
Darin, Bobby, 130
Dave Clark Five, 130, 131
Davidson, Emily S., 200
Davis, Dennis K., 339
Davis, Elmer, 247
Davis, Paul, 49
Day, Benjamin, 36, 39
Day, Doris, 128, 129
Day, Stephen, 20
Day After, The, 155
"Day Tripper," 136
DBS. *See* Direct-broadcast satellites
Dean, James, 219–20
Deep Throat, 205
DeFleur, Melvin, 307
de Forest, Lee, 94, 95, 96
de Gaulle, Charles, 78
DeMille, Cecil B., 204
Demographics: magazines, 80; radio, 108, 114
DeMott, Benjamin, 77
Deneuve, Catherine, 273
Denisoff, R. Serge, 141, 146
Dennis the Menace, 61, 64
Devo, 330
Diamond, Neil, 110
Dick Tracy, 61
Dickey, James, 78
Dickinson, John, 36
Dickson, William, 205, 207
Dierker, Larry, 141
"Different Drum," 137
Dion, 136

Direct-broadcast satellites
    (DBS), 347
Dirks, Rudolph, 61
Disc jockey radio, 101–5; payola
    scandal, 97, 103–4
Disco music, 133
Discs, laser, 355–57
Disney, Walt, 192
Dixie Dugan, 61
Dizard, Wilson P., 341, 351, 360
Dr. Kildare, 180
Dr. Strangelove, 221
Dr. Zhivago, 228
Docu-dramas, 155
Dolby, Thomas, 134
Dominick, Joseph R., 339
Don Kirshner's Rock Concert, 178
Donahue, Phil, 190
Donahue, Tom "Big Daddy,"
    108–9
Donny and Marie, 177
"Don't Be Cruel," 129
Doobie Brothers, 330
Doonesbury, 61, 62–63, 192
Doors, 112
Dorsey, Tommy, 128
Dos Passos, John, 25
Douglas, Mike, 190
Downie, Leonard, Jr., 240
Dragnet, 181, 185
Drake, Bill, 108
Dreiser, Theodore, 25
Dressler, Marie, 213
Dritzehen, Andreas, 3
Dukes of Hazzard, The, 174
Dumont, Allen B., 148
Duran Duran, 134
Dylan, Bob, 64, 126, 132, 138–39
Dynasty, 12, 184

Eagles, 140, 330
"Earth Angel," 136
Earth, Wind and Fire, 345
Earthquake, 205, 222
East of Eden, 220
East Village Other, 46
Eastman, Susan Tyler, 167
Easy Rider, 205, 221–22
Ebony, 80
Edge of Night, The, 186
Edison, Thomas, 94, 126, 127,
    205, 207, 208–9

Edison Speaking Phonograph
    Company, 126
Editor & Publisher, 34
Edmondson, Madeleine, 200
Educational radio, 115–17
*Educational
    Telecommunication*, 115
8½, 229
Eisenhower, Dwight, 78, 282
Electric Company, The, 159, 160
Electronic mail, 353
Electronic media: newspapers
    and, 35; print media vs., 10
Ellery Queen, 98
Ellingsworth, Huber, 102–3
Ellis, Georgia, 103
Ellison, Harlan, 199
Elson, Robert T., 89
Emery, Edwin, 53
Emery, Michael, 53
Emmert, Philip, 339
Empire Strikes Back, The, 205,
    223, 228, 295
Encoding process, 6
Epstein, Brian, 131
Epstein, Julius J., 218
Epstein, Philip G., 218
ESPN, 343
Esquire, 71, 73, 76
E.T., 23, 225, 228
Ethics: in advertising, 261; in
    public relations, 280–81
Ethnic radio, 111–12
Eurhythmics, 112
"Eve of Destruction," 132
Ewen, Elizabeth, 304
Ewen, Stuart, 304
Exorcist, The, 222, 228
"Eyewitness news," 250

Fabian, 130
Fahrenheit 451, 54
Fairbanks, Douglas, 211
Family Circle, 70
Fang, Irving E., 257
Fanny Hill, 26
Fantasy Island, 157, 159
Farber, Myron, 50
Farnsworth, Philo, 148, 150
Farrow, Mia, 229
Fat Man, The, 98

Faulkner, William, 217
FBI, The, 181
FBI in Peace and War, The, 98
*Fear and Loathing: On the
    Campaign Trail 1972*, 37
Federal Communications
    Commission (FCC), 96, 100;
    on direct-broadcast
    satellites, 347; editorials
    and, 97, 254; frequency
    modulation and, 117;
    ownership of media and,
    255–56; radio and, 119–20;
    TV and, 148, 149, 150, 151,
    154, 160, 162, 163–65
Federal Radio Commission
    (FRC), 96, 118–19
Feiffer, 61
Feminine Forum, 120
Fiber optics, 343–44
Field and Stream, 70
"50 Ways to Leave Your Lover,"
    138
Film till Now, The, 212
Films, 203–33; attendance, 205;
    audience age, 219; as books,
    23; complexity, 224–25;
    costs of making, 205; crime,
    213; criticism, 227–29;
    detective, 217–18; disaster,
    222; as electronic media, 91;
    feature, 224–25; form and
    content, 207–9; history of,
    205; horror, 220; money-
    making, 228; music and, 205,
    222–23; musicals, 213;
    obscenity in, 229–30; as
    popular art, 203–33;
    pornography in, 229, 230;
    rating system for, 230; real
    life and, 204–7; self-
    regulation, 229–30; space,
    223; stars of, 211–12;
    talking, 212–13; technical
    basis, 207–9; techniques,
    215–16; TV and, 155–57; in
    U.S.S.R., 302; violence in,
    230; western, 225
Final Days, The, 65
Fiore, Quentin, 304
First Amendment, 49, 65
Fischer, Heinz-Dietrich, 305

Fishwick, Marshall, 279, 289, 294, 296–97, 303, 304
Fiske, John, 198
Fitzgerald, F. Scott, 17, 71, 204
Fixer, The, 26
Fixx, 134
Flacks, 281
Fleetwood Mac, 330, 344
Fleming, John Ambrose, 94
Fleming, Victor, 214
Flintstones, The, 192
Flock of Seagulls, A, 134
Fly, The, 220
Flying Down to Rio, 205, 213
FM, 205
FM radio, 109, 117–18, 328
Follow the Fleet, 213
Fonz, the, 170
Football, 193–94, 295, 296–97
For Better or Worse, 64
"For Free," 139
Ford, Gerald, 281–82
Ford, James L., 89
Ford, Tennesse Ernie, 176
Form/content: in advertising, 268, 270–78; book, 19–20; of communication, 6–7; of films, 207–9; of media, 19–20; of newspapers, 242–43; in pet-food advertising, 268; in rock music, 135; in subliminal advertising, 272–75; of tabloids, 1
Francis, Connie, 136
Franklin, Aretha, 137
Franklin, Benjamin, 20, 36, 70, 72
Franklin, James, 36
Freberg, Stan, 103
Frederick, Pauline, 312, 314–15
Freed, Alan, 129
"Fresno Four" case, 48
Friendly, Alfred W., 257
Friendly, Fred, 247
Frith, Simon, 145
Frost, David, 65
Fuchs, Wolfgang J., 67
Fujiwara, Kristie, 116
Fuldheim, Dorothy, 312

Gable, Clark, 206
Gaines, William, 73, 84

"Gambler, The," 140
Gandhi, 225
Gang of Four, 327
Gangbusters, 98
Gannett Company, Inc., 29–30, 44, 244
Gannett Co., Inc. v. DePasquale, 47
Gans, Herbert J., 304
Garbo, Greta, 213
Garfield, 61, 64
Garner, James, 169
Gasoline Alley, 61
Gatekeepers, in music business, 141–42
Gay Divorcée, The, 213
Gaye, Marvin, 345
Geck, Elizabeth, 15
Gelatt, Roland, 144
General Hospital, 187, 319–24
General Magazine and Historical Chronicle, 70, 72
General manager (GM), radio, 105
Genesis, 330
Gentry, 76
"Georgie," 138
Giant, 220
Gibson, Henry, 223
Gilded Age, The, 23
Gillett, Charlie, 144–45, 146
Gilliam, Terry, 178
Gillray, James, 61
Ginsberg, Allen, 26
Gish, Lillian, 211
Glamour, 70
Gleason, Jackie, 176
Globe, 70
Glyn, Elinor, 210–11
Go Ask Alice, 26
Gobel, George, 176
Gode, Alex, 8
Godfather, The, 156, 228
Godkin, E. L., 72
"Goin' up the Country," 139
Golden Gate North, 80
Goldstein, Richard, 145
Goldwater, Barry, 281
Gone with the Wind, 155, 156, 197, 204, 205, 206, 209, 213–14, 228
Good Housekeeping, 70, 72

Good Morning America, 186
Good Times, 162, 173
"Goodbye Again," 139
Goon Show, The, 103
Gordo, 61
Gordon, Deborah, 136–38
Gore, Leslie, 137
Gospel Carrier, 80
Gourley, Jay, 64
Gourmet, 69
Government, and press, 46–51
Grain Information News (GIN), 244
"Grand Ole Opry," 139
Grapes of Wrath, The, 22
Grateful Dead, 109
Grease, 228
Great Gatsby, The, 229
Great Train Robbery, The, 209
Greeley, Horace, 36, 39, 40, 254
Green Hornet, The, 98
Greene, Graham, 78
Griffin, Merv, 190, 191
Griffith, D. W., 205, 209, 210, 211
Griffith, Richard, 232
Gross, Lynne Schafer, 360
Group W Satellite Communications, 253
Guccione, Bob, 77
Guiding Light, The, 186
Guinness Book of World Records, 17
Guisewite, Cathy, 64
"Guitar Man," 139
Gulfshore Life, 80
Gungles, The, 61
Gunsmoke, 103, 150, 179
Gutenberg, Johann, 1, 3, 4, 9, 18, 20

Hadden, Briton, 72
Haley, Alex, 197
Haley, Bill, 97, 129
Hall, Barbara, 123
Hall, Claude, 123
Hall and Oates, 138
Happy Days, 173, 174
Hard Day's Night, A, 221
Hard news, 30, 33, 57, 61
"Hard Rain's Gonna Fall, A," 139

Harold and Maude, 296
Harper's Weekly, 72
Hart, Lois, 252
Harte-Hanks newspaper group, 48
Hartley, John, 198
Harvey, Paul, 246
Hasling, John, 123
Have Gun, Will Travel, 150, 179
Hawaii Five-O, 181
Hawks, Howard, 217
Hawn, Goldie, 177
Haymes, Dick, 128
Hayworth, Rita, 78
HBO. *See* Home Box Office
Head, Sydney W., 123, 167
Hear It Now, 247
Hearst, William Randolph, 36, 37, 40–43, 72, 215
Heart, 132
"Heartbreak Hotel," 129
Heatter, Gabriel, 246–47
Hefner, Hugh, 73, 76–77
Heighton, Elizabeth J., 167, 285
Help!, 221
Hemingway, Ernest, 25, 71, 78
Hendrix, Jimi, 112
Henry VIII, 24
Hepburn, Katherine, 191
Herman's Hermits, 130
Hersh, Seymour, 240
Hidden Persuaders, The, 269
High Noon, 220
High-definition television (HDTV), 347
Highway Patrol, 181
Hill, Richard J., 309–10
Hill Street Blues, 151, 184, 185
Hispanics, in broadcast media, 162
"History of the Standard Oil Company," 71
Hitchcock, Alfred, 205, 220–21
Hitler's diaries, 55
Hoax, The, 56
Hoaxes, 55–56
Hoffman, Dustin, 225
"Holiday Inn," 139
Hollywood Squares, 186, 189
Home Box Office (HBO), 342, 343, 345, 346, 347
Home video, 353–58
Honolulu Advertiser, 44

Honolulu Star Bulletin, 44
Hot, 345
House Un-American Activities Committee, 218
How to Talk Back to Your Television Set (Johnson), 163, 164, 167
Howdy Doody, 191
Howl and Other Poems, 26
Hughes, Howard, 55
Human League, 134
Humphrey, Hubert, 282
"Hungry Like a Wolf," 134
Huntley, Chet, 239
Hurlburt, Allen, 232
Huston, John, 217
Hutchins Commission on Freedom of the Press, 37, 51
Hutchinson v. *Proxmire*, 65

I Am Curious Yellow, 229
"I Am Woman," 137
"I Can't Get No Satisfaction," 132
I. F. Stone's Weekly, 44
I Love Lucy, 148, 173
"I Saw Her Standing There," 136
"I Should Have Known Better," 136
"I Want to Hold Your Hand," 130
"I Will Follow Him," 136
Ideals, 80
Idle, Eric, 178
"I'm Easy," 223
Imus, John Donald, Jr. (Don), 97, 104, 230
Ince, Thomas W., 211
In Concert, 178
Incredible Hulk, 61
Independent Broadcasting Authority (IBA), 299
Independent Local Radio (ILR), 299
Indiana Jones and the Temple of Doom, 225
Internal specialization, 69–70
Interpersonal communication, 5, 6, 7
Intimate Story, 86
Intolerance, 210
Intrapersonal communication, 5, 6, 7
Iron Worker, The, 79
Ironside, 180, 182

Irving, Clifford, 55–56
Island Trees School District Board of Education, 26

Jack Armstrong, the All-American Boy, 98
Jackson, Andrew, 38
Jackson, Michael, 140, 344
Jagger, Mick, 136
Jakes, John, 22
James, Harry, 128
James, Rick, 345
Japan, 302–3
Jarvis, Al, 96, 101
Jascalevich, Mario E., 50
Jaws, 205, 222, 228
Jazz, 111, 127
Jazz Singer, The, 203, 205, 212
Jefferson, Thomas, 38
Jefferson Airplane, 109, 132
Jefferson Starship, 132
Jeffersons, The, 162, 173
Jennings, Waylon, 140
Jetsons, The, 192
Jeweler, A. Jerome, 286
Joel, Billy, 8, 134, 327
John Birch Society, and book censorship, 26
"Johnny Angel," 137
Johnson, Joseph S., 122
Johnson, Lyndon, 281, 282
Johnson, Nicholas, 147, 163, 164, 167, 255–56, 342
Johnson, Tom, 30
Johnston, Lynn, 64
Jolson, Al, 128, 129
Jones, Donald D., 56
Jones, Kenneth K., 122
Jones, Terry, 178
Joplin, Janis, 126
Journal Company of Milwaukee, 150
Journalism: advocacy, 38, 39; American, 36–46; contemporary, 55–66; early years of, 36, 38; eras of, 36–46; new, 37, 45–46; objective, 37, 44; penny press, 36, 38–40; yellow, 36–37, 40–43. *See also* Newspapers
Joyce, James, 26

"Judgment of the Moon and Stars," 139
Jules and Jim, 229
Jungle, The, 22
"Just the Way You Are," 8

Kadushin, Charles, 28
Kael, Pauline, 215, 233
Kaltenborn, H. V., 247
Kansas City Star, 56, 241
Kasem, Casey, 108, 109
Katzenjammer Kids, 61
Kendrick, Alexander, 122
Kennedy, 155
Kennedy, John F., 282
Key, Wilson Bryan, 269, 272, 275, 286
Key Largo, 217
Keyker, Bob, 107
Keystone Kops, 210
Khrushchev, Nikita, 78
Kilgore, Bernard, 37
King Kong, 222
King, Carole, 132
King, Larry, 113
Kirschner, Allen, 53
Kirschner, Linda, 53
Kirshner, Don, 178
Kiss, 132
Kissinger, Henry, 64
Kittross, John M., 122
Klapper, Joseph, 307
Klein, Lewis, 167
Kline, R. Gerald, 339
Knight-Ridder, 244
Knotts Landing, 184
Koch, Howard, 218
Kojak, 181
Kraft Television Theater, The, 183–84
Kramer vs. Kramer, 228
Krantz, Judith, 22
Krasnow, Erwin G., 168
Kristofferson, Kris, 140
Kubrick, Stanley, 221
Kukla, Fran, and Ollie, 191
Kuriansky, Judith, 114

Lackmann, Ron, 167
Ladies' Home Journal, 70, 72, 74
LaGuardia, Robert, 200
Laine, Frankie, 128

Land of the Giants, 182
Landau, Jack C., 49
Landers, Ann, 59, 60
Landon, Michael, 179
Larson, Carl E., 6, 15
Laser discs, 355–57
Lasswell, Harold, 6
Laugh-In, 151, 176, 177, 179
Laughing Boy, 26
Laverne and Shirley, 173, 174
"Leader of the Pack," 137
Lear, Norman, 151, 173–74
Leave It to Beaver, 296
Led Zeppelin, 330
Lederer, Howard, 77
Lederer, Jules, 60
Lee, Peggy, 128
Lee, Raymond, 231
Legal issues: freedom of the press, 46–51; libel, 64–65
Lehrer, Jim, 253
Leigh, Janet, 221
Leigh, Vivien, 206
Lennon, John, 125
Let's Make a Deal, 189
"Letters from a Farmer in Pennsylvania," 36
Lewis, Fulton, Jr., 247
Lewis, Sinclair, 25
Lianna, 224–25
Libel, 64–65
Liberty, 74
Licensing: of journalism, 51; of radio stations, 118–21
Liebert, Robert M., 200
Life, 71, 73, 74, 78–79, 151
Life of an American Fireman, 209
Lightfoot, Gordon, 132
"Like a Rolling Stone," 132
Linotype, 20
Literacy, 4
Little Caesar, 213
Little House on the Prairie, 153, 179
Little Richard, 140
Living Bible, The, 22
Loggins, Kenny, 330
"Lola," 138
Lolita, 26
Lone Ranger, The, 95, 98
Long, Ray, 72
Longley, Lawrence D., 168

Longstreet, 182
Look, 71, 73, 78, 80
Lorimar Productions, 184
Los Angeles Free Press, 37, 46
Los Angeles Times, 30, 46, 243, 244
Lost in Space, 182
Lou Grant, 174, 184, 185
Loud, Grant, 196
Loud, Lance, 196
Loud, Pat, 196
Loud, William C., 196
Love Boat, 157, 159
Love Story, 23
"Love to Love You Baby," 137
Loving, 187
Lowenstein, Ralph L., 33, 69, 88
LPTV, 160–61
Lucas, George, 223, 226–27
Luce, Henry, 72, 74, 78
Lukas, J. Anthony, 77
Lull, James, 326
Lumber Instant News (LIN), 244
Lumet, Sidney, 222
Lumière, Auguste, 205
Lumière, Louis, 205
Lynn, Loretta, 137
Lynyrd Skynyrd, 140

McCabe and Mrs. Miller, 222
McCall, C. W., 97, 140
McCall's, 70, 71
McCarthy, Colman, 297
McCarthy, Joseph, 25, 45, 247, 248
McCartney, Paul, 138
McCloud, 181, 182
McClure, Robert D., 283, 287
McClure, S. S., 71
McClure's, 71, 72, 78
McGovern, George, 281
McGrath, James B., 122
McGraw-Hill Publishing Company, 55
McGuire, Barry, 132
McKenna, George, 258
McKenzie, Scott, 132
McKinley, William, 37
McLean, Don, 139
McLendon, Gordon, 113
McLuhan, Marshall: on advertising, 259, 270, 276, 286; on environments, 290;

McLuhan, Marshall (*cont.*)
   "global village," 9, 289; on
   media, 7; on news, 29, 55,
   250; on popular culture, 290;
   on the press, 45; on print,
   18; publications of, 53; on
   radio, 93; summary of major
   ideas of, 292–93; on TV,
   250, 293
McMahon, Ed, 190
MacNeil, Robert, 253
MacNeil/Lehrer Report, 253
McVoy, D. Stevens, 360
Mad, 73, 82, 84
Madden, David, 304
Madison, Charles A., 23, 28
Magazines, 69–87; advertising
   rates, 80, 81; without ad-
   vertising, 80–83; in Can-
   ada, 299; circulation, 70;
   history, 70–74; special-
   interest, 69, 79–80; spe-
   cialization, 69–70; in the
   U.S.S.R., 302; writing for,
   83–86
Magnum, P.I., 12, 98, 185
Mail, electronic, 353
Mailer, Norman, 78
Make-Believe Ballroom, 96, 101
Maltese Falcon, The, 217
Man to Man, 80
Manca, Allessandra MacLean,
   272–75
Manca, Luigi, 272–75
Mancini, Henry, 110
Mandell, Maurice, 285
Mankiewicz, Frank, 117
Mannix, 181
Mansfield, Jayne, 220
March, Fredric, 213
March, Hal, 89
March, Peggy, 136
Marconi, Guglielmo, 94, 96
Marcus Welby, M.D., 180
Marey, E. J., 205
Market research, 266
Marlboro, 277
Marsh, Earle, 199
Marshall, Garry, 174
Martino, Al, 129
Marx, Groucho, 103, 213
Marx Brothers, 213, 214

Mary Hartman, Mary Hartman,
   151, 188
Mary Tyler Moore Show, The,
   151, 174
Mary Worth, 61, 64
M★A★S★H, 147, 155, 174, 222
Mass audience, 33
Mass communication, 5, 6, 7;
   birth of, 3–4; future of,
   341–60; phenomena of,
   335–60; popular culture and,
   291, 294; research in,
   307–39; technologies in,
   9–10, 342–58
Mass culture, 8–9
Mass media: censorship in, 176;
   cone effect in, 10–12; effects
   of, 8; newspapers as, 33;
   requirements for, 6–7;
   symbiosis, 35; TV as, 149
Mass message, 7–8
Match Game, The, 186
Maude, 173
Maverick, 150, 169–70, 179
Maxwell, Elsa, 78
May, Elaine, 103
"Maybe I'm Amazed," 138
Mayer, Arthur, 232
Mayflower Decision, 254
Media: control of, 255–56; cross-
   ownership, 255; education
   and research, 12–14; in
   other countries, 298; ownership of, 255–56; power of,
   255. *See also* Electronic
   media; Mass media
Media education, 12
Media Statistics, Inc., 114
Mediated reality, 10–12; in
   advertising, 260; as
   background, 12; con-
   structed, 10–11, 170, 260;
   music and, 106, 125; in
   newspaper stories, 34;
   perceived, 11–12, 170; in
   public relations, 260; in
   radio, 106; real life and, 11–
   12, 194–96; records as, 125;
   in TV, 170–71, 194–96;
   understanding, 10–12
Meet the Press, 103
Melnik, Stefan Reinhard, 305

Men at Work, 134
Mercury Theatre on the Air, 99,
   100, 215
Mergenthaler, Ottmar, 20
Merrill, John C., 33, 69, 88
"Mersey Beat," 131
Messages, mass, 7–8
Metromedia Inc., 251
Metros, 34–35
Mexico, 300–1
Middle-of-the-road (MOR) radio
   format, 109–10
"Midnight Rambler," 136
Midnight Special, The, 178
Miller v. California, 26
Milligan, Spike, 103
Mini-series, 155
Minorities, in broadcast media,
   162. *See also* Women
Minow, Newton, 150, 254
Miss Peach, 61
Mitchell, Joni, 111, 126, 132, 139
Mod Squad, 182
Monday Night Football, 153
Monitor, 103
Monroe, James, 23
Monroe, Marilyn, 73, 77, 220
Monty Python, 177, 178
Moondog's Rock and Roll Party,
   129
Moore, Mary Tyler, 151, 174, 224
Moral Majority, 158
Morality, in TV soap operas,
   317–25
Mork and Mindy, 174, 185
Morris, Desmond, 26
Morse, Samuel, 36
Mother Jones, 71
Motion Picture Association of
   America (MPAA), 230
Motion Picture Patents Company
   (MPPC), 205, 209
"Motown sound," 140
Mott, Frank Luther, 38, 39, 53
Mott, George Fox, 44
Movies. *See* Films
"Mr. Tambourine Man," 132
Ms. 73, 74
MTV, 97, 343, 344–45
Muckraking, 71, 240
Munro, George P., 23
Munsey, Frank, 71

Munsey's, 71, 72, 78
Murphy, Eddie, 178
Murrow, Edward R., 45, 96, 99, 103, 150, 245, 246–47
Music, 125–43; big band, 112, 128; country and western, 110, 139–40, 141; films and, 205; jazz, 111, 127; as a medium, 125–46; phonograph and, 126–28; popular, 326–37; radio demographics, 108; radio formats, 106–13; resistance to new wave of, 326–37; soul, 140; women in, 136–38. *See also* Rock music
Music Television (MTV), 97, 343, 344–45
Mutual Broadcasting System, 95
Muzak, 110–11

Nader, Ralph, 261
Naked Ape, The, 26
Naked City, 181
Name That Tune, 189
Nashville (film), 139, 205, 222–23, 227
Nashville! (magazine), 80
Nashville Skyline, 132
Nation, The, 72
National Association of Broadcasters (NAB), 165
National Association of Educational Broadcasters (NAEB), 115–16
National Broadcasting Company (NBC): early, 95, 96, 98, 99, 150; radio, 245; TV, 151, 155–56, 157, 173, 253
National Enquirer, 1, 57–59, 64, 70, 243
National Football League (NFL), 193
National Geographic, 70, 74
National Lampoon, 84
National Lampoon's Animal House, 228
National Public Radio (NPR), 116, 117
National Tattler, 57
Nazi book burnings, 25
Nelson, Harriet, 100

Nelson, Ozzie, 100
Netherlands, 301
Network, 222, 223
Neuharth, Allen, 29
Neuman, Alfred E. (fictitious *Mad* publisher), 73, 84
New England Courant, 36
New journalism, 37, 45–46
New music, 112–13, 133–34
New Survey of Journalism, 44
New York Civil Liberties Union, 26
New York Daily News, 1, 30, 36, 243
New York Herald, 36, 39
New York Herald Tribune, 37
New York Journal, 36, 40, 42, 43, 61
New York Society for the Suppression of Vice, 24–25
New York Sun, 36, 39, 243
New York Times, 30, 37, 44, 45, 169, 244
New York Times bestseller list, 22
New York Times Co. v. *New Jersey*, 49–50
New York Times Co. v. *Sullivan*, 65
New York Tribune, 36, 39, 40, 254
New York World, 36, 40, 41, 43, 61
New Yorker, The, 57, 72, 79, 87
Newcomb, Horace, 182, 199
Newhart, Bob, 103, 174
Newhouse chain, 44
News: definitional discussion, 237–39; as entertainment, 61; hard, 30, 33, 57, 61; human interest, 238–39; local, 238, 250; printed, 241–44; radio, 113–14, 244–48; reader preference, 56–57; regional interest, 238; selection/suppression, 240; sexism in, 251; soft, 30, 33, 57–61; TV, 237–41, 248–55, 311–15
News and Information Service (NIS), 245
Newsom, Doug, 286, 287

Newspapers, 29–66, 241–44; advertising in, 34; bias in, 34; circulation of, 35; comic strips in, 61–64; economics of, 34; electronic media and, 35; freedom of press and, 46–51, 65; government and, 46–51; information in, 33–34; layout, 242–43; libel and, 64–65; number of, 34; readers of, 33; staff, 241–42; tabloids, 1, 57–61; trends in, 34–46
Newsweek, 55, 70, 72, 80, 131
New-wave music, 327–39
Nicholas Nickleby, 151
Nichols, Mike, 103
Nicholson, Jack, 221
Nicks, Stevie, 133
Nielsen, A. C., Co., 148, 149, 152
Nielsen Station Index (NSI), 152
Nielsen Television Index (NTI), 149
Night at the Opera, A, 214
Night Flite, 345
Nimmo, Dan D., 287
Nine to Five, 228
Nixon, Richard, 37, 50, 65, 177, 281, 282, 283
Noble, Edward, 99
Null hypothesis, 309

Objective journalism, 37, 44
Obscenity: in films, 229–30; Supreme Court and, 25, 26
Ochs, Adolph, 37, 44
Ogilvy, David, 285
Oliver's Adventures, 61
On Golden Pond, 228
On with the Show, 205
Onassis, Aristotle, 59
One Day at a Time, 154
One Flew Over the Cuckoo's Nest, 228
$128,000 Question, 189
Ordinary People, 224
Oregon Journal, 44
Oregonian, 44
Orphans of the Storm, 211
Oswald, John C., 27
Our Gal Sunday, 98

Outcault, Richard, 43, 61
Overbeck, Wayne, 54
Owen, Bill, 122
"Oxford Town," 139

Packard, Vance, 269, 272
Page, Patti, 129
Paine, Thomas, 25
Paley, William, 95, 99, 246, 247
Palin, Michael, 178
Palmer, Volney, 260
Paperback books, 22
Paris, John, 205
Patterson, Joseph, 243–44
Patterson, Thomas E., 283, 287
Paul, Arthur, 76–77
Payola scandal, 97, 103–4
Peanut Farmer, The, 79
Peanuts, 62, 64, 192
Pearson, Drew, 45, 240
Peer, Elizabeth, 67
Pember, Don R., 54
Pennsylvania Chronicle, 36
Pennsylvania Evening Post and Daily Advertiser, 36
Penny press, 36, 38–40
Pentagon Papers, 37
Penthouse, 70, 74, 77
People, 70, 73, 74
Pepper Young's Family, 98
Perceived mediated reality (PMR), 11–12
Perkins, Carl, 140
Permanent press, books as, 17–26
Perry Mason, 180
Personal Computing, 69
Peter and Gordon, 130
Peterson, Theodore, 88
Pet-food commercials, 267–69, 270
Petty, Tom, 134
Phelan, John M., 304
Phillips, Sam, 129
Phonographs, 126–28
Photojournalism, 74, 78–79
Phyllis, 174
Picasso, Pablo, 274
Pickford, Mary, 203, 204, 211
"Pill, The," 137
Pingree, Suzanne, 200
Platters, 140
Playboy, 70, 73, 76–77, 85

Playhouse 90, 184
"Please Please Me," 130
PMR. *See* Perceived mediated reality
Poe, Edgar Allan, 69, 72
Police, 112, 134, 344
"Police Office," 39
Politics: public relations in, 279; TV in, 281–84
Poor Richard's Almanack, 20
Pope, Generoso, 57–59
Popular Computing, 80
Popular culture: Balinese and, 290; cults in, 295; definitional discussion, 290–91; dilemma of, 298; events of, 295; films in, 203–33; mass communication and, 291, 294
Pornography, 26
Porter, Edwin S., 205, 209
Poseidon Adventure, The, 222
Poultry and Egg News (PEN), 244
Powell, Jody, 237
Powers, Ron, 258
Pravda (U.S.S.R.), 302
Presley, Elvis, 109, 126, 129, 130, 140, 175
Press and Foreign Policy, The, 33
Press freedom: responsibility and, 46–50; Supreme Court and, 37, 47–50, 65
Prevention, 70
Price, Jonathan, 271
Price, Vincent, 189
Price Is Right, The, 186, 189
Princess Daisy, 22
Print media: editing of, 87; electronic media vs., 10; in the Netherlands, 301. *See also* Books; Magazines; Newspapers
Printer's Ink, 71
Printer's Ink Model Statute, 263
Printing press, 3, 4, 20
Privacy issue, 64–65
Private Benjamin, 153
Program director (PD), radio, 103–5
Psycho, 205, 220–21
Public Broadcasting Service (PBS), 158–59, 160, 161, 253

Public Enemy, 213
Public radio, 115–17
Public relations, 278–84; ethics in, 280–81; in the global village, 280; jobs/pay in, 280; journalists and, 280–81; mediated reality in, 260; politics and, 279, 281–84
Publick Occurrences both Forreign and Domestick, 36
Publishing business, 23–24. *See also* Books
"Puff the Magic Dragon," 120
Pulitzer, Joseph, 36, 40, 41
Pulitzer Prize, 41
Pullen, Rick D., 54
Punk rock, 134, 327–39
Putnam, George, 249–50

QUBE, 351–52
Quiz shows, 150

Radio, 93–121; advertising, 94–95, 96, 264; criticism, 229; deregulation of, 120; disc jockeys, 101–5; educational, 115–17; in England, 298–99; FM, 109, 117–18, 328; freedom of speech in, 120; future, 118; golden age of, 95–100; history, 94–101; mediated reality in, 106–7; in Mexico, 300; music formats in, 106–13; news, 113–14, 244–48; news commentators, 246–48; newspapers and, 35, 244–48; off-air personnel, 105–6; public, 115–17; ratings, 114–15; regulation of, 118–21; revenues, 118; after TV, 100–1; wire services and, 244–45
Radio Act of 1927, 96, 118
Rado Corporation of America (RCA), 94, 95, 96, 98, 117, 150
Radio 1990, 345
Radner, Gilda, 177
Ragged Dick, 21
Raiders of the Lost Ark, 225, 228
RAM Research, 114
Ramones, 134, 135, 137

Rather, Dan, 62, 237, 238
Raymond, Alan, 196
Raymond, Susan, 196
Reader's Digest, 33, 69–70, 72, 73, 82, 83, 85
Reading: popularity of, 23; television vs., 10
Reagan, Ronald, 281, 283
Real, Michael, 194, 201
Real life, 10; in comic strips, 62–63; films and, 204–7, 222; perceived mediated reality vs., 11–12, 194–96; TV and, 170, 194–96, 291
Real People, 195
Reality, mediated. *See* Mediated reality
Reasoner, Harry, 250
Rebel without a Cause, 219–20
Record(s)/Recordings, 125–43; broadcasting, 96; 45 vs. 78 r.p.m., 130; hit trends, 141–42; as mediated reality, 125
Red Lion Decision, 254
Redbook, 70
Redding, Otis, 140
Reddy, Helen, 137
Redford, Robert, 224, 229
Reed, Lou, 138
Reitberger, Reinhold C., 67
R.E.M., 112, 134
Remington, Frederic, 42
Reporters Committee for Freedom of the Press v. *American Telephone & Telegraph Co. et al.*, 49
Research: design, 309; examples of studies, 310–37; mass-communication, 307–39; procedures and problems of, 308–10; statistical method, 310
Return of the Jedi, 23, 205, 223, 227, 228, 295
Reuters, 244
Revolver, 132
Rex Morgan, M.D., 61
Rhoda, 174
Rhythm and blues, 129
Rich, Charley, 140
Richmond Newspapers, Inc. v. *Virginia*, 47
Right Stuff, The, 226

Rivers, William L., 52
"Roadrunner" cartoons, 192
Roberts, Donald F., 5
Robinson, Edward G., 213
"Rock around the Clock," 97, 129
Rock music, 128–39; birth of, 128–30; British influence, 130–31; content analysis, 135, 138–39; diffusion of, 132–33; form and content, 135; new music and, 112–13, 133–34; radio formats, 108–9, 112–13; renaissance, 131–32; rhythm and blues in, 129; themes of, 135, 138–39; women in, 136–38
Rock videos, 344–45
Rockford Files, The, 182
Rocky Horror Picture Show, The, 296
"Rocky Mountain High," 139
Rocky III, 228
Roddenberry, Gene, 182, 183, 199, 297
Rogers, Ginger, 205, 213
Rogers, Kenny, 140
Roget, Peter Mark, 205
Rohde, H. Kandy, 145
Rolling Stone, 1, 37, 142
Rolling Stones, 132, 136, 137, 330
Romance of Helen Trent, The, 98
Ronstadt, Linda, 132, 134, 137
Roosevelt, Franklin D., 96, 99, 283
Roots, 22, 151, 155, 197
Rose, Billy, 129, 130
Ross, Diana, 140
Rotha, Paul, 212, 232
Rounds, David, 200
Routt, Edd, 122
Rowan and Martin's Laugh-In, 151, 176, 177, 179
Rowlandson, Thomas, 61
"Ruby, Don't Take Your Love to Town," 140
Rucker, Bryce W., 258
Rules of the Game, 229
"Runaround Sue," 136
Rutland, Robert A., 53
Ryan, William, 284
Rydell, Bobby, 130

Sackett, Susan, 304
Sadat, 155
St. Elsewhere, 184
St. Louis Post-Dispatch, 36, 40, 41
Sam Spade, 98
San Francisco Examiner, 36
Sanford, 162
Sanford, Bruce W., 54
Sarnoff, David, 95, 98, 117
Satellite communication, 344–51
Satellite TV Week, 346
Saturday Evening Post, 71, 72, 73, 74
Saturday Night Fever, 23, 205, 228
Saturday Night Live, 177–78, 230
Savalas, Telly, 181
Scaggs, Boz, 109
Schickel, Richard, 211, 232
Schmidt, William, 67
Scholastic Magazine, 70
School boards, censorship by, 26
Schramm, Wilbur, 5, 9, 239, 305
Schudson, Michael, 52
Scott, Alan, 286
Sedition Act, 36, 38
See It Now, 45, 150, 247
Segal, Erich, 23
Seldes, Gilbert, 247
Sellers, Peter, 103
Selznick, David O., 214
Sennet, Mack, 211
Sensationalism, 57–59
Sgt. Pepper's Lonely Hearts Club Band, 205
Service, Robert W., 25
Sesame Street, 159, 161, 162
Settel, Irving, 122
Sevareid, Eric, 99, 163, 245
77 Sunset Strip, 181
Severinsen, Doc, 190
Sex: film ratings and, 230; in rock music, 138; in soap operas, 186
Sex Pistols, 134, 327
"Sextalk," 114
Shakespeare, William, 22
"Shame of the Cities, The," 71
Shane, 220
Shankar, Ravi, 109
Shannon, Claude E., 5

Shannon/Weaver model of communication process, 5
Share numbers, 115
Shaw, David, 28
Shawn, William, 79
"She Loves You," 130
Sheehan, Paul V., 52
"She's Gone," 138
Shogun, 155
Shore, Dinah, 128, 176
Showtime, 343, 345
Siegfried, Tom, 287
Silkwood, 225
Silverman, Fred, 151, 157
Simon and Garfunkel, 132
Simon, Carly, 109, 132, 133, 137
Simon, Howard, 123
Simon, Paul, 133, 138
Sinatra, Frank, 109, 128, 129
Sinclair, Upton, 22, 25
Singleton, Loy A., 311
Siniawsky, Shelley J., 317
Situation comedy, 173–75
60 Minutes, 154, 159, 195
$64,000 Question, 150, 189
Skelton, Red, 100, 176
Skornia, Harry J., 168
Slaughterhouse-Five, 26
Slick, Grace, 132
Smith, Albert E., 208, 231
Smith, G. Albert, 205
Smith, Howard K., 103
Smith, Patrick, 224–25
Smith, Roger, 181
Smokey and the Bandit, 228
Smothers Brothers Comedy Hour, 151, 176–77
Soap opera: daytime, 186–88; mass audience and, 187; moral violations in, 317–25; prime time, 183–84; sex in, 186; TV, 183–84, 186–88, 317–25
Soap Opera Digest, 317, 319
"Soap Talk," 114
Soft news, 30, 33, 57–61
Sommers, Joanie, 136
Sonny and Cher, 177
Sopkin, Charles, 200
Sound of Music, The, 228
Soup music, 140
Southern Jewish Weekly, 80
Southern Living, 70

Space 1999, 182
Speak Up, America, 195
Special-interest audience, 33
Specialization, in magazines, 69–70
Spectrum, 82
Speech Communication, Concepts and Behavior, 6
Speeches, in newspapers, 34
Spelling, Aaron, 157
Spelling/Goldberg Productions, 154
Spielberg, Steven, 225
Spock, Benjamin, 24
Sports, on TV, 193–94, 295, 296–97
Sports Illustrated, 70, 73
Spot advertising, 266
Sprafkin, Joyce N., 200
Springstein, Bruce, 330
Stafford, Jo, 128
Star, The, 70
Stars, The, 211
Star Trek: The Motion Picture, 205
Star Wars, 205, 223, 227, 228, 295
Starsky and Hutch, 181
Statistically significant differences, 310
Steele, James, 240
Steffens, Lincoln, 71
Steinbeck, John, 22
Steinberg, Cobbett, 233
Steinberg, S. H., 27
Sterling, Christopher H., 122, 123
Stern, 55, 56
Steve Canyon, 61
Stevens, Joseph F., 251
Stevenson, Adlai, 282
Stewart, Potter, 49
Stewart, Rod, 138
Stills, Stephen, 3
Sting, The, 228
Stir Crazy, 228
Stokes, Geoffrey, 146
Stokowski, Leopold, 127
Storz, Todd, 97
Street Fighter, The, 230
Stromgren, Richard, 232, 233
Subliminal Seduction, 269, 275
Sullivan, Ed, 130, 148, 175–76

Summer, Donna, 137, 345
Sun Records, 129
Super Bowl, 193, 295, 296–97
Superman, 61, 98, 228
Superman II, 228
"Supermarket journals," 57–59
Supertramp, 330
Supreme Court: libel laws, 65; obscenity and, 25, 26; press freedom and, 37, 46–50
Supremes, 140
Surrealistic Pillow, 132
Sutherland, John C., 317
Swanberg, W. A., 54
Switch, 181
Sykes, John, 345
Synchronicity, 134, 344

Tabloids, 1, 57–59
Talese, Gay, 76
"Talking World War III Blues," 139
Tarbell, Ida M., 71
Taylor, Glenhall, 122
Taylor, James, 109, 132, 139, 330
Tebbel, John, 89
Technologies, in mass communication, 9–10, 342–58
Techno-pop, 134
"Telecaption," 353
Teleshopping, 352
Teletext, 353
Television, 147–201; action-adventure shows, 181–83; cable, 12, 173, 342–45; children's shows, 191–93; color, 150; commercials, 264–66; control of, 163–65; criticism, 149, 229; daytime genres, 184–91; education via, 158–59, 160, 161; FCC and, 148, 149, 150, 151, 154, 160, 162, 163–65; film and, 155–57; FM radio and, 148, 150; game shows, 186, 188–89; genres, 171–84; gratifications derived from watching, 172; growth of, 148–49; history, 150–51; home video, 353–58; influence of, 10, 169–70; licensing and renewals, 148, 160, 163; *Life* and, 151; local

news and, 250; LPTV, 160–61; mediated reality in, 170–71, 194–96; in Mexico, 300–1; mini-series, 155; minorities in, 162; network decision makers, 157–58; new populism in, 195; new technologies, 342–58; news, 237–41, 248–55, 311–15; newspapers and, 35; pioneers of, 148; in politics, 281–84; prime-time genres, 171–83; programming, 154–58; public, 158–59, 160, 161; radio after, 100–1; ratings and, 149–54; reading vs., 10; satellites in, 344–51; set as icon, 294; sitcoms, 173–75; soaps, 183–84, 186–88, 317–25; sponsored programs, 266; sports on, 193–94; talk shows, 190–91; two-way, 351–52; UHF/VHF, 159–60; variety, 175–79; violence on, 8; westerns on, 150, 179–80
Ten Commandments, The, 210, 228
Terms of Endearment, 225
Terry, Herbert A., 168
"Thank God I'm a Country Boy," 139
"That's Alright Mama," 129
That's Entertainment, 213
That's Incredible, 153, 195
Thing, The, 220
Thomas, Lowell, 103, 247–48
Thomas, Terry, 103
Thompson, Hunter, 37
Thompson, Tommy, 79
Thomson, David, 233
Thorn Birds, The, 155
Those Amazing Animals, 195
Three's Company, 174
Thurber, James, 90
Thy Neighbor's Wife, 76
Tichenor, Phillip, 339
Time: advertising rates of, 81; on Beatles, 131; bias in, 44; on "bovies," 23; circulation of, 70; editorial style, 87; on hoaxes, 55, 56; subscribers to, 80; success of, 71, 72

Time Inc., 73, 75, 79
"Time Is on My Side," 136
Tinker, Grant, 151
Titanic, and radio, 98
Today, 150, 186, 253
Toffler, Alvin, 9, 294
Tomlin, Lily, 177
Tomorrow, 191
Tonight Show, 190
Tootsie, 225, 228
Top Cat, 192
Top 40 radio format, 108
Top Hat, 213
Tormé, Mel, 128
Towering Inferno, 205, 222
Townsend, Peter, 125
Tracy, Spencer, 213
Trans LP, 139
Transponders, 347
Treasure Hunt, 189
Treasure of Sierra Madre, The, 217
"Triad," 138
Tropic of Cancer, 26
Trout, Robert, 246
Trudeau, Garry, 62–63, 67
Truman, Harry S, 78
Tuchman, Gaye, 258
Turnbull, Arthur T., 257
Turner, Edward R., 205
Turner, Ted, 245, 252–53, 342
"Turning Japanese," 138
TV-Cable Week, 73, 75
TV Guide, 70, 73, 74, 75, 85, 155, 158
Twilight Zone, The, 184, 296
"Twist and Shout," 130
Two Reels and a Crank, 208
Two-way TV, 351–52
Typesetting, 20

UHF, 159–60
Ulysses, 26
Uncle Don, 98
Uncle Tom's Cabin, 22
"Under My Thumb," 136
United Independent Broadcasters, 95, 96
United Kingdom, 298–99
United Press International, 37, 45, 244
United States Football League (USFL), 193
Unit specialization, 69

Universal Press Syndicate, 62
Upstairs, Downstairs, 151, 159
"Uptown Girl," 327
USA Cable Network, 343, 345
USA Today, 29–30, 35, 37
U.S. News and World Report, 70
U.S. Satellite Broadcasting Company, 350
U.S. Supreme Court, 25, 26, 37, 47–50, 51, 65, 120, 151, 254
U.S.S.R., 301–2
U2, 134

Valentino, Rudolph, 211, 212
Vallee, Rudy, 128
Van Buren, Abigail, 60
Vanity Fair, 73
Vapors, 138
Variables, intervening, 310
Variety, 228
Victor Talking Machine Company, 127
Video cassette recorders (VCRs), 353–55
Video disc players, 355–57
Video games, 351
Videoconferencing, 350–51
Videotext, 353
Village Voice, 37
"Vincent," 139
Violence: in children's shows, 192; in films, 230; football, 193; in TV, 8
Vonnegut, Kurt, 26, 85

Wagenknecht, Edward, 232
"Walk on the Wild Side," 138
Walker, David, 252
Wall, The, 296
Wall Street Journal, 37, 243
Wallace, DeWitt, 72
Wallace, Mike, 103
Walters, Barbara, 250
Waltons, The, 184
"Wanderer, The," 136
War of the Worlds, 96, 99, 100, 215
Warner Amex, 344, 345, 351
Washington Globe, 38
Washington Post, 37, 65, 241, 243, 244
Watergate, 37, 62
Waters, Harry F., 67

Way Down East, 211
Wayne, John, 177
Weaver, Warren, 5
Weiss, Fredric A., 122
Welch, Joseph, 45
Weller, Don, 141–42
Welles, Orson, 96, 100, 214–17
Wells, H. G., 25, 100
Western Electric, 346
Westerns: daytime reruns, 186; films, 220; TV, 150, 179–80
Westheimer, Ruth, 114
Westinghouse, 94, 96
Weston, Martin, 67
What's My Line, 103, 188–89
"Where the Boys Are," 136
Whetmore, Edward Jay, 123, 145, 257
Whetmore Grid for Understanding Communication Relationships, 6, 7
Whitcomb, Ian, 144
Whitehead, Alfred North, 341
Whiteside, Thomas, 286
Whitfield, Stephen E., 199
Who, The, 330
Who Do You Trust?, 188

Whole Booke of Psalms, The, 20
Wild One, The, 219
Wiley, Charles, 23
Williams, Andy, 176
Williams, Frederick, 348, 360
Williams, Martin, 198–99
Williams, Robin, 185
Willis, Fred, 246
Wilson, Dooley, 218
Wimmer, Roger D., 339
Winchell, Walter, 203, 248, 249
Winkler, Henry, 170
Wire services, 243–44
Witt, Linda, 67
Wizard of Oz, 214
WKRP in Cincinnati, 103
Wolfe, Tom, 37, 226
"Wolfman Jack," 112
Wolseley, Roland E., 89
Wolston v. *Reader's Digest Association, Inc.*, 65
Woman's Day, 70
Women: in music, 136–38; in broadcast media, 162; in TV network news, 311–15
Wonder, Stevie, 133, 140
Wood, Donald N., 115

Woodstock, 296
Woodward, Bob, 37, 65, 240
World Series, 193
Writer, The, 85
Writer's Digest, 85
Writer's Market, 79, 85, 86
Wroth, Lawrence C., 28
WTBS, 342, 343
Wyatt Earp, 150
Wylie, Donald G., 115

Yale Daily News, 62
Yellow journalism, 36–37, 40–43
Yellow Kid, 43, 61
Yellow Submarine, 177, 221
You Bet Your Life, 103, 189
"You Don't Own Me," 137
Young, Chic, 61
Young, Neil, 112, 126, 139, 330
"You're Gonna Kill That Girl," 137
"You're So Vain," 137

Zenger, John Peter, 36, 65
Zimbalist, Efrem, Jr., 181
Zurcher v. *Stanford Daily*, 48–49
Zworykin, Vladimir, 148, 150

To the reader:

I'm sure you know by now that *Mediamerica* is somewhat different from most other textbooks you may have read. I have tried everything possible to make this text a positive communication experience for you. Yet communication cannot exist in a vacuum. It is only with the help of your input that I can make *Mediamerica* a better book for future readers. With that in mind, would you take a moment to fill out this postage-free questionnaire and mail it back to me? I'll look forward to hearing from you and to incorporating your suggestions into future editions of *Mediamerica*. Thank you!

SCHOOL _____ INSTRUCTOR'S NAME _____

COURSE TITLE AND NUMBER _____

What features did you like *most* about *Mediamerica?* _____

_____

What features did you like *least* about *Mediamerica?* _____

_____

What were the subjects you would like to have read more about? _____

_____

What were the subjects or sections, if any, you would like to see omitted? Why? _____

_____

Were there any chapters or sections of the book you were not assigned to read? If so, which ones?

_____

How did you feel about the cartoons and graphics in the book? _____

_____

How does *Mediamerica* compare with other college textbooks you have read? _____

_____

Any other comments or suggestions? _____

YOUR NAME _____ DATE _____

May Wadsworth quote you, whether in promotion for *Mediamerica* or in future publishing ventures?

YES _____ NO _____

Thanks again for taking the time to help.

FOLD HERE

FOLD HERE

**FIRST CLASS
PERMIT NO. 34
BELMONT, CA**

BUSINESS REPLY MAIL
No Postage Necessary if Mailed in United States

Dr. Edward Jay Whetmore

Wadsworth Publishing Co. Inc.
10 Davis Drive
Belmont, CA 94002